MW00851533

"I count myself blessed to be among generations of seminary students who have 'basked' in the glory of Christ as we sat under Richard Gaffin's instruction, hearing him unfold the rich theology of Acts and the Pauline epistles. Gaffin models careful attention to, and insightful exposition of, specific New Testament texts as he places each passage within the context of the fulfillment of redemptive work and history in Christ's person. I thank God that this rich lecture material is now offered in print form to the people of God."

> **Dennis E. Johnson,** Professor Emeritus of Practical Theology, Westminster Seminary California; author, *Him We Proclaim*; *Walking with Jesus through His Word*; and *Journeys with Jesus*

"Few living theologians have shaped my own understanding of the deep structures of New Testament theology more than Richard Gaffin. And now in one volume we have the core of his contribution to our generation. He connects the dots for us to see how the apostles understood us New Testament believers to be those 'on whom the end of the ages has come' (1 Cor. 10:11). It is especially in understanding the macrosignificance to Paul's thinking of the resurrection—that of Christ's, and thereby of those united to him—that Gaffin takes twenty-first-century students, pastors, and other readers back into the minds of the apostles with profound clarity. I bless God for giving us this magnificent volume through his faithful servant, Richard Gaffin."

> **Dane Ortlund,** Senior Pastor, Naperville Presbyterian Church; author, *Gentle and Lowly* and *Deeper*

"Sadly, Richard Gaffin's work is a well-kept secret. Well, not entirely. It is known in certain circles, particularly in a portion of the Reformed community, but because of the profundity of his considerations, these labors ought to be known throughout the Christian world and beyond. *In the Fullness of Time* represents the lifework of this seasoned scholar. Like a master craftsman, Gaffin carefully places stone upon stone, which yields a lovely, finished edifice. Comparing the book of Acts to the theology of the apostle Paul is not a project that is immediately evident. After reading this book, it will have become quite patent. The centrality of Pentecost to Paul's understanding of the Holy Spirit—an emphasis that so characterizes all his work—herein becomes manifest. More than that, it becomes vital for the life of the church. Striking are both the depth and the originality of this analysis. This work is destined to be not only the standard but a pacesetter for decades to come."

> **William Edgar,** Professor of Apologetics, Westminster Theological Seminary; author, *Schaeffer on the Christian Life*

"This is the much-anticipated fruit from the author's many decades as a professor of both New Testament and systematic theology. A noble successor of the work of Geerhardus Vos, Richard Gaffin has helped many of us to understand how the Bible should be read. Plus, this volume expounds the climactic events of redemptive history. Read, mark, learn, and digest this work."

> **Michael Horton,** J. Gresham Machen Professor of Systematic Theology and Apologetics, Westminster Seminary California

"Year after year in the classroom, Richard Gaffin radically influenced countless students and would-be pastors in their reading and preaching of Scripture. Those lectures, now happily in print for all to see, if read until absorbed, will change the reader's understanding of Scripture in remarkable and likely surprising ways. No pastor or biblical scholar should neglect the slow digestion of this rich biblical diet. Its truths have been shown to be truly revolutionary."

K. Scott Oliphint, Dean of Faculty and Professor of Apologetics and Systematic Theology, Westminster Theological Seminary

"Some books provide less than their title promises. This one provides more. While it does serve as 'an introduction,' it is not an elementary survey. It rather deftly combines careful exegesis, interaction with scholarship, an integrated view of the whole of Scripture, and awareness of the church's place and mission in the world today. The compelling result, often drawing on the underrated Geerhardus Vos and Herman Ridderbos, is a doctrinally rich exploration and synthesis of how Acts and Paul's letters depict Christ's saving work, in time and for all eternity."

Robert W. Yarbrough, Professor of New Testament, Covenant Theological Seminary

"If in a Qumran-like cave the discovery were to be made of the risen Lord's lecture notes for his forty-day session imparted to his apostles concerning the kingdom of God, they would greatly mirror the truths, themes, and organic union of the Old Testament and the New Testament gospel so perceptively articulated by Richard Gaffin found herein. *In the Fullness of Time* is indeed 'an introduction to the biblical theology of Acts and Paul,' but it is far more. It is the magisterial crescendo of a lifetime of scholarly study, unpacking the realized eschatology of the historical-redemptive revelation of Jesus Christ and his epoch-making grant of the Holy Spirit to his church. This masterpiece of biblical theology will open the word, shape your mind, and bless your heart. No serious student of Holy Scripture should miss the joy of being led by Gaffin and his compelling exegesis into a deeper and fuller understanding of the believer's union with the risen Christ."

Peter Lillback, President and Professor of Historical Theology and Church History, Westminster Theological Seminary

"The first thought that comes to my mind about Richard Gaffin is that he is a reliable interpreter of Scripture. *In the Fullness of Time* thoroughly demonstrates this point. It balances what Christ accomplished at his cross and resurrection in the first century and how that relates to believers now in their own Christian experience. In particular, Gaffin shows how important Christ's death and resurrection are for the Christian's suffering in the present. While many past commentators have focused on the importance of Christ's *death* in Paul's theology, Gaffin explains how important Christ's *resurrection* is, especially for Christian living. Those who read Gaffin's book are in for a 'theological treat.'"

G. K. Beale, Professor of New Testament, Reformed Theological Seminary

In the Fullness of Time

In the Fullness of Time

An Introduction to the Biblical Theology of Acts and Paul

Richard B. Gaffin Jr.

Foreword by Sinclair B. Ferguson

WHEATON, ILLINOIS

In the Fullness of Time: An Introduction to the Biblical Theology of Acts and Paul

Copyright © 2022 by Richard B. Gaffin Jr.

Published by Crossway
        1300 Crescent Street
        Wheaton, Illinois 60187

All rights reserved. No part of this publication may be reproduced, stored in a retrieval system, or transmitted in any form by any means, electronic, mechanical, photocopy, recording, or otherwise, without the prior permission of the publisher, except as provided for by USA copyright law. Crossway® is a registered trademark in the United States of America.

Cover design: Lindy Martin

Cover image: Bridgeman Images

First printing 2022

Printed in the United States of America

Unless otherwise indicated, Scripture quotations are from the ESV® Bible (The Holy Bible, English Standard Version®), copyright © 2001 by Crossway, a publishing ministry of Good News Publishers. Used by permission. All rights reserved.

For other Scripture versions cited, please see Scripture Versions Cited.

All emphases in Scripture quotations have been added by the author.

Hardcover ISBN: 978-1-4335-6334-8
ePub ISBN: 978-1-4335-6337-9
PDF ISBN: 978-1-4335-6335-5
Mobipocket ISBN: 978-1-4335-6336-2

Library of Congress Cataloging-in-Publication Data

Names: Gaffin, Richard B., author.
Title: In the fullness of time : an introduction to the biblical theology of Acts and Paul / Richard B. Gaffin, Jr. ; foreword by Sinclair B. Ferguson.
Description: Wheaton, Illinois : Crossway, 2022. | Includes bibliographical references and index.
Identifiers: LCCN 2021037806 (print) | LCCN 2021037807 (ebook) | ISBN 9781433563348 (hardcover) | ISBN 9781433563355 (pdf) | ISBN 9781433563362 (mobipocket) | ISBN 9781433563379 (epub)
Subjects: LCSH: Bible. Acts—Theology. | Paul, the Apostle, Saint—Theology. | Bible. Epistles of Paul—Theology.
Classification: LCC BS2625.52 .G34 2022 (print) | LCC BS2625.52 (ebook) | DDC 226.6/061—dc23
LC record available at https://lccn.loc.gov/2021037806
LC ebook record available at https://lccn.loc.gov/2021037807

Crossway is a publishing ministry of Good News Publishers.

VP		31	30	29	28	27	26	25	24	23	22
14	13	12	11	10	9	8	7	6	5	4	3	2	1

Contents

Scripture Versions Cited

Unless otherwise indicated, Scripture quotations are from the ESV® Bible (The Holy Bible, English Standard Version®), copyright © 2001 by Crossway, a publishing ministry of Good News Publishers. Used by permission. All rights reserved.

Other Scripture versions cited include the following:

Scripture quotations marked ASV are from the American Standard Version of the Bible. Public domain.

Scripture quotations marked ERV 1885 are from the English Revised Version of the Bible (1885). Public domain.

Scripture quotations marked GNT are from the Good News Translation in Today's English Version—Second Edition Copyright © 1992 by American Bible Society. Used with permission.

Scripture quotations marked HCSB are taken from the Holman Christian Standard Bible®, Copyright © 1999, 2000, 2002, 2003, 2009 by Holman Bible Publishers. Used by permission. Holman Christian Standard Bible®, Holman CSB®, and HCSB® are federally registered trademarks of Holman Bible Publishers.

Scripture quotations marked KJV are from the King James Version of the Bible. Public domain.

Scripture quotations marked NAB are from the New American Bible, revised edition, © 2010, 1991, 1986, 1970 Confraternity of Christian Doctrine, Washington, DC and are used by permission. All rights reserved. No part of the New American Bible may be reproduced in any form without permission in writing from the copyright owner.

Scripture quotations taken from the NASB 1995®, New American Standard Bible®, Copyright © 1960, 1971, 1977, 1995 by The Lockman Foundation. Used by permission. All rights reserved. www.lockman.org.

Scripture quotations taken from the NASB®, New American Standard Bible®, Copyright © 1960, 1971, 1977, 1995, 2020 by The Lockman Foundation. Used by permission. All rights reserved. www.lockman.org.

Scripture quotations designated NET are from the NET Bible® copyright © 1996–2016 by Biblical Studies Press, L.L.C. http://netbible.com. Used by permission. All rights reserved.

Scripture quotations marked NIV 1984 are taken from the Holy Bible, New International Version®. NIV®. Copyright © 1973, 1978, 1984 by International Bible Society. Used by permission of Zondervan. All rights reserved worldwide.

Scripture quotations marked NIV are taken from the Holy Bible, New International Version®, NIV®. Copyright © 1973, 1978, 1984, 2011 by Biblica, Inc.™ Used by permission of Zondervan. All rights reserved worldwide. www.zondervan.com. The "NIV" and "New International Version" are trademarks registered in the United States Patent and Trademark Office by Biblica, Inc.™

Scripture quotations marked NKJV are taken from the New King James Version®. Copyright © 1982 by Thomas Nelson. Used by permission. All rights reserved.

Scripture quotations marked NLT 1996 are taken from the Holy Bible, New Living Translation, copyright © 1996 by Tyndale House Foundation. Used by permission of Tyndale House Publishers, a Division of Tyndale House Ministries, Carol Stream, Illinois 60188. All rights reserved.

Scripture quotations marked NLT are taken from the Holy Bible, New Living Translation, copyright © 1996, 2004, 2015 by Tyndale House Foundation. Used by permission of Tyndale House Publishers, a Division of Tyndale House Ministries, Carol Stream, Illinois 60188. All rights reserved.

Scripture quotations marked NRSV are from the New Revised Standard Version Bible, copyright © 1989 the Division of Christian Education of the National Council of the Churches of Christ in the United States of America. Used by permission. All rights reserved.

Scripture quotations marked REB are taken from the Revised English Bible, copyright © Cambridge University Press and Oxford University Press 1989. All rights reserved.

Scripture quotations marked RSV are from the Revised Standard Version of the Bible, copyright © 1946, 1952, and 1971 the Division of Christian Education of the National Council of the Churches of Christ in the United States of America. Used by permission. All rights reserved.

Foreword

IN 1965, NED B. STONEHOUSE, Professor of New Testament at Westminster Theological Seminary, Philadelphia, introduced his Scottish colleague John Murray's commentary on *The Epistle to the Romans* by writing of his "gratification" with it. More than that, he added,

> If indeed full expression were to be given to my estimate of the volume, my sense of elation might easily result in the use of superlatives. A measure of restraint must be observed, however, considering especially my intimate relationships with the author over a period of thirty-five years. These associations . . . have led to an enthusiastic appraisal of the author as exegete as we all as warm affection for him personally.[1]

Now more than half a century later, it is the turn of a Scotsman to pay the compliment to Richard B. Gaffin Jr., Professor in turn of New Testament and then of Biblical and Systematic Theology at Westminster. I do so with no less pleasure but perhaps feel less restraint than Professor Stonehouse in expressing the undiluted joy it is to see these pages in print.

In the Fullness of Time is a truly wonderful book. It gives so much, and yet—as should be, since its author handles sacred Scripture with faith as well as intellectual rigor and insight—it will leave you feeling, even after four hundred pages, that Dr. Gaffin has only begun, and that there is yet more to discover. It is not because Professor Gaffin has sold you short, but because you feel you are in the presence of one who has mined more deeply and found more precious stones than can possibly be deposited in

---

1 John Murray, *The Epistle to the Romans*, vol. 1 (Grand Rapids, MI: Eerdmans, 1960), vii.

one book. I suspect many readers will feel as they turn these pages that they are gathering sparkling exegetical and theological jewels in both hands and will be encouraged to continue their studies.

A hallmark of *In the Fullness of Time* is its penetration into the deep structures of Paul's thought. There are many pages here where I suspect readers will want to slow down, perhaps reread, meditate, and, best of all, worship. For Dr. Gaffin (to resort to the earlier metaphor) is like a skilled diamond merchant who lends you his loupe and teaches you how to look through it and to admire the multifaceted beauty of the diamond that Paul calls "my gospel."

To change the metaphor, readers will discover that the table of contents provides a map to the theological ascent on which Dick Gaffin is the expert guide. The book itself is like the running commentary of an experienced climber who points out the structures of the mountain and the wonders of the scenery, and occasionally indicates danger points where some climbers have slipped. And in the ascent we are given glimpses of other aspects of the mountain that remain to be climbed on another occasion. Always the ascent is directed toward giving us a memorable view of God's work of salvation wrought in Jesus Christ and applied by the Holy Spirit.

No doubt, such pleasure in reading is partly to be attributed to personal knowledge of the author. It certainly adds to a reading experience to be able to "hear" the writer's accent, to recognize the familiar idiosyncrasies of speech patterns, and on one's mental screen see the familiar facial expressions and gesticulations. And in the case of *In the Fullness of Time*, this is all enhanced by the profound esteem and admiration in which—with a multitude of others—I hold Dick Gaffin as a scholar, a teacher, a friend, and, most of all, like Paul, as "a man in Christ."

But, thankfully, elements of this experience are available to all readers. For, as Dr. Gaffin indicates, he has resisted editing out evidence of the origin of his material in the classroom lectures on Acts and Paul heard by generations of students at Westminster Seminary. For them, part of the enjoyment of these chapters will be the ability to remember having this rich exposition of Paul poured into them *viva voce*. But for those of us who have not had that privilege, hearing the echoes of those class hours as we read *In the Fullness of Time* is surely the next best thing to "being there."

What readers will also sense as they read these pages is that they express the vital, living faith of their author. Mining the apostle Paul's letters has never been for Dick Gaffin a mere intellectual exercise. This teaching has been his lifeblood, as I suspect every student who sat before him in class soon came to realize.

From early years as Dr. Gaffin's junior colleague, I privately coined a verb—used only in the passive—to describe the effect of his teaching on the Westminster student body (I am not sure I ever confessed this secret to him!). To be "Gaffinized" means to come under the influence of Dr. Gaffin's gracious teaching in such a way that it—and he—left a lifelong impress on your understanding of the gospel and its deep structures. It was not difficult to detect this process of "Gaffinization." And it seemed a happy coincidence to me that the Hebrew word for vine, גֶּפֶן (*gephen*), sounds almost indistinguishable from the author's name—for he has truly been the bearer of rich fruit in his family, his colleagues, his students, his denomination, his many friends, and all his ministry. He has humbly embodied the theology he teaches us here and exemplified the life-desire of Paul himself to

> gain Christ and be found in him, not having a righteousness of my own . . . but that which comes through faith in Christ . . . that I may know him and the power of his resurrection, and may share his sufferings, becoming like him in his death, that by any means possible I may attain the resurrection from the dead. (Phil. 3:8–11)

In my mind's eye, I see generations of Dr. Gaffin's students who, instead of taking their newly acquired copy of *In the Fullness of Time* into the study, will carefully place it on the coffee table in full but (out of respect for its author!) not overly obtrusive view. The goal will be that their children or grandchildren may see it, and ask, "Who is Richard B. Gaffin?" As a reward, they will be told tales from the class known as "NT 223" and learn how, for almost half a century, "Acts and Paul" was virtually a single word universally associated with Dr. Gaffin himself.

For these reasons, it is a very great privilege and joy to act as the mouthpiece of a multitude of seminary graduates who are profoundly grateful that *In the Fullness of Time* will give many more people access to the teaching they have gratefully received from their mentor, friend, and example, Richard B. Gaffin Jr.

Sinclair B. Ferguson

Preface

THIS BOOK IS THE EFFORT to put in writing the content of class lectures for a course on the book of Acts and the letters of Paul offered annually at Westminster Theological Seminary from 1977 to 2010 (with much of the section on Paul given in 2015). My thanks to Crossway for providing transcriptions of the audio files for a particular (2005) offering of the course, which together with my lecture notes have almost entirely shaped the book's contents as well as fixed its limits.

Within the New Testament curriculum, the course was sequenced with two other required courses, taught by others, preceded by one on the Gospels and followed by the other on the General Epistles and Revelation. This meant that, at points, I had to presuppose or anticipate, as I do in this volume, conclusions on matters dealt with fully in these and other courses.

As I began teaching the course and continued developing it, the large challenge facing me was how best to use the approximately fifty (fifty-minute) sessions of the course. There is obviously not one right answer to this question. Approaches other than mine that are sound and helpful can be taken, and I can well imagine that some, especially among them those who have taught a similar course or courses, will wonder about or second-guess my approach at a number of points. Why did I not take up this or that topic? Why have I given so much attention to one area, or why not more to another?

This book, then, reflecting as it does the purpose and the time constraints of the course, does not provide a full or rounded-out presentation of the theologies of Acts and Paul. Instead, like the course, its concern is with primary matters, things "of first importance" (cf. 1 Cor. 15:3), in dealing with these theologies.

In that regard, the decision to focus on the significance of Pentecost for the theology of Acts and on eschatological structure, including the resurrection, for the theology of Paul is surely in order and difficult to gainsay. In chapters 13 and 14, from among a number of worthwhile topics on the Christian life, I have singled out the indicative-imperative relationship and suffering for, as it appears to me, their particular timeliness.

In keeping with the structure and flow of the course, I have aimed as well to maintain the classroom level of its content—one large exception being that the lecturing was done from using Scripture in the original languages, which I have kept to a minimum here.

Given this classroom-level aim, I do not see myself as writing for my academic peers, although I hope that some among them may have an interest in my presentation of material. The readers I primarily have in mind are those with some prior familiarity with Acts and Paul's letters, looking for an initial "deep dive," as it were, into their teaching.

Apart from occasional references throughout, I have not sought to provide the complete footnoting and documentation that might otherwise be expected. I want, then, to be clear in acknowledging my considerable dependence on the work of many others, especially Geerhardus Vos and Herman Ridderbos. Over the years, I have seen myself as involved, in large part, in transmitting and building on their insights into the wonderful riches of God's word, and I am deeply grateful to have had that opportunity. Whatever the value of this book depends on how successfully I have done that.

A further word about sources is in order. As noted in the first paragraph above, this book is largely based on class lectures. Some of that lecture material has also appeared in previously published works, including "Redemption and Resurrection: An Exercise in Biblical-Systematic Theology," in *A Confessing Theology for Postmodern Times*, ed. Michael S. Horton (Wheaton, IL: Crossway, 2000), 229–49; *By Faith, Not by Sight: Paul and the Order of Salvation*, 2nd edition (Phillipsburg, NJ: P&R, 2013); "The Resurrection of Christ and Salvation," The Gospel Coalition, https://www.thegospelcoalition.org/; "The Resurrection of the Christ and the Age to Come," The Gospel Coalition; and "Union with Christ," The Gospel Coalition. I have noted throughout where there is a substantial overlap with these previous publications but also want readers to be aware that they are not sources for this book. The class lectures are the primary source for both those previous publications and this book.

Also in order are acknowledgments, with thanks, of my indebtedness to others: to Jared Oliphint, who initiated the idea for the book with Crossway; to Dennis Johnson, Westminster Seminary California, for reading the manuscript and making helpful suggestions; and, at Crossway, to Justin Taylor for his ongoing encouragement and to Kevin Emmert for his careful editing and numerous helpful proposals for improvements.

Finally, I would be remiss not to mention my deep appreciation for the able and devoted students of over three decades whose questions in the classroom, whose answers on examinations, and who in frequent informal discussions often served to sharpen my own thinking and presentation of material.

R. Gaffin Jr.
November 2021

Introduction

SEVERAL MATTERS, supplementary in nature, serve the interpretation of Acts and the letters of Paul.

In addressing them here, some at greater length than others, I do so on the assumption that you, the reader, already have some familiarity with these documents. This prior exposure undoubtedly varies widely from person to person, but most, perhaps all, will have at least some knowledge of them, however minimal.

On this assumption, my interest in this volume may be seen as a *deepening* interest—to grow in understanding Acts and the letters of Paul and to develop in the ability to interpret them soundly. At the same time, this deepened concern ought always to serve a more ultimate concern—that we believe and obey them as the written word of God.

This deepening concern involves challenges, at times difficult and even presently unresolvable problems. Yet the two concerns are not in tension but thoroughly compatible. Whatever problems we inevitably encounter in understanding Scripture, they do not, and never will, diminish its pervasive and abiding clarity and the need for uninhibited submission to its final authority.

INTERPRETATION AND PROCLAMATION

With that said and without at all meaning to eclipse the ultimate concern just indicated—obedience to God's word—I should make clear that the material in this volume should be seen as coming from a lectern, not a pulpit, as belonging in a classroom or study, not a chapel. In other words, I will not be occupied primarily with directly applying to our lives the truth of Acts and Paul's letters.

This, however, hardly means to divorce lectern and pulpit or, in other terms, to drive a wedge between the *interpretation* of Scripture and its *proclamation*. In fact, given that Scripture is the subject matter of both, the line between the two cannot be a sharp one. But that line is a legitimate and necessary one. The difference in view here and its validity and importance may be seen in a number of ways. Here I point that out briefly in terms of the distinction between *historical distance* and *contemporary relevance*.

For interpretation, the distance between the then-and-there of the text in its historical origin and embeddedness, and the here-and-now of the interpreter is *explicit*; its contemporary relevance is *implicit*. For preaching and other ways of ministering the text to and beyond the congregation today, the situation is the reverse: contemporary relevance is explicit, historical distance mostly implicit.

For both—interpretation and proclamation—immediate relevance, whether implicit or explicit, is always guaranteed because the text is God's word and so remains the necessary and sufficient final authority for faith and life for every generation, regardless of time and place, until history ends at Christ's return. This is why the line between interpretation and proclamation, as drawn here, is not a hard-and-fast one, why too our interpretive approach, for reasons that will become ever clearer as we proceed, will inevitably yield results clearly applicable today and personally edifying to my readers.

Interpretation, then, is in order to proclamation; sound preaching presupposes and flows from solid exposition. Negatively, exposition that does not have in view, at least implicitly, what serves the life and witness of the congregation is skewed. On the other hand, preaching devoid of exposition is a travesty. The interpreter primarily serves the preacher; the preacher himself, in turn, must have some competence as an interpreter and as a judge of the interpretation of others. In the spirit (if not the letter) of the apostle (see 2 Thess. 3:10), "If anyone is not willing to exegete, let him neither preach nor teach."

HELPS FOR INTERPRETATION

A variety of topics facilitate an in-depth understanding of Acts and Paul. Here, I do little more than remind readers of some of the major areas.

For one, there is the mix of questions usually designated "special introduction." These deal with matters like authorship, date and place of origin, destination and original recipients, language and style. In the case, say, of

Romans: Who was and what do we know about its author? When, where, and under what circumstances did he write it? Who were the original recipients, where were they located, and what were their circumstances? Such questions appropriately come up for every New Testament document, including all those we will be considering. To be considered additionally for the letters of Paul is the question of their relative chronology. For instance, which was written first, 1 Corinthians or 1 Timothy? Galatians or Romans?

Related to issues of special introduction more broadly is the area of backgrounds. Our concern is with documents whose origin is within the first-century Greco-Roman Mediterranean world. What is the makeup of that environment? What factors—cultural, linguistic, social, political, and so on—constitute it?

In this regard, a particularly important area, one that has become of heightened interest in more recent study of the New Testament, especially Paul, is the Judaism of the time—Jewish life and theology in its various manifestations during the Second Temple period. What about the community at Qumran? Or rabbinic Judaism? Or the distinctions between Palestinian Judaism, the Judaism of the land, and the Judaism of the Diaspora (Hellenistic Judaism)? Attention to such questions serves our basic objective of deepening our understanding of Acts and Paul.

Another important area is the history of the interpretation of Acts and Paul. The interpretation of Scripture—particularly as we are engaged with it as the word of God—ought to be intensely personal. But it is not an individualistic enterprise. We have to be on guard against what may be dubbed the "me and my Bible syndrome," doing my own thing with the Scriptures, more or less in a personal vacuum.

Probably very few, if any, will defend that approach. But among those who would not, many, I suspect, nonetheless fall into something like it, in unreflecting practice if not in theory—a bane arguably of much use of the Bible in contemporary evangelicalism. We can guard against that tendency by remaining aware that a very broad context for our own work is the *church*, which with all that regrettably continues to divide within it nonetheless remains ultimately one in Christ and so is basically unified across the ages and in every place.

The lofty prayer of the apostle at the end of Ephesians 3, we may fairly say, has in view something like a deepened understanding of the knowledge of God in Christ we are concerned for in this book—in its "breadth and length and height and depth" and "to know the love of Christ that surpasses knowledge." An integral aspect of that prayer, not to be missed, is that this deepened comprehension be together "with all the saints" (3:18–19).

"With all the saints" evokes, in the best sense of the word, the ecumenical character of sound biblical interpretation. We are not the first persons or generation to interpret Acts and Paul; we ought not to lose sight of our solidarity with the great host of those who have gone before us and whose work surrounds us. Certainly we should not absolutize any interpreter or interpretive tradition. We expect that we will not always agree, but we also expect to learn, and to learn a great deal, from others. Negatively, in those often-quoted words, variously attributed, "Those who ignore the mistakes of the past are bound to repeat them." That truth, too, surely documents itself as we look at church history and the history of interpretation.

INTERPRETATION PROPER

The topics that I have just been noting, and others that could be mentioned, are important, as they contribute to a careful, methodologically self-aware study of Acts and Paul; they should not be neglected. Without much reflection, however, you can recognize that none of them involves dealing with Acts and Paul's letters in terms of what we could characterize as their intended meaning and function, or the structure of their teaching. Or to qualify that statement a bit, all these areas, like special introduction and background studies, involve us, at the most, only indirectly or incidentally in getting at the intended meaning and function of the text.[1]

A brief, simple example serves to make this point. Especially since the time of the Enlightenment, one of the big issues in the academic study of Paul has been the authorship of the Pastoral Epistles. Who wrote them continues to be a matter of ongoing debate with extensively developed arguments and counterarguments, particularly as so-called historical-critical scholarship in large part denies their Pauline authorship.[2] My point here?

---

1 We need to respect that intention. Reader response techniques have their place, but they must never function, particularly in the case of interpreting Scripture, to override what I am referring to here as the intended meaning of the text.

2 For our purposes here, in its essentials, the historical-critical method applied to the Bible is not simply a matter of being committed to careful, methodical, and methodologically self-aware interpretation of the text; no one ought to object to that. Rather, as its most consistent

For Paul, the authorship of the Pastorals was hardly an uncertain issue or one that greatly preoccupied him!

Topics like background studies and special introduction, in other words, are just that, *introductory*. They are no more than auxiliary in relation to the subject matter of the text. They are helpful to interpretation, but they are not interpretation in the focused or most proper sense. The issues addressed are certainly legitimate and useful, but they are not what is most important in studying Scripture: its intended meaning, what it teaches. This, then, "interpretation proper" of Acts and Paul, is my focus in this volume. I will not deal with introductory matters as such; pertinent conclusions will either be presupposed or noted in passing.[3]

What this focus also means in general terms, then, is that my interest is in these writings for their revelatory character and function, as they are part of the revelation of the triune God that has its climactic focus in the person and work of Christ. We will be occupied with them as, in a single word that captures the essence of their content all told, they are *gospel*, and therefore as—a description applicable to all of them—they are "the power of God for salvation to everyone who believes" (Rom. 1:16).

To transpose this into a more explicitly methodological key, our interpretative approach will be *redemptive-historical* or *biblical-theological*. Both these expressions, more or less interchangeable as I use them, have a broad and widely varying currency today, particularly "biblical theology." So, some account of what in my view constitutes redemptive-historical method or a biblical-theological approach is in order at this point. First, I offer some

---

practitioners make clear, "critical" means a commitment to the autonomy of reason such that (1) the interpreter has not only the right but also the obligation to stand in judgment over the text, either to validate or, failing that, to call into question or even reject the truth claims of its content (so-called *Sachkritik*); (2) the biblical documents, as written texts, have a purely human origin and authorship, and so are to be treated like any other historical text, with at least the presumption and even the expectation of the presence of errors, whether factual or moral.

Of many works that could be cited, two by its advocates have especially shaped my own understanding: Gerhard Ebeling, "The Significance of the Critical Historical Method for Church and Theology in Protestantism," in *Word and Faith* (Philadelphia, PA: Fortress, 1963), 17–61; and Van A. Harvey, *The Historian and the Believer* (New York: Macmillan, 1966); on the requisite autonomy of the interpreter, see esp. chaps. 1–3.

3 For a full treatment of introductory matters see, e.g., D. A. Carson and Douglas J. Moo, *An Introduction to the New Testament* (Grand Rapids, MI: Zondervan, 2005). A briefer discussion, older but still especially useful, is J. Gresham Machen, *The New Testament. An Introduction to Its Literature and History* (Edinburgh: Banner of Truth Trust, 1976), 51–188.

overall comments about biblical theology and then, more specifically but still in general terms, about New Testament (biblical) theology.

BIBLICAL THEOLOGY[4]

Basic Elements

The following factors, subject to some important qualifications made later, bear on and serve to define a biblical-theological or redemptive-historical approach:

First, revelation, in the sense of verbal communication from God, whether spoken or written, has come as a *historical process*, with an emphasis on both "historical" and "process." As the record of this historical process, Scripture—God-breathed in its entirety (2 Tim. 3:16) and so itself fully revelatory—is an integral part of this process, the history of special revelation.[5]

The extent of this history, all that was actually revealed, is larger than the contents of Scripture, as John 20:30 and 21:25 show. At the same time, Scripture expects us to believe that the "pattern found in Scripture reflects the pattern followed in the history of revelation as a whole."[6] The biblical contours are the actual revelation-historical contours. Scripture provides us with a trustworthy revelatory guide to the entire universe of special revelation; there are no revelatory galaxies out there of which we know nothing.

A contrast serves to highlight this factor of historical process. In their divinely authored origin, the biblical documents have not been dropped, as it were, *senkrecht von oben*—straight down from heaven—contrary to the widespread evangelical tendency in practice noted above.

Also, it is worth noting, in this respect the Bible is unlike the scriptures of other major religions—for instance, the Koran, supposedly dictated to Mohammed through a series of night visions in a relatively short time span, certainly within his lifetime, or the Book of Mormon, claimed to be based on gold tablets unearthed in upper New York State, translated,

---

4   The literature is voluminous; for the view taken here, see esp. Geerhardus Vos, *Biblical Theology: Old and New Testaments* (Edinburgh: Banner of Truth Trust, 1975), v–vi, 3–18.

5   Of course, special revelation always takes place within the context of the creation as revealing God (general or natural revelation). The question of the relationship between general and special revelation, important as it is, is beyond our purview here.

6   John Murray, *Collected Writings of John Murray, Vol. 4: Studies in Theology* (Edinburgh: Banner of Truth Trust, 1982), 18.

and published within a short time. The positive significance of revelation coming as an unfolding history and the origin of Scripture as part of that history will be noted presently.

A second factor defining biblical theology, closely related to the first, is that revelation, understood as verbal, is *not an end in itself*. Revelation is never by itself in the sense of giving us information that consists in timeless truths about God, man, and the world.[7] As a fair and important generalization, verbal revelation is always occasioned by and focused on God's activity in history. God's revelatory word is oriented toward his action as Creator and Redeemer.

Further in this regard, revelation can be seen to focus on that action as it attests or, alternatively, interprets, as it either describes or explains. Of course, to describe is already to interpret. The two, description and interpretation, are on a continuum hermeneutically. The difference between them is not a hard-and-fast one, though this relative difference can usually be recognized.

Invariably, then—this is a primary point we are wanting to accent here—God's speech is related to his actions, his word to his work. In this sense—the focus of word on work—verbal revelation, as already stated above, is not an end in itself. Verbal revelation is *derivative*, a function of what God has done in history. Redemption is the *raison d'être* for revelation. "Revelation is so interwoven with redemption that unless allowed to consider the latter, it would be suspended in the air."[8]

In this focus of revelatory word on redemptive deed, of word revelation on deed revelation,[9] lies the deeper reason for our first point above—that revelation comes as a historical process. Verbal revelation is an essential concomitant within that historical process by which God the Creator is

---

7   "Timeless" in this statement is subject to misunderstanding. To be rejected is the notion that the validity of revealed truth is atemporal, independent of what takes place in time and impervious to what occurs in history. Not in question, however, is the abiding truthfulness and permanent relevance of biblical revelation. In that sense, Paul's teaching, say, on the role of women in the life of the church is "timeless."

8   Vos, *Biblical Theology*, 15.

9   This distinction between redemptive deed and revelatory word is also not a hard-and-fast one: verbal revelatory activity is redemptive, and nonverbal redemptive activity is revelatory; this integration or coalescence—of word and deed, of revelation and redemption—is realized consummately in Christ, his person and work, in both his actions and his teaching, as the Word of God (John 1:1; Heb. 1:2).

actually at work in history, accomplishing the redemption of his creation and the salvation of his people. Verbal revelation has its historically progressive character because it is derivative of the historically progressive character that characterizes redemption, the unfolding of the history of redemption.

In view globally, when we speak of redemptive history, is the history that begins in the garden following the fall and the resulting curse on human sin that affects the entire creation (Rom. 8:20-22), largely incorporating in its unfolding the history of Israel, and reaches its consummation in the work of Christ in "the fullness of time" (Gal. 4:4), when "the Word became flesh and dwelt among us" (John 1:14).

Verbal revelation, then, has come as an organic historical whole, as a completed organically unfolding historical process. Negatively, the Bible is not a compilation of disjointed oracles to isolated or unrelated individuals; it is not an anthology of revelatory vignettes more or less independent of each other.

In sum: when we hear the word *revelation*, the history of verbal revelation ought always to come to mind—the history that is an integral stream within the mainstream of the history of redemption and conforms to the contours of that larger flow.

In this sense, then, revelation interprets redemption and the focus of biblical theology is revelation as redemptive-historical.

Biblical Basis[10]

To this point, my comments have been largely assertive. What about their biblical basis? That can be established in a number of ways. Here I focus on perhaps the clearest, most explicit warrant, found in the opening words of the epistle to the Hebrews:

> God, having spoken formerly to the fathers by the prophets at many times and in various ways, has in these last days spoken to us in the Son. (1:1–2, my translation)

This statement is intended, umbrella-like, to cover what the writer goes on to say in the document as a whole. In doing that, it functions as well to

---

10 See also Richard B. Gaffin Jr., *By Faith, Not by Sight: Paul and the Order of Salvation*, 2nd ed. (Phillipsburg, NJ: P&R, 2013), 7–8.

provide an overarching outlook on God's speaking, on his self-revelation as a whole. Four interrelated factors are present in this statement.

First, revelation is plainly in view as a *historical process*.

Second, this historical process is marked by *diversity*; diversity shapes its unfolding. That diversity is highlighted by the two phrases "at many times" and "in various ways." Each of these phrases translates one of two Greek words, adverbs, accented by their placement together at the beginning of the statement in the Greek text. Close to each other in meaning, they likely differ in that the first (πολυμερῶς) indicates multiple parts or times, while the other (πολυτρόπως) different ways or modes.

Briefly here but importantly, the diversity indicated by these words includes various literary genres and so the need to give them due attention in interpreting Scripture. At the same time, it should be recognized that literary approaches and genre concerns have their validity only as they subserve understanding the actual historical occurrence that is the substance of redemption.

Third and climactic is the reference to the Son. Christ is in view both (1) as the endpoint or final goal of the history of revelation, and (2) with all the diversity involved, as he is its integrating focus (cf., e.g., 2 Cor. 1:20). There is no indication here or in what the writer goes on to say subsequently that there are trajectories in revelation leading up to the Son that bypass the consummating fulfillment that takes place in him (see outside Hebrews esp. Luke 24:44–47; cf. 2 Cor. 1:20).

This is true not simply in a relative or limited sense but absolutely, for the Son is said to be nothing less than God's "last days" speaking; the Son is the eschatological endpoint and fulfillment of that revelatory speech. God's revelation in his Son, in his incarnate person and work, both deed-revelation and word-revelation, has a finality that cannot be superseded or surpassed. Christ consummates as he closes the history of revelation.[11] As the hymn line asks rhetorically, "What more can he say than to you he has said?"[12]

---

11 For the writer of Hebrews, the salvation "declared at first by the Lord" includes its attestation "by those who heard" (Heb. 2:3). This attestation is plausibly understood as the ear (and eye) witness of the apostles, authorized by Christ himself (e.g., Acts 1:8; cf. 1:2, 20–21), such that their words are his words (e.g., 1 Cor. 14:37; 1 Thess. 2:13), and others associated with them in the foundational period of the church (cf. Eph. 2:20).

12 "How Firm a Foundation" in *Trinity Hymnal* (Philadelphia, PA: Great Commission, 1990), 94, stanza 1.

Fourth, the history of revelation involves human activity. This activity is not to be depreciated but given due consideration, for it is integral. It explains in large part the existence of the considerable diversity accented by the writer and contributes to the makeup of the history as a whole.

How the writer construes this human activity in general should not be missed. "God has spoken" is the nuclear assertion of Hebrews 1:1–2. He is the sole subject of both verbs for speaking (participle in 1:1 and main verb in 1:2); everything else is subordinate, not only syntactically but also semantically. The human activity in view—"through the prophets"[13]—is *instrumental*.

The way the writer introduces the same quotation from Psalm 95:7 (Ps. 94 in the LXX, Septuagint) illustrates how this instrumentality is to be understood: what God is "saying through David" (Heb. 4:7) is what "the Holy Spirit says" (3:7). The speaking of David and others (oral and written) is neither somehow independent of nor in tension with God's speaking. Rather, God utilizes them so that their speaking is his; their words are to be received as his, entirely truthful and finally authoritative.[14]

Some Basic Qualifications

The biblically supported comments made so far about redemptive-historical or biblical-theological method are subject to the following three necessary and important qualifications and clarifications.

First, it needs to be kept in mind that God is more than his revelation. The focus of the history of revelation is, as noted, on the activity of God as Creator and Redeemer, on who God is in what he does. But with that distinguishing focus, revelation also points us to recognize that the revealing God is more than his revelation, that he exists prior to that activity and is not defined exhaustively by it. As Creator and Redeemer, he is more than Creator and Redeemer, infinitely more. He is not dependent on his creation and what transpires in it or limited by it in any way. Nor is our knowledge of him exhausted by our knowledge of what he does in creation and redemption. Rather, in his aseity—his existing of himself (*a se*) and

---

13 This reference to the prophets is synecdochic for the human instrumentality employed through-out the entire history of revelation; cf. the parallel statements in 2:2 (angels) and 3:5 (Moses).

14 This pattern, for one, sanctions the distinction made subsequently in formulations of the doc-trine of Scripture between God and the human writers, respectively, as primary author (*auctor primarius*) and secondary authors (*auctores secundarii*).

independent of creation—he transcends creation even as he is immanent and active within it.

Attention to the history of redemption will be sound only where this truth is not only not lost sight of but also adequately honored. Isaiah 57:15, for one, beautifully voices this ultimately incomprehensible reality: "For thus says the One who is high and lifted up, / who inhabits eternity, whose name is Holy: / 'I dwell in the high and holy place, / and also with him who is of a contrite and lowly spirit, / to revive the spirit of the lowly, / and to revive the heart of the contrite.'"

Second, verbal revelation is not only redemptive but also preredemptive. The Bible itself is a redemptive revelation in that all the documents date from after the fall. But in order that we properly understand its main theme of redemption, it provides an account of the original creation and its goodness (Gen. 1:31) and the subsequent historicity of the fall, and so the consequent need for redemption from sin and its effects.

That account attests prefall and therefore preredemptive verbal revelation. Specific instances, fairly read as *typical* of the fellowship between God and Adam and Eve before the fall, are Genesis 1:28–30, 2:16–17 (by implication, 2:19), and 3:1–3.[15] This fellowship bond, with the verbal revelation involved, can be shown to be the initial instance of the covenant making that centrally structures God's relationship with humanity before as well as after the fall (covenant of works, covenant of grace). Accordingly, "covenant-historical," covering both prefall and postfall verbal revelation, is a more comprehensive designation than "redemptive-historical."

Third, the distinction needs to be kept clear between redemptive or salvation history (*historia salutis*), the once-for-all accomplishment of salvation, and the ongoing application of that salvation (*ordo salutis*, the order of salvation). The history of redemption, originating in the garden with the fall and moving forward from there toward its completion in the work of Christ, is distinct from its continuing appropriation, regardless of time and place after the fall.

The two are obviously connected. The latter (redemption applied) depends upon the former (redemption accomplished), while the former absent the latter is devoid of its intended efficacy. But neither may the difference between

---

15 See Vos, *Biblical Theology*, 22–23 ("Pre-Redemptive and Redemptive Special Revelation").

them be obscured or blurred. When I speak throughout of the history of redemption or what is redemptive-historical, I have in mind the former, redemption accomplished (*historia salutis*), not its application (*ordo salutis*).

Biblical Theology and Hermeneutics

From the preceding observations it can perhaps be appreciated that a primary significance of a biblical-theological approach is hermeneutical. This prompts some further comment on that significance and the relationship between biblical theology and exegesis.

The Unity of Scripture. Recognition of its unity is essential to a proper view of Scripture. That conviction, then, is integral to its sound interpretation.

That unity, to be clear, is doctrinal or didactic in nature, possessed by the Bible as a whole because God in his unimpeachable veracity is its primary author and as such accountable for every word. The unity of the Bible is a fundamental hermeneutical principle; we could even say its unity is a pre- or metahermeneutical principle. If you do not come to the careful study of the Bible on the supposition of its unity, then you may be able to say a lot, and a lot learned, about what the Bible says, but in the end you will ultimately misunderstand and distort Scripture, especially its central message of salvation in Christ. That does not put it too strongly.

In holding to the unity of Scripture, we speak of the analogy of Scripture (*analogia Scripturae*). "Analogy" functions here for the notion that to understand Scripture, Scripture is to be compared with Scripture; any portion of Scripture has its meaning in the context of the rest of Scripture. This principle has been given classical expression, for one, in the Westminster Confession of Faith: "The infallible rule of interpretation of Scripture is the Scripture itself: and therefore, when there is a question about the true and full sense of any Scripture (which is not manifold, but one), it must be searched and known by other places that speak more clearly."[16]

This principle was grasped and articulated in the original generation of the Reformation. Its Scripture principle (*sola Scriptura*) involves a hermeneutical proposition, expressed by Luther's *Scriptura interpres Scripturae*,

---

16 Westminster Confession of Faith, 1.9. For this and subsequent references to the Westminster Confession of Faith and Catechisms, see, e.g., *The Confession of Faith and Catechisms* (Willow Grove, PA: The Committee on Christian Education of the Orthodox Presbyterian Church, 2005); https://opc.org/confessions.html.

"Scripture the interpreter of Scripture."[17] We need always to appreciate that, as much as anything, the Reformation is about how to interpret the Bible correctly; the Reformation is fairly seen as one large renewed hermeneutical undertaking.

As this principle has also been put, Scripture is self-interpreting or self-elucidating. This does not mean that the Bible may be interpreted in a vacuum, in isolation and without any attention to introductory or background issues like those noted earlier. But any given text (however factored, whatever its length) is located within the context of the unified teaching of Scripture as a whole and has its meaning elucidated as it is embedded within that overall unity and is clarified in the light of other passages. Any given text of Scripture is aptly visualized as the center of increasingly widening circles of context that, as they expand to include the whole of Scripture, have a bearing on understanding that text.

In considering the hermeneutical significance of a biblical-theological approach, then, it is important to see that the unity of Scripture is fundamentally a *redemptive-historical or covenant-historical* unity.

The unity of the Bible may be fairly viewed in different ways. For instance, in affirming that unity, particularly in light of the point made earlier about its doctrinal or didactic unity, we may speak of the unity of the Bible as consisting of a set of mutually consistent, noncontradictory assertions. To say that would be true but clearly does not go far enough when we consider Scripture's *content*.

In speaking of the redemptive-historical unity of Scripture, in view is the unity that lies in back of the Scriptures. Predicating unity of the statements of Scripture in terms of its content recognizes the unity or coherence predicable of the organically unfolding historical process of redemption that Scripture documents. As unity marks the actual unfolding of the history of redemption, as that original revelation process is a unified process, so too the God-authored record of that historical process, itself part of that process, is unified. The unity of the Bible reflects and is an expression of the unity of the organism, the organic pattern, of God's activity in history as Creator and Redeemer.

17 Martin Luther, *The Bondage of the Will*, in *Career of the Reformer III*, vol. 33 of *Luther's Works*, ed. Jaroslav Jan Pelikan, Hilton C. Oswald, and Helmut T. Lehmann (Philadelphia, PA: Fortress, 1972), 25–26.

That entails, then, brought to bear more specifically on the actual work of exegesis, for interpreting a particular biblical text of whatever genre or length (from a single sentence to a larger discourse unit), essential is understanding its place in the history of revelation, its place within covenant history. In terms of the subject matter of the text—what the text is talking about—an all-controlling context is the redemptive- and revelational-historical context.

Terminology

A brief comment on terminology is in order at this point. A certain liability attaches to the expression "biblical theology." For one, it can leave the impression that other theological areas are seen as not or less than "biblical." Also, it can be taken to suggest that in view is a particular theological discipline that can go its own way, as it were, that has its own terrain or turf in distinction from other areas of theological endeavor and can proceed more or less on its own, independent from the other theological disciplines, in particular, say, from systematic theology.

Such misconceptions are to be resisted, because, as I have just pointed out, what is centrally at issue in biblical theology are methodological considerations that involve every aspect of the theological enterprise, because in its entirety that endeavor is staked on sound exegesis. So-called biblical theology is about exegeting rightly, interpreting Scripture correctly.

Vos and others following him, even though they continue to speak of "biblical theology" because of its established currency, have proposed "history of special revelation" as a preferable designation, given its distinguishing concern to consider the original revelation-historical process as recorded in the Old and New Testaments. Further on the matter of terminology, preferable to the substantive "biblical theology" are the adjectives "biblical-theological" or "redemptive-historical" or "covenant-historical"; they better serve to indicate the primarily methodological or functional aspect involved.

Biblical Theology and Systematic Theology (Dogmatics)[18]

The preceding comments bring into view the often-discussed question of the relationship between biblical theology and systematic theology.

18 Of a considerable volume of literature that could be cited, cf. the helpful overview of Lee Irons, "Biblical and Systematic Theology: A Digest of Reformed Opinion on Their Proper Relationship," The Upper Register (website), http://www.upper-register.com/papers/bt_st.html.

Suffice it here to say the following: Biblical theology is the *indispensable servant* of systematic theology, where the latter is understood as providing a presentation, under appropriate topics, of the teaching of the Bible as a whole.[19] Biblical theology is *indispensable* for systematic theology because its distinguishing attention to the text in its redemptive-historical context is indispensable for the exegesis that is the lifeblood of sound systematic theology.

Biblical theology is also systematic theology's *servant*. It is subordinate to systematic theology in the sense that its distinguishing focus on the specific and distinctive revelatory contributions of each of the various secondary, human authors of Scripture (and by others recorded in their writings) is not for its own sake but only as it serves the more ultimate end of presenting the unified and coherent teaching of the Bible in its entirety as the word of God, its primary author. For instance, our interest in Romans or in Paul's theology is not ultimately in what he says but what God says there and elsewhere in Scripture.

Biblical Theology in Historical Perspective

It is worth noting that an *explicitly conceived* application of biblical-theological method or a redemptive-historical orientation is relatively recent, particularly within the tradition of Reformed and, more broadly, evangelical theology. That may be said to date largely, and as much as anyone, from the seminal work of Geerhardus Vos (1862–1949), the first occupant of the newly created chair of biblical theology at Princeton Theological Seminary (1893–1932). Vos is fairly seen as the father of Reformed biblical theology.[20]

---

19 I have discussed this relationship elsewhere over the years (see the source cited in n22 below for some other references). For another brief statement, see, e.g., Richard B. Gaffin Jr., "Redemption and Resurrection: An Exercise in Biblical-Systematic Theology," in *A Confessing Theology for Postmodern Times* (Wheaton, IL: Crossway, 2000), 229–30.

20 The term "biblical theology" begins to occur and gain currency about a century earlier in the mid- to late-eighteenth century, largely within the context of the emerging historical-critical school of biblical interpretation. This biblical theology, which took hold increasingly in ways that proved to be highly influential, particularly in and through key theological faculties of German universities, was self-consciously predicated on a denial of the inspiration and canonicity of Scripture (as taught in Scripture), and so on a denial of the entire truthfulness and unity of its teaching. Over a century later, without our overlooking or depreciating precursors and the pertinent work of others contemporary to Vos, it is fair to say that he led the way in doing biblical theology based on biblically sound presuppositions and principles.

At the same time, however, in highlighting the significance of his work and the explicit biblical theology he developed, it is important not to overlook significant continuity with the past. It is not as if the church was stumbling around in interpretive darkness until suddenly at the end of the nineteenth century Vos and others appeared on the scene.

To enter briefly into what could become a long and profitable discussion, the church has always been sensitive to what is really at stake in so-called biblical theology. Why? Because the church has always been alert to the *historical character* of the salvation come in Christ. That concern—salvation as accomplished in history—as much as anything is the vital nerve of biblical theology.

From its earliest days, particularly in its conflict with gnosticism that raged over much of the second century and beyond,[21] the church has been aware that salvation and saving faith depend vitally not only on who God *is*, or on what he *says*, but ultimately and pointedly on what he *has done*, in history in Christ.

What the church has appreciated, whether implicitly or explicitly, from its beginning is that the knowledge of God, true *cognitio Dei*, is not simply information about God, about the nature of God or man or the world, but at its core is gospel knowledge, knowledge of what has taken place in history in the person and work of Jesus Christ.

So, seen already for instance in the account of Paul in Athens (Acts 17:16–32), the church has perceived that Christianity is not just another competing philosophy. The affront of Christianity is not that it offers another option (however "new" and "strange," 17:19–20). Rather, it soon became evident that the gospel message Paul and others proclaimed, centered on the death and resurrection of Christ, would not simply fold nicely into classical pagan Greco-Roman culture but was destructive at its root of its idolatrous worldview.

The thesis of continuity with later biblical theology may be argued further by showing that, especially beginning with the Reformation, exegesis has often been implicitly biblical-theological.

With this continuity noted, at the same time Vos's epoch-making labors and what he introduced into the life of the church should be recognized.

---

21 In fact, traces of this conflict go back into the New Testament itself, as seen, for instance, in the protognostic errors addressed in the Johannine correspondence (cf. 1 John 4:2) and dealt with by Paul in the church in Colossae.

He is the first, or the most gifted among the first, within historic Christian orthodoxy, certainly the first within the Reformed tradition, to give pointed and programmatic attention to revelation as an unfolding historical process, to grasp the fundamental significance of that fact and to draw out, though not as explicitly as could be wished, its methodological and hermeneutical consequences. The present situation continues to be one where with much profit still to be gained from the work of Vos and its implications, it has yet to have the influence it deserves.[22]

Concluding Observations

The preceding reflections on biblical theology can be rounded out with a couple of concluding observations that serve to reinforce some of what has already been said.

First, by now it can be recognized that, as I view it, biblical-theological method is neither a dispensable exegetical luxury nor an esoteric handling of the text, yielding higher insights reserved for a select group of initiates. Such views, sometimes encountered, betray a serious undervaluing of biblical theology (the theological elitism of the latter is also unedifying). For its concern arises from the subject matter of Scripture itself and has in view methodological issues that are not only appropriate but essential to understanding the text.

In 2 Timothy 2:15, Paul challenges Timothy to be a "worker" with "no need to be ashamed" in "rightly handling the word of truth." *Orthodoxy* and *orthodox* derive from the prefix of the compound word used for this "right handling" (ὀρθοτομεῖν). So, we may say, here Paul expresses a concern for Timothy's hermeneutics to be a correct hermeneutics. At stake in so-called biblical theology is nothing less than what is indispensable for this sound, "orthodox" handling of Scripture.

Second, what has been said so far about biblical-theological method may not have made sufficiently clear that what is in view is better described more loosely as an approach or an orientation rather than a method. Certainly we are not talking about some ironclad methodology, some rigid or stereotyped

22 See further Richard B. Gaffin Jr., "Vos, Geerhardus," in *Dictionary of Major Biblical Interpreters*, ed. Donald K. McKim (Downers Grove, IL: IVP, 2007), 1016–19; Danny E. Olinger, *Geerhardus Vos: Reformed Biblical Theologian, Confessional Presbyterian* (Philadelphia, PA: Reformed Forum), 2018.

set of procedures. Nor is it as if we have in our possession the final word in interpreting Scripture. Rather, as said, in view is an approach to Scripture that recognizes and accommodates a variety of methodological levels and will incorporate various exegetical procedures and techniques.

In this regard with an eye to a misunderstanding that sometimes surfaces, it is not as if we have to choose between grammatical-historical exegesis and redemptive-historical interpretation. That betrays a false disjunction. A redemptive-historical orientation demands or, better, incorporates sound and careful grammatical-historical exegesis.

Looking in a related but somewhat different direction, a redemptive-historical approach readily recognizes the place for a multiplicity of perspectives in handling Scripture. In Ephesians 3:8, the apostle speaks of "the unsearchable riches of Christ," and in 3:10 of "the manifold wisdom of God." No approach, no handling of Scripture can come close to exhausting this multifaceted wisdom of God revealed in Christ with the fullness of perspectives it opens up. With that said, however, I would accent that the redemptive-historical "perspective," with its controlling focus on Christ as central to the whole of Scripture, is not just one among others. It is, if you will, a megaperspective that embraces and accommodates all others.

NEW TESTAMENT THEOLOGY[23]

The preceding comments concern biblical theology in general. Narrowing our focus now, what is involved specifically in a biblical-theological approach to the New Testament? How do we do justice to the New Testament in view of the historically progressive character of special revelation? What is entailed in interpreting the New Testament in terms of redemptive or covenant history?

The Endpoint of the Revelation Process

First, of several observations prompted by these questions, the concern of the New Testament is not so much with the process of revelation as the *endpoint* of that process. In comparison, ongoing development in revelation is much more a structural characteristic of the Old Testament—a difference

---

23 This section builds on and supplements Vos, *Biblical Theology*, 299–304 ("The Structure of New Testament Revelation").

seen simply by noting that the Old Testament documents appeared over the span of roughly a millennium, from Moses to the postexilic prophets. The New Testament, in contrast, is written in approximately one generation. A clear canonical distinction exists between process and endpoint.

Further, to anticipate briefly a major point of what our work in Acts and Paul's letters will show, when we consider the content of New Testament revelation—and that, of course, is preeminently Christ, his person and work—and even more specifically, when we consider the *eschatological* character of his work, then, as we look at the New Testament as a whole, we have reason for speaking of the eschatological character of New Testament revelation, and so of the New Testament as being concerned with the *eschatological endpoint* of the history of revelation. Here we need do no more than remind ourselves of Hebrews 1:2, noted above: God's new covenant speech in the Son occurs "in these last days"; it is his culminating eschatological speaking.

Historical Progression

Taking note of this point, however, should not be at the expense of overlooking the presence of process and development within the New Testament. In fact, historical progression is a critical element there: globally, the movement from the ministry of John the Baptist to the earthly ministry of Jesus to the apostolic church.

In fact, this historical progression is not only present but basic to the gospel. At the heart of the gospel is the historical progression experienced by Christ himself. He moves, pivotally by the cross and resurrection, from his state of humiliation to his state of exaltation—from bearing the just wrath and curse of God that his people deserve for their sins to being restored irreversibly, with that wrath propitiated and removed, to God's favor. The result is the permanent *transition from wrath to grace in history*, effected for the salvation of his people. The gospel stands or falls with the historical sequence of Christ's humiliation and exaltation.[24]

There is, then, a basic, three-phase historical progression in New Testament revelation: John—Jesus—the church. As we look within each of

---

24 This point needs to be affirmed and maintained particularly against views, stemming largely from the influence of the theology of Karl Barth, in which Christ's humiliation and exaltation in their significance for the gospel are seen not as a genuine historical before and after but instead are transposed into an ever-present, dialectically related above and below.

these phases, we may surely recognize that development took place and hypothesize how, more or less probably, it occurred. But such development is not made prominent in the New Testament records. For instance, in considering the church during the time the New Testament was being written, it becomes difficult to establish a precise, fully detailed construction of how its history unfolded—a state of affairs that keeps New Testament scholarship at work revisiting the issues involved. These issues are not unimportant, because they serve to enlighten. But they are not issues to which we are able to provide full and clear-cut answers because of the nature of New Testament revelation.

The controlling concern of the New Testament writers is different. The focus of their interest, "of first importance" for them, is Christ's death and resurrection (e.g., 1 Cor. 15:3–4). They are intent on presenting this event-complex in its immediate and extended historical context and with its immediate and, as it has now turned out to be, long-term historical consequences. In doing that, they provide revelation sufficient for the time until the still-future return of Christ.

At the same time, their collective concern, with its focus on the cross and resurrection, also relates the entire New Testament to the Old Testament as a whole. They document and reinforce in different ways what has taken place in Christ, particularly his death and resurrection, as the fulfillment of Old Testament history. In doing that, it should not be missed, they also understand themselves to be showing the true meaning of Israel's Scriptures—not a new meaning they give to those Scriptures but their inherent and only meaning.

Another factor to keep in mind related to development is that the entire New Testament is written after the cross and resurrection. Every New Testament document, including the Gospels, which deal largely with the period before the resurrection, is written from a post-resurrection outlook. Even the Gospels contain explicit elaboration or commentary from this exaltation perspective. This is particularly evident in John's Gospel: his postresurrection vantage point comes out more explicitly in comparison to the Synoptics (e.g., John 2:21–22; 7:39).

Our observations to this point pertaining to New Testament (biblical) theology may be focused by the following generalization: the New Testament in its various parts, as a record of the consummation of the history of redemption, provides a *variety of witness to Jesus Christ from a postresurrec-tion perspective*. Or to put it in a somewhat more formalized way: the New Testament consists of *diverse and synchronic witness to the exalted Christ*.[25] The task for New Testament interpretation, as fruitful as it is challenging, is to carefully explore this New Testament witness in its full variety.

The New Testament as Witness

This basic characterization of the New Testament prompts a couple of clari-fying comments. The first concerns "witness" as a key category for describ-ing the New Testament, the other about that witness as varied or diverse.

Apostolic Witness

There are some who are properly wary about categorizing Scripture as "witness." That understandable hesitation has come about largely because of the way many apply that term to Scripture. Here, Karl Barth may again be singled out for the widespread and massive influence his doctrine of Scripture has had over the course of the twentieth century to the present, particularly in the academic study of theology.

In this view, dominant particularly in the historical-critical tradition to the virtual exclusion of all other views, "witness" functions to introduce discontinuity between revelation and the Bible, to drive a wedge between them. The use of the term carries the nuance of "only" or "no more than" a witness, with the further elaboration that this witness is purely human and that the Bible, merely human in its origin and character as a written text, is, as such, fallible.

My use of "witness" applied to the New Testament must be careful to distance itself from this view and to make clear how it differs. Due caution, however, should not be allowed to deprive us of the good and proper use of the term, in fact, its biblical use.

Here we do little more than to take note of some key conclusions that a more careful study of the use of the primary New Testament word group for "witness" (μαρτυρία, μάρτυρος, μαρτυρέω) will be able to establish.[26]

---

25 "Synchronic" in the sense that all of the New Testament documents are authored from the es-sentially same-time *redemptive-historical* vantage point.

26 See Herman N. Ridderbos, *Redemptive History and the New Testament Scriptures*, 2nd rev. ed. (Phillipsburg, NJ: P&R, 1988), 58–68.

The witness that we find in the New Testament is more than just an individual's "personal testimony," as that expression is usually used today. Rather, the μαρτυρία encountered there is witness that is transsubjective, witness that is absolutely reliable and trustworthy, that is to be believed, that serves to establish the truth and compels assent; it is the kind of witness that will stand up in a court of law.

Applied to the Old Testament—for instance, the witness of Moses as the immediate context of John 5:39 makes clear (5:45–47)—"The Scriptures," Jesus says to his opponents, "bear witness about me." This witness-bearing of the Scriptures as it accuses them will serve as sufficient grounds to condemn them for rejecting Jesus.

The New Testament, largely considered, is apostolic witness. As such, it is the witness of Christ. The witness of the apostles is the witness the exalted Christ has appointed and authorized, such that he identifies it as his very own (Acts 1:21–22; Eph. 2:20); it is on par with Jesus's own words in truth and authority (e.g., 2 Cor. 13:3; 1 John 1:2 and 4:14 in the light of 1:2).[27]

Apostolic witness as the witness of Christ is, further, the witness of the Holy Spirit as "the Spirit of truth," and that specifically in relation to the witness of the apostles (John 15:26–27).[28] Witness in the New Testament, then, involves the correlate witness of the apostles, Christ, and the Holy Spirit as the same witness. There is a back-and-forth within this triad (Christ—the Spirit—the apostles); the witness of any one implies the witness of the others.

This is the kind of witness that marks the New Testament as a collection of writings (canon), in characterizing it as diverse witness to the exalted Christ—witness that is fully the word of God in its origin, truth, and authority. This, then, is why it is so important to do justice to that witness in terms of its diversity.

27 The New Testament use of "apostle" (ἀπόστολος) varies. My comments here concern those who were apostles of Christ—those chosen and authorized by Christ and having his authority—the original twelve, with Matthias replacing Judas (Acts 1:20–26), Paul (1 Cor. 15:8–9; cf. Rom. 1:5; 1 Cor. 1:1; 9:2; Gal. 1:1, 11–16), and perhaps others. These are the apostles in view in Eph. 2:20 and listed as first in 1 Cor. 12:28 and Eph. 4:11; see the discussion of this apostolate ("apostleship," Acts 1:25) in Ridderbos, Redemptive History, 12–15. In distinction are those "apostles" who served as "messengers" of particular churches (2 Cor. 8:23; Phil. 2:25), on a temporary basis and without the plenary authority of the apostles of Christ.

28 The proximate "you" addressed in these verses, I take it, is not indefinite or general but apostolic (the "you" who "have been with me from the beginning"). Only derivatively and only through the apostles (the church in nuce) is the "you" addressed the whole church.

Diverse Human Instrumentality

To consider the diversity of the New Testament's witness inevitably draws attention to the factor of human authorship, to the various human authors involved in its origin. The great gain in this approach, however—despite the way it is often put—is not that the Bible's humanity is thereby highlighted and "comes closer to us." There is some truth in that, but the primary value of this approach is not that the humanity of the Bible is made to stand out so that the Bible becomes a more human book.

The point that we need to be clear on is that in and of itself, this human instrumentality means nothing. That may seem too strong a statement, and it could be construed in a way that would be unfortunate if it diminishes necessary attention to the human characteristics of Scripture. That is not my intention, but from an ultimate point of view, it does not put it too strongly to say that in and of itself, human authorship means nothing.

What Paul says in 1 Thessalonians 2:13 is particularly instructive for validating the point at issue here. There he gives unceasing thanks to God for the reception of his preaching by the church in Thessalonica. Undoubtedly, it was *his* preaching. It bore the marks of his personality; his personal characteristics were no doubt reflected in its communication. Yet his description of its reception is striking: "when you received the word of God, which you heard from us, you accepted it not as the word of men but as what it really[29] is, the word of God." Ultimately considered, his preaching with which he was entrusted as an apostle is properly assessed in terms of this stark polarity: not the word of men . . . but the word of God.[30]

On balance, approaching the New Testament in terms of the diversity of its witness will undoubtedly draw our attention to its varied human authorship. But the ultimate value in this approach is that in this way, the full riches of divine revelation become plainer and the manifold wisdom of God in Christ (Eph. 3:8, 10) better articulated. God's word will be received in more of its intended precision and penetrating efficacy as the sharp, two-edged sword that it is (Heb. 4:12).

---

29 ἀληθῶς, "truly."

30 To see this verse as expressing what is true of the *content* of his preaching (its "message"), but not its verbal, syntactic-semantic *form* introduces a disjunction completely foreign to Paul's statement.

The Task of Appropriation

Finally, it bears emphasizing that this program of New Testament interpretation—approaching it in terms of the diversity of its witness—has to be carried out with care and discernment. Almost everybody today involved in biblical studies will say that more attention needs to be given to the diversity of the New Testament. But for most—virtually all those committed to historical-critical interpretation—this diversity amounts in large measure to doctrinal confusion, to internal theological contradictions. Pointedly, for many today, diversity is equated with *disunity*. In fact, it seems fair to say that within the current environment of academic biblical studies, the disunity of the New Testament has become a virtual hermeneutical axiom for many; this disunity is more or less an assumption, hardly any longer in need of demonstration.

This contemporary situation can lead to the temptation of overreaction that needs to be resisted. The widespread equating of diversity with disunity must not be allowed to mislead into a too hasty tendency to harmonize or to assert unity. The problem is not with efforts of harmonization where appropriate, and certainly not with seeking to show unity, but with doing that too facilely. To be more specific, we need to be on guard against the tendency of hesitating to stress the diversity and historical particularity of the New Testament materials and all that entails, out of a fear of the specter of a relativizing historicism that would compromise its unity. We ought not to think that we can best defend the unity of the New Testament by toning down on its diversity.

That kind of tactic is wrong, first of all, because it does an injustice to the text, a disservice to the New Testament itself. But also, in the long run, it will result in biblical scholarship that is less credible.

What needs to be recognized and kept in mind is that, at the end of the day, the unity of the New Testament is not something we have to establish or to demonstrate in any constitutive way. Rather, our task is one of appropriation, of accepting what is already there: unity that exists as diversity, diversity that embodies unity. The New Testament is a unity in diversity, an organic wholeness of different parts, a coherence of diverse elements. Unity and diversity are not to be set in opposition or played off against each other.

As noted earlier, the unity in view here is not found in some recurring dynamic action with Scripture, a nonverbal revelatory activity associated with the text but not predicable of the text as text. Rather, it is a doctrinal, didactic unity present precisely as the diversity of New Testament witness.

The task, challenging but also promising, for New Testament interpreters, pastors, teachers, and others is to recognize this diversity and explore it. As a result, the unity of the New Testament will be seen and heard in more of its multiplex depth and truly symphonic power.

PART 1

———

THE THEOLOGY OF ACTS

1

Pentecost and the History
of Redemption

CLEARLY CENTRAL IN ACTS is what took place on the day of Pentecost. There is no better way, then, to gain a sound overall understanding of Acts than to consider the significance of this key event. Exploring that significance brings to light the pivotal place of Pentecost in redemptive history (the *historia salutis*), or, to be thematically more specific with an eye to Luke's narrative in Acts, *the role of Pentecost in the coming of the kingdom of God*. Several observations show the appropriateness of approaching Acts as a whole by focusing on the redemptive-historical significance of Pentecost.

THE PURPOSE AND STRUCTURE OF ACTS:
INITIAL CONSIDERATIONS

The Words of Jesus in 1:8

Without becoming embroiled here in the much-debated question of the purpose(s) of Acts, it seems fair to observe that Luke clearly structures his narrative in terms of the words of Jesus in 1:8:

> But you will receive power when the Holy Spirit has come upon you, and you will be my witnesses in Jerusalem and in all Judea and Samaria, and to the end of the earth.

An overarching concern of Luke, then, is to structure his narration in Acts in terms of this witness-bearing, an activity that has its point of departure in Jerusalem and expands outwardly from there. Or, putting it in clearly intended ethnic terms, a primary aim of Luke, globally considered, is to document how this witness-bearing spread from *Israel to the nations.*

In other words, at least one concern of Luke—surely a basic concern—is to show that history unfolded just as Jesus said it would, to relate certain events that came to pass just as Jesus had prophesied. A bird's-eye survey of Acts bears this out: the basic line of narration moves from Jerusalem to Rome, "the end of the earth," where the narrative ends in Acts 28.

Several facets in this description of the purpose of Acts bear elaborating.

First is the *apostolic* factor. The "you" addressed by Jesus in Acts 1:8 is not indeterminate but specifically an apostolic "you." Its antecedent, working backward in the immediate context from 1:8, is in 1:2: "the apostles whom he [Jesus] had chosen." Also, "you," occurring repeatedly beyond 1:2 through 1:11, refers to the apostles and in those references, it is important to see, is *limited* to them.

This focus on the apostles is reinforced in the rest of the chapter. After describing the return of the "you" to Jerusalem following the ascension (1:11), the eleven apostles are mentioned individually by name (1:13), and the main point to the end of the chapter is the reconstitution of the apostolate (1:25) to its original number of twelve with the election of Matthias. So, as Acts 1:8 is fairly seen as indicating what structures the entire narrative in Acts and the "you" there is an apostolic "you," what Luke documents in Acts *as a whole* is an essentially *apostolic* task.

Second, this task is a *universal* task; the apostolic task is worldwide in its scope. The narrative flow in Acts 1:8, beginning in Jerusalem, reaches to "the end of the earth." Further, the geographic terms of this worldwide expansion have evidently *ethnic* overtones. Acts documents the witness-bearing of the apostles that moves from Jew (Jerusalem-Judea), to part-Jew (Samaria), to non-Jew/Gentile (the ends of the earth).

The essentially ethnic dimensions of this universalism are put beyond question in Acts 13. At Antioch in Pisidia on his first missionary journey, Paul encountered fierce opposition from among the Jews, especially the religious leaders of the Jewish community (13:45; cf. 13:50), a rejection met, in turn, by the bold response of Paul and Barnabas: "It was necessary that the word of God be spoken first to you [Jews]. Since you thrust it aside and judge yourselves unworthy of eternal life, behold, we are turning to the Gentiles" (13:46).

This response, then, is followed (1) by the derivative application to their own witness-bearing ministry of what the Lord says to the messianic servant in Isaiah 49:6: "I have made you a light for the Gentiles, / that you may bring salvation to the ends of the earth" (Acts 13:47); and (2) with Luke's observation, "And when the Gentiles heard this, they began rejoicing and glorifying the word of the Lord" (13:48; cf. 28:28). In the parallelism of the Isaiah quotation, "Gentiles" and "the ends of the earth" correspond to each other and are clearly interchangeable. "The ends of the earth" are specifically Gentile "ends of the earth."

Acts 1:8 and 13:47 are the only New Testament occurrences of the expression "the ends of the earth." It seems likely, then, that its use by Jesus in 1:8 echoes the Isaiah passage (cf. Isa. 45:22) and points to the apostles' impending witness to him as the one who fulfills the promise of universal salvation made to the messianic Servant (see also Acts 26:23). In Acts 1:8, geographic denotation has an ethnic connotation. This ethnic flow of the narrative in Acts points to and reinforces the universality of the apostles' task.

Assuming that in Acts 13 Luke accurately represents what Paul said, it is legitimate methodologically to introduce several statements from Paul's letters as further commentary that reinforces the universality of the apostolic task in which, as Acts documents, he was a key participant.

In Colossians 1:5-6, Paul refers to the "gospel, which has come to you, as indeed *in the whole world* it is bearing fruit and increasing." Later, in 1:23, similarly and more explicitly concerning his own activity, he speaks of "the hope of the gospel that you heard, which has been proclaimed *in all creation*[1] under heaven, and of which I, Paul, became a minister." Similarly, at the conclusion of his ministry, plausibly seen as reflecting on it as a whole, he speaks of his preaching as "fully proclaimed" to "all the Gentiles" (2 Tim. 4:17). As an apostle of Christ (see Col. 1:1; 2 Tim. 1:1), then, Paul knew himself to be involved in a gospel ministry not only worldwide in its scope but also already completed ("which has been proclaimed in all creation under heaven").

Third, then, the universal apostolic task that Acts documents is also a *finished* task. This conclusion follows implicitly from what we have so far been considering about the purpose of Acts and is intimated in the

---

1   Or, "to every creature" (NIV, KJV, NKJV).

statements from Colossians just noted. Acts intends to show that in its universal realization, the apostolic task in view in 1:8 has been completed.

In other words, what Acts does *not* document, what Luke is *not* intending to relate, is an open-ended, partial history that has begun with the ministry of the apostles but is of one piece with and looks for its completion by others who will follow them.

That is the way Acts is sometimes read. Reaching the end of Acts 28, the narrative can appear unresolved and to end on a rather negative note with Paul, its principal subject, a prisoner in Rome under house arrest (28:16, 30). This hardly seems the way to conclude a narrative. What happened to him subsequently? So a part three to Theophilus, no longer extant, has even been hypothesized, in which Luke supposedly wrapped up the loose ends left for us in Acts.

To the contrary, there are no narrative loose ends in Acts. The task as foretold in 1:8 is finished. With the apostolic witness to Christ having reached the Gentile "ends of the earth" (Rome), the narrative that Luke intends is complete; it is not in need of being filled out or supplemented by an Acts 29 and following.

The note on which the document ends signals the successful completion of the apostolic task. The adverb "unhindered" (ἀκωλύτως, 28:31), positioned for emphasis as the last word in the final sentence, has a positive exclamatory force ("without hindrance!").

The New Testament undoubtedly recognizes that there will be a future for the church after the apostles. It makes provision for that postapostolic future, most notably in the Pastoral Epistles and elsewhere. But that provision is not within the purview of Acts, except incidentally. Rather, in the light of 1:8, Acts documents a *completed*, *universal*, *apostolic* task. Acts records the *finished founding* of the "one holy catholic" church as also "apostolic" (the Nicene Creed).

Two Observations

The importance of this basic conclusion about the purpose and composition of Acts and certain of its implications will emerge as we consider how Pentecost and integrally related events are central to the narrative in Acts. Here, before moving on, a couple of other observations pertinent to this conclusion serve to reinforce it.

First, Acts 1:8 should not, as often happens, be made the theme verse for a missions conference or used to challenge a congregation about its responsibility to support missionaries throughout the world today. "Jerusalem" does not stand for or mean just any congregation, whatever its time or location, with "the ends of the earth" extending out from there. Acts 1:8 is not addressed directly to the church today. It is not a mandate for present worldwide witness. The "you" in Acts 1:8 is not a general "you"; it does not include the church of whatever time and place in history. It is addressed specifically and only to the apostles concerning a worldwide task they eventually completed.

This is not at all to deny or even question the worldwide missionary mandate of the church today. In this regard, comparing Acts 1:8 with Matthew 28:19–20 is instructive. Addressed in both is the same group within the same redemptive-historical context, the eleven prior to the ascension, but there is a difference. In Matthew, unlike Acts, the mandate to disciple the nations is in force "to the end of the age"; that is, until the end of history at Christ's return. In Acts, the worldwide witness-bearing in view is unique to the apostles in the initial, foundation-laying era of the church (cf. Eph. 2:20).

In Matthew, discipling the nations includes the activity of both the apostles and, by implication, the postapostolic church as it builds on that apostolic foundation by faithfully ministering it. The two passages complement each other. Matthew 28:19–20, then, is the appropriate theme text for this year's missions conference (and next year's and any year thereafter until Jesus comes again).

Second, the completion of their universal witness by the apostles also has an important bearing on *the overall eschatological outlook* of the New Testament. To note that briefly here without being able to argue it fully or satisfactorily, "the whole world," "all nations" (Matt. 24:14) have been evangelized by the apostles; recall again Colossians 1:6, 23 (cf. 2 Tim. 4:17: "so that through me the message might be fully proclaimed and *all* the Gentiles might hear it.").

To be sure, the worldwide spread of the gospel by the postapostolic church, its extent geographically, has gone well beyond the Mediterranean world, within which the apostles remained in their witnessing. But in terms of its basic ethnic significance in the history of redemption—from

Jew to include non-Jew—the universal spread of the gospel by the apostles (and those associated with them) has already been completed. Through the apostles, the spread of the gospel has, so to speak, come full or, better, closed circle. Its subsequent spread throughout the world in and through the postapostolic church is not the completing of a circle left open and incomplete by the apostles. Rather, it is an ongoing filling in and expansion *within* the worldwide closed circle completed by the apostles.

In terms of these considerations, then, requisite in principle for the fulfillment of biblical prophecy, Christ could have returned at any time subsequent to the completion of the apostles' witness-bearing. The postapostolic mission of the church will continue until that incalculable time—the day and hour known only to the Father (Matt. 24:36; Mark 13:32)—when Christ will return. In this sense, the New Testament teaches his "imminent return."

The Role of Persecution

Worth highlighting in this preliminary assessment of the purpose and structuring of the unfolding narrative in Acts, is the role of *persecution*. Persecution furthers the expansion of the *universal apostolic* witness-bearing until it is *completed*. An important theme in Acts is Jewish unbelief and rejection of the gospel, like the instance in Acts 13 noted above. The effect of this opposition was the exact opposite of what was intended. Rather than succeeding in suppressing the spread of the gospel, the result was its advance.

Instructive in this regard, again, is the ending of Acts. Paul, having reached "the end of the earth" in Rome, was there under some form of house arrest and chained (28:16, 20). Afforded an opportunity by the local Jewish leaders who came to him, he gave them an account of his ministry and sought to persuade them from Scripture about Jesus (28:17–23). The resulting reaction was mixed (28:24), prompting Paul to rebuke with Scripture those who disbelieved (28:25–27), and to declare, "Therefore let it be known to you that this salvation of God has been sent to the Gentiles; they will listen" (28:28).

So, Acts closes on this positive note: over a two-year period, Paul "welcomed all who came to him, proclaiming the kingdom of God and teaching about the Lord Jesus Christ with all boldness and without hindrance" (28:30–31). We have already commented on the upbeat exclamatory force of the final "unhindered." The point is unmistakable: the apostle is "bound with chains as a criminal. But the word of God is not bound!" (2 Tim. 2:9[2]).

The Focus on Peter and Paul

Basic also to the structuring of the apostolic narrative in Acts is its *focus on Peter and Paul.* Peter is central in approximately the first half (Acts 1–12), being phased out after that and mentioned for the last time for the important role he had at the Jerusalem Council (15:7–11, cf. 15:14). Paul, mentioned briefly for his part in the murder of Stephen (7:58), is introduced with his conversion in Acts 9 and is dominant in the last half (Acts 13–28). Several observations may be made about this dual focus.

First, it has been alleged by some that this concentration on Peter and Paul reflects the fact that Luke is involved in unhistorical stylization for kerygmatic purposes. The "Peter" and "Paul" of Acts are seen as Luke's own creations, stereotypes that serve as mouthpieces for the extensive speech materials he attributes to them. Without being able to interact extensively with this viewpoint here, suffice it to say that there are enough variations from the pattern of Peter and Paul dominance to challenge this kind of conclusion.

Limiting myself here to the case of Peter, there are, for instance, repeated summary statements regarding the general state and progress of the church that show a concern to establish genuine historical contours (2:43–47; 4:32–35; 5:12–16; 6:7). Also, there are sections of material, some substantial, where Peter is not mentioned: for example, Barnabas and the sale of his land (4:36–37), the speech of Gamaliel (5:34–39), and the events surrounding Stephen in Acts 7. The narrative in the first half of Acts clearly has in view more than the activity and preaching of "Peter."

On the other hand, it is important to recognize that Luke's presentation is *selective.* In no sense is Acts a comprehensive or complete account of what went on in the church or with all the apostles in the years immediately following the death and resurrection of Christ. If that is not kept in mind, the result will be a distorted picture of the overall dominance of Peter and Paul.

For example, again keeping to the case of Peter and the early chapters of Acts, Luke's intention is surely to communicate Peter's prominence,

---

2   Though written in the context of a later imprisonment in Rome, this verse aptly applies as well to this initial imprisonment.

perhaps even preeminence. Still, we are to infer the activity and influence the other apostles. For instance, John is associated equally and actively with Peter in the various events of Acts 3–4; the speech material in 4:19–20 is attributed to both.[3] In Acts 5, indeterminate "apostles" are involved with Peter in being arrested (5:18) and subsequently responding to the Sanhedrin (5:29–32, 40). We may assume that was not because they were simply following Peter and John around with their mouths shut! Other indications of substantial activity by other apostles are found in 2:37, 42, 43; 4:33–35; 5:12. This activity is left in the background by Luke, selectively and intentionally.

Second, on balance, the deeper motive for Luke's concentration on Peter and Paul is not on them simply as individuals, as prominent and heroic persons in earliest church history. His focus is not to present them as spiritual giants or gifted and charismatic leaders, or to show them as exemplary Christians, although they were certainly that, and that comes through in his account. Acts does not provide spiritual biography (other than incidentally, in a partial fashion).

Rather—and here we are brought back to a key consideration already noted—his focus is on Peter and Paul as *apostles* and the nature of their apostolic commission. As more careful study will show, the apostles, as apostles of Christ, are distinguished as especially authorized and empowered representatives of the exalted Christ, by the unique way they represent him and are identified with him. In particular, the authority of Christ is intimately bound up with the person of the apostle in a unique and incommunicable fashion. They speak for Christ as witnesses of his resurrection, and by their witness they function to establish the church's foundation, understood in a once-for-all historical sense (Acts 1:21–22; Eph. 2:20). In this role, the apostles are personal plenipotentiaries of the risen Christ.[4]

---

3 Unless we make the unlikely assumption that Peter and John recited in unison and word for word what Luke reports, this instance shows that here and arguably often elsewhere throughout Acts, in presenting speech material Luke does not intend to provide verbatim transcripts but gives accurate, fully reliable digests or summaries of what was actually said. Similarly, Acts 4:24–30 is presented as the spoken response of all those ("they," 4:24) who heard the report of Peter and John.

4 Although not everything they say and do is authorized, *ex cathedra*, as the justifiable rebuke of Peter by Paul in Gal. 2:11–14 and Peter's "By no means, Lord" (Acts 10:14) show. My thanks to Dennis Johnson for drawing my attention to the latter incident.

In view of this common personal representation of Christ, then, they necessarily represent each other. In the final analysis, interest in any one apostle is only as he exemplifies the institution of unique authorization and representation established by Christ. Interest in any one apostle is interest in the office by which preeminently the resurrected Christ exercises his authority. In other words, interest in any one apostle and his activity is as he points to *Christ* and what *he*, Christ, is doing.

This is borne out by the opening words of Acts that state that previously, in the first part to Theophilus (cf. Luke 1:3), Luke has given an account of "all that Jesus began to do and teach" (Acts 1:1). As others have observed, this is fairly taken as suggesting that the second part is an account of "all that Jesus *continued* to do and teach." Jesus, not the apostles, is the primary subject or actor in the Acts of the Apostles.

Further in this regard, it should be noted that the title "Acts of the Apostles" (Πράξεις Ἀποστόλων) is not part of the document but the designation it received early on in the church. In light of the preceding comments about the focus being on the office rather than on persons, a better alternative might be "Acts of the Apostolate" (cf. Acts 1:25), despite the abstract ring. Better yet, in the light of Acts 1:1, would be "Acts of the Exalted Christ through the Apostles," or even "Acts of the Exalted Christ by the Holy Spirit through the Apostles"; or, going all out (in quasi-seventeenth-century Puritan style!), "Acts of the Exalted Christ by the Holy Spirit in the Church as Founded by Him through the Apostles."

Playing with the title like this serves to focus, as an overall perspective on Acts, both its central subject (Christ) as well as the manner in which his action is qualified: by the Spirit, through the apostles, in the church.

Third, Acts—it is worth underscoring here—is the history of the *church* in its foundational era (cf. Eph. 2:20). We should not allow the customary distinction between later ecclesiastical history and biblical history to obscure the fact that the history recorded in Acts is *our* history; here are the apostolic "roots" of the church today and of every other postapostolic generation since its beginning.

Our own discussion has already highlighted and will continue to show that real discontinuities exist between the "then" of the church in Acts and the "now" of any subsequent generation of the church. But "apostolic" and "postapostolic," with whatever differences there are between them, have a common denominator: "church."[5] Our place in the church, in the history of the church today, is within the *one* church whose postapostolic *superstructure* continues being built by the exalted Christ, and whose apostolic origins, the *completed* laying of its *foundation*, Acts documents.[6]

Pentecost: A Central and Overall Thesis

A further, reinforcing comment may be made here for focusing on Pentecost in order to gain an overall understanding of Acts. Hardly anyone will care to dispute that Pentecost is the high point and pivotal juncture in the course of events narrated in Acts. It is in order, then, especially in taking a necessarily selective approach to Acts, to concentrate attention on Pentecost and its significance.

In fact, such a concentration will have the advantage of disclosing an even broader and more basic perspective than we might at first expect—namely, the central place of Pentecost not only in Acts but also in the Lucan double work, in Luke-Acts seen as a unit, or in other words, the central place of Pentecost in the entire history that Luke is seeking to relate to Theophilus. Our overall thesis, somewhat overstated, is that "Pentecost is the great turning-point, the hinge, as it were, of the two-volume narrative."[7] If, however, we include Christ's death, resurrection, and ascension as integrally associated with Pentecost, as we will see Luke-Acts does, then this becomes a valid and illuminating thesis.

New Testament Revelation as an Organism

Before beginning to explore this thesis and in order to facilitate doing that, it will be helpful to conclude our preliminary observations about the study of Acts by revisiting a basic point already noted in the introduction: New Testament revelation is an *organism*; the revelation recorded in the New

---

5   An issue, as large as it is important, in seeking to determine how the New Testament applies to the life of the church today is to assess properly both the continuities and the discontinuities between the apostolic and postapostolic periods of the church.

6   Eph. 2:11–22, esp. 2:19–22, suggest this distinction between completed (apostolic) foundation and not yet finished (postapostolic) superstructure to describe the one church-house building project of God, the master architect-builder, underway in the period between the resurrection and return of Christ.

7   G. W. H. Lampe, *The Seal of the Spirit: A Study in the Doctrine of Baptism and Confirmation in the New Testament and the Fathers* (London: SPCK, 1967), 192.

Testament has an organic character as its diverse parts cohere and constitute a unified whole. Among other considerations, this means that, though each part of the New Testament is not equally important—some parts are more important than others—still every part is integral in the specific sense of that word. Each part—no matter how relatively unimportant—belongs to and serves to constitute the whole, so that the whole does not exist without it. No part is dispensable.

This point—the organic composition of the New Testament as a whole—needs to be insisted upon over against a persistent tendency that has manifested itself in the history of interpretation, particularly in the historical-critical tradition stemming from the Enlightenment but even before then. This is the tendency to seize upon the teaching of Jesus and then contrast it with the teaching of the apostles and other New Testament writers in a way that depreciates the latter.

Often at work in this tendency is, as it might be put, a kind of superficially irresistible logic: Because of his person, the teaching of Jesus is more pure and profound, the more basic expression of the truth. Because of the person, because the person is incomparable, therefore—so the reasoning goes—the teaching must be incomparable, in a class all its own and superior to the teaching of all others.

This kind of reasoning is reflected, innocently no doubt for the most part, in red-letter editions of the New Testament. But where this approach takes hold at a deeper or more substantial, I dare say, pernicious level, the aim has been to get in back of the teaching of the New Testament writers, the teaching particularly of Paul and others, to get back behind their allegedly peripheral, less important, and at points erroneous statements to the pure teaching of Jesus. The teaching of Jesus uncovered by this approach then becomes, in effect, a canon within the canon, the corrective standard for judging other teaching found in the New Testament.

A radical instance of this sort of approach in recent decades, one that at one point received a fair amount of media attention, is the work of the Jesus Seminar. Its members cast black, white, or gray marbles regarding the authenticity of statements about Jesus in the New Testament in order to establish what in their judgment he actually said and did (or, more often, did *not* say and do). Another instance is the so-called Jesus-Paul controversy, prominent in the early decades of the twentieth century and by no means dead today. It consists in large part of attempts to play off the teaching of Jesus against that of Paul at the expense or depreciation of Paul.

It is not difficult to point out the fallacy often at work in such approaches. The only access that we have to Jesus is through the apostles and other New Testament writers. Jesus did not leave a written legacy as part of his earthly ministry. We know of Jesus only from what others—namely, the New Testament writers—have told us about him. In that sense, we have no access to the "pure" unmediated Jesus.

It is apparent, then, what this approach is really doing. A reconstructed Jesus—whose teaching, it usually turns out, looks remarkably like that favored by the person the reconstructing critic sees in the mirror—becomes the Jesus for evaluating the teaching of the New Testament as a whole.

In this regard, Vos makes a valuable overall observation regarding the organic makeup of New Testament revelation: In his earthly ministry, Jesus is not "the exhaustive expounder of truth"; rather, he is "the great fact to be expounded." Further, the relationship between Jesus and the apostles is "in general that between the fact to be interpreted and the subsequent interpretation of this fact."[8]

Negatively—contra the critical approach just noted—in his earthly ministry, Jesus did not, nor did he intend to, provide a comprehensive or standalone presentation of the truth. Approached on the assumption that he did, his teaching will inevitably be misunderstood and distorted. Positively, by God's design in terms of the unfolding history of special revelation, which includes the emergence of the New Testament canon with its specific shape, Jesus's person and work, word and deed—his earthly ministry considered in its entirety with its implications—is the subject matter for interpretation and elaboration by the apostles and New Testament writers.

This entails that the teaching of Jesus and the teaching of the apostles complement each other so that in important respects apart from each other their intelligibility is impaired. Each in relation to the other is an incomplete fragment, a truncation.

Instead, on the one hand, the teaching of the apostles and other New Testament writers provides *necessary amplification and elaboration* of the

---

8 Geerhardus Vos, *Biblical Theology: Old and New Testaments* (Edinburgh: Banner of Truth Trust, 1975), 302-3.

teaching of Jesus. This is all the more so since, as we noted earlier, their teaching is from the perspective of fulfillment that has taken place, from this side of the cross and resurrection. On the other hand, correlatively, the teaching of Jesus provides *important roots* for the teaching of the apostles; his teaching supplies key presuppositions and incipient aspects of theirs.

In light of this revelation-historical state of affairs—given this grounding provided by the teaching of Jesus during this earthly ministry—it will be useful both for our further work in Acts and then later in Paul to briefly review the main emphases in the teaching of Jesus, to recall something of its basic structure.

2

The Kingdom of God in
the Teaching of Jesus

An Overview

ESCHATOLOGY AND THE NEW TESTAMENT

One of the important developments in biblical studies, beginning toward the close of the nineteenth century and continuing into the past century, has been the rediscovery of eschatology, a recapturing of the pervasive eschatological force of the message of the New Testament.[1] This development took place across a wide front and has brought about a fairly widespread consensus, at least formally, on certain fundamental points of the eschatology found in the New Testament.

Developments leading to this eventual consensus began largely in reaction to so-called Older Liberalism. Theological liberalism has no place for the supernaturalism of biblical religion, and the eschatology of the Bible is of a piece with that supernaturalism. Over the course of the last half of the nineteenth century, the liberalism then dominant was intent, by one interpretive strategy or another, on either eliminating the eschatological elements in the teaching of Scripture or neutralizing them as peripheral and nonessential.

---

1 Among the voluminous helpful literature available on the kingdom teaching of Jesus, I especially recommend Geerhardus Vos, *The Teaching of Jesus Concerning the Kingdom of God and the Church* (New York: American Tract Society, 1903; repr., Nutley, NJ: Presbyterian and Reformed, 1972)—Ned B. Stonehouse used to tell his classes at Westminster Seminary that every minister of the gospel ought to read this short book once a year; for a fuller treatment, Herman N. Ridderbos, *The Coming of the Kingdom* (Philadelphia, PA: Presbyterian and Reformed, 1962).

But biblical exegesis has a way of moving on, and particularly within the historical-critical tradition there is the interesting development that, without abandoning its commitment to the rational autonomy of the interpreter, the critical descendants often repudiate the views of their critical forebears. Coming into the twentieth century, then, scholars of every stripe, even those whose personal theology remains essentially liberal, recognize increasingly that liberalism's treatment of New Testament eschatology is not sustainable, that eschatology is just too essential to the message of Jesus and the biblical writers. This awareness becomes more and more dominant over the course of the last century to the present in shaping the interpretation of the New Testament.

This trend of reaction against the Older Liberal handling of eschatology may be seen, for one, in the approach of Rudolf Bultmann, widely influential by the middle of the twentieth century and beyond. The one word that has come to be associated with this approach is *demythologization*. But that term, taken literally, suggests the elimination of myth. In that regard it is somewhat misleading and more aptly describes Older Liberalism, like the approach of one of its most of famous exponents, Adolf von Harnack. In trying to establish the morality he deemed to be the heart of the teaching of Jesus, Harnack and others of like mind excised as myth any eschatological elements as nonessential or later intrusions and not truly part of the message of the historical Jesus.

Bultmann, on the other hand, recognized that what he with Harnack agrees is myth, is, unlike Harnack, not dispensable or nonessential but in fact is central to the message of the New Testament, particularly the "myth" of the bodily resurrection of Jesus. So in arriving at the meaning of the New Testament relevant for today, what is required is not the elimination of myth but its reinterpretation (which Bultmann undertook to accomplish with categories largely drawn from existentialist philosophy).

Presently, then, the centrality of eschatology in the New Testament, however it is going to be accounted for further in the historical-critical tradition, whether or not as myth, is broadly recognized in New Testament studies with few, if any, exceptions.

Still, as a matter of general orientation but looking now in a quite different direction, for much Christian theology and preaching seeking to be faithful to the Bible as God's inscripturated word, the rediscovery of eschatology can be seen as having a corrective significance that has resulted in laying hold of biblical teaching in a way that has not been fully appreciated in the past.

For instance, in a standard volume on systematic theology, "Eschatology" is the last chapter. More significantly, coming at the end of the volume, eschatology tends to be defined exclusively in terms of the "last things" having to do with what is still future for the church—Christ's return and matters concomitant with his return, perhaps including as well some treatment of what occurs at death and the so-called intermediate state. Even more significantly, very often little, if any, attention is given to the relationship with what has preceded, to the integral connection between the future hope of the church and its present life and the practical relevance of the former for the latter.

What has become more and more clear is that in an overall presentation of biblical teaching, eschatology is not properly compartmentalized at the end. In particular, the New Testament teaches, as our own work will show, what is often termed a "realized eschatology." Biblical eschatology is to be defined in terms of the first as well as the second coming of Christ. New Testament eschatology has a dual focus. In that respect it is elliptical, defined by two foci, present and future, the proverbial already-not-yet.

ESCHATOLOGY AND THE TEACHING OF JESUS: THE COMING OF THE KINGDOM

The Gospel of the Kingdom

What more than anything else triggered this recapture of eschatology was a renewed look at the teaching of Jesus. Any approach to that teaching, particularly as it is recounted in the Synoptic Gospels, is bound to recognize the centrality of the kingdom of God/heaven. The kingdom is not only central but also a comprehensive and all-controlling theme. Everything in Jesus's teaching dovetails in his teaching about the kingdom.

This is easily seen from the various summary statements of Jesus's ministry in the Gospels. In these statements, both the noun "gospel" (εὐαγγέλιον), for the content of his preaching, or the verb "preach the gospel" (εὐαγγελίζομαι) sometime occur without qualification (Mark 1:15; 13:10; Matt. 11:5). Other summary statements for his preaching and teaching, however, are qualified by references to the kingdom as its content (Matt 4:23; 9:35;

24:14; Luke 4:43; 8:1; 16:16). There is no other similar general qualification of gospel terminology in summary statements. The gospel Jesus preached is the gospel of the kingdom. Further, the parables of Jesus, characteristic of his teaching as a whole, are largely about the kingdom (Matt. 13; Luke 8).

The Kingdom as an Eschatological Reality

What has become clear in Gospel studies is that the kingdom proclaimed by Jesus is not essentially an ideal moral order—the view, for instance, of Older Liberalism, for whom the historical Jesus is seen as a remarkably precocious teacher ahead of his time, a kind of advance advocate of the moralism of Kant's ethical idealism—a view that continues to be widespread in one form or another.

Nor, on the other hand, is the kingdom proclaimed by Jesus simply another way of saying that God is *sovereign*, equated with God's eternal or universal kingship over the creation. Certainly God has always been King—past, present, and future. That is clear, for instance, from a passage like Psalm 145:13: "Your kingdom is an everlasting kingdom, / and your dominion endures throughout all generations." Also, in a particular, covenantal sense, God is said to be "the King of Jacob" (Isa. 41:21); Israel in the Old Testament is properly spoken of as God's kingdom.

With that noted and kept in view, however, it is not in this sense of a timeless kingship—embracing past, present, and future—that Jesus proclaims the kingdom of God. Rather, particularly against the background of Old Testament promise and expectation, for Jesus the kingdom is an eschatological reality. It is a matter of consummation, of the fulfillment at last of the promises made to the fathers. The kingdom that Jesus proclaimed is the actual arrival of the new and final order at the end of history, that order of God's eschatological rule that has begun with Christ's coming and was not before.

Already within Second Temple Judaism, the distinction between "this age" and "the age to come" was coined and used to comprehend the entire unfolding of history from creation to its consummation. In the terms of this distinction, the coming of the kingdom announced by Jesus is nothing less than the dawning of the eschatological "age to come."[2] It is in this sense of

---

2   This two-age construct will be discussed more fully later in considering its use by Paul.

its actual arrival, then, that Jesus's kingdom proclamation is eschatological, a message of realized eschatology.

This note of eschatological realization is sounded from the very beginning of Jesus's ministry. It is on the surface of the Synoptic tradition. In opening the account of the Galilean ministry as a whole, Mark 1:14–15 is fairly seen as summarizing Jesus's proclamation throughout that ministry:

> Now after John was arrested, Jesus came into Galilee, proclaiming the gospel of God, and saying, "The time is fulfilled, and the kingdom of God is at hand; repent and believe in the gospel."

This summary statement is laden with eschatology, both realized and imminent: the use here of "the time" (ὁ καιρὸς) signaling fulfillment, accented by the perfect passive indicative πεπλήρωται ("is fulfilled"), and also the note of the imminence of the kingdom in "at hand" (ἤγγικεν).

The Kingdom as Already-Not-Yet

These observations bring into view the fundamental historical qualification basic to Jesus's kingdom proclamation, the temporal factor essential in it. In this regard, it is crucially important to see how the eschatological kingdom proclaimed by Jesus is both present and future. Several passages, taken together, show the specific pattern of this temporal qualification.

In surveying these passages, it should be kept in mind the Greek word βασιλεία has two distinct meanings: (1) either the concrete, static sense of kingdom or realm, or (2) the abstract, dynamic sense of kingship or rule. These two meanings are obviously closely related; the one implies the other: (1) is the place or sphere in which (2) functions or is exercised. A kingdom without a king and a king without a kingdom are practically meaningless abstractions.

To render βασιλεία uniformly with "kingdom" as most translations do, then, has the disadvantage of masking the dynamic sense where it occurs. In some instances, it is difficult to decide which sense is intended; in others, notably in the Lord's or kingdom prayer (Matt. 6:10), perhaps both senses are in view. In what follows here I will note where the dynamic sense (kingship, rule) is intended.

STAGES IN THE COMING OF THE KINGDOM (THE REALM AND RULE OF GOD)

The Kingdom as Future

There are two strands: statements that have in view an indefinite or distant future and others where the future is seen as immediate or imminent.

The Indefinite Future

From a traditional point of view, least striking are those statements in which the kingdom is in the far future.

MATTHEW 8:11–12 (CF. LUKE 13:28–29)

In the immediate context, Jesus has been sought out by a Roman centurion to have his servant healed—a remarkable act of faith, as Jesus observes (Matt. 8:10). This display of faith prompts him to add, "I tell you, many will come from east and west and recline at table with Abraham, Isaac, and Jacob in the kingdom of heaven, while the sons of the kingdom will be thrown into the outer darkness. In that place there will be weeping and gnashing of teeth."

Here, the kingdom is in view at a time in the future when it will be entered by Abraham, Isaac, and Jacob, along with "many . . . from east and west," the latter a universal reference that includes Gentiles (cf. Luke 13:29); both Jews and non-Jews will enter. This entering is also correlative, negatively, with the time when "the sons of the kingdom will be thrown into the outer darkness." This future time is further described as a time of their "weeping and gnashing of teeth."

In view is Jewish ("sons of the kingdom") rejection of Jesus, those Jews who have spurned the promised kingdom (realm and rule) because of the way, contrary to their expectations, it has arrived with Jesus. Here future entry into the kingdom for some, with the banqueting that will be involved, is coincident with others being cast into outer darkness, marked by weeping and gnashing of teeth.

Subsequently in Matthew 13, in Jesus's explanation of certain of the kingdom parables, occurrences of "there will be weeping and gnashing of teeth" (13:42) serve to fix more specifically and clarify this time of future entrance into the kingdom. In the explanation of the parable of the weeds,

"The harvest is the end of the age" (13:39). The same temporal qualification occurs for the gathering and burning of the weeds by the harvester-angels ("so will it be at the end of the age," 13:40).

"The end of the age" (συντέλεια αἰῶνος) is a fixed designation as part of the two-age construction and as such indicates the crucial transition point between the two ages, the point that terminates "this age," provisional and pre-eschatological and marked by sin and its effects, and inaugurates the eschatological consummation of the "age to come." The ultimate destiny of the weeds/unrepentant law-breakers (13:41), resulting from this fiery conflagration of eschatological judgment, is in the place where "there will be weeping and gnashing of teeth" (13:42), while "the righteous will shine like the sun in the kingdom of their Father" (13:43). So, "weeping and gnashing of teeth" signals what will occur at the end of the age.

Similarly, a few verses later in explaining the parable of the dragnet, the separation of the righteous from the wicked will ensue "at the end of the age" (13:49), at which time the destructive fiery judgment that takes place for the wicked will result in their being where "there will be weeping and gnashing of teeth" (13:50).

In Matthew 8:11, then, the kingdom in view is entered at the end of the age, correlative with the final judgment. From the vantage point of Jesus's earthly ministry this arrival of the kingdom will take place in the remote or distant future.

MATTHEW 25:31-46

This passage provides another, perhaps clearer example of the kingdom arriving in the far future:

> When the Son of Man comes in his glory, and all the angels with him, then he will sit on his glorious throne. Before him will be gathered all the nations, and he will separate people one from another as a shepherd separates the sheep from the goats. And he will place the sheep on his right, but the goats on the left. Then the King will say to those on his right, "Come, you who are blessed by my Father, inherit the kingdom prepared for you from the foundation of the world." . . . Then he will say to those on his left, "Depart from me, you cursed, into the eternal fire prepared for the devil and his angels" (25:31–34, 41).

The kingdom in view here is inherited by the sheep, those at the right hand, and that inheritance is received concomitant with the eternal destruction of the goats, those at the left hand, and subsequent to the coming of the Son of Man and the angels for final judgment. So, again as in Matthew 8:11, the kingdom lies in the remote future, at the end of the age.

The Near Future

More striking from the angle of time are statements in which Jesus speaks of the kingdom as arriving not distantly but in the immediate future. In addition to a number of passages, like Mark 1:15, that speak of the kingdom as being "at hand" (ἤγγικεν) is Matthew 16:28 (cf. Mark 9:1): "Truly, I say to you, there are some standing here who will not taste death until they see the Son of Man coming in his kingdom." Those of that generation—some present there listening to Jesus—will not die until they see the arrival of the kingdom in the coming of the Son of Man.

Worth noting here is the immediately preceding statement: "For the Son of Man is going to come with his angels in the glory of his Father, and then he will repay each person according to what he has done" (Matt. 16:27). With clear indications of the subsequent description of final judgment in Matthew 25:31, this statement likely refers to the remote future. So here, along with 16:28, we see how, looking toward the future, both remote and immediate future are telescoped and seen together, a prophetic perspective much like that often found in the Old Testament.

Another near future reference is Matthew 10:23: The disciples will not have completed their assigned preaching circuit of the city of Israel "before the Son of man comes." This phrase, in light of its occurrence in Matthew 16:28, implies the imminent coming of the kingdom.

The Kingdom as Present

The most striking aspect of Jesus's kingdom teaching in terms of the time of its coming is that it is present.

MATTHEW 13:10–17

This section, inserted between the parable of the sower and its explanation, provides a general explanation of the purpose of parables, an overall clarification as to why Jesus teaches in parables. Noteworthy here for our interest are the statements that bracket this pericope in 13:10–11 and 13:16–17.

"Then the disciples came and said to him, 'Why do you speak to them in parables?' And he answered them, 'To you it has been given to know the secrets of the kingdom of heaven, but to them it has not been given'" (13:10–11). The intervening verses (13:12–15), utilizing Isaiah 6, elaborate on the latter group. Then, in contrast to them, "But blessed are your eyes, for they see, and your ears, for they hear. For truly, I say to you, many prophets and righteous people longed to see what you see, and did not see it, and to hear what you hear, and did not hear it" (13:16–17).

What the disciples, the "you" addressed by Jesus in these bracketing statements, have been granted is not arcane information about the kingdom still in the future. Rather, what they have been given is an experiential knowledge of "the mysteries" (τὰ μυστήρια, 13:11; my translation, though see also NASB, NKJV) of the kingdom. They have been granted to experience "the revelation of the mystery" (Rom. 16:25; cf. Col. 1:26) of the kingdom, to experience the kingdom as a present reality. Their privilege is that for them the kingdom is now the mystery already realized and at last revealed.

Further, in this privilege—this present experiential knowing—the disciples are "blessed" specifically in contrast to "many prophets and righteous people." Surely we are to gloss here, "of the old covenant" (cf. Luke 10:24).

Not to be missed here is how those of the old covenant are characterized in terms of their desire. However inchoately or minimally, what they wanted to see and hear is what the disciples are now seeing and hearing, but did not: the promised fulfillment as it has now taken place in the coming of Christ. Their desire was not yet realized; it remained a future longing. The kingdom was not present for them as it now is for the disciples.

MATTHEW 11:11–13

These verses contain some lexical and syntactical difficulties, but the point I am concerned to bring out—the presence of the kingdom—is clear. They are part of the response of Jesus to clarify an inquiry of disciples of John the Baptist, sent by him from prison since he is apparently perplexed about Jesus and his ministry (11:2–3).

Truly, I say to you, among those born of women there has arisen no one greater than John the Baptist. Yet the one who is least in the kingdom of heaven is greater than he. From the days of John the Baptist until now the kingdom of heaven has suffered violence, and the violent take it by force. For all the Prophets and the Law prophesied until John. (11:11–13)

Looking first at 11:12—for reasons in the immediately surrounding verses that I will point out presently—"from the days" is best taken as exclusive of John; "from" (ἀπό) here has the sense of "following" or "after" the days of John the Baptist, as "until" (ἕως) is inclusive of the present: after or following John the Baptist up to and including "now."

In other words, here Jesus excludes John the Baptist from what he says about the kingdom. Why? Because John belongs to the old order and represents its end, as the immediately following generalization (11:13) shows: "For all the Prophets and the Law prophesied until John." Here and in a parallel statement in Luke 16:16, "until" is inclusive, including John; the old covenant continued up to John and had its prophetic culmination in him. Matthew 11:12, then, is a statement of the presence of the kingdom as it excludes John and points obliquely but unmistakably to its arrival with Jesus.

Matthew 11:12 presents a translation issue. Is what is said about the kingdom meant in a negative or a positive sense? Does it have in view the violent opposition and hostility the kingdom is encountering? Or, alternatively, does it describe its powerful manifestation—thinking, for instance, of the miracles of Jesus—and the determined and vigorous response of those who prize it? Most English translations have the former, unfavorable sense. A good case, however, I believe, can be made for a favorable sense. But that issue does not need to be decided here. On either understanding, the presence of the kingdom is clear.

The preceding observations about the kingdom as present reinforce how that point is already made in 11:11. There, Jesus refers to the "the one who is least[3] in the kingdom of heaven." Surely, we are to gloss: the one who is least in the kingdom presently, right now. In this respect, Jesus says, that person is greater than John. So the kingdom is present in a way that, with

---

3 Here the comparative adjective μικρότερος has a superlative force.

the distinction made between John and the least one, John is outside the kingdom, whereas the least one is in it.

How are we to understand this exclusion of John? Matthew 11:11 illustrates the importance of keeping clear the distinction, noted earlier, between the history of salvation (*historia salutis*) and the order of salvation (*ordo salutis*), between matters having to do with the once-for-all accomplishment of salvation and those matters belonging to its ongoing application.

The point that Jesus makes about John in 11:11 is redemptive-historical. No one "among those born of women" is greater than John because of his function in the history of salvation. No person is greater than John in view of the role that he has been granted in covenant history, where he stands at the end of the prophetic tradition (11:13). Indeed, in that line, he is unique, "more than a prophet." In fulfillment of previous prophecy, he is the "messenger" of the covenant that prepares the way for the Messiah (11:9–10). Nonetheless, in this most privileged of positions that an individual can occupy—immediate forerunner to the Messiah—just in the exercise of that function John is outside of the kingdom. In the role he has carried out, though still alive, he is prior to the coming of the kingdom now present.

John's personal salvation relative to the kingdom (*ordo salutis*) is not in the purview of the passage; his salvation-historical role (*historia salutis*) is. Jesus is hardly saying that John as an individual is excluded from the saving benefits of the kingdom (no more than that was the case for Abraham or any other Old Testament believer) or that in the future he will not be present sitting down together with the patriarchs at the eschatological kingdom-banquet (Matt. 8:11).

MATTHEW 12:28

Though last in the order as we are considering them here, this is Jesus's clearest and most pointed statement of the presence of the kingdom: "But if it is by the Spirit of God that I cast out demons, then the kingdom of God has come upon you."[4] In the immediate context, Jesus has healed a man who

---

4   The parallel statement in Luke 11:20 has "finger" in place of "Spirit." This is fairly read as a figurative description of the Spirit, particularly in light of Lucan references elsewhere to the

was blind and mute because demon-possessed (12:22). This miracle results in a divided reaction. By their reasoning, on the one hand, the Pharisees conclude that Jesus must have been serving Satan (12:24). Jesus, in turn, counters this reaction, negatively, by saying in effect that Satan would never take such a counterproductive action against himself and his interests (12:25–26) and then, positively (12:28), by asserting that this healing is a present manifestation of the eschatological rule of God.

This verse is important not only because it clearly affirms the presence of the kingdom in Jesus's ministry but also because of a couple of key related considerations that come into view here. First, and particularly pertinent for our interest in Pentecost, is the integral association of the Holy Spirit and the kingdom. The Holy Spirit is the power of the kingdom, the dynamic at the heart of the eschatological rule of God. In other words, as the Spirit is linked with Jesus in his kingdom mission, the Spirit in his working is nothing less than the eschatological power of the kingdom as present.

The Spirit, it should not be missed here, does not involve some merely individualistic experience, some isolated principle of religious inwardness, although there is surely a personal experience of the Spirit. But such experience and the activity of the Holy Spirit always has to be understood as occurring within this eschatological kingdom context. We will have occasion to note further the eschatological conception of the Spirit's activity both in Acts and in Paul, but an indication of that conception is already present in the kingdom proclamation of Jesus.

Second, this passage provides an important indication of the nature and program of the eschatological kingdom in its coming. In its arrival, the kingdom is shaped by opposition, specifically by its opposition to the kingdom of Satan and his authority (note the explicit reference to Satan's kingdom in 12:26); the conflict now begun and underway in Jesus's ministry has explicit kingdom dimensions. The kingdom, the eschatological rule of God and its arrival in Christ, manifests itself negatively as opposition to the rule of Satan. This is simply to say positively that the kingdom of God, its agenda of action, is essentially *redemptive*. It arrives for the overthrow of

---

"hand" of the Lord (Luke 1:66; Acts 11:21; 13:11). Note that this is another instance where the sense of *basileia* is clearly dynamic, "reign," rather than static, "realm."

Satan's rule and so to establish definitive, eschatological deliverance from sin and its consequences for those included in its rule and realm.

SUMMARY

The kingdom proclaimed by Jesus is an eschatological entity that is both present and future. In saying that, we should make clear that we are not talking about multiple kingdoms but a single kingdom. Utilizing the Greek word, it is not a matter of multiple *basileiai* (plural) but of one *basileia* (singular). Graphically, this unity may be helpfully represented by an ellipse (if you remember your geometry, a plain figure defined by two points or foci). Within the elliptical unity of the one kingdom proclaimed by Jesus, one of the foci is present, the other future.[5]

Keeping this temporal pattern in mind is essential for understanding the proclamation of Jesus. But presenting it in the somewhat formal manner I have carries a certain liability that requires some further clarification.

Theocentric and Messianic Character

Nothing is as essential for the kingdom as its theocentric and consequently thoroughly messianic character. The kingdom is not a matter of some abstract, preformed independent eschatological schema to which the activity of Christ is then made to conform. It is not as if the Messiah functions for the sake of an already established scheme from which he would be detachable or replaceable by someone else.

Rather, the pattern observable in the present-future structure that we have noted—the unfolding of the *basileia*, the rule and realm of God, in its coming—is determined in its entirety by the Messiah and his activity, by the unique, unrepeatable, and specific task that Christ has come to do and that he alone is able to do. In other words, as it has been put to focus this consideration, Christ is *autobasileia*, literally "self-kingdom," the kingdom itself. Christ is the essence of the kingdom; apart from him, it does not and cannot exist.

---

5 The Westminster Shorter Catechism, 102, distinguishes between the present "kingdom of grace" and the future "kingdom of glory." This distinction is not between two different kingdoms but between two stages of the one kingdom, just as the customary distinction between the church militant and the church triumphant is not between two different churches but between the present and ultimate future of the one church.

"But Christ is the fulfillment, not the product, of prophecy."[6] This distinction—fulfillment and not product—means that it is not as if the Old Testament provides a prophetic agenda into which Christ is made to fit, especially if that would involve the further misunderstanding that someone else might just as equally well carry out that agenda.

Stages of Arrival

Considering the time of the coming of the one kingdom, as we have discussed, shows that it arrives in stages or phases. The kingdom in its arrival is marked by a staging principle, a phasing reality.

How are these stages or phases to be identified concretely? Here, the centrality of the messianic factor just noted provides the answer. The constitutive correlation between Christ and the kingdom prompts us to see that the decisive turns in the ministry of the Messiah determine the stages in the coming of the kingdom.

What are such critical events in Christ's ministry? Two in particular stand out in their significance as transcending in importance compared to other junctures or turns. For one—given the incarnation, the birth of Christ, as the alpha or initiation point—there is the subsequent complex of events, the decisive turn that has taken place in his death and resurrection, his transition from his state of humiliation to his state of exaltation. Beyond that transition and still future is the second event (or second complex of events)—namely, what will come at the end of the age when he returns in glory, what will take place at and concomitant with his second coming.

These two epochal junctures result concretely in a three-stage coming of the kingdom: the period of Christ's earthly ministry culminating in his death and resurrection, the period between his resurrection and return or *parousia*, and the period beginning with his *parousia*.

It is of course in order to identify other stages or phases: within the earthly ministry of Jesus, especially those periods marked out before and after his baptism by John; similarly, subsequent to his death and resurrection, those before and after the fall of Jerusalem. But such events, however climactic, still do not rise to the level of significance and decisiveness true of his death and resurrection and of his return.

6   Herman Ridderbos, *The Speeches of Peter in the Acts of the Apostles* (London: Tyndale, 1962), 26.

Present and future, in themselves abstract terms, can be better expressed concretely in terms of these three stages. So, from the vantage point of stage one of the kingdom as present (Jesus's earthly ministry), stages two and three are future; stage two as present (the period of the New Testament church) is bracketed by stage one as past and stage three as future. The church sees and awaits that future from a decisively different kingdom vantage point than did Jesus in his earthly ministry.

I have already used the figure of the ellipse and concretized its present and future foci in terms of these three stages just noted. By extending the geometry, the pattern of eschatological promise and fulfillment in Scripture, globally considered, may be represented as follows: For the Old Testament, with all of the diversity undoubtedly involved and needing to be accounted for, its kingdom expectation is nonetheless unified in terms of what is entirely future. So, this Old Testament expectation may be represented as a circle (a plain figure defined by a single point) whose center is future.

In the actual fulfillment of that expectation, revealed in the New Testament, the circle is pulled at, so to speak, and takes on the shape of an ellipse as noted, defined both by what is now present as well as still future. Finally, that future—the realization of the church's ultimate eschatological hope—is when everything will be present and the ellipse again becomes a circle, only now with its defining center present. So in terms of the promised kingdom and its realization, the movement from Old Testament to New Testament, from old covenant to new covenant, is from future promise to present-future fulfillment—from circle (future), to ellipse (present-future), to circle (present).

Final Observations

This survey of the kingdom proclamation of Jesus may be rounded off with a couple of concluding observations. First, Jesus's teaching shows that the period between his resurrection and return—that is, the period of the church and its expansion to "the end of the age" (Matt. 28:18–20), when the church is being built as "the gospel of the kingdom" is going "to all nations" (Matt. 24:14)—is not in any sense a postponement of eschatological considerations; it is not a non-eschatological gap, as if things are on hold eschatologically, contrary to some dispensational constructions.

Rather, this period between Christ's resurrection and return, the period of the church, is distinctively and essentially eschatological; it is, in fact, as we have seen, a phase in the coming of the eschatological kingdom. That kingdom significance of the church is apparent by reading Matthew 16:18–19 in the light of the great commission (28:19–20); the keys of the kingdom are to the doors of the church.

Secondly—and this brings us back full circle to a key consideration noted toward the beginning of this chapter—the teaching and preaching of the apostles and those associated with them, their teaching in its entirety, may be fairly seen as varied amplification, as diverse witness to and explanation, of the kingdom proclamation of Jesus. From one angle, apostolic teaching, postresurrection in its entirety, is fairly seen as reflection on the three-stage eschatological structure announced by Jesus, from within stage two of the fulfillment that Jesus proclaimed.

Herman Ridderbos makes the following statement, one that I continue to find particularly helpful for expressing the unity of New Testament teaching, while at the same time recognizing its diverse composition: "It can be rightly said that Paul does nothing but explain the eschatological reality which in Christ's teaching is called the Kingdom."[7] That is as good a way as any for capturing what Paul is all about: expositing Jesus's kingdom proclamation. The same thing, as we will see, may also be said for Luke and the apostolic teaching presented in Acts.

In light of the kingdom proclamation of Jesus and the eschatological structure it provides, then, we are now in a position—a better position than we would be otherwise—to consider the significance of Pentecost and Luke's narration of that central event.

---

7   Herman Ridderbos, "The Redemptive-Historical Character of Paul's Preaching," in *When the Time Had Fully Come: Studies in New Testament Theology* (Grand Rapids, MI: Eerdmans, 1957), 48–49.

3

The Holy Spirit and the
Kingdom in Luke-Acts

THE SPIRIT AND THE KINGDOM IN LUKE'S GOSPEL:
AN INITIAL OVERVIEW

For our treatment of Acts and the significance of Pentecost, it will be useful to take note briefly of those passages in part 1 to Theophilus where a connection or correlation is made between the Holy Spirit and the kingdom.

Luke 1:32–35

> He will be great and will be called the Son of the Most High. And the Lord God will give to him the throne of his father David, and he will reign over the house of Jacob forever, and of his kingdom there will be no end." And Mary said to the angel, "How will this be, since I am a virgin?" And the angel answered her, "The Holy Spirit will come upon you, and the power of the Most High will overshadow you; therefore the child to be born will be called holy—the Son of God.

This passage, part of the interchange between Gabriel and Mary (1:26–38), concerns the son he has told her she will bear and is to name Jesus (1:31), and who will also be called "the Son of the Most High."

On the one hand, notice now how pronounced kingdom language is in what is said here about the Son. The Lord God will give him "the throne of his father David" (1:32); correlatively, "he will reign [βασιλεύσει] over the house of Jacob forever" (1:33a); climactically and with specific reference to the kingdom, "of his kingdom there will be no end" (1:33b).

Further, in response to Mary's wondering question concerning the realization of these kingdom-laden promises, the angel declares concerning the paternity of the royal child who she is to bear that the Holy Spirit, as "the power of the Most High," will "come upon" and "overshadow" her (1:35). So, already from the time of his conception, there is a bond between Jesus and the Holy Spirit essential for the coming of the kingdom. Dating from his conception, Jesus, the Holy Spirit, and the coming kingdom are inseparable.

Luke 3:21–22

Now when all the people were baptized, and when Jesus also had been baptized and was praying, the heavens were opened, and the Holy Spirit descended on him in bodily form, like a dove; and a voice came from heaven, "You are my beloved Son; with you I am well pleased."

This account of the baptism of Jesus by John will occupy us below in greater detail. Here, our interest is to note the connection between the Holy Spirit and the kingdom.

Anticipating what I will discuss more fully later on, the voice from heaven declares approval of Jesus in his identity as the Messiah. Since to speak of the Messiah is to speak of his kingdom, this declaration amounts to his kingdom commission. The voice of the Father addressed to the Son affirms the appointment of his Son as the Messiah on behalf of the kingdom. In integral connection with this affirmation of the Father—his kingdom appointment of the Son—the Holy Spirit descends upon the Son.[1]

This coming of the Spirit on Christ is not merely symbolic, but—symbolized, to be sure, by the dove—the Holy Spirit comes upon him as genuine endowment. Clearly this endowment is for the messianic task that faces him. The Holy Spirit is the equipping that Jesus receives for the kingdom commission ahead of him.

This endowment, it should not be missed, is not merely formal but necessary in view of the needs of the human nature the Son has assumed. All told, we may say that what takes place at the Jordan is the

---

1   Note the unmistakable Trinitarian pattern here.

kingdom-coronation of Jesus. Here, Jesus is marked out publicly as its Spirit-anointed King.

Luke 4:1–13

In Luke 3, the insertion of Jesus's genealogy directly follows the account of his baptism,[2] with the narrative resuming with the account Jesus's temptation (4:1–13). Here, the connection between Spirit and kingdom is more implicit but easy enough to see. Jesus, "returned from the Jordan," goes into the wilderness as he was "full of the Holy Spirit" and "led by the Spirit" (4:1). With the role of the Holy Spirit accented in this way, Jesus enters the desert setting of the temptation.

From what ensues, Jesus, Spirit-endowed and controlled, is drawn into a struggle that, in its largest dimensions, is between the kingdom of God and the kingdom of Satan. Clearly at issue in each of the three temptations is kingdom and kingship. In the second, the devil promises "all the kingdoms of the world" if Jesus will worship him (4:5–8). Similarly, in light of what has previously taken place at the Jordan, in the first and third temptations, the devil seeks to undermine the messianic-kingdom identity and appointment of Jesus as "the Son of God" (4:3, 9).

All told, what took place in the desert was the effort on Satan's part to challenge Jesus in his messianic mission, to get him to abandon his commitment to the kingdom of God. The force of the temptation in each instance was to elicit from Jesus an act of messianic treason, as we might put it, and so in that way to derail the kingdom program with its messianic calling that lay before him.

In passing here but no less importantly, we need to appreciate the uniqueness of this temptation, its redemptive-historical (*historia salutis*) significance. There are, surely, lessons to be learned from this passage for our own lives regarding how to resist temptation, particularly Jesus's recourse to Scripture, his being ready with an answer from Scripture. But what must not be missed here is what is discontinuous with our temptation, its uniquely messianic dimension.

---

2   Luke introduces the genealogy at this point rather than at the beginning of his Gospel; he also traces it all the way back to "the son of Adam, the son of God" (3:38)—both in contrast to Matthew's Gospel (Matt. 1:1–17). It may be plausibly argued that by doing this, Luke intends to indicate that as the Spirit-endowed messianic King, Christ is, as Paul identifies him, "the last Adam," who by virtue of his resurrection, became "the life-giving Spirit" (1 Cor 15:45, my translation).

That discontinuity is highlighted by the reference to the action of the Holy Spirit. Jesus teaches his disciples to pray, "And lead us not into temptation" (Luke 11:4; cf. Matt. 6:13). But here, and pointedly, Jesus himself is "led by the Spirit" into temptation, temptation that unfolds with its singular messianic aspects.

Luke 4:14–44

This lengthy passage describes the Galilean ministry in its opening phases. According to the introductory summary verses (4:14–15), throughout this period Jesus's teaching in synagogues was "in the power of the Spirit." More specifically and no doubt harkening back to what took place at his baptism, "The Spirit of the Lord is upon me, / because he has anointed me / to proclaim good news to the poor" (4:18).

Further, from many indications, some already noted earlier, this Spirit-anointed and -empowered gospel proclamation is described in its fullness as "the good news of the kingdom of God" (4:43; cf. 16:16); it is the gospel that has the kingdom, and particularly the kingdom as a present reality as its subject matter.

Luke 11:20

This is the Lucan parallel to Matthew 12:28, looked at above as the clearest and most emphatic assertion of the kingdom as present in the earthly ministry of Jesus: "But if it is by the finger of God that I cast out demons, then the kingdom of God has come upon you." Where Matthew has "Spirit," Luke has "finger." The latter, particularly considering Luke's usage elsewhere, is a graphic way of picturing the Spirit in his working. For instance, elsewhere in Luke-Acts, similar reference is made to the "hand of the Lord" (e.g., Acts 4:30; 11:21; 13:11). In view in these occurrences, seen in their contexts, is the activity of God, his power either for salvation or in judgment, activity associated specifically with the Spirit. So here, too, a connection between the Holy Spirit and the kingdom is clear.

Luke 11:13 and 12:32

"If you then, who are evil, know how to give good gifts to your children, how much more will the heavenly Father give the Holy Spirit to those who ask him!"

"Fear not, little flock, for it is your Father's good pleasure to give you the kingdom."

What disposes drawing these two statements together is what they have in common in their respective contexts: the needs of the disciples and the Father's concern—the concern of God in his identity as Father—to meet those needs. In 12:32, the greatest blessing that the disciples are to seek (12:31) and that the Father wills to give is the kingdom, while in 11:13 the incomparably highest gift the Father will give to those who ask is the Holy Spirit.

Bringing these two verses together points to a close correlation between the Holy Spirit and the kingdom that amounts to a virtual identification. The Holy Spirit and the kingdom are alternative ways of describing the ultimate blessing, the highest beatitude that the Father has to give. The Holy Spirit and kingdom are two descriptions of that blessing inclusive of all other blessings. Further confirmation for taking these two verses together is that they are the only two places in Luke where Jesus speaks of the Father's purpose or will to give.

This correlation reinforces that the Spirit in the ministry of Jesus and as ministered by him is the inherent power of the kingdom. Also, the reference to the Father anticipates and provides background for the description of the Spirit come on the day of Pentecost as "the promise of [the] Father" (Luke 24:49; Acts 1:4). The promise in these two verses, taken together, is for the coming of the Holy Spirit and the kingdom in the future, a promise, as our subsequent discussion will show, that is fulfilled on Pentecost.

Conclusion

This provisional survey of references to the Spirit in Luke's Gospel has brought to light an integral connection between the Holy Spirit and the kingdom that needs to be explored further in considering the work of the Spirit in Acts generally and at Pentecost in particular.

Also, though our survey has not taken note of it, in the third Gospel (and the other Gospels as well), there is a marked difference during his earthly ministry between Christ and the disciples so far as possession of the Spirit is concerned: for Jesus, the Spirit is clearly a present possession; for the disciples, the Spirit is largely a matter of promise—for them, the Spirit is a future possession (see Luke 11:13). This difference points to a dramatic or historical perspective on the activity of the Spirit that also needs to be further explored and clarified.

LUKE 24 AND ACTS 1

The ending of Luke (24:44–49) and the beginning of Acts (1:3–11) overlap in the attention they give to the period between Christ's resurrection and ascension. Focusing on this overlap serves to reinforce as well as advance our understanding, in important ways, of the link between the Holy Spirit and the kingdom, particularly in Acts and at Pentecost.[3]

In their composition, the Gospel records are so ordered that they tell us relatively little of what transpired in the interval between the resurrection and the ascension.[4] In terms of the history of redemption, this period is fairly seen as a kind of hiatus, a brief pause in which redemptive history is, so to speak, on hold: The Messiah has entered his state of exaltation—he is now resurrected—but he has not gone to his place of exaltation—he has not yet ascended.

This period, then, is in this respect anomalous—being in the state but not yet the destined place of exaltation. Something of that anomaly—if that's the best word—or certainly the transient nature of this period, can be seen from a quick glance at John's Gospel and the interaction recorded there between Jesus and Mary on the day of the resurrection. Having appeared to her, identified himself, and then been recognized by her, he responds, "Do not hold on to me, for I have not yet ascended to the Father" (John 20:17 NIV; "Do not cling to me," NKJV, ESV). As resurrected, Jesus is not to stay with her and the disciples ("my brothers," 20:17). He will not remain here on earth with the church in this kind of face-to-face presence and contact but instead is about to depart in his ascension to what the New Testament calls "the right hand of God" (e.g., Acts 2:33; Rom. 8:34; Heb. 10:12).[5]

---

3   This overlap is an indication that the Third Gospel and Acts are to be taken together as a two-part work, Luke-Acts.

4   Mark, in fact, is totally silent about it (assuming 16:1–7 to be the original ending).

5   The decision of the NET ("Do not touch me") to follow the KJV ("Touch me not") is puzzling. While the Greek (μή μου ἅπτου) can have that sense, it is misleading here because it easily leaves the impression that because of what Jesus has now become, with the glorified qualities of his resurrected body, ordinary, sinful human beings can no longer have close, bodily contact with him. Any such notion is certainly countered, if nothing else, by his dealings with Thomas eight

In light of these observations about the interim between the resurrection and ascension, we will look more closely at the overlap noted above, first in Luke and then in Acts.

Luke 24:44–49

Then he said to them, "These are my words that I spoke to you while I was still with you, that everything written about me in the Law of Moses and the Prophets and the Psalms must be fulfilled." Then he opened their minds to understand the Scriptures, and said to them, "Thus it is written, that the Christ should suffer and on the third day rise from the dead, and that repentance for the forgiveness of sins should be proclaimed in his name to all nations, beginning from Jerusalem. You are witnesses of these things. And behold, I am sending the promise of my Father upon you. But stay in the city until you are clothed with power from on high."

A Cross-Sectional View

These verses form a unit best seen as providing a cross-sectional view of the interval between the resurrection and ascension. While they possibly describe what occurred on one occasion, they are better taken as indicating what was typical during this period, as capturing what marked it as a whole. As one commentator has put it, they give "an extremely succinct account of what happened further."[6] In the words of another, "The activities of the forty days are here compressed into the span of a few verses."[7]

Supporting this view of the passage are the time indications in Luke 24: within the passage, there is none tagging it to a particular time; on its one side, everything in 24:1–43 takes place on the day of the resurrection; on its other side, at 24:50, we are at the ascension, forty days later (cf. Acts 1:3). Luke 24:45–49, then, captures what took place as a whole in the interval between the resurrection and the ascension.

---

days later with the command, "Put your finger here, and see my hands; and put out your hand, and place it in my side" (John 20:27; similarly Luke 24:39); in other words, in that sense, "Touch me."

6 Norval Geldenhuys, *Commentary on the Gospel of Luke* (Grand Rapids, MI: Eerdmans, 1956), 641.

7 In my class lecture notes, this quote is attributed to R. P. Martin but without the source, which I am no longer able to identify and provide.

However temporary and even anomalous this period was, it was hardly unimportant. Luke 24:44–47 shows it to have been largely a time of instruction, in which the resurrected Christ, having succeeded in his kingdom task and triumphed in his messianic suffering, explained its significance and the consequent glory that has now ensued.

What transpired, as it might be pictured, was a forty-day intersession in which Jesus gave a crash course on Old Testament hermeneutics, in how to interpret the Old Testament as a whole from a postresurrection perspective. In doing that, his all-inclusive concern was to point out how the history of redemption, having reached the point that it had, is to be understood. This interpretive activity consisted in showing that his earthly ministry, culminating in his death and resurrection, is the focus of Scripture, the sum and substance of the Old Testament, designated here by its three main divisions: the Law of Moses, Prophets, and Psalms (the latter standing, part for whole, for the Writings).

Jesus was concerned to show that this totality has an essentially prophetic mode. The Old Testament, taken together in all its parts and with its various genres, is looking toward fulfillment and has found that fulfillment in his person and work.[8] This is the key point that he had already made on the day of the resurrection with the two men on the road to Emmaus (24:27).

The Kingdom

While there is no explicit mention of the kingdom in these verses, it is definitely in view from a detail in 24:44, easily overlooked at a first glance. Jesus says that what he is now explaining to the apostles[9]—the necessary fulfillment of the Old Testament, considered in all its parts, is "about me"—is nothing other than what he had taught "while I was still with you."

The wording of this clause, evidently looking back on his earthly ministry, is striking. It shows the importance in exegeting of a redemptive-historical

---

8   That an overall, comprehensive understanding of the Old Testament is at issue is reinforced by 24:45: the object of the mind-opening experienced by the disciples was "the Scriptures"—the Scriptures seen as a whole, not just some Scriptures, not just this or that Scripture in distinction from others.

9   The concrete antecedent of "them" addressed throughout this passage is most plausibly "the eleven and those who were with them" (Luke 24:33)—that is, the apostles and those associated with them.

perspective, of recognizing the history of redemption with its decisive junctures. The event of the resurrection is so pivotal and critical that from the vantage point Jesus now occupies as resurrected, it is as if his presence with them lies in the past. In comparison with the period prior to the resurrection, even though he is right there speaking to the apostles, it is as if he is not "still with them."

A primary concern Jesus has here, then, is for the apostles to understand that what he now has to say to them is what he taught them all along during the period prior to the resurrection. In a word, as our survey in chapter 2 has shown, that teaching centered in the kingdom as its central and comprehensive theme. It follows, then, that everything Jesus taught in this postresurrection period about understanding the Old Testament and himself as its necessary fulfillment was centered on the kingdom and was put in the context of its coming. The fulfillment that he was concerned to impress upon the apostles and others with them consists in events to be understood as the realization of the kingdom.

While I have made this key point here as a matter of inference, implicit in this passage but nonetheless clear in light of the broader Gospel context, it is made explicit in the other side of the overlap in Acts 1:3.

An important aspect of the kingdom comes into view in 24:46–47. There, Jesus speaks of a worldwide ("to all the nations") proclamation of the gospel that is going to take place beginning from Jerusalem, with the message of the gospel being described as the proclamation of "repentance for the forgiveness of sins." As the syntax of the Greek text shows, this gospel proclamation is going to take place as a direct entailment of the sufferings and resurrection of Jesus.

Further, syntactically, these three coordinate elements—suffering, resurrection, and gospel proclamation—are dependent on "it is written." In other words, universal gospel proclamation—the good news that constitutes the church—is part and parcel of the messianic-kingdom expectation of the Old Testament. That church-creating proclamation, Jesus says, will be an integral consequence of the realization of the kingdom to date.

Worldwide gospel preaching, what constitutes the church (cf. Matt. 28:18–20), is the fulfillment of Old Testament prophecy and, as such, is itself a kingdom phenomenon. That preaching, Jesus wants the apostles to understand, is in the interest of the expansion of the kingdom. The church, in its life history, does not represent some kind of non-kingdom state of affairs; it is not in any sense a postponement or a parenthesis so far as kingdom fulfillment is concerned.

The Spirit

Two related points are made in 24:48–49. First, the disciples—the apostles and those associated with them—are to be "witnesses of these things." These things all told, as we have seen, concern the kingdom (rule and realm) as it has arrived in Christ.

Second, to facilitate this kingdom-expanding gospel witness, they are to remain in Jerusalem and wait for what they will receive. This endowment is described in two ways: "the promise of my Father," which Jesus will send upon them, and their being "clothed with power from on high." In other words, as we know from the unfolding narrative in Luke-Acts, what Jesus is promising them, what he is telling them to wait for, is the Spirit as he will come on the day of Pentecost.

Conclusion

Neither the kingdom nor the Spirit is mentioned explicitly in Luke 24:44–49. Nevertheless, a major point in this account of Jesus's postresurrection instruction, one of its "deep structures," if you will, is that the work of the Holy Spirit in the church, specifically his historic coming at Pentecost, is set within the context of the coming of the kingdom. That imminent coming of the Spirit at Pentecost is in view here as a manifestation of the kingdom. Pentecost will be a decisive juncture in that coming.

Acts 1:3–11

Acts 1:3–5

He presented himself alive to them after his suffering by many proofs, appearing to them during forty days and speaking about the kingdom of God. And while staying with them he ordered them not to depart from Jerusalem, but to wait for the promise of the Father, which, he said, "you heard from me; for John baptized with water, but you will be baptized with the Holy Spirit not many days from now."

Turning now from the close of the Gospel to the Acts side of the overlap in Luke's treatment of the period between the resurrection and the ascension, several things about this period are now made explicit or elaborated.

Its length is specified—forty days.

The antecedent of "them" (1:3), to whom Jesus, now resurrected, presented himself is "the apostles" (1:2); as noted earlier, they are the "you" in view in these verses. The apostles, specifically and throughout this passage, are the object and focus of Jesus's attention.

The kingdom was the sum and focus of the teaching of Jesus (what he was "speaking," 1:3) over the forty days. The content of this teaching throughout this period, comprehensively considered, is, literally, "the things concerning the kingdom of God" (τὰ περὶ τῆς βασιλείας τοῦ θεοῦ). This confirms the conclusion already drawn above from Luke 24:44.

Within the context of this teaching about the kingdom and in relation to the kingdom, Jesus tells the apostles they are to wait for "the promise of the Father" (1:4), already mentioned in Luke 24:49. Only now, additionally, Jesus says that this promise will consist in being "baptized with the Holy Spirit" within a few days (1:5). This describes, as the subsequent narrative makes clear, what will take place on Pentecost. So now also made explicit is the link between the kingdom and the Holy Spirit in his coming at Pentecost.

In fact, this link is already intimated in 1:2, where reference is made to Jesus's pre-ascension commands "through the Holy Spirit" to those, the eleven at this point, he had previously appointed as apostles (Luke 6:13–16). The content of this commanding is not specified here. However, within the immediate context and the broader context of Luke-Acts, in view is almost certainly their appointment as witnesses (1:8; cf. Luke 24:48). They will be witnesses to the coming of the kingdom, and for that witness-bearing, as Jesus himself has received the Spirit (cf. Luke 3:22) and through the Spirit has commanded them, they are to wait to receive the Spirit.

Acts 1:6–8

> So when they had come together, they asked him, "Lord, will you at this time restore the kingdom to Israel?" He said to them, "It is not for you to know times or seasons that the Father has fixed by his own authority.

But you will receive power when the Holy Spirit has come upon you, and you will be my witnesses in Jerusalem and in all Judea and Samaria, and to the end of the earth."

THE HOLY SPIRIT AND THE KINGDOM

These verses, fairly taken as a unit or short paragraph, clearly connect the Holy Spirit and the kingdom. Specifically, they set the work of the Holy Spirit and his coming at Pentecost in the context of the kingdom and its coming. That link comes out in this interchange between Jesus and the apostles.

Acts 1:6 sets its tone with a question apparently looming large in the apostles' minds. It is notably a kingdom question: "Lord, will you at this time restore the kingdom to Israel?" Acts 1:7–8 give Jesus's answer to this question—an answer, to keep the issue open at this point, to be seen as either correcting or at least supplementing the apostles' understanding of the kingdom (I will argue the former below).

What needs to be stressed here is that these verses are a genuine answer to the question put to Jesus. He is not avoiding the question; he is not changing the subject. It is not, say, as if the apostles are asking a question about a future millennial kingdom and Jesus says, in effect, "Forget that. I want to talk about the church."

Admittedly, Jesus's reply is indirect; it is an oblique sort of response insofar as considerations involving the kingdom are concerned. As we might put it, the apostles ask a *when* question, and Jesus gives a *what* answer; a *when* question gets a *what* answer.

The force of that answer is this: As the apostles are concerned about the kingdom, their immediate concern is not to be its future but its present, specifically the present or, strictly speaking, impending task before them, the task of their worldwide witnessing. The apostles' concern about the kingdom, Jesus is saying, should be the kingdom task of gospel preaching, and that means with the church as the result of this forthcoming manifestation of the kingdom. Further, to the end of realizing this, their kingdom task, the apostles will receive "power when the Holy Spirit has come upon you"—surely with what will take place at Pentecost in view. So, once again, in this interchange between Jesus and the apostles, linked are the coming of the kingdom and the coming of the Spirit on Pentecost.

THE VARIETY OF EXPRESSIONS

It is worth noting at this point how in the passages we have already considered Pentecost has been described, particularly the variety of description: "the promise of my [the] Father" (Luke 24:49; Acts 1:4); being "clothed with power from on high" (Luke 24:49), the Holy Spirit "coming upon" (Acts 1:8); being "baptized with [or 'in'] the Holy Spirit" (Acts 1:5). There is, then, no single technical or invariable expression that Luke uses to describe what took place on the day of Pentecost. As our discussion proceeds, other variant expressions will emerge.

MANIFESTATION OF THE KINGDOM

One of the basic points I am wanting to bring out from Acts 1:6–8 is that the worldwide proclamation of the gospel by the apostles, the impending task of apostolic preaching to the nations, beginning in Jerusalem, is a manifestation of the kingdom of God. Reinforcing that point is the fact that all further references in Acts to the kingdom, with one exception (14:22), are in summary statements that specify the central content of preaching: 8:12; 19:8; 20:25; 28:23, 31. Each of these statements sums up the preaching taking place in fulfillment of the mandate to the apostles in Acts 1:8.

A brief comment here on the last of these summarizing statements: Acts 28:31 covers Paul's activity in Rome over the course of the two years in which he was there under house arrest (28:27), a summary, as noted earlier, punctuated with the exclamatory final word, "unhindered" (NASB), that concludes Luke's two-part narrative to Theophilus as a whole. This activity, "with all boldness," consisted in "proclaiming the kingdom of God and teaching about the Lord Jesus Christ."

Noteworthy in this description is the connection of verbs and direct objects: preaching the kingdom, teaching the things about Christ. If the kingdom were solely a matter of the eschatological future separate from and not about the present life of the church, then the expected linking of verbs and direct objects would likely be: preaching the things concerning the Lord Jesus Christ—that is, the gospel and its present proclamation—and teaching about the kingdom as some distant and entirely future expectation. But the phrasing is the other way around. That indicates how kingdom and gospel, the church-building gospel, are interchangeable; to proclaim (and teach) the one is to teach (and proclaim) the other. And so, Acts ends on the note with which it begins.

THE MILLENNIUM

First, strictly speaking, the issue of a future millennial kingdom for Israel is left an open question in Acts 1:6–8. If I have been on sound ground in treating this passage so far, then from the apostles' question and Jesus's response, a case cannot be made for a future millennium kingdom for Israel as a geopolitical entity, for a future period of world dominance for Israel as a nation distinct from other nations.

It would perhaps be overarguing to say that this passage excludes that notion. As I put it at the outset, Jesus's oblique answer is either supplementing or correcting the apostles' question. If he is correcting it, then this passage would tell against the notion of a restored kingdom for Israel in a future millennium. But it is perhaps fairest to say that here Jesus does not directly challenge the assumption of the apostles' question, but neither does he affirm that premise.

Second, as we consider the teaching of the New Testament as a whole, most notably Paul's teaching in Romans 9–11, the most plausible conclusion is that New Testament teaching elsewhere corrects the way in which the apostles posed the question and the answer that they appeared to be anticipating. According to the New Testament, the terms of their question need to be reversed. The question to be asked is not, When will the kingdom be restored to Israel? but, When will Israel be restored to the kingdom?

The answer to that question, particularly in light of Romans 11:11–32, is that that restoration takes place by the inclusion of Jews along with the Gentiles in the church. Israel, ethnically considered, has no other future than as Jews, together with Gentiles, are brought into the church, however that is further understood as occurring—whether in an amillennial, postmillennial, or (either dispensational or non-dispensational) premillennial fashion.

Coming back to matters of immediate concern in Acts 1, the apostles' question in 1:6 betrays that they are still too Israel-centered in their outlook on the kingdom. Their understanding of Scripture is still too exclusive, despite the "mind-opening" they had already experienced according to Luke 24:45. Peter, for instance, had still to grasp that adequately as shown by his encounter with Cornelius in Acts 10 and the rebuke he received from Paul (Gal. 2:11–14).

Jesus's reply is calculated to show the apostles that their outlook needs to be all-inclusive. They are to be world-centered, not Israel-centered. In the truest sense of the word, the apostles are to be world-Christians. The holy, apostolic church is also to be the church that is both one and catholic (the Nicene Creed).

Conclusion

The perspective gained by considering the overlap between the end of Luke and the beginning of Acts is that after his resurrection and in view of what has been accomplished by his preresurrection ministry culminating in his death ("while I was still with you," Luke 24:44), Jesus was intent on showing that the coming of the Holy Spirit on Pentecost will be a decisive juncture in the coming of the kingdom of God. A major, overall conclusion to be drawn from this teaching is that the events narrated in Acts all told—the spread of the gospel and Pentecost in particular—are kingdom phenomena. These events take place in the context of the arrival of the kingdom; they exhibit the eschatological rule of God inaugurated by Christ.

LUKE 3:15-18

As the people were in expectation, and all were questioning in their hearts concerning John, whether he might be the Christ, John answered them all, saying, "I baptize you with water, but he who is mightier than I is coming, the strap of whose sandals I am not worthy to untie. He will baptize you with the Holy Spirit and fire. His winnowing fork is in his hand, to clear his threshing floor and to gather the wheat into his barn, but the chaff he will burn with unquenchable fire."

So with many other exhortations he preached good news to the people.

These words of John form the backdrop of the risen Jesus's address to his apostles, "For John baptized with water, but you will be baptized with the Holy Spirit not many days from now" (Acts 1:5). In this statement, Jesus points in opposite directions at the same time—forward to Pentecost and backward to the ministry of John the Baptist. The look back to John, tethered to Pentecost, echoes in part John's prophecy in Luke 3:16. Beyond what we have already gained from Luke's Gospel, taking note of this explicit connection—forged by the resurrected Christ himself—and examining John's prophecy carefully in its immediate context will significantly enhance our outlook on Pentecost and the work of the Holy Spirit.

In all three Synoptic Gospels, John's prophecy not only concludes but also is the climax of the summary account of his ministry that each provides, particularly as his ministry prepares for the ministry of Jesus (cf. Matt. 3:11–12; Mark 1:8).[10]

In 3:15, Luke begins his summary section with the question of "the people" in a state of expectation about John largely because of the considerable attention his ministry, as described in 3:7–14, had attracted. The form of the question in the Greek text—"whether he might be the Christ"—with the verb in the optative mood and its controlling conjunction, has the nuance of something like "perhaps" or "just maybe."[11] It suggests a less likely possibility but at the same time a possibility for which those asking the question are open.

Whatever may be the precise expectation in back of the question, it is a basic question, one that opens up broad perspectives. For the Judaism of this time, this Messiah question is as important as any. It carries associations, some of which we have already noted, so that it can be appropriately rephrased in various ways: Is John the one on whom Israel's expectation, its eschatological hopes, are focused? Is he the one to inaugurate the eschatological rule of God, to bring in the promised kingdom? Or again—as this question loomed large for some—is John the one to deliver Israel from its Roman oppressors, from foreign domination?

Luke 3:16-17 is John's response to this question, a response framed to meet the people's question on the level it was asked. In other words, a *basic* question receives a *basic* answer. His answer—one long sentence in the Greek text—both captures as it summarizes the significance, respectively, of himself and, referring to Jesus, the "coming" one, "he who is mightier than I." In the light of considerations noted earlier and easily established, we may immediately add: *John's response is a one-sentence summary statement of the significance, respectively, of himself and Jesus for the coming of the kingdom.*

---

10 The corresponding account in John's Gospel, though not exactly parallel, is in John 1:19–34, particularly 1:26–27 and 1:31–33.

11 μήποτε αὐτὸς εἴη ὁ χριστός: "if John might possibly be the Messiah" (NIV); "whether perhaps John could be the Christ" (NET).

The broad scope of this statement needs to be underscored. It is not just what John happened to say one day in passing. The text does say that John had many other things to say in exhorting the people (3:18). But surely 3:16-17 does not intend to present just one thing no more important than a number of others. Rather, they get at the heart of what John and Jesus are all about in their respective ministries and so warrant a more detailed examination.

"I baptize. . . . He will baptize."

To bring out that significance, John makes a contrast in which baptism is the common element or denominator. Why baptism? More than one reason is likely involved. Surely one consideration is that John's baptizing activity, particularly the unusual circumstances that marked it, had attracted widespread attention (see Matt. 3:4–6; Mark 1:5–6); his baptism dramatized his ministry. More to the point, however, in his reply John intends to highlight an activity of baptism as central to his and Jesus's ministries; a baptizing activity is a basic index of each ministry.

This conclusion is reinforced, for instance, by Luke 20:4. In the immediate context (20:1–8), Jewish leaders, trying to entrap Jesus, ask him about his authority and its source (20:2); at issue is his overall authority. In response, Jesus turns the table with a counterquestion (20:4): "Was the baptism of John from heaven or from man?" Faced with this "gotcha" question, they are now the ones trapped by whatever direct answer they give and are left reduced to an evasive nonanswer (20:5–7).

This counterquestion of Jesus aims to get at the heart of what John's ministry is all about. Judgment passed on John's baptism amounts to a judgment on his ministry as a whole. Similarly, in Peter's brief survey of the course of recent redemptive history, "the baptism that John proclaimed" references his ministry as a whole (Acts 10:37). In Luke 3:16, then, baptism is the common denominator not simply because of the dramatic, attention-grabbing effect of John's activity but because an activity of baptism serves to point to what is at the heart of the respective ministries of John and Jesus.

In that regard, John first talks about himself, making an essentially negative point. He is not the one the people are looking for. He is not the Christ, he is not the messianic King. Rather, he is the one who anticipates, the one who prepares "the way of the Lord" (Luke 3:4, citing Isa. 40:3). In terms of the conventional designation for John, he is "the forerunner."

Accordingly, as he is not the one but prepares for the one, commensurate with that identity, his baptism is "with water."

In contrast, the one who is "coming," John says, is the one the people are expecting; "he who is mightier than I," not John, is the Christ, the messianic King, the deliverer of God's people. Accordingly, his baptism will be "with the Holy Spirit and fire."

So, then, as John surveys the impending activity of Jesus as a whole, the element that he sees to be central and distinguishing is baptism with the Holy Spirit and fire. The goal of Jesus's ministry in its entirety is put under the denominator of this baptizing activity. To highlight the basic force of John's prophecy with its defining contrast, it is not so much "John the Baptist" as "Jesus the Baptist," Jesus the baptizer. Keeping in mind, as we noted at the outset, Jesus's linking of this prophecy with Pentecost in Acts 1:5, this conclusion about the breadth in outlook of the former (the prophecy) has important implications, as we will see increasingly, for the latter (Pentecost) as its fulfillment.

"He will baptize you with the Holy Spirit and fire."

Zeroing in now further on the one side of the contrast in 3:16, the messianic baptism, first a comment about the verb "baptize." Negatively, with a view to the different ways it has been understood, here the verb does not describe a ritual act or a rite. Nor, for that matter, regarding sacramentally oriented handlings of the passage, does it describe an action that is associated temporally with the administration of a rite or sign.

Rather, what distinguishes this messianic action from John's rite of water baptism so that both are described as baptism is surely their relationship as reality and sign, as the sign pointing to the reality.[12] Just as John's role as pointer, as forerunner, is focused in his water baptism, so Jesus's role as fulfiller and consummator, is focused and realized in his Spirit-and-fire baptism.

It is important at this point to draw attention to a consideration easily and too frequently overlooked, or not considered as it needs to be, in discussions about the Holy Spirit in Luke-Acts and the significance of Pentecost. The reality of the messianic baptism to which John's water baptism as sign

---

12 The particular mode of John's water baptism need not be settled here. Most likely it was by effusion or pouring (cf. Michelangelo's portrayal in the Sistine Chapel); some will argue that it was by immersion.

pointed is fundamentally the reality of *judgment*. The Messiah's baptizing with the Holy Spirit and fire is essentially a matter of judgment; it is a transaction judicial in nature. As we will see, it brings into view a judicial ordeal, an ordeal in which this baptism is central. At the very least, a legal or forensic element is clearly present.

The use of the word judgment here needs some clarification. More often than not, its English usage has in view the outcome of a trial process, particularly as it results in conviction or condemnation. Here I am not using it in that negative sense, but in its broader and open-ended sense as referring to a judicial process that can have either of two opposite outcomes—one positive resulting in acquittal and blessing, the other negative in the sense already indicated, resulting in condemnation and punishment.

This forensic aspect is at the heart of the meaning of the Messiah's baptism and so, it should not be missed, of what takes place on Pentecost. The following considerations from the immediate context bring us to this conclusion.

As the sign related to the reality, John's water baptism is integrally associated with judgment. It points to impending judgment with wrath as an outcome. This is clear from what John says to the crowds coming to him for baptism, particularly in 3:7 and 3:9:

> He said therefore to the crowds that came out to be baptized by him, "You brood of vipers! Who warned you to flee from the wrath to come? . . . Even now the axe is laid to the root of the trees. Every tree therefore that does not bear good fruit is cut down and thrown into the fire."

Emphatic here, as a fundamental aspect of John's ministry associated with his water baptism, is his warning of impending judgment resulting in destruction.

Even more directly to the point of the messianic baptism is 3:17: "whose winnowing fork is in his hand, to thoroughly clean his threshing floor, and to gather the wheat into his barn, but the chaff he will burn with inextinguishable fire" (my translation).

This verse falls totally within the orbit of the prophecy in 3:16. Grammatically, the Greek text of 3:17 is a subordinate clause that begins with a relative pronoun (οὗ), having for its antecedent the subject (αὐτὸς) of the main verb "will baptize" (βαπτίσει) in 3:16. In other words, as he is the

Spirit-and-fire baptizer, Christ will carry out the discriminating activity of judgment in 3:17. Luke 3:17 amplifies what that baptism entails.

This happens with the metaphor of a threshing floor or, by extension, a harvest, which, without taking the time to explore it here, is a favorite Old Testament metaphor for judgment—in fact, eschatological judgment. So, under this metaphor, 3:17 describes the Messiah's baptizing with the Holy Spirit and fire as a judicial transaction that will issue in blessing (the grain), on the one hand, and curse and destruction (the chaff), on the other. Luke 3:17 shows that the messianic Spirit-and-fire baptizer is, as such, a harvester-judge.

At this point, keeping in view the link that Jesus makes (Acts 1:5), we may draw this important overall conclusion about the immediate fulfillment of John's prophecy on the day of Pentecost: Whatever may be the full significance of that fulfillment—and I do not in any way want here to shortchange that significance with all of its outworkings—we are bound to recognize that Pentecost is fundamentally a matter of judgment; Pentecost is a forensic reality. The point of departure for a proper overall understanding of Pentecost, then, is to see it as taking place within the context of judgment, in fact, as will become more and more clear, in the context of nothing less than eschatological judgment. Pentecost is part of the end-time judicial transaction of God. It is of a piece with God's eschatological adjudication. This forensic facet is fundamental for what took place on the day of Pentecost.

From what we have seen so far in considering John's prophecy, several additional observations about Pentecost—three in number—fit in well here.

First is a point in a way obvious but nonetheless needs to be underscored because it tends to get obscured in many discussions about Pentecost. Christ, not the Spirit, is the principal subject on the day of Pentecost; Christ, if you will, is the central actor. It is he who baptizes there. In that respect, Pentecost is primarily a Christological event. Or in order not to set up an undue depreciation of the Spirit, Pentecost is Pneumatological because it is first of all Christological. Certainly, Pentecost is as much about Christ as it is about the Spirit.

Second, in no way does Pentecost represent some sort of additional blessing. It is not the reflex or consequence of the more basic work of Christ, say, in the form of a power experience had by some Christians in distinction from others. Pentecost does not go beyond those blessings secured by Christ essential for salvation. Rather, if we are on target about what may be seen from the prophetic perspective that John provides, what takes place at Pentecost is at the heart of Christ's once-for-all work, essential in the outcome of his earthly ministry seen as a whole. Take away Pentecost, and that once-for-all work is incomplete. What takes place at Pentecost is hardly a matter of some sort of second or second-order blessing. It is a primary blessing secured by Christ, a blessing of the first order.

Third, the forensic element, the judgment aspect essential to the messianic baptism as prophesied by John's prophecy and fulfilled at Pentecost, is reinforced by those promises of Jesus concerning the coming of the Spirit, surely with Pentecost in view, in John's Gospel (14:16, 26; 15:26; 16:7).

Common to these promises is the identification of the Spirit as παράκλητος. The translation of this term has been a matter of some debate. But over the last century or so, increasing and more careful attention to pertinent background material from Second Temple Judaism has made it clear that the term has forensic or judicial associations. So far as its translation is concerned, "Advocate" is preferable, or perhaps "Counselor" in the sense akin to our counselor-at-law. If the option "Helper" is chosen, as a number of translations do, then it needs to be appreciated that in view is not just help of a more general sort but in the sense of providing legal aid and assistance.

Given the associations that the word now has, "Comforter," made venerable by the KJV, is definitely misleading.[13] The promise of Jesus does not concern the subjectivity of the recipient, as if the Spirit is going to engender a sense of psychological well-being (although that may certainly be true on other grounds). It has a more objective reference to the advocacy of the Spirit. That meaning is clear in the only other New Testament occurrence of the term (1 John 2:1), where it is applied not to the Spirit but the exalted Christ: "we have an advocate with the Father."[14]

In passing, it is interesting to note that this forensic sense may well have been within the meaning that the translators of the Authorized Version

---

13 The NKJV has "Helper" for the passages in John.

14 An earlier version of the NIV (1984) has "the one who speaks to the Father in our defense"— a paraphrase that captures the sense. All of the translations cited that have "helper" in the passages from John's Gospel have "advocate" here.

had in mind. At that time in the early seventeenth century, "comfort" had a sense, now obsolete, derived from the Latin *confiteor*, which means "to confess," "to acknowledge," or "to avow," particularly within a legal framework. In that forensic sense, then, the Spirit promised by Jesus and come at Pentecost is the "Comforter."

John's prophecy shows that its immediate fulfillment at Pentecost, connected as the two are by Jesus in Acts 1:5, has forensic as well as eschatological significance. Pentecost is linked with the final judgment. Where that connection is not recognized, to that extent Pentecost is misunderstood.

"With the Holy Spirit and Fire"

The Element of Christ's Baptizing

Focusing further within the messianic side of John's prophecy on this prepositional phrase sheds additional light on the fulfillment that takes place at Pentecost. First, this phrase is not to be understood instrumentally; it should not be translated "by the Holy Spirit and fire." Rather, it describes the substance or material of the baptism, the element used in baptizing. As far as the Holy Spirit is in view, he is the element of Christ's baptizing activity. The Greek preposition (ἐν) should be rendered "with" or "in."

The Nature of Christ's Baptizing

From a brief look at the history of interpretation, there are basically two ways this phrase has been understood. As far back in church history is the view largely associated with the Greek fathers (for instance, Chrysostom in the fifth century) and still found among a number of Roman Catholic commentators. In this view, the phrase describes an entirely gracious outpouring of the Spirit; "fire" is taken as purifying, as a cleansing element.[15]

The great difficulty with this understanding is that in the immediate context, on both sides of the phrase (Luke 3:9, 17), the word "fire" has pronounced and starkly negative associations; it is destructive. The fire in view is clearly the fire of the inextinguishable judgment of destruction.

Much more widespread and in its early expressions more characteristic of the Latin fathers (for instance, Origen in the third century) is the view

---

15   These comments utilize the helpful discussion in James D. G. Dunn, *Baptism in the Holy Spirit* (Naperville, IL: Allenson, 1970), 10-11.

that the phrase describes two baptisms, one positive and one negative: the baptism of the righteous (the grain of 3:17) with the Holy Spirit and the baptism of the wicked (the chaff) with the fire of destruction. This view is clearly much better attuned to the immediate context, particularly the reference to fire as destructive, and its way of taking the phrase is quite plausible. Under any circumstances, it contains a large measure of truth.

The phrase, however, is at least open to the alternative interpretation that in view is not two different baptisms but one baptism with two different, quite opposite outcomes. Upon reflection, I believe this emerges as the preferable understanding—not two baptisms but a single baptism with a dual outcome. Initially, this can seem a rather technical exegetical point. But with a view to our overriding concern on Pentecost, reflecting on it will bring to light an important outlook on Pentecost.

Several grounds support a reference to a single baptism. First is the grammatical observation that the preposition is distributed with both terms; "in" is not repeated before "fire." This by itself is not a decisive consideration, but it does leave open that in view is a single baptism with two elements.

Second and much more decisive is 3:17. Described there is a single judgment or separating activity: the one threshing floor activity with its dual outcome, for the wheat on the one hand, the chaff on the other. This is clearly the metaphoric parallel to the messianic baptizing action in view in 3:16.

Third, the same group "you" is the object of both John's baptism and the messianic baptism. That raises the question, What concretely is the reference of the pronoun "you" (ὑμᾶς)? What is its immediate historical reference? It can be understood in one of two ways: it refers either to those who are actually baptized by John or, more broadly, the potential subjects of his baptism, the "people" mentioned in 3:15 and again in 3:18.

The answer need not be settled here. Either way, the point is surely that those who submit to water baptism do so not somehow as an alternative to Spirit-and-fire baptism or in order to be exempt from it in some way. Rather, they submit to John's water baptism precisely with a view toward receiving the messianic baptism and in preparation for it. They do that, of course, so that for them that baptism will be gracious, that ultimately the outcome will be favorable, that they will be "wheat," not "chaff." To put the point here more simply and negatively, there is nothing in the text grammatically that dissociates "you" from "fire."

Fourth, the parallel statement in Mark 1:8 ("I have baptized you with water, but he will baptize you with the Holy Spirit") makes no mention of fire in describing the Messiah's baptizing.[16] Matthew (3:11) is identical with Luke. So there is a distinction here between Mark ("with the Holy Spirit") and Matthew-Luke ("with the Holy Spirit and fire").

Supposedly, this difference could be viewed in an arithmetical or mechanical fashion: Mark has half of what we find in Matthew and Luke, and by omitting any reference to fire gives what John said a different sense than they have. In light of other Synoptic parallels, however, it is sounder to conclude that Matthew and Luke are best understood as amplifying or expanding on what we have in Mark and so bring out the sense of Mark. Alternatively, positing the priority of Matthew or Luke, Mark can be seen as a compressed statement of what is said more fully in Matthew and Luke. In other words, baptism with the Holy Spirit in Mark is equivalent to baptism with the Holy Spirit and fire in Matthew and Luke.

This reading is supported by the directly following comments about the integration or inseparability of the Spirit and fire in John's prophecy (in Luke and Matthew), as well as by Jesus's allusion to John's prophecy in Acts 1:5, where, like Mark, there is no mention of fire ("but you will be baptized with the Holy Spirit not many days from now"). Luke would hardly see this description of the messianic baptism as having any other sense than what he reported earlier in Luke 3:16. Also, to be discussed later, fire is not absent but notably present at Pentecost.

These four considerations, then, point to one baptism with two facets or aspects. Spirit and fire together represent a unitary complex and bring us to view the messianic baptism as one judgment act with two outcomes: blessing for the repentant and destruction for the unrepentant. With a neat turn of phrase that captures this reality, in view is "the fiery πνεῦμα in which all will be immersed."[17] Or, as I would prefer to put it, the fiery πνεῦμα with which all will be deluged. Significant events earlier in covenant history come to mind here as pointing precursors: for instance, the preservation

---

16   Also missing in Mark is a reference to the threshing floor metaphor in Luke 3:17 (present also in Matt. 3:12).

17   Dunn, *Baptism in the Holy Spirit*, 13.

of Noah in the ark through the deluge of the flood and the deliverance of Israel in the Red Sea event.

The Old Testament Background to John's Prophecy

Further support for a single baptism view—blending or integrating the elements of the Spirit and fire—is found within the broader biblical context of Old Testament prophecy. This is hardly surprising because John surely stands in that tradition. "The Law and the Prophets were until John" (Luke 16:16)—that is, up to and including John. Following the lengthy gap in the Old Testament prophetic tradition earlier during the Second Temple period, that tradition resumes in John, who brings it to its culmination.

Considering the element of fire first, in the prophets fire is forensic; fire stands for judgment. But with this association it symbolizes not only the destruction of the wicked, as it often does, but as well the purification of the righteous. In other words, fire is associated with judgment, but not necessarily with destructive judgment.

Probably the most pertinent and instructive instance is right at the end of the prophets section of the Old Testament, in what is said toward the close of Malachi concerning the coming of the Messiah. Malachi 3 opens with this declaration: "Behold, I send my messenger, and he will prepare the way before me. And the Lord whom you seek will suddenly come to his temple; and the messenger of the covenant in whom you delight, behold, he is coming, says the LORD of hosts" (3:1).

This verse is most plausibly read as (1) distinguishing "my messenger" from "the messenger of the covenant" and (2) identifying the latter with the coming of the Lord. Since the first part of the verse (about "my messenger") is applied explicitly to John the Baptist in Luke 7:27, the messenger of the covenant, whose way John prepares, is the Messiah. Malachi 3:2–3, then, goes on to describe the covenant messenger/Messiah's activity, which, Luke shows, was later realized and fulfilled in Christ:

> But who can endure the day of his coming, and who can stand when he appears? For he is like a refiner's fire and like fullers' soap. He will sit as a refiner and purifier of silver, and he will purify the sons of Levi and refine them like gold and silver, and they will bring offerings in righteousness to the LORD.

Here, the fire in view is associated with judgment (cf. 3:5) with an effect that is positive; it refines and purifies.

Later in the same context,[18] in Malachi 4:5 (3:23 in the Hebrew) the Lord declares, "Behold, I will send you Elijah the prophet before the great and awesome day of the Lord comes." This climactic pronouncement is applied to John in Matthew 11:14 (he is the "Elijah . . . to come"). Now the setting for the coming of the messenger of the covenant mentioned earlier is described as "the great and awesome day of the Lord," the time of final judgment. Malachi 4:1 (3:19 in the Hebrew) describes the judgment as follows:

> For behold, the day is coming, burning like an oven, when all the arrogant and all evildoers will be stubble. The day that is coming shall set them ablaze, says the Lord of hosts, so that it will leave them neither root nor branch.

Now the fire in view is clearly the fire of destruction; its effect is negative, not purifying but destructive.

This Malachi passage foretells the judgment to be carried out by the Messiah in his coming. That judgment will be marked by fire; it will be a fire-day that will be both purifying for some and destructive for others. This passage especially is prophetic background for John's use of the threshing floor metaphor in Luke 3:17 (cf. Matt. 3:12) to describe the goal of Christ's ministry as Spirit-and-fire baptism.

In the prophets, this dual connotation—fire as referring to both purifying and destructive judgment—is similarly the case for the Spirit. Connotations of judgment are plain, particularly in Isaiah's use of S/spirit (רוּחַ, *ruach*). Especially noteworthy is the occurrence in Isaiah 4:4: "when the Lord shall have washed away the filth of the daughters of Zion and cleansed the bloodstains of Jerusalem from its midst by the Spirit of judgment and by the Spirit of burning" (my translation[19]). This will take place "in that day" when "the Branch of the LORD shall be beautiful and glorious" (4:2). Assuming here what detailed study will show, that "the Branch" refers to

---

18 Neither the Masoretic text nor the LXX has a chapter break after 3:18, reflecting that the judgment scene begun in 3:1 continues.

19 Most translations have "spirit" (lowercase; but see NIV mg.). In light of the discussion we are developing here, the Holy Spirit is much more likely in view.

the Messiah,[20] 4:4 describes his activity of cleansing his people (Zion, correlatively Jerusalem) "by the Spirit of judgment and by the Spirit of burning." So, here the messianic salutary cleansing action involves the Spirit, as the Spirit is explicitly associated with both judgment and fire (burning). The means by which the Messiah will carry out this activity of purifying judgment will be, we may fairly say, "with the Holy Spirit and fire."

The Branch reappears in Isaiah 11:1: "A shoot will come up from the stump of Jesse; / from his roots a Branch will bear fruit" (NIV). This Branch is surely "the Branch of the LORD" in Isaiah 4:2, and the parallel description, "the stump of Jesse," makes clear a reference to the Messiah.[21]

Isaiah 11:2 continues: "And the Spirit of the LORD shall rest upon him, / the Spirit of wisdom and understanding, / the Spirit of counsel and might, / the Spirit of knowledge and the fear of the LORD." Now the Branch is described as both anointed and fully endowed with the Spirit. Then follows a description how he will "judge" and "decide disputes" (11:3). As an aspect of that judgment, "with the breath of his lips he shall kill the wicked" (11:4).[22] Now the Spirit-breathed judgment executed by the Messiah is destructive, not purifying.[23] In Isaiah, then, the Spirit functions in the judgment exercised by the Messiah both to purify and to destroy.[24]

This brief examination of the Old Testament background to John's prophecy shows that references there, whether to the Spirit or to fire, are neither exclusively gracious nor exclusively destructive. A certain duality, positive and negative, attaches to both.

The destructive aspect of the Spirit's activity is further illustrated and reinforced as the post-Pentecost narrative in Acts unfolds. Acts 5:1–11

---

20 See Isa. 11:1; Jer. 23:5; 33:15; Zech. 3:8; 6:12.

21 Cf. the reference to Christ: "of the seed of David" (Rom. 1:3 NKJV).

22 Note the interplay in the Hebrew text between the two meanings of רוּחַ, *ruach*: "Spirit," 11:2; and "breath," 11:4.

23 Note the unmistakable echo of Isa. 11:4 in 2 Thess. 2:8: "And then the lawless one will be revealed, whom the Lord Jesus will kill with the breath of his mouth [τῷ πνεύματι τοῦ στόματος αὐτοῦ] and bring to nothing by the appearance of his coming." As with the use of רוּחַ/*ruach* in the Isaiah passage, so here too πνεῦμα/*pneuma*, translated "breath," alludes to the Spirit and reinforces the destructive aspect of the Spirit's activity in the judgment to be carried out by Christ in fulfillment of Isaiah prophecy and his Spirit-and-fire baptism prophesied by John.

24 There are, of course, numerous places elsewhere in Isaiah where the outpouring of the Spirit in view is associated with blessing and the prosperity of God's people. Isa. 32:15–17 and 44:3 are a couple of clear instances.

relates events surrounding the demise of Ananias and Sapphira. There the point made explicitly is first that Ananias had decided to "lie to the Holy Spirit" (5:3) and then similarly that in lying Sapphira had agreed to "test the Spirit of the Lord" (5:9). Surely the inference to be drawn is that the Holy Spirit is the one who has destroyed them.

If, to reflect briefly on this passage and its significance, we ask: Why did Luke include it? How does this incident serve his overall narrative in Acts, anchored, as it is, in the climactic event of the outpouring of the Spirit at Pentecost? Surely the answer lies in recognizing the perennial warning to the church it contains—as it may be put proverbially, echoing John's prophecy: to toy with the Holy Spirit is to play with fire.

What also comes to mind here, tangentially perhaps but nonetheless pertinently, is the warning the writer of Hebrews gives at the close of Hebrews 12. There, he contrasts God's old covenant people assembled at Sinai with his new covenant people who "have come to Mount Zion and to the city of the living God, the heavenly Jerusalem" (12:22). With that privilege and the heightened worship in the Spirit it entails, it still remains true, he reminds the church, "Our God is a consuming fire" (12:29).

The Spirit as Blessing

The preceding reflections have been prompted by the prepositional phrase describing the Messiah's baptism prophesied by John: "with the Holy Spirit and fire." Returning to that point of departure, (1) with all that has been noted, including our dipping into the Old Testament and the not unimportant connections to John's prophecy there, and (2) with our emphasis on one baptism with two elements, it is difficult to avoid the conclusion (3) that in Luke 3:16, the Holy Spirit refers primarily to the positive outcome and fire primarily to the negative outcome of the judgment in view.

Supporting that conclusion for the Spirit is the statement of Jesus noted earlier in our provisional survey of the relationship in Luke's Gospel between the Spirit and the kingdom. The Holy Spirit is the gift that the heavenly Father will give to those who pray for the coming of the kingdom (Luke 11:13, cf. 11:2–4). Also, we are bound to take into consideration here the initial fulfillment of John's prophecy at Pentecost. Later on, we will give attention to the way in which the element of fire is present on the day of

Pentecost in the tongues phenomenon, but at this point, we may note that clearly the Spirit is present there as blessing and as a means of blessing.

Finally, before moving on, whether one sees "with the Holy Spirit and fire" as referring to two baptisms, or, as I have argued as the better, preferable understanding, one baptism with two aspects or outcomes, in John's ministry the phrase is integrally tied to his call to repentance: repentance with submission to John's water baptism is in order that the coming messianic judgment, the coming messianic baptism-ordeal, "the great and awesome day of the LORD" (NKJV)—the description of Pentecost in Acts 2:20, utilizing the language of judgment in Joel 2:31—will mean salvation, not destruction.

It may be helpful here to note (a point to be developed more fully later) that—in keeping with recognizing that the first and second comings of Christ should be seen not as separate events but as two stages of the single eschatological event of the day of the Lord/the coming of the Messiah—the positive side of the fulfillment of John's prophecy occurs at Pentecost, the negative, destructive side at the end of history when Christ returns.

LUKE 3:21–22

> Now when all the people were baptized, and when Jesus also had been baptized and was praying, the heavens were opened, and the Holy Spirit descended on him in bodily form, like a dove; and a voice came from heaven, "You are my beloved Son; with you I am well pleased."

Earlier I touched on this passage in a provisional way, in noting the connection between the Holy Spirit and the kingdom in Luke's Gospel. Now I focus on it in more detail.

Recall that in our interest in Pentecost, we were drawn to examining John's prophecy in Luke 3:16–17 prompted by Acts 1:5, where Jesus explicitly connects that prophecy and Pentecost. It might seem, then, that having explored that connection and gained the resulting perspective it opens up on Pentecost, we can and should move on now to give our attention (finally!) to material in Acts, particularly Acts 2.

To draw that conclusion, however, would be hasty, for it would in fact short-circuit the path that, precisely with the interest that we have in Pentecost and its significance, Luke would have us travel. Here I will follow that path by posing this question: In writing to Theophilus, why doesn't Luke go directly from John's prophecy to its fulfillment? Why doesn't what's narrated in Acts 2 immediately follow Luke 3:18? Why all that is in between? With that heuristic question in mind, a number of important considerations come to light that have a direct bearing on Pentecost.

Messianic Appointment

In all three Synoptic Gospels, the account of Jesus's baptism by John follows directly on their summary accounts of John's ministry, summaries in which, as we have seen, his prophecy concerning baptism with the Holy Spirit and fire is central. More important than this observation about literary flow, however, is the material or inner connection between the two accounts. That connection is the significant redemptive-historical transition that takes place in this baptism event from the ministry of John to the ministry of Jesus, a transition, as the Gospel narratives unfold, that will prove to be of decisive, epochal proportions in the overall flow of the history of redemption.

In that regard—an obvious point perhaps but one about which we need to be clear at the outset—Jesus's baptism is not a merely personal matter. If that were the case, it would make no sense, because as an individual Jesus had no need of repentance, and repentance is what submission to John's water baptism symbolized (Luke 3:3). Luke has been clear from the outset: from birth, Jesus is holy and without sin (1:35). Though not recorded in Luke, we may recall here as well the recoil of John when Jesus comes and asks to be baptized by him. John, no doubt recognizing the significance of his baptism, said, in effect, "I don't need to baptize you; you need to baptize me" (see Matt. 3:14). The event at the Jordan is not personal or merely individual but clearly has epochal, redemptive-historical significance.

Specifically, the baptism of Jesus is his investiture with his messianic task, the occasion of his official installation as the Messiah. Here at the Jordan, the public kingdom-commissioning of Jesus takes place.

The voice from heaven is best seen as having its significance in terms of this messianic installation or kingdom appointment. It is not, as many translations suggest or are often read, a timeless expression of good pleasure—that is, it is not a declaration of the delight of the Father in the Son from all eternity, "before the foundation of the world" (John 17:24), although that sublime delight is surely in the background. Rather, the approval or delighting registered here is to be taken, at least primarily, in a messianic sense.

Further, the heavenly voice is not simply a statement of fact but an effective declaration. The verb (εὐδόκησα), an aorist indicative, is best taken as having a performative force. A timed or concrete reference should not be eliminated, so that the sense of the last clause of Luke 3:22 is properly paraphrased: "whom I have approved as the Messiah," "upon whom the good pleasure of my messianic appointment rests," or in that messianic sense, "with you I am well pleased."

The Roles of the Son and Father

The messianic or, more broadly, redemptive-historical significance of the Jordan event may be reflected on further from two mutually reinforcing angles: from the side of Jesus as the Son, and, correlatively, from the side of the Father.

From the side of Jesus, as already noted, submitting to John's baptism gives expression to his messianic identity and calling. In that way, he identifies with his people, for to speak of the Messiah necessarily implies the messianic community. By submitting to John's water baptism, Jesus identifies himself with those for whom he is Messiah; he shows his solidarity with them.

More particularly, and this does not so much come from what we see in Luke as from what Matthew relates about the recoil of John and about Jesus fulfilling all righteousness: By submitting to John's baptism Jesus shows himself to be the representative of his people. Furthermore, as we reflect on this event in the light of subsequent New Testament revelation— interpretation provided by the New Testament itself that we are bound to take into consideration—here Jesus shows himself to be their representative sin-bearer. Submitting to John's baptism is for the remission of sins. Therefore, in doing that, even though sinless personally, Jesus shows himself to be their substitute. Here at the Jordan, Jesus is marked out publicly as the one for whom it has been true since his birth that he has come "in the likeness of sinful flesh and for sin" (Rom. 8:3), as the one who though "he knew no sin," was "made . . . to be sin . . . so that in him we might become the righteousness of God" (2 Cor. 5:21).

Accordingly, for his part, the Father publicly confirms the messianic identity of the Son and by that declaration inaugurates the public phase of messianic activity that he is about to undergo. At the same time, in close conjunction with this declaration and with a view toward the messianic task before him, the Father endows him with the Holy Spirit. At the Jordan, the Spirit descends on the baptized Jesus as anointing, as gifting, requisite and essential for carrying out his impending messianic mission, the kingdom activity he is about to undertake.[25] That activity, Luke—like the narratives in the other Synoptics—goes on to show, begins in the temptation of Jesus (Luke 4:1–13), the great kingdom struggle enjoined in the desert between Christ, now equipped with the Spirit and led by the Spirit (4:1), and the archenemy of that kingdom, Satan.[26]

The Timing of Christ's Baptizing Activity

Luke's overall perspective, then—in fact, the perspective of the Synoptic tradition as a whole—is that the messianic Spirit-and-fire baptism prophesied by John, the Messiah's own baptizing activity, will not take place immediately.[27] Rather, (1) it will be preceded or, more precisely, be mediated by a period based upon the Messiah's own baptism—an intervening period

25 Note Peter's summary in Acts 10:37-38: "You yourselves know what happened throughout all Judea, beginning from Galilee after *the baptism that John proclaimed*: how *God anointed Jesus of Nazareth with the Holy Spirit and with power*. He went about doing good and healing all who were oppressed by the devil, for *God was with him*." The latter captures the essence of the coming of the Spirit upon Jesus at the Jordan: "God was with him," the one whom he has now approved and endowed with the Spirit, and in whom as the Messiah he affirms his delight.

26 Unlike the other two Synoptics, there is a break in Luke's narrative after 3:22, where to the end of the chapter he inserts the genealogy of Jesus. This differs from Matthew, whose genealogy is not only placed at the beginning of his Gospel but also goes back only to Abraham, while Luke's continues all the way back to "Adam, the son of God" (3:38). It may be plausibly proposed, as already noted earlier (chap. 3, n2), that by placing the genealogy as he does—interposing it between his accounts of the baptism and the temptation and carrying the genealogy all the way back to Adam—Luke in this way identifies Christ, in effect, as Paul does explicitly, as, contrasted with Adam, "the last Adam" (1 Cor. 15:45).

27 This is a point that John himself apparently did not fully grasp or had become uncertain about (Luke 7:18-23). Out of the picture redemptive-historically at this point, in prison and soon to be executed, John receives reports from his own disciples about the shape that Jesus's ministry is taking. These secondhand reports prompt John to send a couple of his disciples on his behalf to ask, in effect, "What's going on?" This uncertainty, stemming from what he has heard about Jesus's ministry, is focused in the single question, "Are you the one who is to come?" (7:20); in other words, "Are you the Messiah?" Jesus then responds affirmatively by pointing to the healing miracles that are marking his ministry (7:21-23).

based on his identification with his people in their sins and as the bearer of the judgment their sins deserve. Correlatively, (2) this mediating period involves his reception of the Holy Spirit, his receiving the Spirit for the full gamut of tasks that lies before him, primarily the sin-bearing task that will eventually bring him to the cross.

The Significance of Jesus's Baptism

From these observations, it is not difficult to appreciate the significance of the convergence at the Jordan for Jesus of baptism with water and endowment with the Spirit. The two are certainly distinct, but they are clearly closely conjoined, in fact inseparable elements in what transpired. In view of this inseparability, then, there should be no hesitation about speaking of Christ's own baptism with the Spirit at the Jordan. For Jesus, the Messiah, being baptized with the Holy Spirit is surely at the heart of the meaning of the Jordan event.

From the vantage point of John's prophecy, then, for the Messiah's Spirit-and-fire baptism to be a saving baptism, for that baptism to be experienced by the messianic community as salvation, as blessing, the Messiah himself must first be baptized with the Spirit in order that he may remove the condemnation and bear away the wrath that their sins deserve.[28] With pointed reference to the Spirit, a basic significance of the Jordan event is this: If the Messiah's people, those for whom he is the Messiah, are to receive the Spirit as gift, as blessing, then the Messiah himself must first receive the Spirit in order to undergo cursing, to bear the curse that their sins deserve.

Confirmation for this close linking in Luke of (1) John's ministry marked by water baptism, (2) his messianic Spirit-and-fire baptism prophecy, and (3) his baptism of Jesus is found in John the Baptist's declaration in the correlative, if not parallel, account in John's Gospel. In response to inquiring Jewish leaders, he denies that he is the Messiah (John 1:19-20) and declares: "I myself did not know him, but he who sent me to baptize with water said to me, 'He on whom you see the Spirit descend and remain, this is he who baptizes with the Holy Spirit'" (1:33).

Furthermore, in bringing these three elements together, this verse is also both linked to and bracketed by the identification of Jesus as "the Lamb

---

28 Cf. Heb. 9:14, where the writer speaks of Christ's death as offering up himself "through the eternal Spirit." Though a reference here to the Holy Spirit is disputed, in my view the more plausible case exegetically is that it does.

of God, who takes away the sin of the world!" (1:29; cf. 1:36). Jesus is the Spirit-baptized and so, consequently, the Spirit-baptizing Christ as he, "the Son of God" (1:34), is the sin-removing Lamb of God.

The Bond Between Christ and the Spirit

What occurred at the Jordan has an integral bearing on the coming of the Spirit on the church at Pentecost, the church's baptism with the Holy Spirit. Along lines seen in Luke's Gospel, the latter will not occur without the former; no Jordan, no Pentecost. Further, in the matter of receiving of the Holy Spirit, there is a certain analogy or parallel between the Messiah and his people; what is true for the Messiah is true for the church. Some important implications of this parallel between the Jordan and Pentecost will occupy us below.

Here we may go on to note that given the messianic character of Jesus's baptism and endowment with the Spirit, it should be appreciated that what took place at the Jordan is hardly just one event among others during the course of Jesus's ministry but has singularly heightened importance. It represents nothing less than an epochal juncture in the history of redemption, a crucial transition in the inauguration of the arrival of the kingdom of God.

In this coming together, this conjunction, of Christ and the Spirit at the Jordan, nothing less than the eschatological climax of history heightens. Here the Messiah begins his final kingdom-struggle. Here he enters the ordeal of eschatological judgment, the ordeal that will culminate in enduring the consummate outpouring of God's wrath on the cross and from which he will emerge successfully and in triumph in his resurrection.

Earlier, I provided a brief sketch of Jesus's kingdom proclamation, his teaching concerning the eschatological rule and realm of God inaugurated in his coming, in his person and ministry. Considered from the angle of the time of the coming of the kingdom, we saw that the present-future pattern observable in Christ's teaching consists concretely in three basic stages: prior to his death and resurrection, between his resurrection and return, and beyond his return.

So far as the Jordan event is concerned, it does not rise to the same level or hierarchy in importance as the two stage-determining events (resurrection and return) just mentioned. But given the alpha point of the incarnation, Jesus's Jordan baptism is surely the most significant transitional event within the first stage of the coming of the kingdom that ends in the cross and resurrection.

Also, to be clear, the epochal endowment of Jesus with the Spirit dating from the Jordan does not mean that previously the Spirit was not present with Jesus. Luke is clear: Jesus was conceived by the Holy Spirit (Luke 1:35); there is a unique conjunction between the Holy Spirit and the incarnate Christ already from the moment of his conception. Consequently, indwelt by the Spirit from birth, as he matured "Jesus increased in wisdom and in stature and in favor with God and man" (2:52). "And the child grew and became strong, filled with wisdom. And the favor of God was upon him" (2:40).[29]

Still, we should not fail to appreciate the heightened stage of Spirit-endowment that begins at the Jordan, the new and deepened dimension in the relationship between Jesus and the Spirit requisite for the public phase of his messianic ministry. This endowment is what the Gospel writers highlight, as does Peter in the summary he gives in Acts 10:37-38, noted above ("after the baptism that John proclaimed: how God anointed Jesus of Nazareth with the Holy Spirit and with power.... for God was with him"). As we continue to explore the significance of Pentecost in Luke-Acts and then later the relationship between the Christ and the Spirit in Paul, we will see that the heightening of this relationship reaches its consummate realization in the bond between Christ as resurrected and the Spirit.

Conclusion

At the outset of this examination of Luke 3:21-22, we asked why all that intervenes between John's prophecy in Luke 3 and its fulfillment in Acts 2? Why doesn't that fulfillment take place immediately? The answer is now clear and may be given in one word: the gospel—the good news about Jesus, the Spirit-anointed Messiah, whose life of obedience culminated in dying on the cross for the sins of his people followed by his resurrection. Because of that intervening gospel reality, the fulfillment of John's prophecy on Pentecost becomes the event of great blessing that it is for the church.

---

29 It always needs to be recognized that such statements, as well as his endowment with the Spirit, apply to the person of Jesus with respect to his human nature, not his divine nature. At the same time—and often this is not sufficiently appreciated—his deity does not eliminate his need of the Spirit, the genuine necessity in his humanity for him to be endowed and equipped with the Spirit. Cf. Geerhardus Vos, *Biblical Theology: Old and New Testaments* (Edinburgh: Banner of Truth Trust, 1975), 348-50 ("The Question of Development").

LUKE 12:49-51

I came to cast fire on the earth, and would that it were already kindled! I have a baptism to be baptized with, and how great is my distress until it is accomplished! Do you think that I have come to give peace on earth? No, I tell you, but rather division.

Connotations of Judgment

These words of Jesus provide striking reinforcement of several key points in what we have so far been considering. Unmistakable here are echoes of John's prophecy and of the state of affairs it brings into view: the reference to "fire," the repetition of baptism language, both noun and verb, and, more importantly, everything said has clear connotations of judgment. The context is that of an ordeal Jesus has to undergo and includes the declaration that his coming is not for peace but for division.

Further, the situation in view is one about which, on the whole, Jesus is experiencing, we may say, a good deal of anxiety. Or if that is not just the right word, he is clearly deeply burdened or distressed. The second clauses in 12:49–50 express a sense of the considerable duress he is experiencing: "would that it were already kindled"; "how great is my distress until it is accomplished."

The Culmination of Jesus's Baptism

Here Jesus speaks of his "casting" fire. There should be no difficulty at this point in recognizing that this is an alternative description of baptism with fire, a variant way of expressing the baptizing activity in view in John's prophecy, an outpouring activity that at this point in Jesus's ministry is still in prospect, still future.

With that noted and given the significance of his own baptism at the Jordan, of equal importance here Jesus also speaks of "a baptism to be baptized with," a baptism he must undergo correlative with his casting fire. In other words, Jesus is saying, "I as the baptizer must be baptized." The messianic baptizer, in order to be that, must himself be baptized.

What is this baptism? In what does it consist? There can be no doubt, as Jesus senses in advance, that in view is the culmination of his sufferings on the cross. Mark 10:38-39 puts that beyond question. In the context, James and John have come with the request, not exactly modest, for places of special prominence in the future glory of Jesus's kingdom (Mark 10:37; cf. Matt. 20:21). Jesus's response includes this rhetorical question: "Are you able to drink the cup that I drink, or to be baptized with the baptism with which I am baptized?" (Mark 10:38) And to their reply, "We are able" (hardly in need of exegetical comment!), Jesus continues, "The cup that I drink you will drink, and with the baptism with which I am baptized, you will be baptized" (10:39).

This shared baptism consists in shared suffering (cf. "with persecutions," 10:30; cf. Rom. 8:17; 2 Cor. 1:5). The synonymous parallel image of drinking the cup reinforces that. This image surely has the sense it has in Luke 22:42, where in the context describing the duress of Jesus in Gethsemane, the "cup" clearly refers to the climax of his sufferings in his death ("Father, if you are willing, remove this cup from me"). The cross is the culmination of Jesus's being baptized.

A Judicial Ordeal

Jesus's declaration in Luke 12:49-51 prompts two concluding observations. First, this passage provides strong reinforcement for understanding the references to baptism in the other related passages we have examined—John's water baptism, the Messiah's prophesied Spirit-and-fire baptism, Jesus's own being baptized at the Jordan—as referring to a judicial ordeal, for seeing them as bringing into view either the reality of judgment or signs pointing to that reality.

Second, the way Jesus expresses himself here also provides substantial warrant for viewing his earthly ministry, certainly from the Jordan through the cross, as one large judicial ordeal, in other words, for putting this entire period under the denominator of this baptism; his entire ministry was a species of baptism.

In this regard, it is of interest and instructive to note how these considerations have found expression in the subsequent life of the church. To cite just two examples here, one confessional, and the other of an individual theologian.

In a section commenting on the Apostles' Creed, question 37 of the Heidelberg Catechism asks, "What do you confess when you say that He suffered?" with this answer in part: "During all the time He lived on earth, but especially at the end, Christ bore in body and soul the wrath of God against the sin of the whole human race."[30] And Calvin writes of Christ, "while he dwelt on earth he was not only tried by a perpetual cross but his whole life was nothing but a sort of perpetual cross."[31]

Christ's entire life, then, is fairly seen as a wrath-bearing cross. This for him was "the baptism with which I am baptized," especially beginning at the Jordan and culminating in his crucifixion—all with a view, in part, to the baptism he would carry out actively at Pentecost.

---

30 Heidelberg Catechism, question 37, Christian Reformed Church (website), https://www.crcna .org/.

31 John Calvin, *Institutes of the Christian Religion*, ed. John T. McNeill, trans. Ford Lewis Battles (Philadelphia, PA: Westminster, 1960), 3.8.1 (1:702).

4

Pentecost (Part 1)

Aspects of Its Fundamental Significance

THE PRECEDING CHAPTER is structured in terms of the key passages we examined. The basic structure of this chapter is topical. This change in format, however, will not mean adopting a substantially different method. As we turn now to focus on material in Acts, my approach will still be largely exegetical but will be developed under these four headings: redemptive-historical, ecclesiological, Trinitarian, and forensic.

Prompted by the words of the resurrected Jesus in Acts 1:5 linking Pentecost and the ministry of John the Baptist, the outlook of the third Gospel explored in the previous chapter centered both in John's prophecy of messianic Spirit-and-fire baptism and the implications of his baptizing of Jesus. In this chapter, we turn our attention to the fulfillment of John's prophecy as it is realized in events narrated in Acts, primarily on the day of Pentecost.

THE REDEMPTIVE-HISTORICAL SIGNIFICANCE OF PENTECOST

We may speak here as well of the eschatological or, more generally, the epochal significance of Pentecost. The value of using the word *epochal* will become more apparent as our discussion unfolds.

The Spirit and the Kingdom

First of all here, articulating further matters we have already been considering: According to Luke, particularly in light of Luke 3:16, what John intimates by prophecy to be nothing less than the sum and substance of blessings bound up with the coming of the kingdom—what the coming of the *basiliea*, the rule and realm of God, is all about in terms of blessing—that is what is realized in the outpouring of the Spirit on Pentecost.

This needs to be highlighted. Nothing less than the central redemptive purpose of the Messiah's activity, nothing less than the meaning of the ministry of Jesus all told at its core, is realized in the baptism with the Holy Spirit on Pentecost. As pointed out in the previous chapter, John's prophecy does not merely indicate one purpose among others that will mark the Messiah's ministry but expresses its overall goal. John is saying, in effect, that the redemptive work of Christ in its entirety, his kingdom ministry, certainly what is at its heart, is to be understood as the comprehensive effort that culminates in securing and then pouring out on his people the Holy Spirit as gift, as blessing.

Putting things this way hardly eclipses the death of Christ and its fundamental significance. As we have seen, the atonement for sin accomplished on the cross is the absolutely necessary basis for what takes place on Pentecost. But in fact, as John's prophecy intends to capture the essence of the Messiah's work in its wholeness, the focus is baptism with the Holy Spirit and fire.

Recall here what we noted earlier in our brief survey of the connection between the Holy Spirit and the kingdom in Luke's Gospel, in particular the connection between Luke 12:32 and 11:13: comparing these two verses shows that the Holy Spirit is, if you will, the kingdom gift par excellence. The fundamental, first order gift, the kingdom gift of all kingdom gifts, is the Holy Spirit, and that donation, that outpouring, takes place on Pentecost.

Pentecost as Climactic

Pentecost, then, ought to receive its fundamental assessment as an epochal or climactic event in the history of redemption. Whatever our fuller understanding of Pentecost, its ramifications and implications, Pentecost always has to be considered first of all in terms of its pivotal place in the flow of redemptive history. Pentecost belongs to the fulfillment of that history as a component in the completed work of Christ. Here we can recall, and perhaps better appreciate, the quote, though somewhat overstated, cited earlier to indicate why in considering the theology of Acts we are focusing on Pentecost: Pentecost is "the great turning point, the hinge, as it were" of Luke-Acts, the two-volume work seen as a whole.[1] Unquestionably, Pentecost is the highpoint, the pivotal event of the entire apostolic history that Luke surveys in Acts.

To reinforce this point further and at the same time to clarify and bring out explicitly the balance that needs to be maintained here: Pentecost is coordinate in a particularly intimate and closely connected way with the death, resurrection, and ascension of Christ; Pentecost is joined inextricably with these other events. Death, resurrection, and ascension inevitably give rise to the outpouring of the Holy Spirit by Christ. Pentecost is climactic on the order that these other events are climactic. These events are temporally distinct—his resurrection three days after his death, his ascension forty days later, and Pentecost ten days after that; nonetheless in their occurrence they belong together. Together they form a unified event-complex, a closely integrated redemptive-historical nexus in which each of these events is part of the whole and any one entails the others.

This state of affairs finds expression in Peter's Pentecost sermon recorded in Acts 2:14-40.[2] It is worth noting that on the occasion of the dramatic events associated with the coming of the Spirit (2:1-13), the primary focus of this sermon, however, is not the Spirit but Christ. The Spirit comes down, and Peter, as every good preacher should, preaches Christ.

Peter does begin by identifying what has taken place in the coming of the Spirit as the fulfillment of prophecy (2:16-21). But then, for the greater part of the sermon, he turns his attention from the Spirit to Jesus. After first mentioning his death as predestined by God (2:22-23; cf. 4:27-28), the verses that follow dwell on his resurrection, documenting it too as the fulfillment of prophecy (2:25-28), and culminates in the declaration of 2:32 that the apostles are witnesses to the resurrection.[3]

Acts 2:32-33 are fairly read as bringing to a focus and at the same time bringing out implications of much of what Peter has said to that point; the verses immediately following (2:34-36) accent as they document the significance of Christ's ascension/exaltation, by appealing to Psalm 110:1,

---

1 G. W. H. Lampe, *The Seal of the Spirit: A Study in the Doctrine of Baptism and Confirmation in the New Testament and the Fathers* (London: SPCK, 1967), 192; see chap. 1, n7.

2 This passage is likely not a verbatim transcript but is best understood as providing a faithful and accurate account of the gist of the sermon in its basic contours.

3 "All" (2:32) is best understood as referring primarily, perhaps exclusively, to the apostles as a group. Cf. Acts 1:22: to be chosen as an apostle is to be authorized as "a witness to his resurrection."

followed by the culminating declaration "Let all the house of Israel therefore know for certain that God has made him both Lord and Christ, this Jesus whom you crucified."

> This Jesus God raised up, and of that we all are witnesses. Being therefore exalted at the right hand of God, and having received from the Father the promise of the Holy Spirit, he has poured out this that you yourselves are seeing and hearing.

Apparent in this compact summarizing statement is the linking of Pentecost with the resurrection and the ascension leading to heavenly session ("exalted at the right hand of God").

Jesus as Spirit Receiver-Giver

In reflecting further on this linkage as it is expressed here, a related reality with important implications should be noted. Grammatically, in 2:33, the aorist participle translated "having received" (λαβών) describes an action prior to the outpouring of the Spirit but also almost certainly what took place with or as a consequence of the ascension. Acts 2:33 does not simply say that following his exaltation, Jesus poured out the Holy Spirit. Rather, it states that in having been exalted and before he poured out the Holy Spirit, Jesus himself first received the Holy Spirit. It asserts a reception of the Spirit by Jesus in his ascension, correlative with his outpouring of the Spirit on Pentecost.

What disposes to drawing this conclusion is not only the grammatical sequence just noted but also the fact that 2:33 states not simply that Jesus received the Holy Spirit but that he received "from the Father the promise of the Holy Spirit." This echoes the language of Jesus, prior to his ascension, in describing the Spirit as he would come at Pentecost: "the promise of my [the] Father" (Luke 24:49; Acts 1:4; cf. 1:5).

The Spirit come at Pentecost is "the promised Spirit" (Gal. 3:14), the Spirit as promised. Prior to Pentecost, the Spirit, in view in this language, was not present but future, a matter of promise still to be realized. Pentecost, together with the ascension, is the fulfillment of that promise, a fulfillment that takes place first for Christ in his ascension and then for the church at Pentecost. In being exalted, Jesus became the receiver-giver of the Spirit.

Here, again, the primarily Christological and once-for-all redemptive-historical significance of Pentecost emerges.

The heightening or phasing principle that marks the coming of the kingdom noted above in chapter 2—the arrival in stages of the eschatological *basileia*, the rule and realm of God, inaugurated by Jesus—helps us here to understand the corresponding coming of the Spirit: At the Jordan, Christ (conceived and so already indwelt by the Spirit; Luke 1:35) received the Spirit as an endowment for the kingdom task that lay before him; in his exaltation, he received the Spirit as the reward for that task behind him and successfully completed.[4] This climactic reward he does not keep for himself ("not for [his] own private use"[5]) but shares. At Pentecost, the Spirit, in turn, becomes the kingdom gift par excellence given to the church, the gift poured out on the church with the accompanying attesting signs that were both seen and heard (Acts 2:33).

No Glorification of Jesus, No Spirit

The single event-complex inseparability in view in Acts 2:32-33—Christ's resurrection, his ascension-reception, and his Pentecost–donation of the Spirit—is notably reinforced outside Luke-Acts in John 7:37-39. In the course of his earthly ministry in Jerusalem, Jesus declares in 7:38 that the hearts of those who believe in him will become sources of "living water." This prompts the parenthetical insertion in 7:39 from John's post-Pentecost perspective that Jesus was speaking about the Spirit whom believers were to receive in the future, with the further explanation that "as yet the Spirit had not been given, because Jesus was not yet glorified."

This explanatory gloss in the latter part of 7:39 is our interest here: (1) in view is a certain "not yet" of the Spirit, a future coming of the Spirit, and (2) this coming of the Spirit is linked to the glorification of Jesus. The Spirit is in view as a fruit or consequence attendant upon Christ's exaltation. Stated here, then, in a more telescoped or briefer way is what is articulated more fully in Acts 2:32-33.

The latter part of John 7:39 should be taken at face value; we should not miss or tone down its epochal absoluteness. Getting its sense may be helped

---

4   See also Richard B. Gaffin Jr., "The Resurrection of Christ and Salvation," The Gospel Coalition, https://www.thegospelcoalition.org/.

5   John Calvin, *Institutes of the Christian Religion* ed. John T. McNeill, trans. Ford Lewis Battles (Philadelphia, PA: Westminster, 1960), 3.1.1 (1:537).

by the terseness of a more literal translation: "For the Spirit was not yet, because Jesus was not yet glorified." The two occurrences of "not yet" are categorical: no glorification of Jesus, no Spirit.

This absoluteness, to head off a misunderstanding, is not to be understood as if John is denying the obvious, as if he means that prior to Christ's glorification the Spirit was not present and active in the creation or not at work among God's old covenant people and in Jesus's earthly ministry. Rather, in view here is a new state of affairs in the future as far as the Spirit is concerned, one that did not exist previously: the Spirit will be present, not as he was before, but on the basis of and as the consequence of the glorification of Christ having actually occurred.

Helpful for our understanding here, again, is the *historia salutis–ordo salutis* distinction, the distinction between the history of salvation and the order of salvation, between what belongs to the accomplishment of redemption in distinction from what belongs to its application. In John 7:39, the "not yet" of the Spirit—the future coming of the Spirit contingent on the glorification of Jesus—has in view a once-for-all event in the *historia salutis*, a climactic event in the history of redemption; it does not belong to the *ordo salutis*, to the ongoing application of redemption and appropriation of its benefits.

This consideration has an important bearing on a matter of ongoing debate and discussion across the face of the worldwide church about the work of the Holy Spirit, particularly with eye to fellow Christians in Pentecostal denominations and groups otherwise associated with the charismatic movement. The coming of the Spirit on Pentecost is not first of all a matter of the individual experience of those believers present there. Their experience is surely involved. It should not be ignored or minimized and needs to be accounted for, as we hope to do subsequently. But their experience—individual experience of the Spirit—is not the primary significance of Pentecost. That significance is Christological, as Pentecost is correlate with Christ's glorification in their once-for-all significance.

Pentecost Is Not a Paradigm Event

These observations concerning the place of Pentecost as a unique epochal event in the history of redemption can be furthered by saying that Pentecost is unrepeatable. In one sense, that really doesn't say very much, because that is true of any event in the linear flow toward consummation essential to the biblical view of history. History is not marked by the cyclical return of past events. Events in history may have striking similarities but, strictly speaking, they do not reoccur.

But the word *unrepeatable* may serve to highlight what needs to be brought out here. Pentecost ought not to be seen as the model for a recurring periodic or episodic event. Pentecost is not a paradigm event. That is, it is not the first in a series of baptisms of the Spirit that need to be repeated or can be replicated. This is so whether that repetition is understood as an occurrence in the individual experience of some Christians in distinction from others, attendant on or subsequent to receiving salvation (about which view, more below), or, more broadly, is seen as an episodic event that recurs periodically throughout history for the life of the church as a whole.

So far as the latter notion is concerned, Pentecost is not an occurrence whose effect ebbs or wears off as it were, so that subsequent renewed outpourings of the Spirit are necessary, whether sought or not. Admittedly, this is the way things may appear to us. It may seem, looking back, that the pattern of church history is a pattern of such repetitions, in effect, of Pentecost. It may appear that characteristic is the resurgence of the Spirit's work after periods of loss or at least dormancy. It might appear, as we look at our experience and on the broader scale of church history as a whole, that what in fact takes place is the return of the Spirit after a time of absence or withdrawal.

But appearances are deceiving. We need to look deeper. Certainly, the way in which the Spirit works does vary—in the life of the individual believer and, more broadly, in the life of the church over the centuries. How the Spirit manifests himself and is experienced does and may fluctuate in its effects and intensity from time to time, from place to place, both in the history of the church and in the lives of individual Christians.

Worth recalling here is Jesus's statement in his interchange with Nicodemus that the Spirit is like the wind that blows where it wills (John 3:8). This points to the incalculability that marks the Spirit's working, a dimension of what is unpredictable and unexpected in the sovereign working of the Spirit. This carries the important reminder that sound theologizing about the Spirit's activity must honor this incalculability. Any theology of the Spirit true to Scripture will have a certain remainder of what is unexplained.

With that reminder, however, the point I am wanting particularly to bring out—given the redemptive-historical character of Pentecost—is that all the undeniable variety observable, with all the ultimately incalculable fluctuations involved, does not amount to a capricious whimsy of the Spirit. Rather, all this variety is to be seen as constituting the large, single, and indelible pattern of the Spirit's activity. This singular pattern is nothing other than the ongoing concrete outworking in all its details of what has been given to the church at Pentecost, and, to stress the point yet again, given to the church once for all as the culmination of Christ's work in his death and resurrection.

Pentecost is an event that has eschatological finality. That means, if it means anything, that the Holy Spirit will not abandon the church. Pentecost means that the Holy Spirit is here to stay. The Spirit will always be present with the church, with believers. We can count on that.

Outside the Lucan context, in Matthew 28:20, Jesus, now resurrected and soon to ascend, declares, together with 28:18 ("All authority in heaven and on earth has been given to me")—the bookends, so to speak, that sanction the Great Commission—"I am with you always, to the end of the age."

This is not, at least in the first place, a declaration of Christ's divine omnipresence, what is true in terms of his deity, though that is surely involved. Rather, within the context of the Gospel, that declaration, as it authorizes and grounds the Great Commission, is a promise of Pentecost, a promise of what will soon be the case. Matthew's Gospel doesn't have a sequel; it ends on that note. But Luke will pick up and document in part 2 to Theophilus just how Christ begins to make good on that promise. Christ is with his church in the power of the Spirit to the end of the age. He will always be with the church, active in and with the Spirit, until his return. This enduring presence of the resurrected Christ is primary for the meaning of Pentecost.

So, the church—or, more personally, you and I—are not in need of repeated Pentecosts. One is more than enough. Does that mean, then, that Christians should not hunger and thirst for more of the Spirit in their lives? Not at all. That will concern us subsequently. But as believers have that concern for an ongoing richer and deeper experience of the Holy Spirit, they must set that longing, that aspiration, within the perspective of the fulfillment that has taken place on the day of Pentecost and the permanent prospect that holds for the church in every place and age until Jesus comes.

To reinforce the basic point that I am concerned with bringing out here, Pentecost is no more capable of repetition, of being viewed as a typical event or model, a repeatable paradigm, than are the death but particularly the resurrection and ascension of Jesus with which Pentecost is so closely conjoined (Acts 2:32–33). Pentecost, as we have seen, is definitive on the order that Christ's death, resurrection, and ascension are definitive. So, as his death, resurrection, and ascension are unrepeatable, once-for-all events, so too the outpouring of the Spirit at Pentecost is an unrepeatable, once-for-all event.

This emphasis need not and should not be perceived, as some do, as distancing the church today from Pentecost, as if stressing its singular redemptive-historical significance leaves us as more or less detached spectators on what happened back then. That is no more the case than that we are simply spectators on the death, resurrection, and ascension of Christ. Particularly as we look into Paul's theology, it will be clear how he defines the very existence of the believer in terms of being united with Christ in his once-for-all death, resurrection, and ascension, and so also sharing in the Pentecost gift of the Spirit received by him in his ascension.

One significant implication of all that we have been considering is that we, the church, may continue, and may continue confidently, in the discipling and church-building task of extending the gospel to the nations, and to that end, then, may continue confidently in praying for and expecting revival. I mention revival specifically at this point because it has been objected that to stress the nonparadigmatic, redemptive-historical significance of Pentecost eliminates the expectation and motivation to pray for revival today.

That objection betrays a misunderstanding of the once-*for-all* character of Pentecost, in terms of which we not only may but are bound to be praying for revival. The objection stems from the perception that emphasizing the redemptive-historical, as I am, necessarily turns one into a detached observer, whereby Pentecost becomes an interesting event in the past with uncertain, if any, relevance for the present.

That is hardly the outcome, nor should it be. Rather, we can be confident—despite adverse circumstances, despite repeated discouragements, despite the opposition that the church will inevitably encounter, not only from without but all too regrettably from within, despite times of spiritual decline and poverty—we can be confident in the commission given by the

resurrected Jesus to the church because we know of the once-for-all finality of Holy Spirit baptism that occurred at Pentecost. This gift, this great
gift come at Pentecost, is irrevocable, unlosable. For that reason, it is an
ever-present dynamic sufficient for every task that the church encounters,
every difficulty that Christians may experience.

Here we may apply the principle that Paul enunciates in Romans 11:29, as
he comes to the close of his long discussion of God's saving purposes in his
dealings with Jew and non-Jew, his faithfulness to Israel and the inclusion
of the Gentiles. "For the gifts and the calling of God are irrevocable" (ἀμε-
ταμέλητα), not capable of being retracted. God will not change his mind. He
will not have a change of heart about or undo what he has done at Pentecost.

Romans 11:29 is not focused specifically on the gift of the Spirit. But it
surely voices the same broad redemptive-historical sweep we have been
considering. When Paul says the "gifts" (χαρίσματα) of God are irrevocable, we are on sound ground in seeing, by implication, a reference to the
irrevocable gift of the Holy Spirit given at Pentecost.

Supposed Repetitions of Pentecost

But now after all I have been saying—stressing that Pentecost is a once-for-
all, nonrepeatable, nonparadigmatic event—doesn't Acts show plainly just
the opposite, precisely what I have been denying? Doesn't Acts teach what
are clearly certain repetitions of what took place on the day of Pentecost?

That question may be addressed here by considering together along
with what we find in Acts 2, passages from elsewhere in Acts—from Acts
8, 10–11, and 19. Other passages could also be viewed as relevant, but
those who raise this question will agree that those just mentioned are the
most important. The material in Acts 10 and 11 can be viewed as a single
instance since both deal with the same events in the house of Cornelius:
first the account of what occurred (10:44-48) and then Peter's subsequent
retelling (11:15-18).

Looking first at this instance, in 11:15 Peter, in describing events that
had previously taken place for Cornelius together with his household
and friends, says, "the Holy Spirit fell on them just as [ὥσπερ καὶ] on us
at the beginning." Such language suggests a repetition. Backing up to the
account of the same events in 10:47, Peter speaks there of "these people,
who have received the Holy Spirit just as [ὡς καὶ] we have." Again, this

language suggests a parallel, a repetition for "them" of what first occurred for "us." Or further along in Peter's account in Acts 11, he puts it this way: "God gave the same gift to them as [ὡς καὶ] he gave to us" (11:17). Later, at the Jerusalem Council, reflecting on the events related in Acts 10–11, at least primarily, Peter speaks of "God . . . giving them the Holy Spirit just as [καθὼς καὶ] he did to us" (15:8).

These descriptions—repeatedly drawing explicit parallels that suggest repetition—are reinforced in 8:15-17. Peter and John "came down and prayed for them that they might receive the Holy Spirit, for he had not yet fallen on any of them, but they had only been baptized in the name of the Lord Jesus. Then they laid their hands on them and they received the Holy Spirit." Similarly, at a later point in Ephesus (Acts 19:1), "when Paul had laid his hands on them, the Holy Spirit came on them, and they began speaking in tongues and prophesying" (19:6).

These passages, as I've said, are widely recognized as key on the issue in dispute: whether Pentecost is a paradigm event. In assessing them (and other texts deemed pertinent), however, despite what may seem apparent and many argue, they do not in fact demonstrate a pattern of repetitions of what took place on the day of Pentecost. Or to be more precise, they do not establish Pentecost as a model event for baptism with the Holy Spirit understood as an experience to be replicated for individual Christians subsequently throughout church history regardless of time and place.

Certainly these passages present what in one sense are fairly described as repeats or repetitions of Pentecost. But what they are called is not really the issue. The decisive question is how further to conceptualize these repetitions, if we choose to call them that, how to explain them and what implications are then drawn.

In this regard, several related points from our introductory comments in chapter 1 concerning the study of Acts as a whole are decisive and in fact take on an overriding importance for properly assessing these passages. These considerations, restated briefly here, are the following: (1) Acts, by its design, documents a history that is both apostolic and complete, a completed apostolic history. (2) This history and the narration that Acts provides unfolds according to the commission given by the resurrected Jesus to the apostles in Acts 1:8. (3) This commission and its fulfillment by the apostles is universal ("Jerusalem . . . to the end of the earth"). (4) This universal fulfillment is ethnic (Jews → half-Jews/Samaritans → Gentiles)—from Israel to the other nations.

Seen in the light of these four key points, taken together, the events under consideration in Acts 8, 10–11, and 19, along with those in Acts 2, are not in the first place a matter of the empowering of individuals or even primarily about their experience. Although their empowering or experiencing is no doubt involved, the significance of what occurred does not lie in establishing a perennial model for an individual experience of the Spirit. Their experience is not intended to be directly applicable to or replicable by just any Christian "us" or "them"—regardless of time and place.

Rather, the experience of the "we"/"us" and "they"/"them" encountered in these passages is tied to the monumental turn of events that has taken place in the history of redemption. This epochal turn has its basic significance in terms of the broad redemptive-historical consideration: "to the Jew first and also to the Greek" (Rom.1:16). This once-for-all redemptive-historical expansion anchors the pronouns in these passages and give them their meaning. The we/they in view is not indefinite or indifferent to time and place; it is a redemptive-historical we (Jews)/they (Gentiles).

A second look at these passages will bring this anchoring to light. Some readers may have already noted that in citing them I focused rather narrowly on certain language within them, omitting some language and saying little about their contexts. The omission of this language was deliberate, in order to highlight it now in giving these passages our further attention.

Looking first at the Acts 11 passage (Peter's report of what transpired for Cornelius and others with him), 11:1 and 11:18 bracket this account and in doing so emphasize the significant point that Luke intends to bring out: "The apostles and the brothers who were throughout Judea heard." In other words, those who heard—the apostles and those with them—were all Jewish Christians. And what they heard was "that the Gentiles also had received the Word of God" (11:1).

The point of 11:1, then, setting the stage for what follows, is that Jewish Christians heard that Gentiles had become Christians. As a result, when Peter eventually came up to Jerusalem, "the circumcision party"—a group within, if not all, Jewish believers—faulted Peter for having had table fellowship with those who were "uncircumcised"—that is non-Jews, Gentiles (11:2-3).

Peter counters this criticism by going on to explain (11:4) that what had occurred was the undeniable expansion of the church to include Gentiles together with Jews and to conclude with the rhetorical question, "Who was I that I could stand in God's way?" (11:17). This validating explanation led to the bottom-line outcome among his critics—the other statement bracketing this pericope (11:18): "When they[6] heard these things they fell silent," a silence, however, that was then broken by their glorifying God. Why? Because "to the Gentiles also God has granted repentance that leads to life."

It should not be missed that what is accented in these bracketing statements is not that the Gentiles had received the Spirit, as noteworthy as that with the accompanying phenomena was, but what that reception documented, what was more basic and had saving significance: they "received the word of God" (11:1) and so were "granted repentance that leads to life" (11:18).

Similarly, in the Acts 10 passage, "believers from among the circumcised"—that is, Jewish believers who had accompanied Peter to the home of Cornelius—"were amazed." Why? Not because certain random individuals had believed and received the Holy Spirit, but "because the gift of the Holy Spirit was poured out even on *the Gentiles*" (10:45).

In Acts 8, the activity of John and Peter in 8:15-17 that we noted earlier is marked by the introductory statement in 8:14: "Now when the apostles at Jerusalem heard that Samaria had received the Word of God." Again, as with Peter in Acts 10-11, here too the involvement of Peter and John, as apostles, is central. The apostles, who remained in Jerusalem as the remnant of the persecuted Jewish Christian church otherwise "scattered throughout the regions of Judea and Samaria" (8:1), heard what had transpired in Samaria through Philip (8:4-13).

What prompted the apostles to send Peter and John and their subsequent activity was that Samaritans—not Jews, but those who were of mixed Jewish and Gentile ethnicity—had responded to the gospel. And the pericope closes on the note that Peter and John "returned to Jerusalem, preaching the gospel to many villages of the Samaritans" (8:25). The fulfillment of the

---

6 Grammatically, the subject ("they") of the participle ἀκούσαντες ("heard") is the same as the participle λέγοντες ("saying") in 11:3. Those Jews who had criticized Peter were silenced and then brought to praise God by his explanation.

witnessing mandate given to the apostles in 1:8 had in fact expanded from "Jerusalem and in all Judea" to now include "Samaria."

What about Acts 19:6, quoted above, and the events in Ephesus narrated in 19:1-7? While this passage presents some difficulties for interpretation, these need not detain us here from making the following observations relevant for the issue we are discussing.

First, in light of the way Luke frequently uses "disciple(s)," the "some disciples" (19:2) Paul encountered and on whom "the Holy Spirit came" when he laid his hands on them (19:6) are likely to be seen as Christians (cf. "when you believed," 19:2). They were uninformed or not fully informed believers, in that respect like Apollos mentioned just previously (18:24-28).

Second, these disciples had been baptized by John (19:3). This is fairly understood as indicating that they had responded as they should have to John's call to repentance; his baptism, as Paul says, was a "baptism of repentance" (19:4). So in that sense they were initially John's disciples.

Third, the historical uniqueness of their circumstances as disciples is apparent. By the nature of the case, given the onetime role of John as forerunner in the history of redemption, there were disciples of John only for one generation. As, redemptive-historically, John was to "decrease" in order that Christ might "increase" (John 3:30), so John's disciples were not to remain his but become Christ's disciples. As Paul either reminds or, as the case may be, instructs, these disciples in Ephesus, those baptized by John were, as John himself had instructed, "to believe in the one who was to come after him, that is, Jesus" (19:4).

Fourth, in view, then, are not just any disciples, indifferent to time and place, whose experience in receiving the Spirit provides a permanent paradigm for believers subsequently throughout church history. Rather, what occurs here is, as we might put it, the tying up of a redemptive-historical loose end in the apostles' completing the mandate of Acts 1:8, in light of the fulfillment on Pentecost of John's prophecy of Spirit-and-fire baptism in Luke 3:16.

Some who had received John's water baptism—the sign associated with that prophecy in anticipation of its fulfillment—had so far remained unaware of its fulfillment on Pentecost. Now, by the agency of Paul the apostle, they are brought within the scope of that fulfillment. They are baptized as Christians (19:5), accompanied by receiving the phenomena (tongues and prophecy, 19:6) that document that fulfillment. The situation—unique and anomalous—is removed and resolved for those who had received the sign (John's water baptism) but had not (yet) been made aware of and included in the reality (the Spirit come at Pentecost) to which it pointed.[7]

Manifestations of Salvation for All Nations

At this point, it is perhaps worth drawing attention again to the point made in Acts 11:18: God gave the Gentiles repentance unto life.[8] In all of the events described in the passages we have been considering, at issue is not some sort of endowment with the Spirit auxiliary or additional to salvation. Rather, in view—in Jerusalem on Pentecost, in Samaria, among the Gentiles exemplified in Cornelius and his household, and in the unique situation in Ephesus of the removal of the redemptive-historical anomaly for former disciples of John the Baptist—are manifestations of the Spirit that show the dawning presence of salvation for non-Jews as well as Jews. These manifestations are Spirit-worked epiphenomena that attest the arrival of the more basic phenomenon of salvation for all nations, Gentiles as well as Jews.

Again, what transpired in the key passages we have been considering—Acts 2, 8, 10–11, and 19—has to be assessed in light of Acts 1:8, the statement of purpose that structures Acts as a whole and provides its rationale as a complete document. In other words, these passages are not chosen more or less at random. It is not as if Luke is concerned to give us incidents that are part of a loose collection of episodes intended to edify, inspire, and challenge Christians in subsequent generations to emulate them. Viewing these passages as providing perennial examples for experiencing the Spirit reflects the way Acts is too often read and dealt with. On this view, what we have in Acts is a kind of anthology of vignettes, as I might put it, from "the good old days when Christians were really Christians."

---

7   In the answer of these disciples ("No, we have not even heard that there is a Holy Spirit," 19:2), it is highly implausible to take the anarthrous reference to the Holy Spirit as indefinite and their answer as expressing complete ignorance of the existence of the Holy Spirit. That would entail the difficult assumption that, though recipients of John's baptism, they had heard and knew nothing about the coming reality (Spirit-and-fire baptism) to which it pointed, as John in his preaching made that tie explicit. The ASV and ERV 1885 fairly capture what these disciples meant: "Nay, we did not so much as hear whether the Holy Spirit was given."

8   Cf. Acts 14:27—at the heart of what Paul and Barnabas reported back to the church in Antioch about their first missionary journey was "how he [God] had opened a door of faith to the Gentiles."

This sort of approach carries the tendency to view Acts as incomplete. Acts will seem, in effect, to be a fragment whose ending remains a question, perhaps with speculation, noted earlier, about a possible lost part 3 to Theophilus. When Acts is viewed in a fragmentary fashion and not as documenting a completed apostolic task, the risk of imposing some other rationale on the book foreign to it is high.

The Expansion of Pentecost

The events in the passages we have been discussing reflect the program of Acts 1:8, specifically its once-for-all foundational, apostolic realization. This happens as the gospel witness of the apostles and others associated with them moves outward from Jerusalem/Judea (beginning in Acts 2), to Samaria (Acts 8), to the nations (Acts 10–11), and deals with the "loose end" disciples of John (Acts 19).

Luke provides an even broader perspective on these events in Acts by linking them to John's prophecy in Luke 3:16 as its fulfillment—a link, recall, that is made explicit by the resurrected Christ in Acts 1:5. The fulfillment prophesied by John takes place in its full apostolic scope in the events of Acts 2, 8, 10, and 19, and others in Acts that might be considered pertinent.

Undoubtedly, what occurs on the day of Pentecost (Acts 2) is the initial and primary fulfillment of John's prophecy, but that fulfillment is such that it is has an echoing or rippling effect extending outward to include the events in the other passages under consideration. So as we might put it as an overall outlook: the events in Acts 2, 8, 10, and 19 together constitute a single once-for-all event-complex that fulfills John's prophecy.

I find this conclusion the most satisfactory exegetically in addressing those passages that come up for discussion in considering the significance of baptism with the Holy Spirit in Acts.

With reference to the question we raised above about the repetition of Pentecost, it would be better or more accurate, and also, I believe, more faithful to the language of these passages, to view them not as describing repeats of Pentecost—a second, third, and fourth baptism with the Holy Spirit in series, as it were—but extensions of Pentecost. Within the context of the narration in Acts as a whole, these passages document an expansion. They describe an expansion or a spreading of the scope of Holy Spirit baptism.

Keeping in mind, as we always must, the correlativity of the Holy Spirit and the kingdom noted earlier, we ought to see the events in these passages as extensions of the dominion of the Spirit as the dynamic of the *basileia*, the eschatological rule and realm of God, in its once-for-all arrival, in the foundational establishment of the church through the apostles.

When I speak here of extension or expansion rather than repetition, we may also recall, in light of the mandate of Acts 1:8, that Luke is concerned to document the ethnic universality of the spread of the gospel through the apostles from Jerusalem/Judea to Samaria to the ends of the earth—that is, as the bringing of the nations together with Israel into the kingdom and so under the universal dominion of the Spirit. Acts 1:8 expresses a clear principle of expansion, an expansion realized in the incorporation of half-Jews and non-Jews along with Jews into the fellowship of the Spirit-baptized church. To speak here of completed expansion rather than ongoing repetitions is hardly just playing with words or splitting hairs.

A Unique Generation

The view of Holy Spirit baptism that we have been calling into question involves an assumption that many readers carry in coming to Acts, an assumption that needs to be but is too seldom questioned as a source of considerable confusion. This is the assumption that events recorded in Acts—particularly events in the life of the church that are seen to be positive or beneficial—are normative for the life of the church and Christian experience in subsequent generations.

This assumption prompts the effort to incorporate the narrative material of Acts into an *ordo salutis*, using that expression broadly here—that is, as a model or pattern for individual Christian experience regardless of time and place in the history of the church. This effort to incorporate narrative material in Acts in an exemplary or a normative way for Christian experience leads to difficulties that seem, to me, to be insoluble, even though they are often not noted or ignored.

These difficulties can be seen by taking yet another look at our key passages—in Acts 2, 8, 10, and 19—and posing three questions, questions that are pertinent to seeing the events in them as establishing a pattern or having a paradigmatic significance for individual Christian experience.

First, does Holy Spirit baptism take place before or after water baptism?

Acts 2: uncertain
Acts 8: after
Acts 10: before or perhaps coincidently
Acts 19: after

Second, does Holy Spirit baptism take place with prayer and the laying on of hands?

Acts 2: uncertain; more likely, no
Acts 8: yes
Acts 10: no
Acts 19: yes

Third, and a more significant question, does Holy Spirit baptism take place at conversion, with the initial exercise of faith, or later? Is it a post-conversion experience?

Acts 2: yes
Acts 8: uncertain, depending on whether faith in response to Philip's preaching (cf. 8:12–13) was genuine
Acts 10: no
Acts 19: yes, on the assumption that they were already Christian "disciples"; see our discussion above

What is my point with this brief taxonomy? These are questions that arise and need definite and consistent answers if these passages are to be used to establish a permanent pattern for being baptized with the Holy Spirit as an individual experience, particularly as a postconversion experience. But these are questions that cannot be answered as they need to be because they are the wrong questions. They are seeking in Acts what Acts does not intend to provide.

In contemporary discussions about the work of the Spirit, often much is made of the fact that the recipients of the Spirit at Pentecost were already believers before Pentecost. This then is taken as evidence pointing to a postconversion paradigm and that at least regeneration and faith are prerequisites or preconditions for subsequently receiving Holy Spirit baptism.

In this regard, consider the following, which does involve bringing in my earlier conclusion that Pentecost together with the death, resurrection, and ascension of Christ constitute a once-for-all event-complex in the history of the accomplishment of redemption (*historia salutis*): some of those at Pentecost—Peter and, we can fairly suggest, at least others of the original circle of apostles—had saving faith in Christ and were converted before his death, resurrection, and ascension.

Peter declares not only for himself but also for others of the twelve (John 6:67, 70), when many other disciples had turned back from following Jesus (6:66), "Lord, to whom shall we go? You have the words of eternal life, and we have believed, and have come to know, that you are the Holy One of God" (6:68-69). Or Peter's words, representative as well for other disciples at the time, "You are the Christ, the Son of the living God" (Matt. 16:16), is a confession, Jesus says, that did not come by "flesh and blood" (16:17)—that is, implicitly, it was by the Spirit of God.

Few are going to say that the faith of Peter and the other disciples was a prerequisite for the death and resurrection of Christ to take place. No more is it so, then, that what occurred at Pentecost was on the basis of or in view of their faith and conversion. What took place on the day of Pentecost does not have its primary significance in terms of the application of salvation, as an accompanying benefit in the *ordo salutis*.

The experience of the 120 or so (see Acts 1:15) on the day of Pentecost is surely postconversion. They had an experience; it was postconversion. But that experience is extrinsic, an epiphenomenon that attests the significance of what took place there: the permanent, once-for-all sending of the Spirit by the ascended Christ to be with the church until he returns.

So concerning the experience of those present at Pentecost and the related events in Acts we have looked at, we need to recognize its historically unique character. It was the experience of those living within that one generation of which by the nature of the case there could only be one. They were those who lived at that time when the redemption promised was actually and finally accomplished in Christ and the church was founded once for all.

There could be only one such generation. As they were of that unique transitional generation, different terms can be used to label their experience. It was "epoch-crossing, and consequently atypical and non-paradigmatic in nature,"[9] bound up with the once-for-all redemptive-historical developments of that time, the inception of what the New Testament calls "the fullness of time" (Gal. 4:4; Eph. 1:10), in which they were living.

Pentecost Brings the Spirit as the Eschatological "Firstfruits"

I have been stressing at some length, with important implications for understanding Acts, that Pentecost—seen together with the death, resurrection, and ascension of Christ—is a once-for-all event in the history of redemption. That stress now needs to be given a fundamental qualification. Accenting, as we have, the eschatological or epochal significance of Pentecost does not mean that Pentecost has brought to the church the Spirit and his consequent working in full finality or total completeness.

The qualification in view here can be seen by recalling the correlation between the Spirit and the kingdom discussed earlier: the Spirit is the dynamic or power of the *basileia*—the rule and realm of God—in its eschatological advent in the person and work of Christ (cf. esp. Matt. 12:28; Luke 11:20). As we noted, this coming is fairly seen as arriving in three basic stages delineated by the messianic activity or history of Jesus: (1) the period from his baptism at the Jordan culminating in his death and resurrection, (2) the intervening period until his return, and (3) the period beyond his return. Accordingly, the coming of the Spirit at Pentecost, correlate with the coming of the kingdom, forms, together with Christ's death, resurrection, and ascension (Acts 2:32–33), the nexus that inaugurates the second stage of the eschatological kingdom. Pentecost brings, the church can be assured, the abiding presence of the Spirit in all of his working "to the end of the age (Matt. 28:20)."

But what Pentecost does not do is bring the even greater fullness of the presence and working of the Spirit that will come at Christ's return, and not before, with the third and final stage of the kingdom: the full finality of the Spirit's work realized in the bodily resurrection of believers and the attendant renovation of the whole creation (Rom. 8:19–22) as "a new heaven and earth" (Rev. 21:1).

---

9 Sinclair B. Ferguson, *The Holy Spirit* (Leicester: Inter-Varsity Press, 1996), 80.

In this regard, a brief look ahead into Paul's theology provides an instructive perspective on Luke's. To describe the Spirit present in the church and at work in believers, all told, Paul uses a couple of metaphors, the one commercial, the other agricultural: the Spirit as a "deposit," "down payment," "guarantee" (ἀρραβών; 2 Cor 1:22; 5:5; Eph. 1:14)[10] and as "firstfruits" (ἀπαρχή; Rom. 8:23).

These terms—"firstfruits," the initial portion of a harvest, and "deposit" on a full amount—are calculated to express both the partial nature of our present possession of the Spirit and equally the organic connection, the integral tie, there is between this present partial possession and its future fullness at Christ's return.

This organic linking of present and (eschatological) future is explicit in Ephesians 1:13-14: "The promised Holy Spirit," with which believers "were sealed" is "the guarantee of our inheritance until we acquire possession of it." For Paul, this future possession, this consummate working of the Spirit, centers on the resurrection of the body—the "Spiritual"[11] body, the one-word label by way of eminence that Paul uses (1 Cor 15:44), because that body itself will be, as well as exist within an environment, totally transformed by the Holy Spirit.

This is the qualification—the eschatological reservation—we need to keep in view when stressing the epochal and eschatological significance of Pentecost. Required is this balancing of this already-not-yet state of affairs, so far as Holy Spirit baptism is concerned. Pentecost is the down payment on the eschatological inheritance of the church, not its full inheritance. Pentecost brings the firstfruits of the eschatological harvest, itself fully eschatological but not the full harvest.[12]

---

10 "a deposit, guaranteeing what is to come" (2 Cor. 1:22; 5:5 NIV).

11 I have capitalized this adjective to make clear that it has in view the activity of the Holy Spirit, and not the sense that "spiritual" (lowercase) has: either (1) what is immaterial, nonphysical in contrast to what is physical or (2) the human spirit, the inward aspect of human personality. In order to keep this distinction clear, I follow the practice throughout of capitalizing the adjective where it refers to the Spirit and his activity.

12 What prompted Paul to choose firstfruits as a metaphor for the Spirit is uncertain. But it is of interest—and may not just be coincidental—that in the calendar of annual festivals of Greek-speaking Judaism at this time, Pentecost (as in Acts 2:1), the "fiftieth" (πεντηκοστή) day counting from the beginning of Passover, is in the Hebrew calendar "the day of the firstfruits" as part of the Feast of Weeks or harvest festival (Num. 28:26; cf. Ex. 23:14-17; Lev. 23:10, 15-21). Hence, the appropriateness of "firstfruits" for the Spirit come at Pentecost, fulfilling the typology of Israel's annual harvest festival. Pentecost is the day of the firstfruits eschatological arrival of the Spirit.

The Continuing Relevance of Pentecost

Emphasizing Pentecost as a nonparadigmatic, nonrepetitive event, as I have, may leave the impression, at least initially, that we are no more than disengaged spectators on something that happened in the past and wondering what, if anything, Pentecost has to do with the life of the church today. That impression needs to be dispelled, for Pentecost is not simply an event in the past but a once-for-all past event. Like Christ's death, resurrection, and ascension with which it is inseparably linked, it has permanent and enduring consequences and relevance.

This raises the question of how what took place on the day of Pentecost relates to the ongoing experience of believers and the life of the church until Jesus returns. As the question could be put, given the integral place that Pentecost has in the *historia salutis*, its redemptive-historical significance, what is the *ordo salutis* or applicatory significance of Pentecost? In other words, What place does the Spirit come at Pentecost have in the benefits of salvation actually appropriated? How does the Spirit of Pentecost affect and shape the lives of Christians today? What ought to be our expectations for our own experiencing the work of the Spirit?

My comments here in addressing an obviously large question are necessarily partial. My aim, in the light of Pentecost, is to identify some controlling considerations that provide a basic framework essential for arriving at sound answers about our expectations for the work of the Spirit in the church today. Our question, again, concerns the *ordo salutis* significance of Pentecost. What bearing does Pentecost have on the individual and corporate appropriation of salvation, specifically on the ongoing and permanent work of the Spirit in the church?

This, as we have seen, is a question that Acts itself is not calculated to answer. Given its purpose as a whole—to document the "to the end of the earth" witnessing mandate not only given to the apostles but also completed by them—the concern of Acts is not, at least directly or primarily, to address the situation of the church beyond the time of its apostolic or foundational beginnings.

This is by no means to deny that there are any number of ways in which, in the light of the rest of the New Testament, Acts provides important and timely lessons for the church in all times until Christ returns. To mention just several: the essential role of prayer and fellowship (Acts 1:14; 2:42; 14:23), the importance of preaching and teaching God's Word (e.g., 15:35; 20:27; 28:31), and the necessity of Christian suffering (14:22). However, to answer our question concerning the *ordo salutis* implications of Pentecost, we need to look outside of Acts elsewhere in the New Testament. To that end, we are better served by using two passages prominent in Paul's theology as a lens.

1 Corinthians 12:13

> For with one Spirit we were all baptized into one body—whether Jews or Greeks, whether slaves or free—and we were all given one Spirit to drink (my translation).

First Corinthians 12–14 is concerned primarily with the multiple gifts of the Spirit present in the church. At 12:12, Paul begins a comparison of the church to the human body. The central point of this analogy (continuing through 12:27) is that as a body has various parts with different functions, so too does the church. The church is one, but this unity is not an undifferentiated uniformity consisting in the sameness of every member. Rather, it is a unity in diversity; by God's design the church is (to be) a unity composed of various parts with different gifts functioning as a harmonious whole. In context, then, 12:13 is an emphatic affirmation of this unity that also points to its source.

In establishing a basic framework for understanding the *ordo salutis* or ongoing applicatory significance of Pentecost, I begin with this verse primarily for the following reason. Apart from the six occurrences we have considered in Luke-Acts and their parallels in the other Gospels,[13] this is the only other place in the New Testament where the prepositional phrase beginning with the Greek preposition ἐν and referring to the Holy Spirit modifies the verb for baptism (βαπτίζω). It is fair, then, to surmise that this occurrence is calculated to instruct us specifically how the baptism with the Holy Spirit at Pentecost as a once-for-all event relates to those who were not in the unique historical and geographical circumstances of the original recipients.[14]

---

13 Matt. 3:11; Mark 1:8; Luke 3:16; John 1:33; Acts 1:5; 11:16.

14 My comments here overlap with those in my *Perspectives on Pentecost: New Testament Teaching on the Gifts of the Holy Spirit* (Phillipsburg, NJ: P&R, 1979), 28–31.

A translation issue in 12:13 needs to be addressed. It concerns the preposition ἐν. A number of versions have "by."[15] This easily leaves the impression, which some in fact affirm, that the preposition has an instrumental sense, and that the Spirit is the active agent of the baptism in view. However, the preposition should instead be rendered "in" or—preferably, like the six occurrences in Luke-Acts in virtually all translations—"with." In view is not the agency of the Spirit but the Spirit as the element of the baptism, the material with which one is baptized.

This understanding is put on a firm basis by the latter half of 12:13: "we were all given one Spirit to drink"—a statement best seen as parallel to the first half in order to reinforce the unity in view. Here the Spirit is similarly viewed materially, now like a potable liquid. As the one Spirit is poured out upon or deluges all in the church (12:13a), so all in it imbibe the one Spirit (12:13b)—alternative ways of expressing sharing in the baptism-gift of the Spirit, as that sharing grounds the unity of the church. The second half of 12:13 does not make a different point about the Spirit from the first half but restates the same basic thought for emphasis.

With that understanding, two further questions may be put to 12:13 concerning the baptism with the Spirit in view. First, who is it that has been baptized with the one Spirit? The answer is plain, even emphatic: not just "we," but "we all" (ἡμεῖς πάντες). This "all" is, of course, not indiscriminate; within the context of 1 Corinthians 12, in view are "all" in the church. But with that qualification noted, there is no further restriction or limitation on "all"; it is comprehensive for those in the church-body. Paul, then, is unmistakably clear: all believers, not just some in distinction from others, have been baptized with the Spirit. All believers, without exception, have been Holy Spirit baptized. All believers, all in the church as it is in view here, are on a par in the matter of Holy Spirit baptism.

Second is a time question. If it is the case that all have been baptized with the Spirit, when does that take place? At what point in the Christian's life does baptism with the Spirit occur? At first glance, it may not seem that 12:13 addresses that question. But a definite indication of time is present. It is there in the use of the preposition "into" (εἰς), suggesting motion or movement

---

15 E.g., NIV, NASB, NKJV, KJV, NLT; as marginal entries, the NIV has "Or *with* or *in*," and the NASB, "Or *in*."

toward. Baptism with the Spirit, Paul is saying, is tied to the moment of being brought "into" the one body; it is coincident with coming "into" the church.

Nothing is more central in Paul's teaching on receiving salvation than being "in Christ," being united with Christ by faith—a teaching that will occupy us extensively later, when we consider Paul's theology as a whole. Here I simply note that for Paul, to be united with Christ is to be incorporated into his body. To be "in Christ" is necessarily to be in the church; the two cannot be separated.

So, in the light of Paul's teaching elsewhere, 12:13 is saying we are baptized with the Spirit when we are first united with Christ. This union, note, is specifically with the exalted Christ—the Christ who is what he is because of his death, resurrection, ascension, and Pentecost—all told, the "life-giving Spirit" (1 Cor. 15:45; cf. 2 Cor. 3:17). Christ, who at Pentecost reveals himself to the church as the baptizer-giver of the Spirit, grants believers a share in that baptism, that gift—the Pentecostal Spirit—at the point they are united to him. For the believer, the time of my conversion is my Pentecost experience, when I am baptized with the Spirit.

It is not at some later point, then, subsequent to being first united with Christ by faith, that believers come to share in the gift of the Spirit, but at the point that union begins. Being baptized with the Spirit is not a postconversion experience but occurs at the time of conversion. The church is not made up of "haves" and "have nots," some who have been Spirit baptized and others who are lacking that baptism, lacking the gift of the Spirit, and presumably to be seeking it. Every believer in Jesus Christ, not just some in distinction from others, everyone united to him by faith, has been baptized with the Spirit, has received and shares in the gift of the Spirit.

As Paul immediately adds, emphasizing this point, "we were all given one Spirit to drink." First Corinthians 12:13 accents what all believers have in common and unites them: All in the church are in possession of the gift of the Holy Spirit as the foundation of their Christian life and experience. In the church, some do not lack that gift in relation to others. The whole church, not just part of it, is made up of those who are Holy Spirit baptized. We may say along with the Nicene Creed (without proposing to revise it!) that the "one holy catholic and apostolic church" is also the Pentecostal church. All Christians, regardless of their church denomination, are Pentecostals!

Ephesians 5:18

This is a second passage to consider in answering our question regarding a basic perspective on the *ordo salutis* or applicatory implications of Pentecost.

> And do not get drunk with wine, for that is debauchery, but be filled with the Spirit.

A primary implication of 1 Corinthians 12:13 is that all believers are to presuppose that they have been baptized with the Holy Spirit. As believers, they are not to be seeking to experience that baptism.

This presupposition expresses an important truth about the Christian life. From it, however, the conclusion hardly follows that believers may take the Spirit's activity in their lives for granted. Such a conclusion amounts to one of those proverbial half-truths that results in complete error—in this instance, a serious error. Certainly, believers may, indeed must, presuppose the Spirit's presence and working in their lives—devoid of that they would not be believers—but they may not presume on his presence and power as something they can count on as automatic, as something that they need not be concerned about or can be indifferent toward. There is a categorical difference here between presupposition and presumption. Believers must presuppose, but they may not presume on the Spirit in their lives—there is a world of difference.

This difference is seen from the fact that the New Testament—we will confine ourselves here to Paul—repeatedly commands believers concerning the Holy Spirit in their lives. Some of those commands are even negative: "And do not grieve the Holy Spirit of God" (Eph. 4:30); similarly, "Do not quench the Spirit" (1 Thess. 5:19).

It should not be missed that these prohibitions are given to the church, not to those outside the church. That there is a sense in which their content could be directed to unbelievers would certainly be true theologically. But from their contexts, it is clear that these prohibitions are not addressed generally to include unbelievers but specifically to believers, to those who "were sealed [with the Spirit] for the day of redemption" (Eph. 4:30; cf. 1:13).

First Corinthians 12:13 and Ephesians 1:13-14, then, must be taken together with these and other commands concerning the Spirit. In terms of a grammatical distinction, in the lives of believers, the Holy Spirit is both an indicative and an imperative. The two must be kept together; the one may not be allowed to eclipse the other. The indicative is the basis of the imperative, not the reverse, but the indicative does not exist without the imperative.

Here we will explore this imperatival aspect further by focusing on Ephesians 5:18 and the command there addressed to the church to "be filled with the Spirit." I begin with a couple of initial observations: First, as in 1 Corinthians 12:13, here the preposition ἐν is not instrumental; it does not mean "by" but, as virtually all translations have, "with." Although, as we will see, the Spirit is the active agent of filling, the thought of the command is not being filled by the Spirit with something other than the Spirit, but being filled with the Spirit himself; the Spirit fills with himself. In view is the Spirit as indwelling, the presence of the Spirit at work within believers.

Second, it is apparent that Paul does not equate being filled with the Spirit and being baptized with the Spirit—contrary to the misunderstanding that sees them as the same. Being baptized with the Spirit is the indicative, being filled with the Spirit is the imperative.

A similar observation may be made about Luke's usage in Acts. True, what takes place for the recipients on the day of Pentecost, fulfilling John's prophesied baptism with the Holy Spirit, is described as being "filled with the Holy Spirit" (Acts 2:4). Seemingly for Luke, then, being baptized with the Holy Spirit and being filled with the Holy Spirit are the same.

The following, however, has to be taken into consideration. At least some of those described in Acts 2:4 are subsequently said to be filled with the Holy Spirit again. For instance, Peter, among those in view in Acts 2:4, is said at a later point to be "filled with the Holy Spirit" (4:8), and, yet again, he is among those who, as they spoke, "were all filled with the Holy Spirit" (4:31). So, while "filled" with the Holy Spirit is a way of describing action otherwise spoken of as "baptized" with the Holy Spirit, the two are not equivalents. Baptizing was filling or had a filling effect, but not all filling is baptizing—unless we are to take the view, implausible at best, that in Acts 4:8 and 4:31 Peter and others were "rebaptized" with the Spirit in the sense of John's prophecy and its fulfillment at Pentecost.

Similarly, and supporting the preceding observations, in Luke's account, the converted Paul ("Brother Saul") was "filled with the Holy Spirit" in an initial way (9:17). Subsequently, in the context of his activity during the first missionary journey, as he began to speak, he was "filled with the Holy Spirit" (13:9). There is every reason to see this description as likely typical, as what was repeatedly true of the apostle in his ministry. All told, both in Acts and in Paul, "filling" captures an ongoing and repeated aspect of the Spirit's working in believers. In light of this usage, we may generalize: the New Testament commands believers to be filled with the Spirit, but it nowhere commands believers to be baptized with the Spirit.

A further look at Ephesians 5:18 in its immediate context brings to light several facets of being filled with the Spirit. Three may be noted here. As an imperative reality in the lives of believers, being filled with the Spirit is to be (1) controlling, (2) continuing, and (3) comprehensive.

A CONTROLLING REALITY

Ephesians 5:18 has both a positive command and a prohibition. "Be filled with the Spirit" is set in opposition to "Do not get drunk with wine." This juxtaposition serves to highlight an important consideration about being filled with the Spirit. That consideration is clear enough in the use of "filling," which of itself suggests no room for anything else. But Paul accents that thought by contrasting being filled with the Spirit with what, in effect, believers are not to be filled with, for that is what drunkenness amounts to—being full of wine. Believers are to be full of the Spirit, not wine.

Paul is certainly concerned about drunkenness as sinful (Rom. 13:13; Gal. 5:21; 1 Thess. 5:7). But it misses his point to think that being drunk is his only or even primary concern here. The reference to drunkenness on the negative side of his contrast is surely illustrative. It instances any number of things that can find their way into the lives of believers and become so controlling and dominating that their effect, indicated in the relative clause, is captured by ἀσωτία—a forceful word that indicates what debauches, dissipates, disintegrates, or is destructive in its tendency.

The apostle's primary concern in this command is that the Holy Spirit be dominating and controlling in the life of the believer to the exclusion of any and all other competitive and ultimately destructive dominations or, we may say, idolatries—idolatries that compete with and seek to supplant the all-controlling work of the Spirit. So, as it could be put to make the point, Ephesians 5:18 is the first of the Ten Commandments, "You shall have no other gods before me" (Ex. 20:3), applied explicitly to the Holy Spirit.

A CONTINUING REALITY

As being filled with the Spirit is to be the controlling reality in the life of the believer, so, secondly, it is also to be a continuing or ongoing reality. This can be seen in Ephesians 5:18 from a grammatical point, indicated by the verb form used for being filled (πληροῦσθε), a present passive imperative. In the Greek New Testament, imperative forms are of two different kinds, one in the aorist tense, the other in the present tense. The aorist imperative, much like imperatives in English, presents the matter commanded in a simple or indefinite way, without indicating anything about duration or repetition of the action commanded.

In distinction, the present imperative, for which English has no grammatical equivalent, indicates that what is being commanded is to be done repeatedly or continually. This is the form that Paul uses here so that its force in English has to be brought out by paraphrases, like the following: "Constantly be seeking the filling of the Spirit." "Seek to be filled with the Spirit again and again." "Be concerned with a constant, ever greater outworking of the filling work of the Spirit in your life."

Such paraphrases, prompted by the grammatical form of the verb Paul uses, point to an important implication of Ephesians 5:18: One of the marks of a Spirit-filled Christian is that that Christian is not preoccupied with some past experience of the Spirit in my life—as real and memorable as that experience may be—but with what the Spirit is doing in my life right now, today, in the present, and out of that preoccupation with the present is oriented toward the future and what may be the even greater filling work of the Spirit in my life.

The filling of the Spirit operates, we might say, according to a "physics" all of its (his) own. As a Christian, you can never be too filled with the Holy Spirit. You can always be filled more and more. You can never be filled to a capacity that does not have the potential for an even greater "volume," an even fuller capacity. The filling of the Spirit is to be a continuing reality as well as a controlling reality.

A COMPREHENSIVE REALITY

Third, being filled with the Spirit is a comprehensive reality. This comes out in the verses that immediately follow the command to be filled with the Spirit (5:19-21).

In their composition, these verses consist of four parallel subordinate clauses (my translations):

"speaking to one another in psalms, hymns, and spiritual songs" (5:19)

"singing and making melody from your heart to the Lord" (5:19)

"giving thanks always for all things to God the Father in the name of our Lord Jesus Christ" (5:20)

"being subject to one another in the fear of Christ" (5:21)

In each of these clauses, the verbs are participles. Participles in Greek function much as they do in English. As subordinate verb forms, they do not stand on their own syntactically but are dependent on a main verb. In this instance, the main verb on which the participles (5:19-21) depend is the imperative, "be filled with the Spirit" (5:18).[16]

By this pattern of grammatical dependence, the four participial clauses (5:19-21) draw attention to matters associated with being filled with the Spirit, things that are expected in those who are Spirit-filled. It would certainly be wrong to conclude that Paul intends to be exhaustive here or is saying everything that is true about being filled with the Spirit. Still, keeping in mind that this is the only place where he commands believers to be filled with the Spirit, it seems fair to conclude that he singles out what are among the important results of being filled with the Spirit, what one should expect to find in those who are Spirit-filled.

We may consider each of these four clauses—only briefly as it must be here—primarily in the interests of seeing the overview that emerges. The first of the two clauses in 5:19 has worship in view, seen from the angle of the singing involved, particularly corporate or at least communal worship of some kind ("speaking to one another"). A first mark of Spirit-filled Christians, then, is that that they are present when God's people are gathered for worship.

---

16   In the Greek text, the four participles on their adjectival side (nominative, masculine, plural) modify the unexpressed second person plural subject ("you" in translation) in πληροῦσθε. This grammatical subordination is obscured in some English translations (e.g., the NIV) that break up 5:19-21 into several sentences.

The second clause, closely associated with the first, also concerns worship, again in song. Only now made explicit is both that the focus of worship is "the Lord" and that worship is to be "from the heart." So, a second mark of those Spirit-filled is that while matters of form in worship are a legitimate concern (cf. 1 Cor. 14:33, 40), their worship is never just a matter of form; it involves them in being God-centered and engaged from the core of their being.

The third participial clause (5:20) broadens Paul's outlook considerably, beyond communal or corporate worship into a matter that concerns all of life. A third mark of being filled with the Spirit is "giving thanks." Spirit-filled Christian are known by the thanks they give to God as their Father.

Just how unqualified and unlimited that thanksgiving is, is apparent: "always for all things." Whatever the circumstance, no matter how dark and difficult in itself, those Spirit-filled are (to be) filled with gratitude because they know God intends it for their good (cf. Rom. 8:28). Here, as often throughout Paul's exhortation to the church, thanksgiving is singled out for emphasis; thanksgiving is an especially important fruit of being filled with the Spirit.[17]

The last of the clauses is "being subject to one another in the fear of Christ" (5:21). A fourth characteristic of being filled with the Spirit is mutual subjection within the church. Those who are Spirit-filled are known by the fact that they are ready to serve other members of the body, as that is, ultimately, their reverent service of its head, Christ.

This fourth mark, mutual subjection, is evidently at the forefront in Paul's mind, for in the long section that directly follows, beginning in 5:22 and continuing through 6:9,[18] he spells out specifically what this Spirit-filled subjection involves for believers in their various basic life relationships, how that filling work is realized in these relationships.

First, he looks at family life, starting with its nucleus and what mutual subjection looks like in a marriage filled with the Spirit (5:22–33). Spirit-filled husbands and Spirit-filled wives are those who in their marriages, in their respective roles as head and helper, given at creation (Eph. 5:31,

---

17 Even from this brief survey, it should be apparent by now the potential sermons, even sermon series, that can be developed from these participial clauses. Subordinate syntactically, they are hardly that semantically!

18 The chapter break—not part of the original text but introduced later in the course of the transmission of the Bible, is not in the best place; it breaks up what is clearly a unit.

quoting Gen. 2:24), mirror the "mystery" (Eph. 5:32) of mutual service and submission between Christ and the church.

Next, with life in the home still in view, is the relationship between children and parents, in the leading role of fathers, and how children and parents serve each other (6:1-4). Spirit-filled children[19] are those that obey their parents as part of their obeying the Lord (cf. "being subject to one another in the fear of Christ," 5:21). Parents filled with the Spirit, in turn, raise their children with discipline that is constructive by being neither excessively exacting nor unduly permissive.

Addressed finally, looking out now beyond family and home into the larger world, is the mutual subjection that ought to mark the inevitably fundamental economic dimension of human life (6:5-9). That dimension is considered here in terms of the relationship between slaves and masters—for our own cultural situation, this transposes as roughly equivalent to the relationship between labor and management. What marks both employers and employees as Spirit-filled in their respective positions is what they have in common: the same Lord and Master they serve in the opportunities and responsibilities they have to serve each other (5:9). Negatively, in this mutual service, they avoid every form of cheating, on the one hand, exploitation and intimidation, on the other, that so often burdens and ruins economic life.

Even from this survey, necessarily brief and providing little more than an overview, the trajectory of these verses is unmistakable and leads to an important observation. The filling of the Spirit is not—at least not in the first place or primarily—some sublime and memorable experience of the Spirit on the periphery of the lives of believers.[20] Rather, that filling occurs within the "everydayness" of our lives as it shapes our normal routines and common responsibilities. The filling of the Spirit ought to leave no area of life untouched; it should permeate and transform the whole of our lives. Being filled with the Spirit is not, as it were, the icing on the cake of the Christian life but is of the substance of that cake

---

19 The "in the Lord" identity (on the most likely reading of this verse) of the children of Christian parents points to their inclusion in the new covenant (cf. elsewhere in Paul, "as it is, they are holy," 1 Cor. 7:14), and so implies that as infants they should be baptized as the sign and seal of that inclusion.

20 This is not to deny that such dramatic workings of the Spirit may occur in the lives of some believers. At issue is the primary and controlling pattern of his filling work, a pattern that is to be realized in the basic relationships and everyday activities of every believer.

The filling of the Spirit come to the church at Pentecost, then, is (to be) a comprehensive as well as controlling and continuing reality in the lives of believers.

HOW TO OBEY THE COMMAND

Ephesians 5:18 commands believers to be filled with the Spirit and, as we have been seeing, the immediately following verses point to some important and characteristic results of that filling. But this passage leaves unaddressed, at least explicitly, the means for being filled with the Spirit. How, after all, are believers to obey this command?

The command is odd grammatically. How does one obey a passive command? The command is not to fill ourselves with the Spirit as if we can help ourselves to the Spirit at will. This grammatical form is an indicator that the Spirit is not at our disposal, that being filled is beyond our own resources and capacities, even as believers. Being filled with the Spirit does not happen by some regimen of steps we can master of ourselves or by some set of spiritual exercises we can determine and control.

Still, the question remains. How are believers to obey this command? The answer, for one and an important one at that, is prayer. Pray for the filling of the Spirit. In light of Pentecost, Luke 11:13, for instance, "how much more will the heavenly Father give the Holy Spirit to those who ask him!" takes on full, we may say, filling dimensions in light of Pentecost.

Of a great deal more that could be said in this regard, we may remind ourselves of the integral tie noted earlier between the kingdom and the Spirit—the essential link that exists between the eschatological rule and realm of God established by Christ in his coming and the Holy Spirit as the power or dynamic of that kingdom (Matt. 12:28; Luke 11:20). So, to pray, as Jesus has taught his disciples, "Your kingdom come" (Matt. 6:10; Luke 11:2) is, in effect, a prayer for the Spirit, for God's rule to be established and maintained with ever increasing fullness in our lives.

There is this to be said as well about the command to be filled with the Spirit. Ephesians was written about the same time as Colossians, during a period of house arrest in Rome. Moreover, a literary interdependence between them is apparent. It appears that Paul made some use of the one letter in writing the other. For instance, Ephesians 5:18–6:9 clearly corresponds to Colossians 3:16–4:1. While the latter passage is shorter and more condensed, an overlap between the two, both in wording and in the flow of the discourse, is unmistakable.

Setting the passages side by side is one way of seeing that overlap. Specifically, in place of "be filled with the Spirit" in Ephesians 5:18, Colossians 3:16 has "Let the word of Christ dwell in you richly." This replacing of the one command with the other shows that they are closely correlative and condition each other in some way.

"The word of Christ" occurs only here in the New Testament. Whether its immediate reference is to the word proceeding from Christ (Christ as its source) or to the word about Christ (Christ as its content)—a case can be made for either—for the church today, that word exists and is accessed as the inscripturated Word.

How, then, to obey the command to be filled with the Spirit? In a word, be filled with Scripture. Where Scripture, "the word of Christ," is present and heard, there the Spirit is at work.

This is the liberating reality that re-entered the life of the church with renewed power and efficacy with the Reformation: *Spiritus cum verbo*—the Spirit working with the word. The key to experiencing the filling of the Spirit is a rich appropriation of the truth of Scripture, an ongoing prayerful endeavor to "lay it up in our hearts and practice it in our lives."[21] In this endeavor, the Spirit is sovereignly active to ensure that the passive command will be fulfilled in and by believers, and in doing so, he will leave no area of their lives untouched, no aspect that isn't affected and transformed.

Conclusion. These reflections prompted by 1 Corinthians 12:13 and Ephesians 5:18 point to how recognizing the epochal and redemptive-historical nature of Pentecost leaves believers today as anything but mere spectators on Pentecost. To the contrary, the once-for-all place of the baptism with the Holy Spirit in the *historia salutis* has inevitable and far-reaching consequences for the *ordo salutis*, for the ongoing appropriation in the life of the church of the work of the Spirit come at Pentecost.

THE ECCLESIOLOGICAL SIGNIFICANCE OF PENTECOST

An important implication of the redemptive-historical significance of Pentecost, just considered in some length, is its ecclesiological significance. This

---

21 Westminster Shorter Catechism, answer 90.

bears emphasizing here, even if only briefly. Pentecost is for the church—for the whole church, not just for some in the church, for all believers, not only for some believers in distinction from others.

The Power for the Whole Church

This ecclesiological significance follows from "you shall be my witnesses" in the key theme verse, Acts 1:8. Earlier we stressed that this statement is addressed specifically to the apostles in view of the unique foundational task of worldwide gospel witness entrusted to them, a task that Luke is concerned to document as completed by them. But what is true for the apostles as the foundation of the church (Eph. 2:20) is also true derivatively for the church as it subsequently builds on the apostles in nonfoundational ways. So, we can say that the Spirit come at Pentecost is, among other considerations, the power for the ongoing activity of worldwide witness given to the church as a whole.

With an eye to 1 Corinthians 12:13, all believers, baptized with the Spirit, share in the potential power for witness, as that power is exercised in whatever appropriate ways and with all the variety that is involved—the exercise Paul has in view, for instance, in Ephesians 5:19–6:9. So, once again, it is not that Holy Spirit baptism is an imperative for the church. For the church, Holy Spirit baptism is an indicative with the potential for witness, and so witness in all its dimensions is the imperative that is to mark the church as a whole.

The Link Between the Jordan and Pentecost

The ecclesiological significance of Pentecost also appears along a somewhat different but still related line. Earlier in this chapter, we explored the important bearing that John's baptism of Jesus has on Pentecost: at the Jordan, Jesus received the Holy Spirit as empowering for the messianic task that he faced and that culminated on the cross; in his ascension, he received the Holy Spirit as the reward for that task successfully completed—his just reward, in turn, that he shared as his great gift to the church on Pentecost.[22]

This link between the Jordan and Pentecost in Jesus's ministry entails an analogy or parallel between his baptism and receiving of the Holy Spirit

---

22 See also Richard B. Gaffin Jr., "The Resurrection of Christ and Salvation," The Gospel Coalition, https://www.thegospelcoalition.org/.

and the church's receiving and being baptized with the Holy Spirit. What the Jordan was to Jesus, Pentecost was to the church.[23] As the Jordan was the Father's *confirmation* of Jesus as Messiah and in inseparable conjunction with that confirmation, his *endowment* with the Spirit for the kingdom task that lay before him, so Pentecost is the *constitution* of the church and also at the same time its *equipment* with the Spirit for the kingdom task of worldwide gospel ministry that lies before it.

The Church Constituted at Pentecost

To spell out the ecclesiological side of this parallel a bit further, Pentecost constitutes the church as "a dwelling place of God in the Spirit" (Eph. 2:22 NKJV), using the language of Paul but surely a narrative point that Luke is concerned to make as well. In fact, given, as we noted earlier, that Pentecost must be seen in the context of the coming of the kingdom, fully eschatological in its arrival in the person and work of Christ, the church is the dwelling place of God in the Spirit in its consummate form short of the return of Christ. When we ask where we find the citizens of that kingdom obediently submissive to its King, there we have the church.

We may say, then, that the church—specifically as the new covenant community of God's people—comes into existence at Pentecost. By itself, this statement is subject to misunderstanding and in need of immediate qualification. Within the larger framework of biblical teaching, since the fall, there has been and is only one way of salvation—by grace through faith—and so there has always been only one people of God. In view of this oneness or unity, we may properly speak of the old covenant church. Israel and the church are not dual parallel, nonintersecting realities in God's purposes for history.

Old Testament Israel and the New Testament church made up of those from all nations are related as the latter embodies the fulfillment of promises made to the former. As Christ is the culmination of Israel's history and of God's purposes with Israel in history, the church is Israel's future; in all that is realized in and through the church, Israel finds its true destiny.

Avoiding any disjoining of Israel and the church, and failing to recognize the basic unity of unfolding covenant history, is important. At the same

---

23 Slightly rephrasing Dunn, "What the Jordan was to Jesus, Pentecost was to the disciples" (James D. G. Dunn, *Baptism in the Holy Spirit* [Naperville, IL: Allenson, 1970], 40), in order to make the ecclesiological dimension explicit.

time—and this is what I am primarily concerned to accent here—we must not so emphasize that unity that we lose sight of the newness of the new covenant. In fact, we properly maintain the underlying oneness of God's old and new covenant dealings only as we appreciate the newness of the new covenant and the church.

Here, the statement in John 7:39—"The Spirit was not yet, because Jesus was not yet glorified" (my translation)—is instructive. In the sense that statement has, discussed earlier in this chapter, the church, correlatively, was "not yet," because Jesus was not yet glorified. There is no church, as the new covenant people of God, until Jesus is glorified and pours out the Spirit on Pentecost.

A key biblical metaphor for the church is the church as a house, as God's large-scale building project underway in the period between the resurrection and the return of Christ. In terms of that metaphor, and recalling here the language of Jesus in Matthew 16:18, we may capture our point here by saying that the immovable rock upon which Christ, now glorified, is building his church is the permanent and abiding foundation of the Spirit that Christ himself poured on the day of Pentecost. To mix metaphors appropriately here, by pouring out the Holy Spirit at Pentecost, Jesus, along with this death and resurrection, pours the foundation, the firm foundation, of the church (cf. Eph. 2:19–22).

In the Peter who acts and speaks so powerfully and boldly in Acts 2 and subsequent passages—not just Peter alone, but Peter as apostle *primus inter pares*, as first among apostolic equals—we have a clear fulfillment of the prophecy of Jesus in Matthew 16:18: "I will build my church." In what Acts documents, that prophecy finds its initial, undeniable, and totally impressive fulfillment.

Much more could be developed at length concerning the ecclesiological significance of Pentecost, but I leave it here with these indications.

Conclusion

The ecclesiological significance of Pentecost reinforces its redemptive-historical significance. Pentecost—along with Christ's death, resurrection, and ascension—is an essential part in the once-for-all event-complex in the history of redemption that forms the culmination of his saving work. The events in Luke-Acts related to Pentecost have their primary significance in terms of the once-for-all accomplishment of salvation, not its ongoing application. Pentecost belongs to the *historia salutis*, not the *ordo salutis*.

The significance of Pentecost, then, is not first of all experiential but epochal. Pentecost, as we have seen, does not provide the model or pattern for Holy Spirit baptism understood as a "second blessing" in addition to salvation by faith, to be sought by all believers but experienced only by some believers in distinction from others. As a climactic event in the history of redemption, Pentecost is constitutive for the church as a whole and so is the basis and has a bearing on the experience of the Spirit of not just some but everyone in the church, of not only some but everyone united to Christ by faith and in that union baptized with the Spirit.

If, finally, we ask: What more than anything else constitutes the unprecedented reality of Pentecost? Wherein does the newness of Pentecost lie? In answer, two things above all are to be highlighted.

First, Pentecost means that the Holy Spirit is now present and at work among God's people as a result of the finished work of Christ, that the Spirit is now present as the Spirit of the exalted Christ. Recall the "not yet . . . not yet" of John 7:39; no glorification of Christ, no Pentecost.

The point here is not that the Spirit was absent or inactive among God's people prior to Pentecost. There is ample evidence to establish his activity under the old covenant order, for instance in justifying and generating justifying faith in Abraham and David (Rom. 4 and Gal. 3), as prime examples of what was true in every generation, both before and after Sinai, for each one of the remnant in Israel.

In all of the undeniable pre-Pentecost activity, the Spirit, however, was out of season, ahead of time, as it were. The work of the Spirit under the old covenant is proleptic; it occurred in advance of the basis for the saving activity of the Holy Spirit in God's people. That basis is the actual accomplishment of their salvation centered in the cross and resurrection of Christ. There is no saving blessing of any sort whatsoever for God's people, before as well as after the coming of Christ, that is not grounded in the sole sufficiency and finality of his saving work in "the fullness of time" (Gal. 4:4).

When we ask, then, about the newness of Pentecost, the point above all to be made is this Christological point: From now on, the Spirit is the Spirit of the now exalted Christ. This is to say, then, that the Pentecostal Spirit is the *eschatological* Spirit, the Spirit now at work at last, finally, and in proper and fulfilled redemptive-historical order.

Second, the newness of the Spirit come at Pentecost is also seen as the Spirit is now the Spirit poured out on all flesh. In view of Pentecost, the people of God are now a fellowship of the Spirit made up of Gentile as well as Jew, a people gathered from every nation, kindred, tribe, and tongue. The eschatological Spirit is as such also the *universal* Spirit. And so—even though I am unable to develop it here, this is hardly an ancillary consideration—the universal Spirit of Pentecost is the Spirit of missions, the *missiological* Spirit.

As the Spirit come to the church at Pentecost, the Spirit is who he was not previously: the Spirit of the now exalted Christ, and so, as such, he is now the eschatological and universal Spirit.

The watchword of the church is not "Back to Pentecost." That is not what should be on our banners. The church is not to be caught up in a redemptive-historical anachronism—what that backward look would be in terms of the inexorable forward movement of redemptive history toward its consummation at the end of history. The church is not to be marked wistfully by a return-to-Pentecost nostalgia, longing to recapture the good old days of the church and seeking to replicate the Pentecost experience of the 120 and others in Acts, unique to their day. Rather, the marching orders for the church are "Forward from Pentecost" in the ever-present power of the Holy Spirit until, as the eleven were told, that final day when Jesus "will come in the same way as you saw him go into heaven" (Acts 1:11).[24]

THE TRINITARIAN SIGNIFICANCE OF PENTECOST

The obviously central and extraordinary activity of the Holy Spirit in the Pentecost event-complex—Pentecost and the other related events in Acts

---

24 Several things may be said here to the question sometimes raised concerning the difference in experience of the Holy Spirit between New Testament believers and the believing remnant in the Old Testament. For one, it is fair to say that Scripture does not spell out this relative difference. With that noted, however, many of the psalms, for instance, provide an important window that shows in an edifying and challenging way the essential continuity in experience there is and ought to be between old and new covenant believers. Further, what differences there are, are comparative, not categorical (distinctions like OT: "the Spirit on," NT: "the Spirit in," are misleading at best). The difference for post-Pentecost experience of the Spirit is best captured by adjectives like "deeper," "richer," "fuller," "freer." For a fuller discussion of this and related issues, see Richard B. Gaffin Jr., "Pentecost: Before and After," *Kerux: A Journal of Biblical-Theological Preaching* 10, no. 2 (September 1995): 3–24.

discussed earlier—should not cause us to overlook the equally important involvement of the Father and the Son. Pentecost has fully Trinitarian significance. It is a climactic act of the triune God in history.

The Son

The Christological importance of Pentecost is abundantly clear from its redemptive-historical significance. Among other factors already noted, the sermon that Peter preached on the day of Pentecost is Christocentric, not Spirit-centered, or if that overstates, it is at least much more the former than the latter. The sermon's climactic point is Jesus's own reception of the Spirit from the Father in his ascension and his consequent action in pouring out the Spirit on the church, confirming that as crucified and now exalted, he is "both Lord and Christ" (Acts 2:36).

To put this point in more formal theological jargon, according to Acts—and this would be true of the New Testament as a whole—there is no Pneumatology independent of Christology; any such stand-alone concern with the Holy Spirit or reflection on his work is misplaced. In the New Testament, Christology and Pneumatology belong together; they inevitably interpenetrate.

In addition to what we have so far considered, the connection between Christ and the Spirit revealed at Pentecost is even more central and integral than is explicit in Peter's sermon. In his resurrection and ascension, Christ—already man of the Spirit from birth and further endowed with the Spirit at the Jordan—has become so completely *transformed and indwelt by* the Spirit and come into such permanent and complete *possession of* the Spirit that, anticipating a fundamental element in Paul's theology to be considered later in detail, it can be said that he, as the last Adam, "became the life-giving Spirit" in the sense of the Holy Spirit (1 Cor. 15:45, my translation; cf. "the Lord is the Spirit," 2 Cor. 3:17). Dating from his resurrection—or more broadly, his exaltation—the incarnate Son and the Spirit in much of their activity are now one in a way they were not previously. They are to be seen as one in their redemptive functioning; specifically, they are identified in the work of giving eschatological, resurrection life.

From this perspective, then, when on Pentecost Jesus baptizes with the Holy Spirit, in a manner of speaking he baptizes with himself, with his own indwelling and surrounding presence. To put it in a Trinitarian way: at Pentecost, the exalted Christ sends the promise of the Father by coming himself in the presence of the Spirit.

Recall here the connection to Matthew 28:20 noted earlier and the promise there of the resurrected and soon-to-be-ascended Jesus to the church, sanctioning the Great Commission, "I am with you always, to the end of the age." While this statement no doubt entails the divine omnipresence of Jesus as the Son of God, it is also to be understood—I would not be hesitant to say primarily—as a promise realized by the presence and power of the Holy Spirit. Jesus makes good on that promise of his own presence by sending the Spirit on Pentecost.

In terms of these considerations, then, there is an element of truth in the otherwise quite serious error held by some critical scholars that Pentecost is the parousia. I say an element of truth in that, in a manner of speaking, Pentecost is truly the return of Christ. Pentecost is a parousia in the sense that it is the coming of the glorified Christ to be with his church.[25] Pentecost, if it has any significance, means that Christ is present with his people.

Admittedly this functional unity between Christ and the Spirit is not explicit in Peter's sermon or from a strict exegesis of Acts 2, as it is in the teaching of Paul. But in the light of the latter, it is implicit in Peter's statements, and that should not be missed.

A BRIEF EXCURSUS ON JOHANNINE THEOLOGY

This functional oneness or unity of Christ and the Spirit comes out pointedly in the teaching of Jesus himself in John 14–16. For instance, in John 14:18–20:

> "I will not leave you as orphans; I will come to you. Yet a little while and the world will see me no more, but you will see me. Because I live, you also will live. In that day you will know that I am in my Father, and you in me, and I in you."

25 We might even say that the New Testament teaches three, rather than two, comings of Christ: in his incarnation, at Pentecost, and at the end of history. This correlates with the three stages in the coming of the kingdom discussed earlier. It also serves to show once again the primarily redemptive-historical rather than experiential significance of Pentecost.

The larger context unit, John 13–17, is John's account of Jesus's final teaching before the climactic events of the cross and the resurrection. In this context, these statements have a clear bearing on what took place at Pentecost.

In the immediate context, Jesus tells the disciples that he is about to depart to the Father ("because I am going to the Father," 14:12). Further, he goes on to say—what will surely be coincident with his going to the Father in his ascension—that at his request, the Father will send the Spirit, the Spirit particularly in his identity as "Helper" (παράκλητος), in the sense of an advocate or intercessor (14:16, 26; cf. the other references to the Spirit as παράκλητος in 15:26; 16:7).[26]

John 16:7—still in the same context of Jesus's final instruction to the disciples—reinforces this point: "Nevertheless, I tell you the truth: it is to your advantage that I go away, for if I do not go away, the Helper will not come to you. But if I go, I will send him to you." Clear here is the linking of the departure of Jesus previously mentioned in 14:12—his departure in going to be with the Father in his impending ascension—and the coming of the Spirit.

In passing here, but hardly insignificant, John 16:7 has perennial importance for the church. It is for the church's good that for now Jesus is not with the church in the sense of his words here. It is for its good that Jesus has departed, because if that were not the case, the church would be at a substantial disadvantage. We would be without the Spirit present with us as our Helper-Advocate.

Back in John 14, with the promise that the Spirit will come as the Paraclete, Jesus surely intends to assure the disciples that they will not be abandoned. More particularly, they are not going to be without support, without "paracletic" assistance, without the Spirit present with them as Advocate. But along with this accent on the advantage of the Spirit coming to be present and helping, Jesus immediately adds in 14:18, "I will not leave you as orphans; I will come to you." Likewise, later in the passage, he says—telescoping, I take it, from 14:12 ("because I am going to the Father") and 14:18—"You heard me say to you 'I am going away, and I will come to you'" (14:28).

The verses immediately following contain several statements that are fairly taken as amplifying 14:18. These include a couple of time references:

---

26 See the discussion of the meaning of παράκλητος earlier in chapter 3.

"Yet a little while and the world will see me no more, but you will see me." (14:19)

"In that day you will know that I am in my Father, and you in me, and I in you." (14:20)

"Whoever has my commandments and keeps them, he it is who loves me. And he who loves me will be loved by my Father, and I will love him and manifest myself to him." (14:21)

"If anyone loves me, he will keep my word, and my Father will love him, and we will come to him and make our home with him." (14:23)

The time references are "a little while" (μικρόν, 14:19) and, correlatively, "in that day" (ἐν ἐκείνῃ τῇ ἡμέρᾳ, 14:20). How concretely are we to understand these references that qualify the time of Jesus's coming in view? In addressing that question, I proceed negatively by eliminating a couple of proposals that have been made.

For one, the reference is not to the second coming. The second coming is likely in view back at the beginning of the chapter in 14:2–3. But that is not the state of affairs that Jesus has in view here for the following reason. The coming of Jesus in 14:18 is such that the world is excluded from the "seeing" (14:19) or "manifest[ing]" (14:21) of Jesus involved, while regularly throughout the New Testament, the second coming is an event that is visible to all. For instance, Revelation 1:7: "every eye will see him." So the second coming, an open and universal event, is hardly in view in these statements.

Nor in 14:18 and 14:28 does Jesus have in mind his postresurrection appearances to the disciples. It is difficult to see how the resurrection appearances, temporary in their nature, can be described as the mutual indwelling of Jesus and believers (14:20) or as Jesus and the Father making their home with the believer (14:23).

So, discounting proposals that in 14:18 and 14:28 Jesus is referring either to his second coming or to his temporary postresurrection appearances, the situation in view instead pivots around Jesus going to the Father and, correlatively, the coming of the Spirit. This, a main thread in the context, is a further instance of John 7:39: "The Spirit was not yet, because Jesus was not yet glorified."

A key point, then, of Jesus in 14:18 and following is this: The impending course of redemptive history is going to be such that he must leave bodily in order that the Spirit may come. But at the same time, that also means that he, Jesus, will come and, in coming, will share his life with believers—the life he will then have as resurrected and ascended (14:18-19). For Jesus to depart bodily is for the Spirit to come, and in the coming of the Spirit, Jesus comes: "I will not leave you orphans; I will come to you." John 14:28 brings together from what is said in 14:12 and 14:18: "You heard me say to you, 'I am going away, and I will come to you.' If you loved me, you would have rejoiced, because I am going to the Father, for the Father is greater than I."

This functional identity of Christ and the Spirit comes out further in John 16. There in 16:7, as already noted above, he speaks of the coming of the Spirit as Paraclete, contingent on his going away. In coming, the Spirit "will convict the world concerning sin and righteousness and judgment" (16:8). Of these three elements, conviction concerning righteousness will occur "because I go to the Father, and you will see me no longer" (16:10).

At 16:16—the intervening discourse prompted, in part, by the statement in 16:10—Jesus says, "A little while, and you will see me no longer; and again a little while, and you will see me." This, along with what was said in 16:10, leaves the disciples thoroughly perplexed:

> So some of his disciples said to one another, "What is this that he says to us, 'A little while, and you will not see me, and again a little while, and you will see me'; and, 'because I am going to the Father'?" So they were saying, "What does he mean by 'a little while' [τὸ μικρόν]? We do not know what he is talking about" (16:17-18).

These disciples sense, as it might be put, that Jesus is playing a kind of theological shell game with them: "Now you see me; now you don't."

In the verses that follow, Jesus goes on to address their perplexity, clarifying for them his statements and the impending future, beyond his death and resurrection, when the Spirit—previously identified as "the Spirit of truth," who "will guide you into all the truth" (16:13)—comes. A principal benefit, among others, of this coming of the Spirit is that "your sorrow will turn into joy" (16:20).

Conclusion. According to the teaching of Jesus in John, for the Spirit to come is, in that mode, for the ascended Jesus himself to come. The requisite balance here is between the bodily absence and the Spiritual, in the sense of the Holy Spirit, presence of Christ. In passing here but hardly unimportantly, this required balance Reformed theology maintains sacramentally in its view of the real presence of Christ in the Lord's Supper. He is really and truly there as the Spirit is present and also indwells those who partake by faith.[27]

The Father

No less prominent is the role of the Father at Pentecost. My brief comments here touch on a couple of points that, given the important implications they have, warrant much more attention.

As the fulfillment of promise, Pentecost is specifically the fulfillment of "the promise of my/the Father" (Luke 24:49; Acts 1:4), "the promise of the Holy Spirit" "from the Father" (Acts 2:33); note as well Luke 11:13: "the heavenly Father" will "give the Holy Spirit." As Acts 2:33 makes clear, in the expression "the promise of the Father" in 1:4 (τὴν ἐπαγγελίαν τοῦ πατρός), the reference to the Father is a genitive of source or origin. It indicates the promise that comes from the Father, the promise that the Father makes and then fulfills. The Spirit, then, is the content of that promise; the Spirit is what—or better, whom—the Father promises.

This identification of the Spirit as promised by the Father in fact opens up the widest possible perspective on Pentecost, because it links Pentecost to the fulfillment of the promise that is at the core of Old Testament expectation. To identify Pentecost as a matter of promise marks out Pentecost as the fulfillment of the promise that is at the foundation of covenant history and has shaped its course and outcome from the beginning. That is the promise of Genesis 12:3, that in Abraham all the families or nations of the earth will be blessed. Pentecost as the promise of the Father, as promised by

---

27 It is perhaps worth observing here once again, to avoid possible misunderstanding, that this functional oneness between Christ and the Spirit is consistent with the continuing personal distinction between them as the second and third persons of the Trinity. That distinction and the essential inner-Trinitarian relationship between them remain unchanged. In view is a unity effected redemptive historically and true only in terms of the human nature assumed by the Son.

the Father, points back to the promise made to Abraham, a promise basic to the architecture or design of the covenant.

Galatians 3:14—note that Genesis 12:3 is quoted in Galatians 3:8—helps to clarify and reinforce this point. In the brief section (3:10-14), 3:13 has just stated that "Christ redeemed us from the curse of the law" by his death on the cross. This redemption, 3:14 then concludes, has a twofold purpose: "in order that in Christ Jesus the blessing of Abraham might come to the Gentiles, in order that we might receive the promise of the Spirit through faith" (my translation).

There is some debate whether these two purpose (ἵνα) clauses, grammatically parallel, are epexegetical—that is, are different ways of saying (nearly) the same thing—or whether the second expresses a consequence of the first. The latter seems likely because the blessing promised to Abraham is connected directly with justification in 3:8. But however that question is settled, for our purposes here the basic consideration is the same: the connection that is made between the promise of Genesis 12 to Abraham and the promise of the Spirit. The blessing of Abraham to the Gentiles entails receiving of the Spirit as a matter of fulfilled promise.[28]

Taking Pentecost as the reference point, then, there is an expanding horizon of promise and fulfillment concerning the Spirit: not only the nexus between Luke 3 and Acts 2, which we have considered in some detail, or even between Joel 2 (cf. the quote in Acts 2:16-21) and Acts 2, but in its broadest sweep, between Genesis 12 and Acts 2.

This pattern of connections, whether or not recognized, lies in back of the observation often made that Acts 2 points to the reversal of the Babel confusion of languages that occurs in the narrative flow in Genesis (11:1-9), just prior to and in stark contrast with the initiation of God's covenantal dealings with Abraham in Genesis 12, with its overarching inaugurating promise in 12:3.

The phenomenon on the day of Pentecost—"Jews . . . from every nation under heaven" (Acts 2:5) hearing, representatively we may say, "in our own tongues" (2:11; cf. "each one . . . in his own language," 2:6)—is a striking signal that the promised Spirit from the Father (Acts 1:4) will unify those

---

28 Note, too, that in the argumentation in Gal. 3, the promise of the Spirit in Gal. 3:14 is anticipated by the references to the gift of the Spirit in 3:2-5.

from every nation who, in the diversity of human languages, hear and confess the one gospel of the *magnalia Dei* ("the mighty works of God," 2:11).
This arresting phenomenon indicates the beginning of the Spirit's reversing
of the disunity and confusion associated with this linguistic diversity that
originated as God's curse on human sin and rebellion in Genesis 11. In
this Pentecost reversal, it is also fair to see an anticipation, linguistically,
that points to the ethnic universalism of the apostolic mandate in Acts 1:8
(from "Jerusalem . . . to the end of the earth").

Returning briefly to John's Gospel and the passage in John 14 that we
have examined, the Father's involvement in sending the Spirit is evident. It
is the Father who will give the Spirit at the request of Jesus in his ascension
(14:16), and the Father will send the Spirit in the name of Jesus (14:26).
Additionally, there is the promise in 14:23, to be understood in terms of the
coming of the Spirit, to the one who loves Jesus and keeps his word: "we"—
plural, Father and Son—"will come to him and make our home with him."

In concluding these reflections on Pentecost as fully Trinitarian, an
important caveat of sorts is in order. The roles of the Father and the Son
in sending the Spirit should not be seen as parallel, as if they exist side by
side. Rather, the Son has priority in the sense of his mediatorial indispensability for the coming of the Father to dwell with believers in view in 14:23.

An indication of this indispensability is clear from his interchange with
Philip earlier in the chapter, in 14:8–9. To Philip's request, "Lord, show us
the Father, and it is enough for us," Jesus responds, "Have I been with you
so long, and you still do not know me, Philip? Whoever has seen me has
seen the Father. How can you say, 'Show us the Father'?"

"Whoever has seen me has seen the Father."[29] This statement is not
reversible. There is no ground in this passage (or elsewhere in Scripture),
and it would run counter to its entire thrust to imagine Jesus also saying,
"Whoever has seen the Father has seen me." This irreversibility reflects
the mediatorial indispensability of Jesus and so his priority, in that sense,
to the Father in the coming of the Spirit. In terms of the language of John
14:20 and 14:23, only as it is the case that Jesus is in the Father and indwelt
by the Father, and indwells believers by the Spirit, is it true that the Father
indwells believers.

---

29 Cf. earlier in John 12:45: "And whoever sees me sees him who sent me."

All told, from a Trinitarian perspective, Pentecost belongs to the fulfill-ment of the ultimate design and expectation of the covenant: God consum-mately in the midst of his people in triune fullness. Pentecost is the initial realization on an eschatological scale of the Emmanuel principle—"God with us"—at the heart of and that controls covenant history.

THE FORENSIC SIGNIFICANCE OF PENTECOST

My discussion under this heading has a more provisional character. My interest is in sketching a framework to promote recognizing and reflecting on the forensic or judicial dimension of Pentecost—an aspect that often goes unrecognized and is surely in need of more discussion than my comments here. Some background from systematic theology provides a helpful frame-work for facilitating some pertinent observations about the theology of Acts.

From the viewpoint of systematic theology, the benefits of salvation in Christ applied to believers—in distinction from the once-for-all accom-plishment of salvation by Christ—are of two basic kinds: those benefits categorized variously as forensic, judicial, juridical, or declarative and, in distinction, those benefits that have to do with renovation, renewal, and transformation. This basic distinction, put another way, is between those blessings having to do with our status or standing before God and those dealing with our subjective condition and functioning. Negatively, the former blessings remove the guilt of sin and the estrangement from God it causes; the latter blessings eradicate and suppress the power of sin as it corrupts and enslaves. Specifically in view are justification and adoption, forensic benefits having to do with our standing before God, and, in dis-tinction, renovative benefits, particularly regeneration and sanctification.

In passing here, it is important not to eclipse either one of these strands by so stressing one to the neglect the other, and, on the other hand, not to blur or lose sight of the distinction between them. Serious error is involved in either case. The most prominent instance of the latter error is the Roman Catholic suspension of the forensic on the renovative—basing justification and removal of the guilt of sin on the process of sanctification in the sin-ner—an error leading to the need for the Reformation and its recapturing of the heart of the gospel with its doctrine of justification.

The former error appears in an observable long-standing Protestant tendency toward isolating these two strands of benefits from each other

as if our salvation more properly resides in one than the other—specifically, stressing justification and the gospel as the gospel of justification—
and consequently failing to see that sanctification is no less integral to
the good news of salvation revealed in Christ. Where that separation
occurs, what becomes further obscured is that both justification and
sanctification have their foundation in Christ and that in the believer's
union with him these two benefits are united and inseparable without
being confused.[30]

With this systematic-theological sketch in hand, we may observe that
while at Pentecost the Spirit is obviously present as a power indwelling the
church and transforming believers, that should not cause us to overlook a
forensic or judicial facet in what takes place. That may be seen along two
lines, one having to do with justification, the other with adoption.

Pentecost and Justification

This judicial facet is already indicated and prepared for by John the Baptist's
programmatic prophecy in Luke 3:16-17, as that prophecy is fulfilled on
Pentecost. Here we may recall and draw together the basic threads of our
earlier detailed discussion in chapter 3: The Messiah's Spirit-and-fire baptism is essentially forensic, a matter of judgment. This baptism is an ordeal
that has a judicial character. It is, in effect, a trial process that separates
wheat from chaff, the righteous from the unrighteous.

Against the backdrop of John's prophecy, the overall picture leading to
its fulfillment, as we saw, is this: For the Messiah's people, those he came to
save, to escape the destructive aspect of his Spirit-and-fire baptism—that
is, that the messianic people not be consumed like chaff, that they not be
destroyed by the fire of eschatological wrath, to put it bluntly, that there
be a messianic people at all—it was necessary that Christ himself suffer on
behalf of his people.[31]

For the messianic people to be baptized for salvation, he, the Messiah,
must be baptized with condemnation and curse. It was necessary that

---

30 On this issue, see, for instance, the excellent formulations in the Westminster Larger Catechism,
question and answer 69 and 77.

31 This necessity for the fulfillment of John's prophecy is expressed by Jesus in Luke 9:22, a statement I have not previously cited: "The Son of Man *must* suffer many things and be rejected by
the elders and chief priests and scribes, and be killed, and on the third day be raised."

Christ himself pass through judgment and, moreover, that in that process he endure the just eschatological wrath of God on the sins of his people. That was intimated by the statement of Jesus in Luke 12:50: "I have a baptism to be baptized with." It was necessary, further, not only that he endure that baptism of judgment culminating in his death but also that he emerge from this exposure to eschatological wrath triumphant and vindicated, as he did in his resurrection.

Returning to Acts 2, when at Pentecost Christ comes to baptize his people—triumphant as he now is from his baptism ordeal—for them the just wrath they deserve has been removed. For them, the church, the judicial fire of destruction has been exhausted, quenched by his death. What takes place in his baptizing activity on Pentecost, then, is entirely positive and saving; it is exclusively a baptism of blessing. It involves the coming of the Spirit as blessing along the various lines we have previously discussed and others that we haven't touched on.

But what about the presence of fire on the day of Pentecost? How are we to account for the fire phenomenon coincident with the outpouring of the Spirit at Pentecost?

For one thing, we should carefully note the terms of the description of what occurred. The fire phenomenon itself was "tongues as of fire" (γλῶσσαι ὡσεὶ πυρὸς, Acts 2:3).[32] These tongues are further described in 2:3 as "divided."[33] However this is to be envisioned exactly, the result was a distribution so that the tongues, it is said, "rested on each one of them."

The description—"tongues *as of* fire"—points to the Pentecost fire phenomenon not as a reality in itself or for its own sake but as a sign, a sign that signifies the reality of the Spirit. That said, of course, raises the further question: What specifically is signified? What is the signifying significance of the fire-like tongues at Pentecost?

Proposals made most often are that the fire symbolizes either the empowering or, alternatively, the purifying work of the Spirit. Against the broader biblical background, it is less clear that the former view (empowering) is immediately in view in Acts 2. But in light of the forensic context in terms of which Pentecost is to be understood, as I have

---

32 "what seemed to be tongues of fire" (NIV); "tongues . . . like a fire" (NET).

33 Here διαμεριζόμεναι may be taken either as passive ("divided") or in the middle voice: "spreading out" (NET); "distributing themselves" (NASB).

made some effort to show, the fire phenomenon at Pentecost shows that for those on whom the tongues rested, the fire of destructive judgment has been dissipated and quenched. For them, indicative for the church as a whole, so far as exposure to eschatological wrath is concerned, that fire has been exhausted and will not consume them. The fire tongues are pictured as resting or hovering benignly, not as in any way incendiary. Without pushing the text unduly, we may say that the fire at Pentecost is domesticated fire; it no longer has the potential to harm, to destroy, to consume.

At any rate, the fire tongues at Pentecost are to be accounted for in terms of the forensic factor essential in John's prophecy and so in its fulfillment at Pentecost. It seems difficult to see how there would not be some connection.

In this regard, I would add that when it comes to the significance of the fire, there is no need to choose between the various views I noted—between its dissipated judgment significance, or as a sign of purification, or signifying empowering. It seems fair to see all those aspects there. Only we should not fail to recognize the forensic aspect, perhaps as primary.

Additionally, earlier we noted how in the Malachi 3–4 passage, the integration of fire and Spirit ("fiery *pneuma*") as well as the eschatological significance of fire there provides Old Testament background for these elements prominent in John's prophecy. That, I think, disposes us to see in the fire of fulfillment on Pentecost the dimensions of both judgment and purification. Picking up on the language in Malachi 3:3, we may say that what is revealed on the day of Pentecost is the church as made up of the "purified sons of Levi"—cleansed through the fires of judgment that Christ has gone through on their behalf.

The outpouring of the Spirit at Pentecost, as we have noted repeatedly, has clear affinities with the Messiah's baptism ordeal, pointedly his death and resurrection. In fact, Pentecost is an element in the complex of events that makes up that climactic ordeal—judicial and judgment-bearing in nature—and its outcome (Acts 2:32–33 again). In view of that, it seems difficult not to conclude that Pentecost not only results in the *efficacious empowering* of the church for kingdom service but does that as it is also the *effective demonstration* that the church is no longer subject to God's just wrath.

Pentecost reveals the church as made up of those who are no longer in fear of the destructive side of the Messiah's baptism—that destructive judgment that Christ will finally execute at his return on those unrepentant and outside the church. The church, in other words, is made up of those who are no longer under sentence of condemnation (cf. Rom. 8:1), and that is simply to say, those who are justified.

With an eye to ongoing and often heightened discussions of the doctrine of justification today, the New Testament, particularly Paul, clearly spells out how individual sinners are justified—solely by faith and solely on the basis of Christ's righteousness imputed to them. But that truth need not be played off against the corporate emphasis I am making here. Pentecost reveals what is true of the community of those who are justified by faith. Together with the resurrection and ascension of Christ, and the eschatological life in the Spirit that Pentecost reveals, Pentecost is also the de facto justification of the church.

A couple of statements, both in Paul, point in the direction of this conclusion and provide background for it. In Romans 4:25, bringing much of his discussion beginning at 3:21 to its conclusion, he speaks of Christ "who was delivered up for our trespasses and raised for our justification." Here, without exploring it in detail now, Christ's resurrection—part of the death-resurrection-ascension-Pentecost complex—is connected with the Christian's justification.

In 1 Timothy 3:16—a six-part formulation, perhaps an already existing hymn or confessional fragment that he has taken over—Paul affirms, clearly with Christ as exalted in view, that he was "justified in the Spirit."[34] Brought together here because of what has taken place for him in his exaltation are the Spirit and Christ's vindication-justification. We may say, then, that it is this justifying exaltation-vindication experienced by Christ for the good of the church that is manifested in the outpouring of the Spirit at Pente-

---

34 KJV/NKJV; ἐδικαιώθη ἐν πνεύματι. Other translations (e.g., ESV, NIV, NASB) have "vindicated" instead of "justified" (some with "justified" in the margin), but the latter is the preferable translation in light of Rom. 4:25 and the use of the verb elsewhere. Christ's resurrection is his own justification. His resurrection is the de facto declaration of his righteousness, that he is righteous because of his obedience culminating in his death—the righteousness he shares by imputation with those who are united with him by faith. See also Richard B. Gaffin Jr., "The Resurrection of Christ and Salvation," The Gospel Coalition, https://www.thegospel coalition.org/.

cost. The Spirit of Pentecost is the Spirit of justification in the sense that the Spirit come at Pentecost is the forensic seal on the justification of the church (cf. Eph. 1:13).[35]

These stanzas from T. S. Eliot's "Little Gidding," drawn to my attention by a student, are obviously prompted, it would seem, by Pentecost and provide a commentary, as fitting as it is striking, to conclude our discussion to this point of the forensic significance of Pentecost:

> The dove descending breaks the air
> With flame of incandescent terror
> Of which the tongues declare
> The one discharge from sin and error.
> The only hope, or else despair
>> Lies in the choice of pyre or pyre—
>> To be redeemed from fire by fire.
> Who then devised the torment? Love.
> Love is the unfamiliar Name
> Behind the hands that wove
> The intolerable shirt of flame
> Which human power cannot remove.
>> We only live, only suspire
>> Consumed by either fire or fire.[36]

Pentecost and Adoption

Pentecost can also be viewed as the adoption of the church, as having adoptive significance. While the New Testament understanding of the adoption of believers is fairly seen as having renovative as well as forensic dimensions, our focus here will be limited to the latter, how adoption as judicial or legal bears on Pentecost.

This judicial consequence of Pentecost does not so much follow from the forensic character of the baptism, as we just traced that out for justification,

---

35 For a fuller treatment elaborating the comments in this section, see my "Justification in Luke-Acts," in *Right with God: Justification in the Bible and the World*, ed. D. A. Carson (Grand Rapids, MI: Baker, 1992), 106–25.

36 T. S. Eliot, "Little Gidding," in *Collected Poems: 1909–1962* (New York: Harcourt, Brace, & Co., 1991), 207.

but from the basic analogy we have already noted: between the Jordan and Pentecost, between Jesus being baptized with the Holy Spirit—the descending of the Spirit on Jesus when he was baptized by John—and the church's being baptized with the Holy Spirit on Pentecost.

At his baptism, the coming of the Spirit upon Jesus is joined with the Father's declaration, "You are my beloved Son" (Luke 3:22), a declaration of sonship. This voice of the Father at the Jordan asserts the identity of Jesus as the divine Son. At the same time, that heavenly voice also has a definite performative force. It is effective, commensurate with his being anointed with the Spirit, as the investiture of Jesus into the new, public phase of his *messianic* sonship that begins at the Jordan.

In the sense of this investiture, the declarative voice of the Father has adoptive significance. It is a form of adoption or perhaps better, reaffirmation of adoption—Jesus has been the messianic Son since his birth—as it inaugurates the momentous final stage of the earthly ministry of Jesus as the messianic Son.[37]

This has nothing to do with advocating some form of adoptionist Christology, where Christ is not God's Son until what takes place at the Jordan. That is no more the case than Peter, in saying that by exalting Jesus to his right hand, "God has made him both Lord and Christ" (Acts 2:36), means he was not Lord and Christ before his exaltation. Rather, in view in each instance—his baptism by John and his exaltation—is the appointment and in that sense the (re-)adoption of the Son in his identity and status as the messianic Son.

In a statement we will consider in detail later, Romans 1:4 captures this adoptive sense: by his resurrection through the action of the Spirit, Christ, the preexisting divine Son (1:3; cf. Rom. 8:3, 32), was "appointed" (NIV, NET; or "declared" ESV, NKJV) "Son of God in power." By virtue of the climactic heightening he experienced in his exaltation, Christ, as the messianic Son, is now who he was not prior to the resurrection: "the Son-of-God-in-power" (NET).[38]

---

37 It is essential to keep clear that speaking about the adoption of Jesus by the Father applies to him only as he is the Messiah and in terms of his human nature, not to his divine Sonship, as he is the Son from all eternity—the same in substance and equal in power and glory with the Father and Spirit.

38 The adoptive significance of the exaltation is made even more explicit in Hebrews 1. The name, more excellent than that of the angels, that "the Son" (1:2) "inherited" in his exaltation (1:3-4) is *Son*. The writer makes that clear by the rhetorical questions in 1:5, citing Ps. 2:7: "You are

As that is the case for Jesus at the Jordan and in his resurrection and exaltation, so at Pentecost the church comes into its inheritance as sons. With the coming of the Spirit at Pentecost, the church receives the "down payment" on its inheritance (cf. Eph. 1:14 ESV mg.), the inheritance of sons. At Pentecost, the church receives the fulfillment of that promise that in Luke-Acts, as we have noted repeatedly, is specifically the promise of the *Father* (see again, e.g., Luke 24:49).

At Pentecost, then, the Son receives son and daughters, brothers and sisters. To borrow again from Paul, in Romans 8:29, the goal of predestination, all told, is for believers "to be conformed to the image of his Son, in order that he might be the firstborn among many brothers." At Pentecost, the exalted Christ shows himself for who he now is: "firstborn among many brothers," the firstborn to whose now eschatologically exalted image his many brothers are to be conformed.[39]

Believers, then, as they are adopted sons, have received and share in the gift of the Spirit come at Pentecost. Accordingly, in Romans 8:15 and Galatians 4:6, the Spirit is identified as "the Spirit of adoption" and "the Spirit of his Son." As such, he engenders in believers their "Abba" cry to God as Father—the totally fitting response of those who share in having received "the promise of the Father" fulfilled at Pentecost. The Spirit of Pentecost is the Spirit of adoption.

Conclusion

Recognizing the forensic significance of Pentecost reinforces how little the experience of those at Pentecost and those involved in the unique Pentecost event-complex in Acts provides an ongoing model or is intended as an example to be replicated in the subsequent life of the church in the experience of some Christians, in distinction from others, whether sought or not.

Rather, once again, Pentecost emerges as an event in the history of redemption (*historia salutis*) at the heart of the salvation once-for-all accomplished by Christ. In bringing to the church the Holy Spirit as the abiding *source* of renewal and sanctification, Pentecost also provides the permanent *seal* on the justification and adoption of the church.

---

my Son, / today I have begotten you" and 2 Sam. 7:14 (cf. Ps. 89:26–27/LXX 88:27): "I will be to him a father, and he shall be to me a son." In view in Heb. 1:4–5 is the adoptive-messianic sonship of the Son, eschatologically heightened by his exaltation.

39 Cf. Col. 1:18: As resurrected, Christ is now "the firstborn from the dead."

5

Pentecost (Part 2)

Two Related Issues

ACTS 2 AND JOHN 20:22

John 20:22 reads, "And when he had said this, he breathed on them and said to them, 'Receive the Holy Spirit.'" A perennial question in interpreting the New Testament concerns the relationship between this verse and the account in Acts 2.

The problem is apparent. In Luke-Acts, the Spirit is given on Pentecost, fifty (or approximately fifty) days after the resurrection; in John, on the day of the resurrection (cf. 20:19). Perhaps predictably, then, some modern, historical-critical scholarship has concluded that John 20:22 is the "Johannine Pentecost" and with that a classic instance of contradiction within the New Testament, evidence of conflict between the theology of John and the theology of Luke-Acts.

In considering this issue here, the following factors should be noted:

Differences in the Accounts

On any construction, the differences between the two passages need to be kept in view. Despite apparently similar references to the Holy Spirit, these differences are multiple and pronounced. Not only is there the difference in time already noted. The circumstances are quite different. In John, in the evening and in secrecy, behind closed, even locked doors (John 20:19); in Acts, in the middle of the morning (Acts 2:15), perhaps in the outer (Gentile) court of the temple (2:1-2), and with immediate public consequences.

The recipients are also different. In John, only the closest circle of disciples is present; of the eleven apostles, Thomas is absent (John 20:24). In Acts, the entire Jerusalem church is present or represented, as "all" (Acts 2:1) is likely to be understood (cf. the 120 persons mentioned in 1:15).

Then there is the notable difference concerning the person of Jesus. In John, not yet ascended, he is present bodily; in Acts, now ascended, he is not present bodily.

This combination of factors points to the fact that we are dealing with something other than varying or contradictory accounts of the same event but rather with accounts of two different events and how they are related.

Johannine Structure

John's Gospel records more fully than do the Synoptics, including Luke, Jesus's own promise concerning the coming of the Spirit. For instance, the promised sending of the Spirit as "Helper" is dominant in the teaching of Jesus in John 14-16. There, as we noted earlier, in the context beginning at 14:12, the giving of the Spirit is contingent on the fact that Jesus is about to go to the Father in his ascension. This is made most explicit in John 16:7: "Nevertheless, I tell you the truth: it is to your advantage that I go away, for if I do not go away, the Helper will not come to you. But if I go, I will send him to you." John's account of Jesus's teaching is clear: the sending of the promised Spirit follows and is contingent upon the ascension.

In John 20:22, however, Jesus is clearly not presented as ascended. To the contrary, as he says to Mary on the same day, "I have not yet ascended to the Father" (20:17). So, to view John 20:22 as the Johannine Pentecost not only brings him into conflict with Luke but also, implausibly, with himself, with his own theological structure.

Lucan Structure

Pertinent to the issue under discussion is the following state of affairs. Customarily, considerable stress is put on the decisive impact of Pentecost on the experience of the disciples. Rightly so—although, as we have seen, the decisiveness or significance of Pentecost is first of all redemptive-historical and objective rather than experiential and subjective. On this view, Pentecost transforms the disciples from anxious and cowering timidity to unshakeable boldness, seen notably in the case of Peter.

This view of the significance of Pentecost for the experience of the dis-ciples needs to be shaded considerably. Luke 24:52–53 reads, "And they worshiped him and returned to Jerusalem with great joy, and were continu-ally in the temple blessing God."

This is the note that Luke sees as a fitting way to end part 1 to Theophilus: with this description of the activity of the disciples—likely of a consider-able number of disciples (there were at least 120 before Pentecost, Acts 1:15)—in the ten-day period between the ascension and Pentecost. This activity was marked by blessing or praising God, praise that was no doubt influenced by the heart-burning, mind-opening effect of exposure to Jesus and his teaching following his resurrection (see Luke 24:32, 45). In other words, it seems fair to conclude, the content of their praise was the gospel, centered in the death and resurrection of Christ and with its call to repen-tance for the forgiveness of sins (24:46–47).

Further, this gospel-centered praise took place "in the temple"; it was public or at least open. It also occurred "continually" and was accompa-nied "with great joy." In other words, it was both ongoing and exuberant, a persisting activity not easily contained or suppressed.

So, in closing his Gospel as he does, Luke highlights a transforming experience of the disciples after the resurrection yet prior to Pentecost that during this period resulted in an open and positive witness to the gospel.

Conclusion

John likely makes no mention of Pentecost because it falls outside the scope of what his Gospel intends to cover. A more difficult question is why Luke, given the broader range of his two-part work, does not mention the event of John 20:22.

At any rate, the two events stand in some relationship to each other. A plausible proposal is that the state of affairs described in Luke 24:53, just noted, is due in part to the experience of at least some disciples on Easter Sunday described in John 20:22.

The relationship between the two events is perhaps best understood in terms of the staging or phasing principle, discussed earlier, that marks the coming of the (one) kingdom and the associated giving of the Spirit. From this perspective, the event of John 20:22 may be seen as a kind of "firstfruits" toward the firstfruits of the Spirit come at Pentecost (the day of firstfruits in the Jewish ceremonial calendar). In this regard, note that John 20:23 echoes Matthew 16:19, connected there with the promise of Jesus that he will build his church (16:18), a promise whose fulfillment begins on Pentecost.

Additionally, there is weight to the observation that in John 20:22, Jesus shows himself to be the giver of the Spirit by virtue of his resurrection, anticipating Paul's description that, as resurrected, he is "the life-giving Spirit" (1 Cor. 15:45, my translation). In this connection, as others have pointed out, the use of "breathed on" (John 20:22) that describes the action of Jesus is striking. This, the only occurrence of the verb (ἐνεφύσησεν) in the New Testament, echoes its use in Genesis 2:7 in describing the creation of Adam and so points to Jesus as the resurrected last Adam and source of the new creation.

Among alternative proposals is the view that John describes the gift of the Spirit to the apostles as the foundation of the church, while Acts relates the gift of the Spirit to the whole church. This view seems less plausible. According to Luke-Acts, the apostles were waiting with the rest of the church for the Spirit to come on Pentecost. Also, in John, Thomas, an apostle, was missing, and while the other apostles were no doubt central in what took place, other disciples who were not apostles were likely present.

Another view is that the breathing of Jesus on the disciples in John was purely symbolic, a prophetic action for what was to take place on Pentecost. This might seem plausible initially. But it is difficult not to conclude from the text that an actual communication of the Spirit is involved.

There is no warrant for seeing the relationship between these two passages, as do some Pentecostals, as providing the basis and model for a "second blessing" reception of the Spirit by some in the subsequent life of the church. On the assumption, not to be doubted, that the disciples present in John 20:22 and at Pentecost were already previously regenerated by the Spirit (cf. John 6:68–69), this view would make what took place for them at Pentecost to amount to a "third blessing" of the Spirit.

To reiterate a point I have already made, these events to do not serve as a model for an experience of the Spirit to be replicated in the lives of believers subsequently throughout church history. Rather, they are part of the epoch-crossing experience, unique to those who were living when the death and resurrection of Christ occurred and who were a part of the first, foundational generation of the church.

THE HISTORICAL RELIABILITY OF ACTS

Perceptions of Acts

Historical-critical interpretation of Acts has concluded that—to a greater or lesser degree, depending on the individual interpreter—Acts is not a historically reliable account of the events it describes.

Developments leading to this conclusion began to emerge increasingly in the latter part of the eighteenth century as the opinion began to be voiced that the conventional way of viewing Acts is too simple and unreflecting. According to this traditional view, Acts is the first church history. It chronicles the church in its foundational, apostolic era and is an authentic presentation, a reliable record, of the earliest Christianity.

However, the conviction began to grow that Acts is not to be viewed as a chronicle of church history, that it is not even really an "Acts of the Apostles" in the sense of a history of all the apostles, and that it deals to any extent with only two (Peter and Paul) and even then hardly provides a complete picture of their work. In short, especially those working with the recently emergent historical-critical method, driven by presuppositions calling into question the inspiration and final authority of Scripture and calling for the rational autonomy of the interpreter, became impressed with what they perceive to be the incomplete and fragmentary character of Acts, when Acts is judged by modern standards of sound historiography.

For this perceived state of affairs, basically two alternative lines of explanation suggested themselves: The author—whether or not Luke— either *would* not (did not want to) say more than he did or, alternatively, *could* not say more than he did. In other words, it has been maintained, the fragmentary nature of Acts is to be explained by limitations placed on the author either by himself, voluntarily, in terms of his purposes and interests, or involuntarily by the insufficient sources that were available to him. Neither of these approaches excludes the other, and a survey of the variety of positions taken on Acts down to the present will show that they are often combined.

Luke's Concern for Historical Truth

In assessing developments in the history of the interpretation of Acts, the following should be noted.

First, the title "The Acts of the Apostles" is not part of the text penned by Luke. To be sure, in its variant forms, it is quite ancient and became a fixed designation at an early point. The earliest extant list of New Testament books, The Muratorian Canon (late second century), has "The Acts of All the Apostles" (*Acta . . . omnium apostolorum*), and the earliest list of the twenty-seven book New Testament canon, the Easter Letter of Athanasius in 367, has what has become the standard title, "The Acts of the Apostles" (Πράξεις Ἀποστόλων).

This title reflects the response of the church; it is not a canonical given. It is not Luke's but the church's assessment of the document and, though early, should not constrain interpretation of part 2 to Theophilus.

Second, it is not accurate to maintain that in the premodern or "precritical" era there was no awareness of the issues that have subsequently concerned those taking a historical-critical approach, that in this period, without exception, the author of Acts was viewed simply as a chronicler of the earliest history of Christianity. Rather, in the works of Calvin (1552–1554), Bengel (1742), and others, though not emphasized or dwelt upon, there is a recognition of matters that subsequently occupied the study of Acts, for instance, that the historical accounts in Acts are selective and partial in nature, that theological themes and motives are observable in the composition of Acts, and that the speeches are not necessarily verbatim reports of what was said.[1]

Where these earlier commentators do differ from most subsequent critical interpreters is in their conviction that however limited its scope or theological its design, Acts presents an accurate, historically reliable account of the early church.

Third, it is certainly the case that Luke knew a great deal more about the matters he deals with in Acts than he reports. Further, as our own work has shown, doctrinal purposes shape what he wrote, and apologetic interests govern his selection of material. From this state of affairs, however, the conclusion almost invariably drawn by historical-critical scholarship does not follow—namely, that to the extent Acts displays doctrinal interests or an apologetic *Tendenz*, it is historically unreliable. The explanation for this

---

1   This observation is based on W. W. Gasque, "The Historical Value of the Book of Acts," *Evangelical Quarterly* 41 (1969): 67–88.

well-nigh universal conclusion, polarizing history and theology, is rooted in its critical presuppositions and commitments rather than in anything in the subject matter of Acts.

Fourth, with all the variations and fluctuations in viewpoints that mark historical-critical interpretation from its inception in the late Enlightenment to the present, there is one pervasive constant: Acts, for the most part, is historically unreliable. This means, then, that the course of criticism amounts to one long and continuing rejection of Luke's own claim in Luke 1:1-4, or at least fails to take that claim seriously.

> Since many have undertaken to compile a narrative of the things that have been fulfilled among us, just as those who from the beginning were eyewitnesses and ministers of the word have delivered them to us, it seemed good to me also, having followed everything closely from the beginning, to write an orderly account to you, most excellent Theophilus, that you may have certainty concerning the things you have been taught. (my translation)

Whether or not a direct literary connection exists between this prologue to the third Gospel and Acts (it likely does), a close connection between the two is undeniable; part 2 to Theophilus is plainly a continuation of what was begun in part 1 (cf. the wording in Acts 1:1). The prologue, then, provides an at least indirect indication of Luke's procedure in Acts; it puts Acts in the same "ballpark" of literary endeavor. Taking the following aspects of that endeavor into consideration is essential for properly interpreting Acts.

Luke 1:1 indicates the setting or context. At hand for Luke were the efforts of others, in fact "many," to provide an account of what had occurred "among us"—that is, to narrate events of the recent past.

Luke 1:2 gives the basis of Luke's own narrative. It rests on the testimony handed down by those who were involved in and observed these events at the time they occurred. "Those who from the beginning were eyewitnesses and ministers of the word" is plausibly read as including the apostles (cf. Acts 1:21-22; Heb. 2:3). In other words, Luke used reliable tradition about what occurred, tradition that was both oral and written.

Luke 1:3 shows the procedure Luke followed. His investigation (1) was done "carefully," (2) took into consideration "everything," (3) did so "from the beginning," and (4) all in order to provide "an orderly account"[2] of the events in question. In other words, his use of the sources and traditions concerning these events was both careful and comprehensive.

Luke 1:4, finally, states Luke's purpose. It is that his reader might have "certainty." Certainty in this instance plainly has to do with the accuracy of information communicated, the full truthfulness of what had been "taught," teaching that dealt with what had recently been "fulfilled" or taken place (1:1).

All told, the prologue to his Gospel highlights Luke's concern for historical truth; factual certainty is a paramount objective for him. Luke-Acts is not a disinterested, neutral chronicle. It, like the rest of Scripture, is undoubtedly theologically and apologetically driven so that readers "may believe that Jesus is the Christ, the Son of God, and that by believing . . . may have life in his name" (John 20:31). But precisely to that end Luke is intent on providing a reliable, entirely trustworthy historical account of the events he reports. Any study of Acts that questions or slights that intention and, more importantly, its successful realization will be correspondingly impoverished.

2　This "order" is not always chronological, nor is Luke claiming that it is. The adverb used (κα-θεξῆς) need not be taken as having an exclusively temporal sense; it can refer to other kinds of order, logical or topical.

PART 2

THE THEOLOGY OF PAUL

6

Preliminary Remarks

FUNDAMENTAL CONSIDERATIONS

This chapter begins our consideration of the theology or teaching of Paul. Two aspects or sides of this objective ought immediately to be highlighted. These are fundamental considerations that apply to all of the biblical authors and so need to be kept in mind when our concern is with Paul. They can be highlighted here by reflecting on what Paul himself observes about the reception of his preaching and teaching by the church in Thessalonica. He says, with thanksgiving to God, "that when you received the word of God, which you heard from us, you accepted it not as the word of men but as what it really is, the word of God" (1 Thess. 2:13).

Paul's Teaching Is *God's* Word

This statement looks back to when he was present and speaking with them. But there is no good reason not to see it as applicable to what he wrote as well as to what he spoke. Later he wrote to the same Thessalonians, urging them to "stand firm and hold to the traditions that you were taught by us, *either by our spoken word or by our letter*" (2 Thess. 2:15). Paul's oral and written teaching are on a par with each other. Both are the word of God.

This above all, then, is true of any sound consideration of the teaching of Paul: that it is received, first of all and finally, as the word of God. Our interest in the letters of Paul is because they are Scripture, inscripturated revelation. In the strictest sense of the word, they are the words of God, because they have God, not Paul, as their primary author.

Our ultimate interest in our focus on Paul, then, is not Paul. We are not primarily interested in either his religious experience, although from every indication that was deep and exemplary, or his theological genius as such, although we are bound to recognize that it was, in fact, profound. Rather, in a word, our interest is Paul the *apostle*. Our focus is on his role in the history of special revelation as that role was an aspect of his unique ministry to the church as ἀπόστολος Χριστοῦ 'Ιησοῦ, an apostle of Christ Jesus.

It should be quite clear, then, that my making this point at the outset is not merely a matter of lip service—as if it is no more than a pious patina that we can strip off, as it were, and forget about as we go about our study of Paul. Rather, the word-of-God character of his teaching is what matters, as he says, "really," "truly" (ἀληθῶς). Recognizing and always keeping that in view in the in-depth study of Paul is a methodological necessity, a non-negotiable *academic* demand.[1]

Paul's Teaching Is *His* Teaching

In 1 Thessalonians 2:13, Paul does not mean to deny that what he taught was *his* teaching. "Not the word of men but . . . the word of God" is hyperbole that serves to highlight what is ultimately true about his teaching. At the same time, in his instrumental role in bringing God's word, he identifies himself as the author of the letter (1 Thess. 1:1), as he does in all his letters. In all of them, the stamp of his person is pronounced. His individual circumstances and aspects of his personality are evident throughout. All this warrants speaking of *Paul's* theology and also prompts the following important biblical-theological observation.

Scripture in its composition is not an amorphous conglomeration of statements. Its unity is not a shapeless uniformity. The history of revelation

---

1   It is worth noting, with an eye to different and opposing views about the nature of Scripture in the modern era (especially since the Enlightenment), that there is no indication in 1 Thess. 2:13 (or anywhere else) that Paul is thinking in terms of a distinction between content and form—as if he is saying, the important thing is that you received the divine content or substance somehow contained or present in my message, despite the fallible and questionable human verbal form in which that message came to you. That introduces a disjunction that he would not recognize. Here, Paul affirms that his teaching is the word of God in both its content and linguistic form. Entailed by this affirmation is a commitment necessary for the sound overall interpretation of Paul.

in its unfolding has a definite shape or profile. These contours are in large part determined by the writings of each of the biblical authors.

Accordingly, the writings of each author, or those writings taken together if there is more than one, as is true for Paul, constitute important contextual units within the Bible as a whole. In terms of the principle of context, so important for sound interpretation, a given verse or a passage ought, first of all, to be understood in the light of other relevant passages from the same writer. A given unit of text ought to be considered within the framework or context provided by the rest of what that writer has written before it is related to relevant passages from other writers.

In this regard, the effort ought to be made to identify the distinctive emphases of each biblical writer. What are the linguistic and conceptual distinctives of each group of writings? What, considered as a whole, are its primary concerns and basic contours? Addressing such questions is particularly important when considering the teaching of Paul because it makes up such a substantial part of the New Testament.

ACTS MATERIAL

Our primary source for Paul's teaching is his thirteen letters. But pertinent material from Acts is to be considered as well.

This decision to include material from Acts as a reliable source for the theology of Paul is not shared by many today. This is especially so among those who take a historical-critical approach. For them, this material is regularly dismissed as having little usefulness in determining his teaching. Depending on the interpreter, the Paul of Acts and the Paul of his letters are deemed to be more or less at odds with each other; the former is said to tell the reader more about the theology of Luke than of Paul.

In my view, such construals are not persuasive or sustainable. There is no conflict between Paul's theology and Luke's. Luke accurately represents Paul's teaching and provides important material for our understanding of it.

THE SIGNIFICANCE OF PAUL'S TEACHING

The dominant place that Paul's letters occupy in the New Testament is obvious. His letters make up approximately 60 percent of the nonnarrative portions of the New Testament (excluding the four Gospels and Acts). No other New Testament writer comes close to Paul in terms of size of contribution, except Luke. About the same quantity of material—the third Gospel and Acts together—is from his pen. But then the latter half of Acts, for the most part, is about Paul and his activity. As an overall perspective on the New Testament, apart from Jesus, Paul is the most dominant figure in the New Testament. As we consider the teaching of the New Testament, Jesus and Paul constitute its central axis.

There is, of course, a danger in accenting this observation unduly; namely, that the other parts of the New Testament get eclipsed. We need to be on guard against the tendency for that to happen. Preaching and teaching should take an overall approach to the New Testament that endeavors to give due attention to these other writings. Still, from a biblical-theological, revelation-historical perspective, how the teaching of Jesus during his earthly ministry—reliably presented in the four Gospels—and the teaching of Paul relate to each other is a key question for understanding the New Testament as a whole.

That there is a considerable quantity from Paul in the makeup of the New Testament is not so significant in itself. What is important is not *how much* he has to say but *what* he has to say, the *material* dominance of Paul's teaching.

In this respect, within the New Testament as a whole, Paul's teaching has a notable prominence, and the nature of that prominence will emerge as we go about exploring something of the basic contours and central themes of his theology. Here I simply assert that material dominance at the outset as more or less self-evident, at least for many readers.

For instance, the experience of many Christians is that it is principally from Paul's letters that they have gotten their understanding of the basic realities of the gospel, of the significance of the death of Christ, and of the forgiveness of sins. Quite rightly, it is often taught that in Romans 1–8, we have the fullest, most extensive single statement of the gospel in the Bible. That emphasis can become a problem if it results in unduly isolating Romans 1–8 within the larger context of Romans, particularly from chapters 9–11. But, while guarding against that sort of sequestration, the heightened gospel significance of Romans 1–8 is apparent.

What is true in the individual experience of many reflects what has taken place more broadly in the history of the church. It is easy to see the great impact that Paul's teaching has had down through the centuries, especially since the Reformation. As an example, in a number of places in systematic theology (dogmatics)—particularly in the area of applied soteriology or redemption applied—in formulating basic doctrines, like justification and sanctification, again and again it is Pauline materials particularly that the church has been drawn to and that have captured its attention in a dominant way. As a fair generalization, we may say that the course of church history since the Reformation is largely unintelligible apart from the impact of Paul's letters, or at least from the way in which those letters have been understood.

THE PROBLEMATIC HISTORY OF PAULINE INTERPRETATION

The prominence of Paul's writings in the New Testament and in the life of the church hardly means, however, that the church has been or is presently characterized by unity in its interpretation of Paul, that there is a uniform or universal consensus on how Paul is to be understood. In fact, the contrary is the case. As it could be put, while virtually everybody appeals to Paul, everybody's Paul does not say the same thing.

As we look from the past down to the present, the history of Pauline interpretation is a history of ups and downs. By the way, this fluctuating history—commensurate with Paul's dominance—serves as about as accurate a barometer as any for understanding the history of the church as a whole, particularly the history of doctrine. How Paul has been understood has regularly been a mirror of how the church and its role in the world have been understood. So our own work should take some account of this lack of consensus and the divergent understandings of Paul there have been and continue to be.

This divergence has led to some rather negative and discouraging assessments. For instance, "No one has ever understood Paul, and the only one who did understand him, Marcion, misunderstood him"![2] "No one has understood Paul if he thinks he can agree with him."[3] For Herman Ridderbos, Paul's recounting of the hardships that marked his ministry in 2 Corinthians

---

2 Franz Overbeck to Adolf von Harnack, reported by Albert Schweitzer, *The Mysticism of Paul the Apostle*, trans. William Montgomery (New York: Holt, 1931), 39n1.

3 Anthony C. Thiselton, *New Horizons in Hermeneutics* (Grand Rapids, MI: Zondervan, 1992), 256. In "today's church, where [Paul] is more honored than heard" (Leander Keck, "Käsemann on Romans," *Interpretation* 36, no. 4 (October 1982): 419.

11:23–26 aptly describe the history of the interpretation of Paul: "countless beatings, and often near death . . . Three times shipwrecked; . . . in danger . . . from my own people, . . . from Gentiles . . . from false brothers"![4]

My point here is not to what extent these and other similar statements that could be cited are accurate. Certainly, the paradoxical pessimism expressed by Overbeck is unwarranted, as is Thiselton's comment without considerable qualification. Still, such assessments do point to an undeniable state of affairs: the problem-laden nature of the history of Pauline interpretation.

In fact, the New Testament itself anticipates this problematic history. This not only shows the antiquity of this history but also and, more importantly, puts it in an explicitly canonical perspective. In view here is Peter's generalization about Paul's letters: "in all his [Paul's] letters" (whatever may have been the specific contents of the Pauline corpus circulating at that time), "there are some things in them that are hard to understand" (2 Pet. 3:16). These things, Peter goes on to add, bringing out the dark side of the picture as a permanent warning to the church, "the ignorant and unstable twist to their own destruction, as they do the other Scriptures."

Notice, pertinent to our earlier point about Paul's theology as God's word, that this statement is New Testament evidence that already at the time 2 Peter was written, Paul's letters as a whole were put on a par with the Old Testament and viewed as Scripture.

Peter's assertion of difficulties encountered in Paul's letters prompts us to ask what constitutes that difficulty. Immediately, all the limitations there are on the side of the interpreter come to mind, including the ignorance, sometimes culpable, and the sinful perversity brought to the text in varying degrees.

But implicit as well in Peter's statement is a consideration distinct from the culpable distortion he mentions: an *inherent* difficulty, a difficulty intrinsic to the subject matter of the text. When we ask about that difficulty, no doubt more than one factor is involved. For instance, according to 1 Corinthians 2:10, in a context where Paul brings into view considerations basic to his ministry as a whole, he says that the revelation granted to him through the Spirit involves "the deep things of God" (NIV), "What no

---

4 Herman Ridderbos, "Terugblik en uitzicht," in *De dertiende apostel en het elfde gebod: Paulus in de loop der eeuwen*, ed. G. C. Berkouwer and H. A. Oberman (Kampen: Kok, 1971), 190.

eye has seen, nor ear heard, / nor the heart of man imagined, / what God has prepared for those who love him" (2:9). As the sublime doxology in Romans 11:33–36 intimates, Paul's theology flows out of, as it is rooted in, the impenetrable depths of God's incomprehensibility.[5]

Two factors, then, combine to explain the problematic history of Pauline interpretation: limitations—ignorance, sometimes sinful, and sinful willfulness—on the side of the interpreter, but also an intrinsic difficulty, a difficulty rooted in the subject matter of the text.

A balancing caveat is in order at this point. Peter's generalization about Paul's letters does not say "*everything* . . . hard to understand." We must keep that in mind, and our own work will show that there is an essential and pervasive clarity to the apostle's teaching. The difficulties encountered do not threaten or impair that clarity. We must avoid being so preoccupied with the former, what is difficult, at the risk of missing or obscuring the latter, what is clear.

The preceding comments about the problems encountered in understanding Paul suggest two areas worth giving some attention to before becoming involved in our own interpretation of his theology: (1) attention to the history of the interpretation of Paul and (2) a more precise identification and clarification of the difficulty inherent in interpreting Paul.

---

5   See also Richard B. Gaffin, *By Faith, Not by Sight: Paul and the Order of Salvation*, 2nd ed. (Phillipsburg, NJ: P&R, 2013), 11–12.

7

Paul and His Interpreters

SURVEYING THE HISTORY of the interpretation of Paul may be done from different angles and in varying depths. The brief survey in this chapter is highly selective and in rather bold—some may think too broad—strokes. It does little more than take note of certain issues and developments that are particularly significant for how Paul's theology has been and is to be treated. For reasons that will soon become clear, the Reformation serves as my primary point of reference. Our survey is done from both positive and negative angles in order to provide a context for our own work that also sets much of its basic direction.[1]

BEFORE THE REFORMATION

We may generalize by taking the first fifteen hundred years of church history in a single bound, as it were. Like most generalizations, this one is inevitably in need of any number of qualifications and amplifications. That needs to be kept in mind. Still, it is permissible to say that over this long period, Paul is read, and often cited and even commented on, but only infrequently is he really understood, and at times it can appear that his influence is virtually nonexistent.

The most notable positive exception of course is Augustine. In view is not only his own work but also the important tradition that builds upon

---

1 For developments up to around 1970, I make considerable use of the survey of Herman Ridderbos, *Paul: An Outline of His Theology*, trans. J. R. de Witt (Grand Rapids, MI: Eerdmans, 1975), part 1 ("Mainlines in the History of Pauline Interpretation").

that work and remains alive over the period up to the Reformation and beyond to the present.

In Augustine and this tradition, we find a clear grasp of basic elements of Paul's anthropology and soteriology, forged in his controversy with Pelagius, particularly Paul's understanding of sin, with its stress on the radical depravity of man, and the sovereignty of God's grace in salvation. With good right, the Reformers—Luther, Calvin, and others—appeal to Augustine in their emphasis on *sola gratia*, grace alone, though the Reformers' understanding of saving grace and Augustine's is not identical. The necessary and crucial correction and clarification the Reformation made concerns how grace is effective particularly for justification. In ongoing debate, then, it is understandable that both Protestants and Roman Catholics appeal to Augustine.

Perhaps the most notable negative exception to the neglect of Paul in this period, glaring but perennially instructive, occurs already in the second century in Marcion (d. 160). He exhibits a peculiar and distorted kind of preoccupation with Paul. That distortion is apparent formally in the canon he created. Rejecting the entire Old Testament and the New Testament canon incipiently recognized and accepted throughout much of the church by this time, his canon consisted of only ten of Paul's letters, excluding the Pastorals, and a version of Luke's Gospel, no longer extant, apparently edited in terms of his understanding of Paul.[2]

The substance of Marcion's misunderstanding is the sharp and sweeping antithesis he made between law and love, rooted in his radically disjunctive notion that the God of the Old Testament, seen as the Creator of the material world, and the God and Father of Jesus Christ, the God of the New Testament, are not the same.

Marcion provides permanent lessons for the church. For one, he serves as a warning against what could be dubbed a one-sided Paulinism, a skewed and imbalanced preoccupation with Paul. His work shows that a tendentious appeal to Paul in support of a distortion of the gospel is by no means an imaginary danger. Already in the third century Tertullian made the pungent comment, largely with an eye toward Marcion

---

2   In denying the Pauline authorship of the Pastorals, Marcion is the first precursor of record in anticipating what has become the standard post-Enlightenment, historical-critical view.

and Gnosticism, that "Paul is *haereticorum apostolus*," "the apostle of heretics."[3]

A further development in this period is noteworthy. In the earliest literature at our disposal, that of the Apostolic Fathers, dating from the end of the first and early second centuries, the eschatological significance of Christ's death and resurrection and the present situation of the church is largely lost sight of. Striking is the fact that an appreciation of the realized or inaugurated eschatology—so central in Paul's teaching as our own work will show—appears to have virtually vanished in such a short passage of time. Why and how that happened will have to remain unexplored here.

THE REFORMATION

In its basic dimensions, the Protestant Reformation may be seen as a rediscovery of Paul. The New Perspective on Paul disputes that, or would agree only with a considerable amount of qualification, but it would certainly not deny that is largely how the Reformation understood itself.

Surely such a discovery was in large measure what Luther felt himself to be doing. All one need do is pick up and read portions of his lectures on Romans or of his commentary on Galatians to appreciate something of the thrill of discovery, at times overwhelming, that Luther experienced. One celebrated evidence is his often-cited comment that he "had entered paradise itself through open gates," prompted by his dawning understanding of the righteousness of God in Romans 1:17 as saving.[4]

Given his historical context, it was inevitable that Luther was captured by the forensic aspect of Paul's teaching, specifically his doctrine of justification as that doctrine is found and developed extensively in Romans 3–5 and Galatians 2–3.

What so burdened Luther and what he was seeking release from was the soteriological legalism and, to a certain extent, the mysticism of Roman Catholicism. So it was Paul's teaching that justification is by faith alone that especially gripped him. He saw an all-too-evident similarity between the Jewish and Judaizing reliance on the works of the law, the works

---

3 Tertullian, *Against Marcion*, in *The Ante-Nicene Fathers*, vol. 3, ed. Alexander Roberts and James Donaldson (Grand Rapids, MI: Eerdmans, 1973), 324.

4 Martin Luther, "Preface to Latin Writings," in *Martin Luther: Selections From His Writings*, ed. John Dillenberger (New York: Anchor Books, 1961), 11.

righteousness, that Paul was opposing and the Roman Catholicism of his own day. And, perceiving that similarity, he saw that Paul's doctrine of a fully gracious justification solely by faith is the answer to both.

The New Perspective on Paul calls into question the validity of this perception of Luther. Suffice it here to say only that it is likely true that Luther's experience should not be read into Paul's experience, particularly his pre-Damascus Road experience, as if Paul underwent the same kind of psychological distress that so burdened Luther. Concerning Paul's pre-Christian psychology, it is best to remain silent or at least cautious, since neither Acts nor his letters disclose enough to enable us to draw fully developed conclusions. We will consider the New Perspective on Paul further later in this chapter.

It might be said that, if anything, Luther was too gripped by Paul. That imbalance is seen in his approach to the New Testament canon, formally akin to Marcion's but for far different reasons. Luther equated his understanding of Paul's doctrine of justification with his use of *was Christum treibet*—"what urges (or 'impels' or 'presses home') Christ"—as a criterion of canonicity. As a result, Hebrews and James are judged as not measuring up to this Christological criterion and are depreciated to a deuterocanonical status. In his translation of the New Testament, they are taken out of the traditional order and printed along with Jude and Revelation at the end as a kind of appendix.

In Calvin, there is nothing like Luther's approach to the New Testament canon. But what needs to be underscored here is their basic and substantial agreement. That is apparent in the conflict with Rome. Calvin stands together with Luther in the dominant place given to Paul's doctrine of justification as key to the gospel. While Calvin is clearer than Luther that justification flows from union with Christ, for Calvin justification by faith is "the main hinge on which religion turns."[5]

Mention of Luther and Calvin, these two major figures of the Reformation, brings into view, as well the tradition flowing directly from it, Protestant orthodoxy. For this tradition, too, it is fair to say, Paul is primarily the preacher of justification by faith. This is a generalization to be sure and so

---

5   John Calvin, *Institutes of the Christian Religion*, ed. John T. McNeill, trans. Ford Lewis Battles (Philadelphia, PA: Wesminster, 1960) 3.11.1 (1:726).

subject to qualification. But as a basic profile, insofar as Paul's teaching was considered as an entity, the tendency was to view his doctrine of justification as central to his teaching as a whole.

This entails a broader perspective, one important for our own work on Paul's theology and that also bears on the large issues raised by the New Perspective on Paul. The tendency of the Reformation tradition, as it may be put, has been to approach Paul in light of the question of the Philippian jailer, "What must I do to be saved?" (Acts 16:30), for which Paul had a ready answer, "Believe in the Lord Jesus, and you will be saved, you and your household" (16:31)—and, by the way, it should not be overlooked, Paul went on to spend time explaining, likely at some length (16:32).

A prevailing tendency of the Reformation tradition, then, has been to approach Paul in terms of the question how the individual sinner comes to experience the saving grace of God, particularly how the guilt of my sin can be removed, how I can receive the free forgiveness of my sin. Or, to put it in a more explicitly Pauline way, how in my life do I come to experience the decisive transition from no longer being a child of wrath (Eph. 2:3) to becoming a child of God, an adopted son delivered from the bondage of fear (Rom. 8:14–16)?

All told, more broadly, the Reformation tradition has read Paul largely for what he has to teach concerning the application of salvation to the individual sinner—or, in more formal theological idiom, concerning the *ordo salutis* and particularly within the order of salvation, the decisive place of justification by faith.

SINCE THE REFORMATION

The period until about the middle of the seventeenth century witnesses the rise and flourishing of Protestant orthodoxy, particularly as the Reformation consolidates and spreads throughout the north of Europe and even beyond to North America and elsewhere, largely through immigration from Great Britain and Holland. However, in the period that follows, over the next hundred years until approximately the middle of the eighteenth century, factors come increasingly into play that have the combined effect of progressively undermining the vitality of the Reformation.

Among these factors, two especially influence the understanding of Paul: pietism and rationalism. Pietism, understood here in a church-historical sense, was a development, beginning in Germany within the churches of the Reformation, especially Lutheran churches. It can be fairly seen largely as a reaction movement to what was felt to be the dead orthodoxy of these confessional churches.

Leaving to the side here to what extent that charge is true, what marks this pietism is its pronounced stress on Christian experience in the sense of what takes place in the inner life of the believer. The effect of this absorption with experience was that the focus tended to drift away from Christ's work for me in the past and onto Christ's work in me now, presently. Whether or not intentionally, this stress on the experience of being a Christian happened in ways that tended to eclipse the finished sufficiency of Christ's work in his death and resurrection—what was at the heart of the Reformation's recapture of Paul.

Along with this pietistic focus on experience is the rationalism that during this time increasingly surfaced in the life and theology of the Protestant churches. To speak of rationalism raises a large and many-sided issue. For our purposes here, this rationalistic tendency, seen globally, is a legacy of the Renaissance, of the recovery and influence of the classical pagan tradition that occurs in the centuries just prior to the Reformation. Along with the Reformation, the Renaissance confronted the domination of medieval Roman Catholic Christendom.

However, given if nothing else the Reformation's Scripture alone principle, this alliance in opposition to Rome was always at best an uneasy one. Already at the time of the Reformation, that tension is focused instructively in the conflict between Luther and Erasmus on important points, especially on the bondage or freedom of the human will as fallen.

That conflict, in its basic dimensions, has its eventual and inevitable outworking in the sharp separation between Reformation and Renaissance that subsequently becomes apparent in the open and aggressive commitment of the Enlightenment, as the heir of the Renaissance, to the autonomy of human reason. This autonomy commitment engulfs wide stretches of the Protestant church by the late eighteenth century but is increasingly at work already a century or so earlier.

What is particularly pertinent here about this rationalism is its pronounced moralistic tendency. Rationalism and pietism, then, despite real differences between them, had a common effect. Together they fostered moralism and mysticism—the combination that Luther struggled against. Their resulting influence was a stress on human effort and moral accomplishment that brought about a shift in the center of gravity of interest in Paul.

This shift consists in moving away from the forensic aspects of his teaching to its ethical or transformative aspects. In other words, what took place was a shift away from the Reformation's focus on the free, unmerited forgiveness of sins and the graciously imputed righteousness of Christ. Instead, as already noted above, the emphasis now falls on those passages where Paul speaks about the Holy Spirit and his work in the Christian. The activity of the believer and, correspondingly, the imperatives of the Christian life are increasingly accented. These are now judged to be what is central, even basic, for Paul.

As I have already indicated, the full outworking of this shift takes place in the context of the late Enlightenment and the increasing influence of rationalism, developments that we will take note of below. But for now, with an eye to our own work, these developments have had the effect of highlighting a fundamental issue for understanding Paul and, in doing that, more broadly for the soteriology of the church, since the teaching of Paul figures so prominently in that area of doctrine. That issue is the relationship in the application of salvation (*ordo salutis*) between what is definitive and completed, and what is ongoing and incomplete—in terms of key doctrines, the relationship between justification and sanctification.

To be sure, it is not as if the Reformation was not alert to that question. In my judgment, book 3 of Calvin's *Institutes*, chapters 1–19, for instance, has some of the best and most enduring discussion concerning that relationship.[6] But subsequent developments made that a prominent question for understanding Paul.

Subsequently, as the teaching of Paul came increasingly to be considered as a distinct entity, this question was formulated in terms of two basic lines identified in his teaching on salvation, often with each held to be more or less independent from the other and complete in itself: one line with a forensic focus, the other with a transformative or renovative emphasis.

---

6   See in particular the summary statement of the relationship between the "double grace" (*duplex gratia*) of justification and sanctification (which he calls "regeneration") in the first section of chapter 11.

Further, seen to be central in each line is righteousness (δικαιοσύνη); along both lines, the driving concern is the acquisition and expression of righteousness.

This inevitably prompted the question of the relationship of these two lines and their relative importance: How in the life of the believer does Paul relate the forensic and the transformative, justification and sanctification, imputed righteousness and inwrought righteousness?

On the assumption that these two lines are not virtually independent of each other and so at odds with each other—as some historical-critical interpretation of Paul has argued—there is a positive relationship between them. As our own work will show, requisite, in order to be true to Paul, is to maintain the forensic (justification) in a way that does not allow it to be undermined by making the transformative, the renewal that takes place in the believer, somehow the basis for justification, yet at the same time without viewing the renovative (sanctification) as secondary or nonessential or even dispensable in salvation. In other words, balance is called for: to maintain the integral place of both the forensic and the renovative, properly understood, in a way that does not eclipse or compromise one or the other.

That balance has often been lacking in the interpretation of Paul. The tendency, in one way or another, has been to suppress or ignore one line or to reduce it to the other.

In that regard, by far the predominant tendency has been to stress the renovative—the transformation that takes place in the believer and the resulting activity of the believer—at the expense of the forensic. In view here are all views that put the stress in salvation on what human beings contribute by their own unaided efforts or by those efforts cooperating with God's grace.

This occurs most often where interpreters approach Paul with views about the sinner's ability and freedom of the will that, in terms of historical precedent, may be fairly characterized either as Pelagian or semi-Pelagian. Such views hold that ability is the measure of responsibility. Responsibility before God is understood either in terms of the unimpaired ability, the freedom of the will, that human beings have (the Pelagian view), or as that ability or freedom, seen as impaired by sin but still viable, is aided or supplemented by God (the semi-Pelagian view). In other words, in this view, God does not expect anything more from me than what I am able to achieve either of myself or by his assisting my own willing efforts.[7]

The classic example of this way of reading Paul is reflected in the Roman Catholic doctrine of justification that was formulated already at the Council of Trent (1547) in opposition to the Reformation and continues to the present to influence much Catholic interpretation of Paul. On this reading, the difference between justification and sanctification is blurred, and the two are merged such that justification is suspended on a process of sanctification; in this sense, justification is equated with sanctification.

In this view, which denies that Paul teaches the definitive imputation of Christ's righteousness, justification is seen rather as a continuing process, in which infused righteousness becomes the basis for justification. Justifying righteousness is what the sinner merits by the ongoing use of the sacramental system of the Church, especially the mass and penance. This view does not so much deny the forensic character of justification as undermine its unmerited graciousness by suspending it on a continuing process of infusing grace in the sinner. In this way, Paul's understanding of justification is eclipsed.

While the depreciation or distortion of the forensic results in soteriological legalism (salvation by works), the imbalanced stress in the opposite direction—on the forensic at the expense of the transformative or renovative—leads to antinomianism, whether in quietistic forms or indifference to holy living.[8]

---

7   Variously attributed (to Charles Hodge, for one) is the statement "I don't so much fear the ghost of Pelagius as the ghost of Semi-Pelagius"! In view is the notion that became dominant in late-medieval Roman Catholicism and underlies its doctrine of justification: "to the one who does what is in himself God does not deny grace" (e.g., Gabriel Biel)—a variant of "God helps those who help themselves."

    In opposition, the Reformation tradition, based on its biblical understanding of the radical depravity of human sinfulness, holds that in the sinner's relationship to God, ability is *not* the measure of responsibility. Rather, in their total *inability* sinners are unable to meet their *responsibility* before God. Where this inability as total is not acknowledged (usually in the interests of maintaining some measure of free will despite the fall), the "alone" in the Reformation's *sola gratia* is not understood and effectively denied.

8   The most extreme instance I have come across related to the study of Paul is what has been called Neo-Kohlbruggianism. Hermann Freidrich Kohlbrugge (1803-1875) was an important figure in his day in resolutely opposing the rising tide of moralistic Christianity. Under his influence, others, particularly his son-in-law, Eduard Böhl, pushed beyond Kohlbrugge's defense of the forensic to the point of maintaining that all human beings, including believers, are completely

In this connection, it could be observed that a continuing character-istic of the Reformation tradition, perhaps more so in the Lutheran and free church evangelical traditions than in the Reformed tradition, is the failure to emphasize adequately the integral place of sanctification in salvation, which raises this question: Is that only a practical shortcoming or oversight, or are there considerations bound up with the formulation of doctrine that explain that failure? This question will occupy us in our own work.

One takeaway from looking at how Paul was understood in the period following the Reformation is that a careful study of Paul has to keep these questions in mind: What is the relationship between justification and sanctification? How does Paul maintain the due place of each? Or as the question may be put in terms of righteousness (δικαιοσύνη), How, for the apostle, are imputed righteousness and imparted or inwrought righteous-ness related?

HISTORICAL-CRITICAL INTERPRETATION

In large part, the scholarly study of Paul's letters as a distinct unit has unfolded within the so-called historical-critical tradition, the method of interpreting texts that becomes dominant by the late-eighteenth century as an outworking of the Enlightenment with its commitment to the autonomy of human reason.[9] One important factor determining this method is the historical consciousness that emerges with the Enlightenment. Specifically, this consciousness was marked by a sense of historical distance between the perceived superior modernity of the interpreter's present and earlier less enlightened and unenlightened times, including texts from the past like the Bible.

In biblical studies, this historical consciousness—the interpreter's sense of detachment, even disaffection for some, from the past, especially the distant past—is what gave rise to the call for "biblical theology." It is in this late Enlightenment, historical-critical context that the expression begins to be used for the first time, at least with any frequency, and eventually

---

and entirely sinful flesh. Justification was stressed to the extreme of denying that in this life the believer experiences sanctification, ongoing personal renovation and renewal.

9   On the basic commitments of the historical-critical method in its approach to Scripture, see the description in this book's introduction, footnote 2.

gains widespread currency.[10] The aim of this biblical theology was a study and presentation of the teaching of the Bible in terms of the distinctive and historically situated contributions of each of the biblical writers.

This aim expresses a formally correct insight, sound in itself. However, what perverts its execution from the outset is that this call for biblical theology is inseparable from a denial of the inspiration and canonicity of the Bible. The biblical theology sponsored by the Enlightenment goes hand in glove with a rejection of the divine origin and authorship of the Bible, a denial that God is the primary author of Scripture as a whole and of the individual documents that constitute that whole. The "enlightened" demand is for the Bible to be treated like any other book and to recognize that its various documents are of purely human origin, so that the presence of errors and contradiction among various writers or even within a given writer is a necessary methodological presumption.

In terms of the distinction that Paul makes in 1 Thessalonians 2:13, discussed above, we may say that biblical theology in the historical-critical tradition focuses on the "word of men" character of Paul and the other biblical writers such that the "word of God" character of their writings is eclipsed, distorted, or even denied. On this view, biblical theology is seen as a purely descriptive historical discipline, with no inherent or necessary normative value. Dogmatic or systematic theology, in distinction, has the task of providing a statement for contemporary Christian faith (cf. the title of Gabler's lecture), determined as often as not by what the philosophy of the day in vogue dictates.

This necessarily negative assessment in principle of historical-critical biblical theology is not meant to deny the often-careful attention to the text of those who take this approach and the resulting value of reading and studying numerous works produced. In what follows here, however, my primary purpose is not to note such valid viewpoints but rather to provide a survey that makes readers aware of the basic thrust of the major and most

---

10 Often cited from this period for the considerable influence it had is the 1787 programmatic address (in Latin) of J. P. Gabler, "On the Correct Distinction Between Dogmatic and Biblical Theology and the Right Definition of Their Goals." For a full English translation, see John Sandys-Wunsch and Laurence Eldredge, "J. P. Gabler and the Distinction between Biblical and Dogmatic Theology: Translation, Commentary, and Discussion of His Originality," *Scottish Journal of Theology* 33 (1980): 133–44. The expression "biblical theology" apparently occurs for the first time, though sporadically, earlier in the century within Lutheran pietism.

influential views of Paul's theology that have emerged in the historical-critical tradition in the last two hundred years or so.[11]

F. C. Baur and the Tübingen School

Ferdinand Christian Baur (1792–1860) has the distinction of being the first to write a theology of Paul (1845, *Paul, The Apostle of Jesus Christ*; English translation 1876). Baur is best known for his highly influential views on the origin and nature of Acts, giving rise to the so-called Tübingen School dominant in the historical-critical tradition through roughly the middle third of the nineteenth century, with a waning but in many respects enduring influence beyond.

In terms of the distinction made between the two lines in Paul's teaching noted in the preceding section, Baur's reading is characteristic of the way developments subsequently unfold in the historical-critical tradition: the focus is regularly on the line having to do with renovation or transformation, the non-forensic, on what takes place within the Christian; the forensic line is minimized or discounted in various ways as not most true to Paul's real intention and interests.

Baur's assessment of Paul, as well as of Acts, is through the lens of the philosophy of G. W. F. Hegel (1770-1831), particularly the historical dialectic (thesis-antithesis-synthesis) of Hegelian idealism. Accordingly and hardly surprisingly, Baur finds that central in Paul is his teaching on the Spirit and the closely associated antithesis between the Spirit and flesh, found particularly in Romans 8 and Galatians 5.

Reading Paul through the grid of Hegelian philosophy results in a fundamental misunderstanding of Paul. The Spirit is not seen, as Paul does, as the person of the Holy Spirit, who while immanent and active within history and creation is at the same time transcendent over creation and all that transpires in history.

Instead, Paul's statements are misconstrued in the Hegelian sense of spirit (*Geist* in German): spirit is the absolute seen as totally immanent in history,

---

11 I proceed in this largely descriptive manner convinced that for those who do not share its un-biblical commitments and rationalistic procedures, diagnosis of the true intent of criticism is the best prophylaxis ("To have correctly diagnosed criticism in its true [rationalistic] purpose is to possess the best prophylaxis against it"; Geerhardus Vos, *Biblical Theology: Old and New Testaments* [Edinburgh: Banner of Truth Trust, 1975], 17).

the infinite or universal that exists only in the finite particulars of history, the divine that *is* only in its *becoming* in the unfolding process of history.[12]

Accordingly, for Baur, the spirit-flesh antithesis is not, as it is for Paul, between the Holy Spirit and flesh as the sinful nature of human beings. Rather, that antithesis expresses the dialectic in history between absolute and relative, universal and particular, infinite and finite. This dialectical interplay and tension gives history its meaning as the manifestation of the absolute in the unfolding historical process; the ongoing process of history is the self-realization of *Geist*.

The pantheism, or panentheism, of this view is apparent. The various themes in Paul's teaching—for example, the indwelling of the Spirit, freedom in the Spirit, and reconciliation, whether between God and man or Jew and Gentile—are all read through the lens of this view: the essential oneness (*Gottmenschheit*) of God and human beings, the mediation of absolute spirit through human consciousness.

Paul's Christianity, as Baur understands it and also wants to identify with, is a stage in the development of religion on the basis of a principle immanent in human beings. This is what makes Christianity the absolute religion, the religion of *Geist*, because what Christianity offers the world is recognition of the advance of the spirit to the freedom of self-consciousness within human beings.

In this recasting of Paul's theology, Baur sees considerable continuity between it and the teaching of Jesus, in contrast to the Christianity of the original apostles, who are seen as still too locked into their Jewish particularism and as failing to pick up on the universalizing tendencies already advocated by Jesus and further spelled out in Paul.

Older Liberal Interpretation

In terms of broader philosophical developments, moving on toward the latter part of the nineteenth and into the twentieth centuries, Hegel's speculative, metaphysically oriented idealism, dominant earlier in the nineteenth century, gave way increasingly to an ethical idealism. This occurred

---

12 Note that on this construction, the divine can never be identified exclusively with any single historical particular, with any one person or event in history. This excludes the uniqueness of the incarnation, of God become man exclusively in the person of Jesus, as taught by Jesus, Paul, and the other New Testament writers.

primarily through a renewed influence of the philosophy of Kant, with a less speculative and more dualistic orientation. One outworking of this neo-Kantian revival is seen in theological Liberalism.[13] Its interpretation of Paul proved much more influential and enduring than that of Baur.

As we noted briefly in chapter 2, this older Liberalism is convinced that Jesus was a remarkably precocious individual, well ahead of his time as an advocate in advance, as it were, of Neo-Kantian morality. It sought to show that in his teaching, and his actions consistent with that teaching, Jesus's true concern was a rationally derived morality, the universal values of an ethical idealism, focused primarily in his emphasis on the fatherhood of God and the brotherhood of man. The accent of this Liberalism is on the timeless, abiding moral truths identifiable in the proclamation of Jesus that can be made directly applicable to modern man and relevant for contemporary Christianity.

With this understanding of Jesus, Liberal interpretation of Paul undertakes to mold him according to its image of Jesus. This proved difficult to do, for it involved concluding that there is a fundamental inconsistency in Paul, a basic internal contradiction in the structure of his teaching.

Picking up on the traditional debate concerning the relationship between justification and sanctification in Paul, Liberalism maintains that there are two basic lines or strands of teaching in Paul—most often designated as the mystical-ethical and the juridical—but then with the emphasis that these two lines are contradictory. In more or less deliberate, self-conscious opposition to the Reformation, Liberalism sees the former, the mystical-ethical line, as best expressing, though imperfectly, Paul's true concerns, his real interest.

Like Baur but with a characteristic difference, Liberalism finds the key to Paul in the concept of spirit. This is seen to be at the heart of the

---

13 In assessing historical-critical treatments of the Synoptic Gospels prior to and around 1960, Ned B. Stonehouse spoke of "what may with very little exaggeration be characterized as the persistence of Liberalism" (*Origins of the Synoptic Gospels. Some Basic Questions* [Grand Rapids, MI: Eerdmans, 1963], 154). This observation is made concerning the widespread and continuing tendency within historical-critical scholarship, despite considerable differences in successive and ever-changing approaches to interpreting Scripture, either to advocate or otherwise offer support for contemporary Christianity as self-help moralism in one form or another. The truth of Stonehouse's observation concerning this persisting moralistic tendency will be borne out as this survey continues. I capitalize "Liberal(ism)" in this section to distinguish from subsequent liberal approaches to Paul.

mystical-ethical line of his teaching. Unlike Baur, however, the background is not speculative metaphysics but the pagan Hellenistic anthropology of the first-century Mediterranean world. Within that context, for Paul, the contrast between flesh and spirit is not primarily, as it was for Baur, the contrast between the absolute and relative, the infinite and finite, but rather a contrast within the makeup of human beings. On the one hand, flesh is seen as our lower, sensuous nature; spirit, on the other hand, is our higher, rational nature, the principle that strives to keep the flesh in check.

This view of spirit in Paul is thoroughly anthropological. It is not too difficult to see, then, how it serves the overall outlook of Liberalism, as it may be fairly put, that salvation is by ethics. Salvation is the moral betterment capable of being achieved by the dominance of the human spirit, by self-discipline and self-improvement through the influence of the higher ethical impulse in human beings.

H. J. Holtzmann

The lengthy treatment in the section on Paul in the two-volume work on the theology of the New Testament (1911, *Lehrbuch der neutestamentlichen Theologie*, 2) by Holtzmann (1832–1910) provides a classic statement of this Liberal understanding of Paul. Basic is the distinction between the *religion* of Paul and the *theology* of Paul.

In fact, what Holtzmann finds in Paul is a disjunction between his religion and theology: his letters contain a confused conglomeration of conceptions—ethical emphases, on the one hand, and juridical emphases, on the other; a realistic eschatology focused in the resurrection of the body, here, and the release of the soul from the body as a prison house, there; throughout are metaphysical speculations about Christ, including his preexistent deity. Paul's teaching is seen as a remarkable incorporation of various Jewish and Hellenistic viewpoints, resulting in all sorts of antinomies and internal contradictions. This gives Pauline theology its distinguishing character.

However, for Holtzmann, the key to understanding Paul is not his confused theology but his peerless religious experience beginning on the Damascus road. This experience consisted in recognizing and rejecting his Pharisaical pride and Jewish particularism, replaced by a love for and sense of brotherhood with all human beings in light of his newfound understanding that the love of God is universal. If one takes Paul's statements at face value, it is impossible to discover a coherent unity. But if one has an eye for the religious genius and profound religious experience seeking to find expression in them, then the whole of his teaching becomes intelligible.

Paul's theology is the (largely unsuccessful) projection or objectification of his religious experience. In terms of this distinction between his theology and his religion, Holtzmann seeks to account for Paul's Christological and eschatological views and yet at the same time show him to be at heart an exponent of a rational, idealistic religiosity in agreement with the Liberal conception of Jesus.

The Waning of the Older Liberal Interpretation

During the late nineteenth and early twentieth centuries, developments in historical-critical interpretation gave rise to the so-called History of Religions School (which was not so much a school as an orientation or methodology). Its agenda was what it considered a consistent historical explanation of the New Testament, which it found lacking in the Liberal approach. It was occupied largely in the radical undertaking of seeking to show that in its origin and content, the Christianity found in the New Testament is to be explained almost exhaustively within its immediate historical context—that is, in terms of factors already resident in the existing culture and religions of the first-century Mediterranean world. Its tendency was to argue that there is little unique or new in the teaching of the New Testament, that the New Testament is largely an amalgam of elements appropriated from its largely pagan environment.

Wilhelm Wrede

The influence of this approach, calling for a more radical or at least more consistent historical approach, led increasingly to a recognition that the Liberal conception of Paul's theology is not sustainable. This can be seen in the short study, *Paulus* (1907) by Wrede (1859–1906), a work that proved to have a considerable impact.

Wrede's basic thesis is simple and easy enough to establish: Paul's theology is his religion. In other words, Wrede breaks with Liberalism's distinction in Paul between an outer husk of theological conceptions at odds with an inner core of religious conviction and experience. Rather, Wrede argues, Paul's theology is an adequate expression of his religion. The preexistent, incarnate, and exalted Christ, the Son of God about whom Paul writes and speculates—this is the Jesus Paul worships and serves.

For Wrede, the heart of Paul's theology is his Christology, his explication of Christ's person and work, and the foundation of his religion is the redemptive accomplishment that takes place in the incarnation, death, and resurrection of Christ. The backbone of Paul's conception of Christianity is the historical character of redemption; his religion is a religion of redemption, supernaturally wrought in history. When this is recognized, Wrede maintains—and this can only be read with a certain degree of poignancy by someone standing outside the historical-critical tradition—everything in Paul fits together. There are no basic contradictions, no gaping antinomies.

However, for Wrede the history of redemption at the heart of Paul's theology is a myth. For instance, he recognizes that fundamental for Paul was the historicity of the bodily resurrection of Jesus, but that resurrection never took place.

Further, as part of a larger developing picture, Wrede and many who became convinced about what may be fairly characterized as his redemptive-historical assessment of Paul, remained committed theological Liberals personally; they continued holding to the Liberal conception of Jesus. This contributed to a large-scale upheaval in New Testament studies as a whole, to developments that are front and center beginning around 1910 and continuing to the mid-century and beyond, even to the present in some quarters.

The Jesus-Paul Controversy

Early on among these developments, pertinent to our survey, is this controversy, with the central point at issue the growing conviction among historical-critical interpreters that there is a fundamental religious and theological cleavage within the New Testament, especially between Jesus and Paul.

Earlier critical interpretation (Baur, Liberalism) sought to show, albeit in different ways: (1) that there is an essential harmony between the religion of Jesus and the religion of Paul and (2) that this religion was compatible with the ethical idealism of modern Protestant Christianity. Now, it is maintained, if we follow Wrede in his convincing assessment of Paul, then we must recognize the fundamental religious and theological discord there is within the New Testament, discord for which Paul is largely responsible.

Paul is now seen, as it was put, as the second founder of Christianity in the sense that he is the perverter of the teaching of Jesus. Paul is said to have transformed the simple, down-to-earth morality of Jesus of Nazareth into alien speculation about a heavenly Christ and cosmic eschatology. In doing this—an implication that was drawn—Paul, not Jesus, is the real founder of traditional orthodox Christianity, particularly of the ecumenical creeds.

Several slogans that emerged and began circulating capture the tenor of this development: Paul turns the religion of Jesus into the religion about Jesus. Jesus preached the kingdom, Paul preached Christ. At a later point in a different context: "The proclaimer became the proclaimed."[14] The Jesus-Paul controversy begins as a kind of back-to-Jesus movement, as an effort to preserve the Liberal conception of Jesus in light of the increasingly persuasive assessment of Paul advanced by Wrede.

As we move on to the middle of the twentieth century, this controversy unfolds and then softens in what is fairly predictable historical-critical fashion. Groundbreaking developments in the study of the Gospels proved decisive.

Especially influential, for one, is the so-called consistent eschatology assessment of Jesus's kingdom proclamation, initially advanced by Johannes Weiss (1863–1914) and Albert Schweitzer (1875–1965). They argued that, far from being Liberalism's paragon proponent of timeless morality, Jesus was an apocalyptic visionary who died expecting the cataclysmic end of the world in the near future. In this view, Jesus is no more capable of being modernized or made a Liberal than, as Wrede argues, Paul is.[15]

In other words, the contradiction between Paul and Jesus created by the historical-critical tradition is now eliminated. But that elimination comes at a cost. Now Jesus, like Paul, is no longer serviceable to modern theology, to contemporary theology after Kant, as the Liberal interpretation was intent on trying to show. Criticism first gives up on modernizing Paul (Wrede), then on modernizing Jesus (consistent eschatology). The result is to make

---

14 Rudolf Bultmann, *Theology of the New Testament*, trans. Kendrick Grobel (New York: Charles Scribner's Sons, 1951) 1:33.

15 Weiss's work on the kingdom in Jesus (1892, *Die Predigt Jesu vom Reiche Gottes*; English translation: *Jesus' Proclamation of the Kingdom of God*, 1971) antedates Wrede's on Paul (1907). But the latter takes hold more quickly than the consistent eschatology of the former. Those with a Liberal conception of Jesus, it appears, had more at stake and so a greater resistance in having to abandon modernizing Jesus rather than Paul.

Jesus as well as Paul irrelevant, not more or less relevant for contemporary Christianity.[16]

1930–1980 and Beyond

In the wake of Wrede's work, historical-critical interpretation, with its controlling presuppositions, is marked by various efforts to explain Paul's theology within his immediate historical context. As major works have their influence—like that of Schweitzer, *The Mysticism of Paul the Apostle* (1931), the section on Paul in the *New Testament Theology* (1953) of Rudolf Bultmann (1884–1976), and others—the eventual result is fairly widespread recognition that a redemptive-historical framework, as Wrede showed, is basic in Paul's teaching. A critical consensus forms that central for Paul is his eschatological orientation, his view that the new creation has begun, inaugurated by the death and resurrection of Jesus, and will be consummated by his return in the near future. A recognition that this basic already-not-yet eschatological outlook structures Paul's teaching (as well as Jesus's kingdom proclamation) becomes more and more predominant.

However, this historical-critical consensus concerning the redemptive-historical content of Paul's theology is a purely historical assessment. As such, in principle, it does not decide but leaves an open question: What, if anything, is normative about his theology, what is its continuing truth value for contemporary Christianity?

Consequently, from the middle of the twentieth century on, a wide spectrum of viewpoints emerges on this question: How and to what degree is Paul with his redemptive-historical theology relevant or serviceable in today's world? For our purposes here we can note the poles of that spectrum, as seen in the representative works of Oscar Cullmann (1902–1999) at the one, more moderate end, and of Bultmann at the other, radical end.

In *Salvation in History* (1967), for instance, Cullmann argues for a high degree of continuity between Paul's teaching and the outlook of

---

16   Another influential factor insofar as Jesus is concerned is the emergence in the decades after 1920 of form criticism in the study of the Gospels, with its basic conclusion that the Gospel accounts of Jesus and his teaching are heavily overlaid with subsequent unhistorical viewpoints of the post-Easter church. The effect of form criticism in its history-of-traditions approach is to leave a large question mark on the historical Jesus: e.g., the bottom-line conclusion of Bultmann in his *Jesus* (1929) that we can know next to nothing about the actual history of Jesus. As consistent eschatology makes the historical Jesus *irrelevant*, form criticism makes him *irretrievable*.

contemporary Christianity. In doing that, however, he maintains that Paul, like Jesus, was mistaken in expecting an imminent parousia—a view that is a virtual commonplace for historical-critical interpretation of the New Testament. The work of others often provides helpful insight where their concern, like Cullmann's, is to show continuity between Paul's theology and the theology of the church today.

Bultmann

In the years around 1950 toward the end of the twentieth century, the section on Paul in Bultmann's *New Testament Theology* and his other writings proved to be the single most influential treatment of Paul since Wrede. Here, however, my focus will not be on the details of Bultmann's historical analysis but rather on providing a brief sketch of how he thinks Paul is to be appropriated in the modern world. This view, which proved to be highly influential for a time among those with historical-critical commitments, is made clear in a number of places in his voluminous writings, like *History and Eschatology* (1957).

Bultmann's hermeneutical stance derives from the position that was articulated beginning especially with Friedrich Schleiermacher (1768–1834), and developed by others coming into the twentieth century. It holds, as a basic tenet, that the interpreter of a text, particularly a text from the past, is to seek to understand its author better than the author understood himself.

This leads Bultmann to make a categorical distinction between what Paul *said* (or wrote) and what Paul *meant*.[17] On the one hand, what Paul said is the redemptive-historical, eschatological outlook already demonstrated by Wrede. But that outlook, Bultmann, like Wrede, maintained, is an outdated piece of mythology. In its understanding of what has transpired in history and its historical expectations, it is in error and as such has no meaning or direct relevance for the modern world.

But, Bultmann continues, what readers of Paul today need to appreciate and can appropriate for their lives is what Paul *meant*, the intention implicit in what he said. That intention, the significance of his redemptive-historical

---

17 It is fair to ask how dissimilar really this distinction is from that, like Holtzmann's, between Paul's theology and religion.

mythology for today, is the intention of faith resident in the mythology and expressed through it.

Bultmann finds this demythologized faith intention best expressed in Paul's anthropology, his view of human existence. If we look for what Paul means in what he says, then we discover pronounced continuity between him and the modern reader, a continuity that is readily translatable for our own times, particularly by utilizing the categories of existential philosophy.

To illustrate this approach further, we can note how Bultmann construes the flesh-spirit antithesis in Paul—this provides a point of comparison with F. C. Baur's and the Liberal understandings. Its true intention is this: Flesh, on the one hand, has reference to what is visible, phenomenal, what is at my disposal and over which I can exercise control, what and whom I can manipulate. Flesh has to do with all my efforts in life to secure myself but in which I can never find authentic existence, true personhood.

Spirit, in contrast, stands for what is invisible, what is not at my disposal, over which I have no control, and what is beyond my capacity to manipulate. As such, spirit is the possibility of authentic existence, the experience of transcendence that is mine in the moment of decision, only as I decide for it and not for the flesh.

The spirit-flesh antithesis, then, is Paul's way of expressing the decision-determined historical nature (*Geschichtlichkeit*) of specifically human existence. The antithesis is Paul's way of expressing that at every moment, my existence as a human being is at stake. I am ever faced with actualizing the decision between spirit and flesh—that is, choosing for authenticity instead of inauthenticity, for persons other than myself rather than for myself and things, for a commitment of openness to others in love (spirit) and not a selfish, self-serving commitment (flesh).

Bultmann similarly construes the realized and future elements in Paul's eschatology. His already-not yet eschatology is transmuted into the existential dialectic just noted. The demythologized intention of living between the first and second comings of Christ is the present situation where the decision for authenticity has been made (the already), but has ever to be re-actualized (the not yet).[18]

---

18 It is not difficult to see how this construal—where what is loving or unloving, right or wrong, cannot be known in advance by an objective standard outside the self but can be determined only in the moment of deciding—lays the foundations for autonomous, self-determining morality

Subsequently within historical-critical circles, there has been increasing pushback against this position, against its anthropologically reductive reading of Paul, particularly its radically individualistic cast (which of course is to be expected with existential philosophy made the lens through which Paul is read). In reaction to this anthropological narrowing, a corrective has been sought by giving renewed attention to the corporate aspect of Paul's theology and to reevaluating more positively the cosmological and apocalyptic dimensions, eclipsed by Bultmann, of his eschatology.

THE NEW PERSPECTIVE

The major development in interpreting Paul in recent decades is the New Perspective on Paul (NPP). Subsuming it as I do here largely under the umbrella of historical-critical interpretation may seem questionable, since not everyone with a positive assessment of at least aspects of the NPP takes a historical-critical approach.[19]

Looking at matters from a historical distance, when the dust of the details has settled, often provides a clear perspective that is lacking when one is still immersed in issues presently being explored and debated. That lack of a distanced perspective is the case with the NPP, and I make no effort here to treat it in anything like a full or finished way. In keeping with the limited and selective scope of our survey of the history of Pauline interpretation, I confine myself to what appears to me both clear and primary.

---

and the various kinds of subjectively defined situational ethics that have emerged and become increasingly dominant in recent decades.

19 One of the most influential proponents is N. T. Wright. At the outset of *The New Testament and the People of God* ([Minneapolis, MN: Fortress, 1992], 1-144), the first in a major four-volume series, Wright puts his epistemological and methodological cards on the table. Doing that in some fullness, as he has there and elsewhere, is helpful, and I appreciate that his aim is to challenge and rein in the presumed sovereignly legislative objectivity of the Enlightenment view of reason that has given rise to the historical-critical method.

But that attempt is inadequate. As I might put it, the critical realism for which Wright advocates is insufficiently critical of the autonomy of reason inherent in the "critical" of the historical-critical method. The requisite critique and distancing in this regard requires affirming and maintaining consistently that God is the primary author of Scripture (cf. Westminster Confession of Faith 1.4), and that, as God's word, Scripture is *self-attesting* and its entire truthfulness and final authority *self-validating*.

As far as I can see, that affirmation or recognition is lacking or at least not sufficiently clear in Wright's work. Any approach to Scripture marked by that lack has not fundamentally abandoned the legislating autonomy of the historical-critical method.

The New Perspective on Paul: Orienting Observations

First, the NPP is antecedently and more basically a new perspective on Second Temple Judaism, on Judaism in the period of the rebuilt temple before its destruction in AD 70. This perspective has then been brought to bear on the study of Paul over the past forty years or so.

Revealing in this regard is the unequal distribution of attention in the seminal work of E. P. Sanders, *Paul and Palestinian Judaism* (1977), which has proven to be highly influential in triggering the NPP. With the subtitle *A Comparison of Patterns of Religion*, most of its five-hundred-plus pages is spent on Jewish sources with only a relatively brief (less than a hundred pages) section on Paul, in the light of conclusions drawn from those sources. In light of this imbalance, the better title might have been *Palestinian Judaism and Paul*.

In fact, this new perspective on Second Temple Judaism is only new relative to non-Jewish scholarship. It is new for other, mainly historical-critical scholars catching up on key points that many Jewish scholars have been making since much earlier in the twentieth century (e.g., G. F. Moore), in some instances even earlier.

It is certainly true that sound exegesis of the biblical documents never takes place apart from attention to the historical environment in which each emerges. However, it is difficult to overemphasize that the NPP does not derive primarily from careful study of the letters of Paul themselves ("primarily" is the key word here). Rather, the NPP results from reading Paul through a controlling grid provided by the new assessment of Second Temple Jewish sources. That is clearly the case, I would say, with Sanders and arguably so, at least at crucial points, for others, such as James Dunn and N. T. Wright, whatever differences there are among them. Certainly, these scholars do careful exegesis of Paul; that is not at issue. But the lens through which they largely do so is.

Second, as basic as anything for the NPP is its view that Second Temple Judaism in its various mainstreams is a religion of grace. For Judaism in this period, it is argued, salvation is by grace and not by works, not by a merit-based system of keeping the law.

This conclusion, then, entails a significant reassessment of the conversion of Paul as traditionally understood: When Saul the Pharisee became Paul the Christian, he did not renounce a religion of meriting salvation by works for a religion of salvation by grace. Rather, he went, as it could be put, from grace to grace. His former ethnically (Israel) limited understanding and experiencing of God's grace was replaced with a new understanding and experience of the universal scope of that grace. Certainly, the NPP maintains, Paul has substantial criticisms to make of Judaism, but despite these criticisms, Paul the Christian sees himself as essentially in continuity with Judaism.

This conclusion carries with it a historical-theological implication of considerable moment. If the NPP is correct in its assessment of Judaism and Paul, then, as many of its proponents point out, in regard to salvation by grace, the Protestant Reformation, beginning with Luther, has significantly misunderstood both Judaism and Paul.

The Reformation tradition has always seen substantial continuity between merit-oriented late medieval (as well as subsequent) Catholicism, from which it was freed, and the Judaism and Judaizing tendencies that Paul opposed. But in holding that view, the NPP characteristically argues, the Reformation tradition has missed the central concern of Paul's teaching about the righteousness of God and justification. The fundamental change that faith in Christ brought Paul to see, it is alleged, is the broadening scope of God's grace: that in Christ, the God of Israel has also become the God of the Gentiles, that the righteousness of God already graciously manifested to the Jews is now for the Gentiles as well, that the people of God is a people made up of all nations, not just one.

The New Perspective on Paul: Some Assessment

The assessment that follows, which will also bring out further details of the NPP, is necessarily largely negative. In making it, I am aware that it is partial and that not every point applies equally or even at all to everyone aligning in one way or another with the NPP. I hope to avoid overgeneralization or misrepresentation.

The NPP is undoubtedly of value in contributing to a better and more nuanced understanding of the Second Temple context in which Paul emerges and was active. Renewed attention has been given to various materials from that period, especially in the aftermath of the discovery of the Qumran materials around 1950. That study, in which prominent advocates for the NPP have been intensively occupied, has led to a clearer picture of aspects of Judaism in the Second Temple period. That should be recognized and appreciated.

Still, it is the case that in several areas characteristic of the NPP and its most identifiable and influential proponents, it is wrong and misleading.

A Religion of Grace

The NPP is wrong and misleading in its assessment of Second Temple Judaism as pervasively a religion of grace. My observations here are tethered to this overall consideration: From the vantage point of the covenantal religion of the Bible, specifically from the vantage point of *normative* Old Testament religion, the revealed religion of the Jewish Scriptures, God's grace is given and received only by faith in his promises to Israel. Those promises have their focus and fulfillment in the Messiah to come, who is Jesus of Nazareth, come in the fullness of time. Biblically, saving grace is given and received only by faith in Christ—either by way of promise (Old Testament faith in the Messiah to come) or in light of its fulfillment (New Testament faith in the Messiah who has come).

Apart from such Christ-centered faith, be there ever so much talk of grace, the reality is and will always prove to be its opposite. Without faith in Christ as the fulfillment of God's promises to Israel, there is no salvation (cf. Paul's sweeping declaration in 2 Cor. 1:20; cf. Acts 4:12). Rather, salvation will be sought either based on what amounts to self-serving and self-securing efforts, however refined and veiled those efforts may be, perhaps even from one's self, or based as well—as in Judaism, at least in part—on ethnic identity and status. Conceiving of salvation by either human performance or ethnic pedigree—projects in self-justification *coram Deo*—is the inevitable result when Christ is rejected as the meaning and fulfillment of God's saving promises to Israel.

On the historical theological point, then, I remain persuaded that the Reformation is essentially correct in its understanding of Paul's opposition to Judaism. It continues to puzzle me that proponents of the NPP characteristically perceive a radical dissimilarity in soteriology between Second Temple Judaism in its various forms and Roman Catholicism. Both speak of grace, but for both, that grace amounts to assisting me either for who I am in myself or for doing what I'm capable of doing for myself. Apart from the resurrecting grace of God in Christ, the human heart, even in its best moments and its presumably most altruistic expressions, is both inherently semi-Pelagian and perennially merit-oriented and self-justifying.

In fact, further study has shown that the NPP has characteristically failed to recognize sufficiently the pronounced strand of merit-oriented thinking found throughout the soteriology of Second Temple Judaism, particularly with the final judgment in view.[20]

Paul's Relationship to Judaism

The NPP is wrong and misleading in its assessment of Paul's relationship to Judaism, particularly the Pharisaic Judaism of his pre-Christian past. This criticism is related to the preceding point but brings out a further aspect.

The NPP characteristically equivocates on "Judaism," what is meant by Judaism. For instance, N. T. Wright says repeatedly that in becoming a Christian, Paul, while he strongly critiques Judaism, does not reject or abandon it but rather sees Christianity as the fulfillment of Judaism.

That way of putting things is ambiguous at best. Certainly, Christianity as taught by Paul is the fulfillment of Judaism in the sense that it is the fulfillment of the promises constitutive for the religion revealed by God in the Old Testament (as noted above). But precisely for that reason, Paul's Christianity is and requires the utter rejection of the Judaism of his day in its various streams, the Judaism in which he was raised and which rejected Jesus of Nazareth as its Messiah and Savior.

For Paul, Judaism in the sense of normative Old Testament religion, *that* Judaism and Christianity are the same religion (e.g., Acts 24:14; 26:6, 22). The mainstream Judaism of his day and Christianity, he came to see, are two quite different religions. They are as opposed as the latter is the way of blessing and life, and the former the way of destruction and death. They are as opposed as the excellence of the salvation (the full, experiential knowledge) gained in his newfound union with Christ is opposed to his past Jewish-Pharisaic pedigree and performance, now considered to amount to excrement (Phil. 3:3-9; cf. 1 Tim. 1:13).

Paul on Justification

The NPP is wrong and misleading in its assessment of Paul on justification, certainly on what is central in his teaching on justification. Major NPP pro-

---

20 An important work in showing this is Simon Gathercole, *Where Is Boasting?: Early Jewish Soteriology and Paul's Response in Romans 1–5* (Grand Rapids, MI: Eerdmans, 2002).

ponents, like N. T. Wright and James Dunn, argue that in Paul, justification is about ecclesiology, not soteriology—or, as it is sometimes put, primarily about ecclesiology rather than soteriology, although this modulated wording ("primarily") leaves unanswered just what soteriological significance justification has.

Pivotal in this view is the understanding of *righteousness* in Paul, particularly his use of righteousness language as it is associated with justification terminology. According to this view, righteousness is a relational category. Righteousness for the Christian connotes being included in covenant with God and entails being faithful to that covenant identity. Accordingly, with this relational understanding of righteousness, for God to "justify" means for him to declare that one is righteous in the sense of being included in the covenant, with the nuance—not to be missed— that to justify means to recognize that one is already in the covenant, to affirm one's already existing covenant identity, not how one enters that covenant relationship.

On this view, then, justification does not have to do with establishing or bringing one into a state of salvation but is the de facto recognition of that state, the state of being righteous—that is, of being in covenant with God. Justification is about being and living as a Christian, but it is not definitive for becoming a Christian. Paul's gospel, including the good news of justification, is not "a message about 'how one gets saved,' in an *individual* and ahistorical sense."[21]

So, for instance, in Romans and Galatians, Paul says that Gentiles are "justified by faith in Christ and not by works of the law" (Gal. 2:16). According to the NPP, this means that Gentiles (as well as Jews) are declared to be in covenant with God because they have confessed and are seeking to follow Jesus as Lord. But they do not have to assume the obligations of the law as given by God to Israel (including circumcision) as necessary for belonging to God's people, for being in covenant with God.

For the NPP, the heart of Paul's understanding of justification is that now in view of the coming of Jesus as Israel's Messiah, God's covenant embraces all nations, not just one, Gentiles as well as Jews. That Gentiles are justified

21 N. T. Wright, *What Saint Paul Really Said* (Grand Rapids, MI: Eerdmans,1997), 60; emphasis added. Cf. 40–41, 45, *passim*.

by faith and not by works means, to put it bluntly, that a non-Jew does not have to become a Jew in order to be Christian. Justification is about whom you may eat and have fellowship with as a Christian, not how you become a Christian. In this sense, the NPP maintains, for Paul, justification is (primarily) about ecclesiology rather than soteriology.

In response to this view, for Paul, justification undoubtedly has ecclesiological implications, implications that are as inalienable as they are important. No doubt, these are clearly a prominent concern for him, particularly in Galatians. No doubt, too, these implications have not always been appreciated in the past as they should. The NPP serves to alert us to that neglect where it occurs. The ecclesiological and corporate *consequences* of justification must not be downplayed or eclipsed by an ecclesiologically indifferent and unduly individualistic soteriological mindset. Properly understood, there is no salvation, including justification, outside the church with the fellowship with others involved.

But with that said and kept in view, Paul's teaching on justification is essentially soteriological. It most definitely has to do with "how one gets saved." To justify is, in the idiom of current discussion, a "transfer term." Justification is a component, "redemption, the forgiveness of sins," in what occurs and is effected at the point of being "delivered . . . from the domain of darkness and transferred . . . to the kingdom of his beloved Son" (Col. 1:13-14).

Justification concerns what takes place in an individual's transition by faith from being under God's just wrath on sinners to being a beneficiary of his saving mercy and grace (Eph. 2:3-10). Justification includes the imputation to faith (that is, to those who believe) of the righteousness of Christ as the basis for justification that entitles to eschatological life in the Spirit (Rom. 4:5, in the light of 5:18-19; Gal. 3:1-14).[22]

Paul's teaching on justification in Galatians has its stark urgency not simply because church unity was at stake, but because of what that threatening disunity revealed. Paul's rebuke of Peter's conduct in drawing back

---

22 Troublesome is the failure to recognize or the outright rejection of many NPP advocates that essential to Paul's teaching on justification is the imputation of Christ's righteousness—dismissed, e.g., by Wright as "a cold piece of business" (*What Saint Paul Really Said*, 110). Instead, a positive, justifying verdict at the final judgment is seen as based on "faithfulness"—the Spirit-worked conduct of the Christian, over a lifetime of obedience.

from eating with Gentiles is so unsparing not just because unity between Jew and non-Jew was being jeopardized, as wrong as that was, but because such conduct contradicted "the truth of the gospel" (2:14).

That gospel truth, as Paul expresses it programmatically elsewhere, is not the ex post facto ecclesiological reflex of salvation, of having been saved, but "the power of God *unto* salvation" (Rom. 1:16 KJV), or even more tersely, "the gospel *of* your salvation" (Eph. 1:13). At issue in Paul's understanding of justification is soteriology, and of ecclesiology only derivatively. The NPP is in error in making this derivative point, as important as it is, the main point of justification.

Making ecclesiology not soteriology the primary focus of Paul's teaching on justification leaves unclear where else in Paul, then, if not here in his teaching on justification, are we to locate the soteriological substance and core of his teaching—teaching that the Reformation was confident to have found and contended for in his teaching on justification.

The NPP has the effect of begging this question, or at least of being unclear about it, about key questions of the *ordo salutis*, of the application to the sinner of the salvation accomplished by Christ: What is the gospel in the sense of the good news about what effects my actual appropriation of salvation? How does one "get saved"? "What must I do to be saved?" (Acts 16:30). What effects in my life the transition from wrath to grace so that I am no longer a child of wrath but an adopted child of God?

I may have missed it, but I have yet to find clear answers to such questions in the work of NPP proponents, including the extent to which I have looked into their more popular writings and public lectures, where we might most expect to find these questions addressed. An appeal is often made to union with Christ. Well and good. But how is that union effected and, in particular, what are the essential saving effects that occur at the "transfer" point of being united to Christ, at the moment of transition from previously being outside Christ to now being "in Christ" (cf. "they were in Christ before me," Rom. 16:7). That, as far as I have seen, is not made clear.

The Clarity of Scripture

Finally, a presumptive observation that has to be given some weight: the NPP is defective in the effect that it has, like so much of historical-critical scholarship, in compromising confidence in the clarity of the Bible.

In its Scripture principle, the Reformation tradition contends for the Bible's clarity as essential to maintaining as well its authority, its necessity, and its sufficiency as God's word. For the Reformation, that clarity has been located, prominently, in the doctrine of justification taught in Scripture, principally in Paul.

If in its doctrine of justification—in fact, in its view a doctrine so clear and central that it is among the articles of a standing and falling church— the Reformation has substantially missed Paul's point, as the NPP holds, then it is difficult to evade the implication that the Bible's central message of salvation is obscure.

Conclusion

The final paragraph of the lengthy study of the NPP by Stephen Westerholm aptly serves to round out this survey:

> At the end of Part Two I summed up the issue that divides the "Lutheran" Paul from his contemporary critics [the NPP] as "whether 'justification by faith, not by the works of the law' means 'Sinners find God's approval, by grace, through faith, not by anything they do,' or whether its thrust is that 'Gentiles are included in the people of God by faith without the bother of becoming Jews.'" As I see things, the critics have rightly defined the occasion that elicited the formulation of Paul's doctrine and have reminded us of its first-century social and strategic significance; the "Lutherans," for their part, *rightly captured Paul's rationale and basic point*. For those (like Augustine, Luther, Calvin, and Wesley) bent on applying Paul's words to contemporary situations, it is the point rather than the historical occasion that is crucial. Students of early Christianity must attempt to do justice to both.[23]

This strikes me as a fair and balanced summary—in identifying what at the heart of the Reformation is true to Paul, along with what within

---

23 Stephen Westerholm, *Perspectives Old and New on Paul: The "Lutheran" Paul and His Critics* (Grand Rapids, MI: Eerdmans, 2004), 445; emphasis added. Westerholm's composite "Lutheran" (Augustine, Luther, Calvin, and Wesley) may seem questionable (particularly in bringing together a Calvinist and an evangelical Arminian!), but in this instance, it works because of the nature of the issues raised by the NPP.

the Reformation tradition has heretofore been missed or insufficiently recognized.[24]

HISTORICAL-CRITICAL INTERPRETATION: TWO FINAL NOTES

Sources

It needs to be kept in mind that for those taking a historical-critical approach to Paul's theology, only seven of his thirteen canonical letters are universally accepted as authentic: Romans, 1 Corinthians, 2 Corinthians, and Galatians—the so-called *Hauptbriefe* (main or major letters)—as well as Philippians, 1 Thessalonians, and Philemon, although in their present form, some of these letters, particularly Philippians, are viewed by some as having undergone varying degrees of post-Pauline redaction.

A spectrum of dispute exists about the authenticity of the remaining six letters. The Pastorals are almost universally viewed as non-Pauline. Ephesians, though to a lesser degree, is generally seen as inauthentic, with less doubt about the authenticity of 2 Thessalonians and even less about Colossians.[25]

In assessing any study of Paul's theology, then, one always needs to be alert to what sources are considered genuinely Pauline and whether denial of the authenticity of one or more of the thirteen canonical letters limits or distorts the presentation of his theology.

Background

A major debate within the historical-critical interpretation of Paul has long been whether the background that influenced the development of his theology is primarily pagan Hellenistic religion or Judaism. The older

24 For another in-depth treatment of the NPP on justification, see esp. Guy Prentiss Waters, *Justification and the New Perspectives on Paul: A Review and Response* (Phillipsburg, NJ: P&R, 2004); on literature concerning the NPP, see my *By Faith, Not by Sight*, 1n1.

25 Denials of authenticity can lead to some interesting and, for someone accepting the authenticity of all thirteen letters, quite ironic assessments, like the following: "Colossians is therefore almost more Pauline than Paul himself" (Fritz Neugebauer, "Das Paulinische 'in Christo,'" *New Testament Studies* 4, no. 2 [January 1958]: 136). Or, "There is no second document which would stand closer to Paul inwardly and would have brought particular tendencies of his theology to expression in so relatively a pure form as the Pastoral Letters" (Hans Von Campenhausen, "Polycarp von Smyrna und die Pastoralbriefe," *Aus der Frühzeit des Christentums: Studien zur Kirchengeschichte des ersten und zweiten Jahrhunderts* [Tübingen: J.C.B. Mohr (Paul Siebeck), 1963], 210).

Liberal view and the history of religions approach, followed by a figure like Bultmann, emphasized Hellenistic religion and philosophy, and to a certain degree Oriental (Middle Eastern) mystery religions, as the seedbed or stimulus for Paul's theology. Subsequently, from the latter part of the last century to the present, the stress increasingly has been on its roots in Judaism. The NPP, of course, argues that emphatically.

This latter development is certainly salutary, but only with the important caveat that the Jewish Scriptures (the Old Testament) and postcanonical Second Temple sources must not be homogenized into a single overarching notion of "Judaism" as the primary source of Paul's theology, as the NPP for the most part does.

It is telling, for instance, that nowhere does Paul cite noncanonical Jewish sources in support of his teaching, while his extensive use of the Old Testament throughout provides the basis in large part for that teaching. As noted earlier, Saul the Pharisee become Paul the Christian came to see that the religion of Second Temple Judaism in its mainstreams was for the most part antithetical to the normative religion of the Old Testament, as antithetical as false and true religion.

Also on the issue of background, Greek and Hebrew is not a true dichotomy. Questionable is the view, often encountered, that makes a categorical distinction between a Hebrew and a Greek conception of truth, corresponding to contrasting Hebrew and Greek mindsets, whereby the former is seen to be concrete and historically oriented, the latter abstract and ahistorically disposed.

In Paul, for instance, we see nothing of a tension between Jewish and Greek cultural influences. Instead, present in his person as a Hellenistic Jew is a blending of those influences, a blending that forms the matrix or seedbed, if you will, used by the Holy Spirit for the revelation that comes through Paul as an apostle.

The issue here is the same one that comes out, for instance, in the Jesus-Paul controversy touched on earlier, the issue of continuity between New Testament teaching and subsequent church doctrine. Has the church substantially fallen captive to a Greek mindset and conception of truth alien to Hebrew-oriented biblical revelation, as many are still ready to argue today? Or has the church proven in the main to be faithful to that revelation? For Paul and the other biblical writers, the answer is the latter.

RECENT REFORMED AND EVANGELICAL INTERPRETATION

Some remarks about recent interpretation of Paul in the Reformed and broader evangelical tradition will serve to round off our historical survey and at the same time indicate further something of the direction our own work will take.

Within this tradition, the emergence of biblical theology, of an explicit biblical theological approach, is relatively recent. And, just to remind again, by a biblical theological approach, I mean exegesis, recognizing and taking into account the fully God-breathed origin and authority of Scripture, that is controlled by a recognition of the historically progressive and differentiated character of special revelation, the history of special revelation. In the case of the New Testament, this approach entails focusing on the particular contributions of each writer and their distinctiveness.

Within a Reformed and evangelical setting—among other efforts to deal with Paul's letters as a whole, to set out in some measure of fullness the teaching of Paul as a distinct entity—two deserve special mention: the work of Geerhardus Vos and subsequently of Herman Ridderbos. To single out their work is not meant to overlook or depreciate the valuable work of others. But I have been particularly influenced by these two, especially Vos; my own work in large part builds on theirs.

Geerhardus Vos

Vos (1862–1949), as I noted earlier, was the first occupant (1894–1932) of the chair of biblical theology, created with him in view by the faculty of Princeton Theological Seminary. The work on Paul's theology that draws our attention is primarily *The Pauline Eschatology*, appearing in 1930.[26] That work provides the fullest single statement of his views and of his basic approach.

A bit of "source criticism" on *The Pauline Eschatology* shows that it incorporates some material that appeared earlier, most notably the valuable chapter with the short title "Paul's Eschatological Concept of the

---

26 Geerhardus Vos, *The Pauline Eschatology* (Grand Rapids, MI: Baker, 1979); original edition, Princeton, NJ: Princeton University Press, 1930; repr. Grand Rapids, MI: Eerdmans, 1961.

Spirit" in the 1912 volume commemorating the centenary of Princeton Seminary.[27]

The title, *The Pauline Eschatology*, can be misleading to someone who understands "eschatology" in the traditional or conventional sense and will therefore be expecting a more or less specialized study limited to Paul's teaching about "the last things" concerning Christ's future return and matters concomitant with his return. However, one does not have to read very far into the volume before recognizing that Vos intends something much more, that he is working with a broadened understanding of eschatology that includes the past as well as the future coming of Christ.

For instance, he says of the book as a whole, "It will appear throughout that to unfold the Apostle's eschatology means to set forth his theology as a whole."[28] Or again:

> Not only the Christology but also the Soteriology of the Apostle's teaching is so closely interwoven with the Eschatology that, were the question put, which strand is more central, which more peripheral, eschatology would have as good a claim to the central place as the others. In reality, however, there is no alternative here; there is backward and forward movement in the order of thought in both directions.[29]

An interwoven reciprocity between Christology, soteriology, and eschatology marks Paul's theology—a fundamental consideration that we will highlight and explore in our own work.

To take note of one other sampling here, the title of the second chapter is "The Interaction between Eschatology and Soteriology." The thesis developed is that fundamental benefits of salvation *presently experienced* by the believer in the application of salvation—namely regeneration, justification, and the ongoing work of the Holy Spirit in sanctification—are eschatological realities. These benefits, Vos shows in detail, are eschatologically grounded and are themselves eschatological anticipations presently realized.

---

27 Geerhardus Vos, "The Eschatological Aspect of the Pauline Conception of the Spirit," reprinted in Richard B. Gaffin Jr., ed., *Redemptive History and Biblical Interpretation: The Shorter Writings of Geerhardus Vos* (Phillipsburg, NJ: P&R, 1980), 91-125.

28 Vos, *The Pauline Eschatology*, 11.

29 Vos, *The Pauline Eschatology*, 28-29.

Herman Ridderbos

Ridderbos (1909–2007), after a short period as a pastor, was a professor at the Theological Seminary of what during that time was the Reformed Churches in the Netherlands (Synodical) from 1943 until his retirement in 1976.

Paul: An Outline of His Theology is his major work on Paul,[30] to which his brief chapter "The Redemptive-Historical Character of Paul's Preaching" in another work[31] provides a helpful introduction. The former amounts to an expansion of over six hundred pages of the overview provided earlier in the twenty-three pages of the latter.

By any standard, *Paul* is a milestone in the history of interpretation. A case can be made that it is as important as any major work on Pauline theology, for both its scope and depth of insight.[32] It is a work, like Vos's, that repays carefully reading and re-reading.[33]

The overall, pervasive emphasis of *Paul* is that the particular themes of his teaching taken as a whole, those themes seen in their totality, are embraced and interrelated within an "eschatological" or, correlatively, a "redemptive-historical" framework or viewpoint. Chapter 2 on "Fundamental Structures" makes this overall orientation clear.

Taking in the work of Vos and Ridderbos as a whole, then, it is noteworthy that these two Reformed scholars, who have worked with Paul in a comprehensive way, have arrived at the same basic conclusion, a conclusion

---

30 Herman Ridderbos, *Paul: An Outline of His Theology*, trans. J. R. de Witt (Grand Rapids, MI: Eerdmans, 1975); original, *Paulus. Ontwerp van zijn theologie* (Kampen: Kok, 1966). Along with *The Coming of the Kingdom*, trans. H. de Jongste, ed. Raymond O. Zorn (Philadelphia: P&R, 1962), an in-depth study of the kingdom proclamation of Jesus in the Synoptic Gospels, these two works are his major contributions to New Testament theology.

31 In Herman Ridderbos, *When the Time Had Fully Come: Studies in New Testament Theology* (Grand Rapids, MI: Eerdmans, 1957), 43–60.

32 E.g., James Dunn, in the opening chapter of his large volume on Paul's theology, where he briefly surveys the history of the discipline and positions his own work, sees Ridderbos's *Paul* in its scope as "probably" its most important recent predecessor (James D. G. Dunn, *The Theology of Paul the Apostle* [Grand Rapids, MI: Eerdmans. 1998], 5).

33 With my great appreciation for *Paul*, I do have some reservations. A matter of lesser concern is his understanding of the struggle described in Rom. 7:14–25 as taking place not in the believer but in a typical Jew under the impact of the law. Of much deeper concern is his handling of election in Rom. 9–11, Eph. 1, and elsewhere, and his conclusion that Paul is concerned primarily with redemptive-historical or corporate election and teaches nothing about the irrevocable pretemporal election of individuals.

that represents a certain shift in accent so far as the tradition of Reformation orthodoxy is concerned.[34]

On the one hand, as we have noted, the approach for the most part of the Reformation and subsequent Reformation tradition to Paul has been in terms of justification by faith, and where a distinct Pauline theology has been in view, to see justification as its center. Or to broaden this observation, the Reformation tradition has seen an issue of the *ordo salutis*, of the application of salvation to the individual, to be Paul's central concern, and, in particular, a specific aspect or element of that *ordo*, his teaching on justification.

Vos and Ridderbos, on the other hand, maintain—Ridderbos does this more self-consciously and programmatically than Vos in drawing a distinction from the Reformation—that central in Paul is the death and resurrection of Christ in their eschatological significance. In other words, what they find to be the center of Paul's teaching is the history of salvation, *historia salutis*,[35] the once-for-all accomplishment of salvation by Christ. Controlling for Paul is not a particular point in the individual application of salvation (the *ordo salutis*), however undeniably crucial and important, like justification, but its finished accomplishment (the culmination of the *historia salutis*).

Availing himself of an adjectival distinction in Dutch, Ridderbos emphasizes this point explicitly, that Paul's basic orientation is *heilshistorisch* (salvation-historical), not *heilsordelijk* (having to do with the order or application of salvation). Repeatedly, he says on a given issue of interpretation that Paul's concern is the former, not the latter. In fact, the way he stresses this point leaves the impression that the two concerns are in tension, when, as I will try to show, it is not a matter of tension between differing concerns but of the concern or point of departure that is primary.[36]

---

34 That has happened more or less independently. Ridderbos is aware of Vos and occasionally refers to his work but apparently was not significantly influenced by him.

35 Ridderbos apparently coined this Latin expression to contrast with the conventional and well-established usage in theology of *ordo salutis*. I am not aware of *historia salutis* occurring prior to Ridderbos. It is a significant coinage because it captures that the once-for-all accomplishment of redemption (in distinction from its application) is not a one-time isolated event but consists in the unfolding of old covenant history that leads up to and culminates in the unique work of Christ.

36 I have addressed this issue at some length in my review article of the Dutch original of the book, "Paul As Theologian," *Westminster Theological Journal* 30, no. 2 (May 1968): 204–32; see esp. 228–32.

Vos, too, in the chapter noted earlier, "The Interaction Between Eschatology and Soteriology," argues, in effect, that for Paul the application of salvation, including justification, is a function of the accomplishment of salvation; the *ordo salutis* derives and has its efficacy from the *historia salutis*. That, then, is an issue with its undoubtedly broader systematic-theological implications that will be on the horizon in our own work: the relationship in Paul's theology between *historia salutis* and *ordo salutis*, between the accomplishment and application of salvation and what belong to each.

8

Paul as Pastor-Theologian

PETER'S GENERALIZATION about the letters of Paul that in them "some things . . . are hard to understand" (2 Pet. 3:16), led us to survey the history of their interpretation. Now some further reflection on the intrinsic nature of that difficulty is in order.[1]

THE FIRST CHRISTIAN THEOLOGIAN

The more you become involved in studying and reflecting on the letters of Paul, the more you are bound to become impressed with the fact that you are dealing with a systematic thinker, that his teaching reflects a structure of thinking as profound as it is penetrating. Encountered in his teaching is a pattern of thought characterized by careful reflection and penetrating analysis. In the words of Vos, Paul's is "the genius of the greatest constructive mind ever at work on the data of Christianity."[2]

But saying that—accenting Paul's mind as logical and orderly—is not at the same time to suggest that he presents us with an articulated systematic theology, that in their format his writings are doctrinal treatises. Rather—and this "rather" is obvious, though often overlooked or slighted in practice—his writings are genuine letters and primarily pastoral in their purpose. They are directed to concrete life conditions and problems in specific church situations. This pastoral concern is always present, even in sections of Romans where evidence of theoretical reflection and precise conceptualization is unmistakable.

---

1 Some of the content in this chapter overlaps with my *By Faith, Not by Sight: Paul and the Order of Salvation*, 2nd Ed. (Phillipsburg, NJ: P&R, 2013), 8–17.
2 Geerhardus Vos, *The Pauline Eschatology* (Grand Rapids, MI: Baker,1979), 149.

In other words, Paul's letters are "occasional," in the quasitechnical sense that that word is often used in biblical studies—that is, targeted to specific, concrete situations. As fully occasional, however, they are not intended, as is often the case with letters, simply to be read and then discarded.

Nor are his letters (and sermons recorded in Acts) a tangled mass of ad hoc formulations. What we encounter in them is not a conglomeration of unrelated conceptions, an unreflecting and largely unthinking doxology. One simply cannot get away with doing what, for instance, nineteenth-century Liberal interpretation tried to do with Paul: to separate his religion from his theology, to try to free a core of religious conviction or doxology from a disposable shell composed of all sorts of presumably confused and contradictory theological viewpoints that had not really been thought through very carefully.

Rather, in all of their occasional character and pervasively doxological tone, the letters of Paul reflect a unified structure of thought, a coherence of theological thinking. As Albert Schweitzer—however otherwise substantial his misunderstanding of that thinking was—has memorably put it, "Paul is the patron saint of thought in Christianity."[3]

The preceding observations—taken together along with a recognition of the relatively substantial quantity of material we have from him—provide us with warrant for viewing Paul as the first Christian theologian, the first theological thinker of Christianity. That warrant will become increasingly apparent as our own work unfolds.

THE PROBLEM OF INTERPRETING PAUL'S THEOLOGY

We are now able to be more precise about what we could call the real or proper problem of Pauline interpretation, in distinction from all those factors on the side of the interpreter that tend to mar and produce so much confusion and misunderstanding. That inherent difficulty resides in the depth dimension—"the deep things of God" (1 Cor. 2:10 NIV)—that pervades the subject matter Paul is concerned with, and as that difficulty is further compounded by the occasional nature of his writings.

Paul the theologian provides us with letters, not with theological treatises. A real difficulty in interpreting Paul, then, is that in his writings we encoun-

---

3 Albert Schweitzer, *The Mysticism of Paul the Apostle*, trans. William Montgomery (New York: H. Holt, 1931), 377.

ter a thinker of undeniably reflective and constructive genius, someone with a decidedly doctrinal bent or disposition, but only as he addresses specific church situations and problems, and does so in a theologically nonformalized manner, in a nonsystematic and largely nontopical format. The problem is that Paul is a theologian accessible only through his letters and sermon records. As it could be put, although his letters are not theological treatises, they present us with Paul the theologian.

Another factor, bound up with the occasional nature of the material that we have from Paul and that also adds to the difficulty we are considering, is that we are not its original recipients. A number of his letters are written against the background of previous personal contact, in some instances of extensive time spent in oral instruction with those he is writing to. The content of that instruction in its details, now unknown, is unavailable to us.

An example, as good as any, will suffice to illustrate this problem. In 2 Thessalonians 2:1-12, matters are addressed related to the return of Christ, particularly as that will entail the activity of "the man of lawlessness" (2:3; "the lawless one," 2:8). Concerning this figure and what and who is presently restraining him, Paul writes, "Now you know" (2:6 NIV). What he assumes the Thessalonian church knows, presumably from the time he spent with them during his second missionary journey, is exactly what the subsequent history of interpretation has been trying to figure out. That long, complicated, and inconclusive history prompts Vos toward the close of his own lengthy treatment of this passage (over forty pages) to comment to the effect that its best interpretation will be its fulfillment!—a comment no doubt true about a number of other passages as well.[4]

CONCLUSION

Since early on in my own study of Paul, I have continued to find it a useful analogy to compare Paul's letters to the visible portion of an iceberg. What projects above the surface is but a small fraction of the total mass, which remains largely submerged. What is taken in, particularly at a first glance, can prove deceptive (reference the Titanic!).

4   "2 Thess. 2 belongs among the many prophecies, whose best and final exegete [sic] will be the eschatological fulfillment, and in regard to which it behooves the saints to exercise a peculiar kind of eschatological patience" (*The Pauline Eschatology*, 133).

Stated less pictorially, the conception or line of thought with relatively little explicit textual support may upon careful examination prove to have basic and constitutive significance. Perhaps the best instance is Paul's identification of Christ as the last Adam (1 Cor. 15:45; cf. Rom. 5:12-19). In terms of the hermeneutical principle expressed in the Westminster Confession of Faith 1:6—that the teaching of Scripture is not only its express statements but also what follows from them by good and necessary consequence—one makes full sense of Paul's letters as a whole, of his theology, only by being prepared to wrestle with matters of good and necessary consequence, with the difficult and sometimes thorny questions that involves.

In terms of the categories of structural linguistics—and I do not understand myself to be saying anything really different here from what already in its own time the Westminster Confession has in view—the question that especially confronts the interpretation of Paul concerns the deep structures that give rise to the surface manifestation that are his letters, the competence level of which his letters are a performance, the generative matrix from which his letters emerge. It is this state of affairs that in large part makes the effort of an extensive, overall interpretation of Paul the inherently arduous, even precarious, enterprise that 2 Peter 3:16 already alerts us to.

9

The Question of Entrée and the Center of Paul's Theology

A SURVEY OF THE HISTORY of interpreting Paul, such as we have made, coupled with recognizing the inherent difficulty involved (2 Pet. 3:16), serves to impress on us an important question: How should we proceed in our own interpretation? Where should we begin? Is it, for example, with his teaching on justification by faith? Or with his teaching on the work of the Holy Spirit? Or somewhere else?

To put the question another way, How can we minimize the inevitable tendency to constrict our understanding of the apostle and the impact of his teaching? How should we approach Paul so that our understanding is opened in ways that are appropriately broad and enable us to gain a perspective on the whole of his teaching, so that our understanding is deepened as we process his teaching and respond to it for our lives?

With this question of approach in view, Ridderbos uses a helpful analogy.[1] He compares the teaching of Paul to a vast imposing building, a large edifice with a number of entrances. What, then, is the main or intended entrance, in distinction from other possible places of entry? What is the door or set of doors that, when we enter, enables us to discover the floor plan of the entire structure so that we do not end up wandering about confused or semiconfused in what amounts to a maze?

---

1 Herman Ridderbos, "The Redemptive-Historical Character of Paul's Preaching," in *When the Time Had Fully Come: Studies in New Testament Theology* (Grand Rapids, MI: Eerdmans, 1957), 44.

To vary the image, what is the center of that circle whose circumference is not improperly restrictive and sufficiently broad to enclose the whole? Does Paul's theology have such a center? If so, how do we go about identifying it?

THE CENTER OF PAUL'S THEOLOGY

Despite the reservations some have about affirming that Paul's theology has a center, it seems difficult to deny that it does, particularly if that notion is not maintained rigidly or too narrowly. It is certainly not the case that there is a single key concept—like election or salvation or even God—a *Zentraldogma* ("central doctrine") from which everything can be shown to be deduced. At the same time, however, the ad hoc, occasional character of his letters clearly does not provide us with a proverbial wax nose, so that we can make of them whatever we will.

By the metaphor of a "center," then, I mean that in Paul's letters an overall set of concerns is identifiable, in which some matters are plainly more important for him than others. Certainly, Paul may be approached from a variety of perspectives, and it is valuable to do so, but each of his various concerns is not equally important or controlling. Recognizing this state of affairs points to a circle of interests, in which each is more or less central, with room for debate in some instances as to relative centrality.

Assuming, then, that in this sense Paul's theology has a center, what is it? What is the locus of his centering concerns, and, more importantly, how do we go about properly identifying that center?

There is perhaps more than one way to answer this question. But it seems that we proceed most safely and usefully by identifying passages in Paul that have a summarizing or synoptic function, whether these be in his own words or whether he may be utilizing an already existing formulation. Our interest, in other words, is those statements that express, more or less clearly, his core concerns.[2]

Among such places, 1 Corinthians 1:18–3:22 is a passage in which Paul is concerned to provide an important overall perspective on his ministry as an apostle and in doing that highlights factors basic to it, including what may be seen as the heart of his theological epistemology. This concern

---

2   See also Richard B. Gaffin Jr., *By Faith, Not by Sight: Paul and the Order of Salvation*, 2nd ed. (Phillipsburg, NJ: P&R, 2013), 24–25.

leads him to declare, "For I resolved to know nothing while I was with you except Jesus Christ and him crucified" (2:2 NIV). Paul's epistemic commitment—as *exclusive* as it is *comprehensive*—is the crucified Christ. In a similar sweeping vein is Galatians 6:14: "May I never boast except in the cross of our Lord Jesus Christ." (NIV). Second Timothy 2:8, perhaps adapting an existing creedal summary, similarly asserts, "Remember Jesus Christ, raised from the dead. . . . This is my gospel" (NIV).

Such statements point to the overall centrality of Christ's death together with his resurrection. What further would seem particularly useful—with an eye toward identifying the center of Paul's theology—are statements, like these, that are sufficiently nuclear, yet, unlike them, with enough additional detail to enable identifying an appropriate and adequately inclusive circumference of issues and concerns.

In this regard, the passage that commends itself as perhaps most helpful and forthcoming, or at least more so than others, is 1 Corinthians 15:3–4. There Paul, perhaps though not certainly, utilizes an already existing confessional fragment:

> For I delivered to you as of first importance what I also received: that Christ died for our sins in accordance with the Scriptures, that he was buried, that he was raised on the third day in accordance with the Scriptures.

Within the overall context of Paul's teaching, this statement prompts several observations:

First, in the prepositional phrase, literally "among first things" (ἐν πρώτοις), "first" almost certainly has, as virtually all commentators take it, a qualitative, not a temporal, sense, and most English translations properly render it "of first importance." So, Paul tells us explicitly, his paramount concerns have their focus, their "center," in Christ's death and resurrection.

In light of 15:1–2 ("Now I would remind you, brothers, of the gospel I preached to you."), this center is the center of his gospel. That, in turn, prompts an even broader observation: At 15:1, Paul is best read as beginning to reflect on his ministry as a whole among the Corinthians (as he did earlier in 1:18–3:22). In view, then, is not just a part or aspect of his proclamation but that preaching and teaching in its wholeness.

That disposes saying, perhaps risking a certain degree of reductionism, that Paul's theology is his gospel; his is a "gospel-theology." Or, better, viewed in terms of expanding concentric circles, the center of Paul's theology is the gospel, and at the center of that gospel are the death and resurrection of Christ. The focus of the whole of his teaching, its gospel-center, is Christ's death and resurrection.

Second, the death and resurrection are not in view as bare, isolated, and uninterpreted facts. In that regard, two things are stipulated. For one, their occurrence is "according to the Scriptures" (15:3 NIV). That is, they have their meaning as they fulfill the Jewish scriptures, as they involve fulfillment of the Old Testament—a fulfillment, as will become clear as we proceed, that is nothing less than eschatological.

Also, the death is said to be "for our sins." At the center of Paul's gospel-theology, Christ's death, together with his resurrection, as the fulfillment of Scripture, has its significance in relation to human ("our") sin and its consequences. This points, we may note here, to their applicatory, *ordo salutis* significance. That *ordo* is rooted in and flows from the *historia* centered climactically in Christ's death and resurrection.

This brings us, then, to this baseline conclusion, following from this passage and reinforced by others already noted: At the center of Paul's theology, constituting that center as much as anything, are Christ's death and resurrection—or, more broadly, messianic suffering and glory, his humiliation and exaltation, in their saving and Scripture-fulfilling, eschatological significance. The center of Paul's theology is determined by the triangulation of his Christology, soteriology, and eschatology.

This provides important substantiation for the observation of Vos, noted above, that "not only the Christology but also the Soteriology of the Apostle's teaching is so closely interwoven with the Eschatology, that, were the question put, which of the strands is more central, which more peripheral, the eschatology would have as good a claim to the central place as the others."[3]

JESUS, PAUL, AND THE KINGDOM OF GOD

The question of proper entrée into the teaching of Paul may also be addressed by considering its overall place in the history of special revelation.

3 Geerhardus Vos, *The Pauline Eschatology* (Grand Rapids, MI: Baker, 1979), 28-29.

This suggests specifically considering its relationship to the teaching of Jesus, which it follows more or less directly in the flow of that history. This relationship is an important question, as noted earlier, for arriving at an overall unified understanding of the New Testament and so for understanding Paul. That relationship may be considered both from the vantage point of his letters as well as a pertinent passage in Acts.

The Letters of Paul

As we noted in our survey in chapter 2, according to the Synoptic Gospels, the central and integrating conception in the teaching of Jesus is the kingdom of God—the *basileia* as the rule and realm of God. There we saw that the kingdom in view is not to be understood in the sense of the constant providential rule of God over the creation from its beginning—a typical historic Christian construal. Nor, considering earlier historical-critical assessments, is it a message of timeless morality, an ideal moral order.

Rather, the kingdom proclaimed by Jesus is the eschatological rule of God, the final order in and for the creation that has been inaugurated by his own coming and work in fulfillment of the Old Testament promises, a work, eschatological in its dimensions, that will be consummated at his return. The controlling framework of Jesus's proclamation is eschatology—eschatological fulfillment that is realized in a present-future pattern.

In the letters of Paul, however, we find that kingdom terminology has noticeably receded; it is not central as it is in the teaching of Jesus. This has sometimes been taken—for instance, in the Jesus-Paul controversy within historical-critical circles in the early twentieth century—as an indication of a basic conflict between Paul and Jesus, giving rise to slogans like "Jesus preached the kingdom, Paul preached Christ."

Such an assessment is superficial because the language and certainly the concept of the *basileia* are there in Paul, and they are there with the same present-future pattern that we find in the teaching of Jesus. Distinctive are places where the kingdom is connected with the vocabulary of "inheritance," noun and verb, in statements that have in view the future inheritance of believers. These statements are cast in a negative form, referring to unbelievers as those who will *not* inherit the kingdom of God. Instances are 1 Corinthians 6:9-10, Galatians 5:21, and Ephesians 5:5, where the conduct of unrepentant sinners is characterized in various ways. Plainly, in such statements the kingdom is, as in the teaching of Jesus, a comprehensive future reality, a future inheritance of eschatological dimensions.

Less frequent but occurring are references to the kingdom as present. A key statement here is Colossians 1:13: "He has delivered us from the domain of darkness and transferred us to the kingdom of his beloved Son." This describes comprehensively the fundamental transition, effected by their redemption in Christ (cf. 1:14), already experienced by believers.

In 1 Corinthians 4:20, concerning his interactions with the Corinthian congregation and the problems he is having to deal with there, Paul makes the point that "the kingdom of God does not consist in talk but in power." Paul knows himself to be ministering in the power of the kingdom as already present.

Particularly instructive for its implications is Romans 14:17: "For the kingdom of God is not a matter of eating and drinking but of righteousness and peace and joy in the Holy Spirit." Within the immediate context, Paul is addressing a specific issue in the church in Rome: the problematic relationship between those he categorizes as "the strong" and "the weak," and how they are to relate to each other with their differences. In doing that, he does something typical for him and, we should recognize, is highly effective pastorally. He deals with the immediate, "practical" problem at hand by bringing to bear on it the wide-angle, overarching perspective that needs to be kept in view.

Here that overall, controlling consideration is the kingdom of God, note, clearly in view as a present reality. The kingdom, presently manifested, does not consist in "eating and drinking" (referring to the particular matter in dispute in the Roman congregation; cf., 14:2-3, 6), but, positively, is marked by "righteousness and peace and joy in the Holy Spirit."

Commentators debate whether "righteousness" here has a forensic or ethical/renovative meaning. Most likely it is the latter, although the forensic sense, so prominent earlier in Romans (1:16-17; 3:21-5:21; 9:30-10:6), is surely in the background. So, Paul tells us here, in effect, his conception of the *basileia*—the eschatological rule and realm of God as presently manifested—is to be amplified by what he has to teach about righteousness and the work of the Holy Spirit in the context of the church.[4]

---

4   "Peace" and "joy" surely echo some of the "fruit" of the Spirit that are to mark believers and their conduct (Gal. 5:22).

Anticipating at this point results of our own work, more careful study will be able to show that on any construction, categories like righteousness and the Holy Spirit are plainly basic to Paul. So, Romans 14:17 shows, righteousness, particularly as it bears on justification elsewhere in Paul, and the sanctifying work of the Holy Spirit brought into view here—both fundamental areas of interest for him—amplify his understanding of the kingdom. The two basic strands of Paul's teaching on salvation applied to believers—the forensic and the renovative—are in view here, together yet distinguished, as explicating the present reality of the kingdom.

The *basileia*—the eschatological rule and realm of God, present and future—though not lexically, is *conceptually central* in the letters of Paul.

By way of comparison, looking back at the kingdom teaching of Jesus in the Synoptic Gospels, while righteousness terminology as well as references to the Holy Spirit are relatively infrequent there, where they do occur they are always associated with the *basileia* as its essential manifestations: For instance, "But seek first the kingdom of God and his righteousness, and all these things will be added to you" (Matt. 6:33), and in the healing of the man blind and dumb, "But if it is by the Spirit of God that I cast out demons, then the kingdom of God has come upon you" (Matt. 12:28). We may note here as well, looking at the records of Paul's preaching in Acts, that repeatedly, a central theme is the kingdom (Acts 19:8; 20:25; 28:23, 31).

Acts 20:25

And now, behold, I know that none of you among whom I have gone about proclaiming the kingdom will see my face again.

On the question of proper entrée into Paul's teaching as a whole, this verse, reflected on in its immediate context, is instructive. It reinforces what we have seen in his letters: the centrality of the *basileia*—the eschatological rule and realm of God, already present and yet still future—for his theology.

The context (20:17-38) recounts what is sometimes referred to as Paul's farewell address to the Ephesian elders, in Miletus on the return leg of his third missionary journey back to Jerusalem. Aware that he will not see them again (20:25, 38), he is clearly intent on giving an overall accounting of his ministry in its main points, not only among them but also elsewhere. This passage, then, is fairly read for the comprehensive perspective it gives on key elements in his teaching throughout the whole of his ministry as an apostle.

A number of indications in the passage underscore this concern to provide an all-inclusive outlook on his ministry: In view is Paul's activity "the whole time from the first day" he was among them (20:18), "for three years . . . night and day" without ceasing (20:31 NIV), and with the aspiration he has, all told, to "finish my course and the ministry that I received from the Lord Jesus" (20:24), and that ministry involved teaching, as to its venue, both public and private ("in public and from house to house," 20:20), and, as to its audience, both "to Jews and to Greeks" (20:21). "With tears" (20:19, 31) gives a measure of the intensity of his involvement.

Concerning this intended comprehensive apologia, 20:27 provides the single most sweeping, all-embracing summation: "for I did not shrink from declaring to you the whole counsel of God." By itself, "the whole counsel of God" is a general and somewhat abstract designation. If we ask after more concrete and explicit indications of its content, several other statements in the passage provide that clarification.

Linguistically, these statements are parallel in that, on the one hand, in each, the verbal idea describing his ministerial activity is, with slight variations, the same. On the other hand, in each, the direct object differs. This pattern of similar verbs with different direct objects can be highlighted as follows:

I did not shrink from declaring . . . *anything that was profitable* (20:20)

testifying . . . *of repentance toward God and of faith in our Lord Jesus Christ* (20:21)

to testify to *the gospel of the grace of God* (20:24)

proclaiming *the kingdom* (20:25)

I did not shrink from declaring . . . *the whole counsel of God* (20:27)

This pattern enables drawing the conclusion that the content of the "whole counsel of God" is, still generally, "anything profitable," but what this involves materially is "repentance toward God and faith in our Lord Jesus Christ," "the gospel of the grace of God," and "the kingdom."

If, further, we ask about the relationship between these various factors, the answer, negatively, is that they are hardly more or less independent sectors within the "whole counsel," side by side like pieces of a pie. Rather, as is clear from both Luke-Acts and Paul's letters, and need not be spelled out again here, the kingdom is clearly basic and encompasses the other elements. The gospel of God's grace is the gospel of the kingdom and its coming. Likewise, repentance and faith are primary blessings of the kingdom, the way of entrance into and continuance in the kingdom. Again, as already noted, elsewhere in Acts the kingdom is a summary description of the content of Paul's preaching (Acts 19:8; 28:23, 31).

For any overall understanding of Paul's preaching, then, and so for any preaching that would be faithful to his and build on it, the following series of propositions hold:

> To preach the whole counsel of God is to preach the kingdom of God.
> To preach the whole counsel of God is to preach the gospel of the grace of God, with its call to repentance and faith.
> So, to preach the gospel of the grace of God is to preach the kingdom of God.
> Or, all together, to preach the whole counsel of God is to preach the gracious gospel of the kingdom of God by calling sinners to repentance and faith.

It should not be overlooked that doing this is, all along, to be doing "everything profitable." There is no place in Paul's teaching for a dichotomy between truth and utility; the truth he is concerned with is always eminently practical.

The Acts 20 passage also shows the wholeness or largeness of the proclamation of the *gospel* for Paul. Here he goes on record against "essential core" or common-denominator reductions of the gospel. For him, like Jesus before him, the gospel as the gospel of the kingdom is a comprehensive message, embracing the whole of life.

To be sure, Paul knows, as we must know, how to distinguish between center and periphery in that gospel message with its implications and so within the whole counsel of God. We do not have to, or need not try to, say everything at once. Clearly the call to repentance and faith (20:21) for the forgiveness of sins (Luke 24:47) must always be present and prominent, as well as those matters "of first importance" in view in 1 Corinthians 15:3–4.

With that said, however, within the wholeness of the whole counsel, the periphery, because peripheral, is not thereby disposable or nonessential or unimportant, for it is *integral* to the whole in the sense that without it the center ceases to be truly central. Just as periphery, it is essential, "peripherally essential," we might say. Within the whole counsel of God, everything is necessary, but not equally necessary or necessary in the same way.[5]

CONCLUSION

In his letters, largely considered, Paul is fairly seen as explicating the kingdom proclamation of Jesus with its already-not-yet eschatological structure. He does that by his central focus ("of first importance"): the death and resurrection of Christ in their eschatological significance. This focus, in turn, he amplifies substantially by the themes of righteousness and the work of the Holy Spirit, primarily in the church. In their respective conceptions of the kingdom, then, there exists a deep and pervasive continuity in the history of revelation between Jesus and Paul.

These observations about the letters of Paul bear out the accuracy of the comment of Herman Ridderbos: "But however different the modality in Paul's ministry may be as compared with Jesus Christ's, it can be rightly said that Paul does nothing but explain the eschatological reality which in Christ's teaching is called the Kingdom."[6] This statement, as I noted earlier, is particularly helpful for the incisive perspective it provides on the unity in diversity of the teaching of the New Testament. It recognizes in Paul and Jesus the distinctiveness of each, and yet at the same time sees their unity as Paul, as much as anything, is explicator of the kingdom proclamation of Jesus.

---

5   This discussion of Acts 20:25, based on my class lecture materials, may also be found in large part in my chapter, "The Whole Counsel of God and the Bible," in *The Book of Books: Essays on the Scriptures in Honor of Johannes G. Vos*, 2nd ed., ed. John H. White (Pittsburgh, PA: Crown & Covenant, 2019), 23–33 (originally published by P&R, 1978).

6   Ridderbos, "The Redemptive-historical Character of Paul's Preaching," in *When the Time Had Fully Come*, 48–49.

10

Eschatological Structure

THE CENTER OF PAUL'S THEOLOGY, as we have seen, is at the intersection of his teaching about Christ (Christology), his work (soteriology/redemption accomplished), and the redemptive-historical context of this saving work (eschatology). Any one of these three themes, then, may be made the vantage point for exploring the other two and so the heart of Paul's theology, those things "of first importance" (1 Cor. 15:3). Here, as a preferable way of proceeding for my purposes, his Christology and soteriology will be considered in the light of his eschatology.

PAUL'S USE OF THE TWO-AGE DISTINCTION: BACKGROUND[1]

Paul's use of the distinction between "this age" and "the age to come" is perhaps the best way, certainly a helpful way, of showing the eschatological structure of his thinking and how it shapes his teaching.

The Origin of the Distinction between the Two Ages

This distinction first emerged in Second Temple Judaism during the intertestamental period, where it functioned to facilitate reflecting on the overall historical-eschatological outlook of the Old Testament, especially the prophets. From there, it is taken over by Jesus, Paul, and the writer of Hebrews.[2]

---

1   Some content in this section, based on my class lecture materials, may also be found in Richard B. Gaffin Jr., "The Ressurection of the Christ and the Age to Come," The Gospel Coalition, https://www.thegospelcoalition.org/.

2   This is not a problem, as it might at first seem, for the doctrine of the inspiration of Scripture. At issue is whether or not this development in later, postcanonical Jewish theology, though

On the one hand, this age is provisional and pre-eschatological. It is the time of the present world, originally "very good" (Gen. 1:31), but now subsequent to the fall, marked fundamentally by the presence of sin and its consequences—corruption and death. The age to come, in contrast, is the final world order for the creation, the eschatological age of righteousness, incorruption, perfection, and life. It is coterminous with the coming kingdom of God, the arrival of the day of the Lord, and the new heavens and new earth.

The division point between the two ages—"the end of the age," when this age ends and gives way to the age to come—is tied to the coming of the Messiah (in the New Testament, Matt. 24:3).

As used in the two-age construct, the words for "age"—in Hebrew (עוֹלָם), Aramaic (עָלְמָא), and Greek (αἰών), and subsequently after the New Testament was written, in Latin (saeculum)—took on as well the sense of "world" or "universe."[3] In other words, a comprehensive time word gained an all-inclusive spatial connotation. The distinction, then, expressed more fully, is between this world-age and the world-age to come, between the present world order and the coming world order.

In what follows here, when discussing the use of this distinction, I will often use aeon, a derivative of the Greek αἰών, interchangeably with age, its primary meaning, as a way of keeping in view the "world-age" sense, the spatial as well as the inherently temporal sense of the contrast, and that the contrast is between two comprehensive spatiotemporal orders, one provisional and pre-eschatological, the other final and eschatological.

In sum, in their relationship, the two aeons are *comprehensive* (together they cover the entire flow of time, the whole of history, from its beginning

---

uninspired, accurately reflects the teaching of the Old Testament as God's word. In fact, the distinction between the two ages does that. This observation about Paul's usage applies as well to its presence elsewhere in the New Testament: "There is no escape from the conclusion that a piece of Jewish theology has been here *by revelation* incorporated into the Apostle's teaching" (Geerhardus Vos, *The Pauline Eschatology* [Grand Rapids, MI: Baker, 1979], 28n36; emphasis added). For a thorough discussion of the two-age construction, see Vos, *The Pauline Eschatology*, chap. 1, esp. 36–41, including the diagrams in 38n45. My treatment here is largely taken over from his.

3 E.g., in the New Testament, Heb. 1:2; 11:3. This development in Greek shows the semantic link between the temporal and spatial senses of αἰών, since Greek had available several words for "world." Of these, κόσμος, in turn, can substitute for αἰών—e.g., in Paul, 1 Cor. 7:31: "For the form of this world [τοῦ κόσμου τούτου] is passing away" (NKJV).

at creation up to and including its consummation), *consecutive* (no other period intervenes between them), and *antithetical* (due to the entrance of sin with its effects into this age).

Modifications of the Two-Aeon Distinction

While the two-aeon construction was at hand in the Judaism contemporary to Jesus and the New Testament writers, they could not simply take it over unchanged. The reason is not difficult to see: for Judaism (as continues to be true for Orthodox Judaism today), the coming of the Messiah—the turning point of the two ages, the great inaugurating eschatological event—has not yet occurred; it is still future. However, for the New Testament and for Paul specifically, this decisive turn-of-the-ages event has already taken place; the Messiah has already come in the person and work of Jesus. While his coming does have a still-future component to it, the crucial eschatological event—the coming of the Christ marking the end of this age—has already taken place.

Consequently, for Paul, to continue using the two-aeon distinction as a basic structuring element in his theology, correspondingly fundamental modifications of the construct were necessary. These modifications with the changed pattern that results are best spelled out after we survey and reflect on some pertinent passages. These are passages where Paul either makes explicit use of the distinction, or it is clearly in the background and shapes what he has to say.[4]

SOME KEY TEXTS

Galatians 1:4

A number of passages could serve to begin our survey. Galatians 1:4 does that as well as any. The immediate context unit is1:1-5, the so-called *exordium*—the opening section characteristic of letters written during the Hellenistic period, extrabiblical as well as biblical—with its fixed format of three elements: first identifying the sender (in the nominative case in Greek), then the recipient(s) (in the dative case), and then a greeting or salutation.

---

4 In fact, the distinction with both its parts expressed occurs only once in Paul in Eph. 1:21 (cf. Matt. 12:32; Mark 10:30; Luke 20:34-35): "not only in this age but also in the one to come" (οὐ μόνον ἐν τῷ αἰῶνι τούτῳ ἀλλὰ καὶ ἐν τῷ μέλλοντι). Elsewhere, he refers only to this age, but the contrast with the age to come is implicit.

Here, the sender is Paul (including others associated with him) (1:1–2a), and the recipients are the churches of Galatia (1:2b), followed by the salutation (1:3–5).

For this standard format, it would have sufficed for Paul simply to write, "Paul, to the churches of Galatia, greetings" (cf. Acts 23:26; James 1:1). Instead—and this is characteristic of what happens in all his letters—he elaborates within the basic format, and in doing so gives it a distinctively Christian cast; we might say he "Christianizes" his use of the form.

Importantly—a point to be highlighted here—his elaborating often serves to signal in advance matters of substantial importance that either underlie or will be prominent in the main body of the letter, and so for his theology as a whole. That is particularly the case in Romans, as we will see later on.[5]

Here expansions are present in the first and third elements, in describing the sender and within the salutation. For the former, Paul identifies himself as "an apostle—not from men nor through man, but through Jesus Christ and God the Father, who raised him from the dead," and then associates others in sending the letter ("all the brothers who are with me").[6]

The pronounced negative form of expression here—"not . . . nor" . . . but"—striking and unique in comparison with the openings of his other letters, signals what will occupy him throughout the letter, particularly in the first two chapters: the need, in the face of the serious opposition he is encountering from some—often called Judaizers, with their gospel-denying undermining of his teaching on justification—to defend the divine origin and authority of his apostleship.

Following the identification of his addressees, "the churches of Galatia," without further comment, a fully expanded salutation follows in 1:3–5. Where something like a simple "Greetings" would have satisfied the form, we read instead,

> Grace to you and peace from God our Father and the Lord Jesus Christ,
> who gave himself for our sins to deliver us from the present evil age, ac-

---

5 These elaborations in his letter openings, some more substantial than others, make an interesting and worthwhile Bible study series, going through these openings and considering the expansions that occur in each.

6 As the rest of the letter makes clear, these others are not co-authors and certainly not being identified as apostles. They share in the salutation and, we may infer, agree with the contents of the letter.

cording to the will of our God and Father, to whom be the glory forever and ever. Amen.

Positioned as it is as part of the expansion of the salutation, 1:4, it is fair to say, intends to provide a summary description of salvation, what lies at the heart of the salvation accomplished by Christ. That salvation is said to be effected by his death ("who gave himself for our sins") and tied to his resurrection, mentioned as part of the expansion in 1:1 ("God the Father, who raised him from the dead"). Here, as in 1 Corinthians 15:3–4, Christ's death and resurrection are gospel matters "of first importance."

Galatians 1:4 further specifies the purpose that is at the heart of salvation as willed by God the Father and accomplished by Christ in his death and resurrection. That purpose is "to deliver us from the present evil age." This description of purpose prompts a couple of questions. First, When will this deliverance take place? The immediate context does not say, but as will become clear as we look at other passages, the reference is not solely or primarily to what will take place in the future. Paul is not saying that Christ gave himself for our sins, so that at some future point he might deliver us from the present evil age. Rather, Paul sees this deliverance—again, other passages will make this clear—as a deliverance that is realized, that has already taken place.

The way this deliverance is expressed here also raises another question. This expression is negative; it tells us what believers have been delivered from. But what, positively, have they been delivered to? Here, too, the explicit answer is found in other passages we will look at. But for now, keeping in mind the background considered above, we should not hesitate to recognize that Paul would expect his original and also subsequent readers—particularly Jews, those with a background in Judaism, as well as others familiar with the Old Testament and its ongoing interpretation and appropriation—to make this immediate connection: In having been delivered from the present evil age, believers have been brought into the age to come. As Christians are those who have been delivered from the age of sin and death, so they have now been brought into the final, consummate age of righteousness and life. To have been delivered from this present evil age is to have entered the dawning age to come.

We must appreciate, then, the broad, quite comprehensive perspective that Paul opens here on the death of Christ for sin, including the forgiveness of sins, and so on the transition experienced by believers in what Christ has done for them. The forgiveness of my sin is personal, preciously personal, but it is not an isolated transaction, occurring in an individualistic vacuum. Not only does that forgiveness have a corporate connection with others within the fellowship of the church. Its context is nothing less than cosmic in its proportions. The forgiveness of sin ushers the believer into the eschatological order of the aeon, the world-age, to come.

Colossians 1:13-14 is instructive here. Though the language of the two-age construct does not occur, that distinction is present in the reference to the kingdom, an equivalent description of the age to come. In "redemption, the forgiveness of sins" in Christ (1:14), God the Father (1:12) "has delivered us from the domain of darkness and transferred us to the kingdom of his beloved Son" (1:13). Redemption in union with Christ has brought believers out of one *basileia*—the regime of sin and death, "the present evil age" (Gal. 1:4)—and into another quite opposite rule and realm, that of the righteousness and life of the age to come.

Ephesians 2:2

In the opening verses of Ephesians 2, Paul reminds those in the church of their pre-Christian past, when they "were dead in the trespasses and sins in which you once walked" and "were by nature children of wrath" (1–2, 3). Among the multiple descriptions he gives of their former condition as the "walking dead," that conduct was literally "according to the age of this world" (2:2, my translation). Most translations have "course" instead of "age," an interpretative rendering that masks the clear and pronounced allusion to the two-aeon distinction Paul intends here.

Looking ahead in the passage to 2:5-6, there, repeating the description in 2:1, Paul says that what those formerly dead in trespasses have experienced is nothing less than resurrection. Just "when we were dead in our trespasses," God "made us alive together with Christ . . . and raised us up with him and seated us with him in the heavenly places in Christ Jesus."

We will consider this passage and the resurrection described here in greater detail later on when we explore in some depth Paul's theology of resurrection. But for now, several further observations can be made. For one, the already-experienced resurrection in view is nothing less than deliverance from the "walk," the sinful way of life, characterized as being "according to the age of this world." This compounding expression has a certain redundancy, perhaps for emphasis.[7] But it also makes explicit the spatial aspect of the two-age construct; believers have been released from the life of this aeon.

Also, from this passage, what is implicit in Galatians 1:4 is now made clear. Deliverance from the present evil age has already taken place. The resurrection in view is not future but in the past; note the past (aorist) tenses for resurrection in Ephesians 2:5-6. In a sense still to be further clarified, the life into which believers have already been introduced is the life, the way of life, that is nothing less than that of the new and final aeon.

Here again, salvation is set in a broader context. Salvation experienced, while it is individual and personal, has as well not only corporate but also comprehensive aeonic and eschatological dimensions.

Romans 12:2

Romans 12:1-2 forms a major transition in the letter. As many have commented, there is probably no more heavily weighted "therefore" in the entire Bible than in the opening words of 12:1: "I appeal to you therefore. . . ." It may be taken as looking back on all that Paul has had to say so far in the letter through to the end of Romans 11 about the magnificent sweep of God's dealings with Israel among the nations to accomplish the salvation of the church, made up of both Jews and Gentiles.

At the same time, in the light of these manifold "mercies" (12:1; cf. esp. 11:30-32), these verses also look forward. In general terms, they exhort the church concerning the Christian life. The implications of this overarching exhortation for sanctification are then made more specific on various issues in the remainder of the letter, especially through 15:13.

This sweeping exhortation begins with the appeal that believers present themselves to God in their bodily existence "as a living sacrifice" (12:1). This exhortation entails the prohibition at the beginning of 12:2, equally comprehensive: "Do not be conformed to this age" (my translation),[8] and the flip-side positive command, "be transformed by the renewal of your mind."

---

7   Paul could have made his basic point just by saying "walking according to this age."

8   Translations typically opt for the spatial sense of αἰών instead of "age" (e.g., ESV mg.) The phrasing of the original, τῷ αἰῶνι τούτῳ, shows the two-aeon distinction is in view.

Implicitly but plainly here, this transformation—set explicitly in opposition to conformity to this aeon—is that of the aeon to come. In its deepest dimensions, the present renewal and sanctification of the believer is eschatological. As it may be put, beginning here in Romans 12 and continuing in the chapters that follow are the apostle's new creation ethics.

1 Corinthians 1:18–3:23

In this part of the letter, Paul takes his point of departure in the division that has been created by his preaching of the cross ("For the word of the cross is folly to those who are perishing," 1:18). The passage then goes on to expand on this division created by this preaching of "Christ crucified" (1:23). His purpose, in part, is to bring out the true nature of the division the gospel brings, in light of the false divisions that have emerged in the church in Corinth and are being manifested and exploited in the party spirit that has taken hold there (cf. 1:10–17).[9]

Such divisive and counterproductive rivalry is not the division the gospel should produce. The gospel, however, does result in division, and Paul proceeds to spell that out beginning at 1:18. Doing that, as we noted earlier, is also in the larger interest he has in this section of giving an overall account of what he is about as an apostle.

The division created by the gospel arises because of the conflict that exists between God and unbelievers, so that they hear the gospel, "the word of the cross," as foolishness. Rhetorically, much of the discourse beginning at 1:18 is structured around this opposition between God and unbelief, in which the key categories are wisdom and power, on the one hand, foolishness and weakness, on the other. What holds for the one is the opposite for the other. What is wisdom and power for God is foolishness and weakness for unbelief and vice versa (1:19–28).

Our particular interest here is the way in which Paul describes the wisdom of unbelief in opposition to the wisdom of God:

Where is the one who is wise? Where is the scribe? Where is the debater of this age? Has not God made foolish the wisdom of the world? (1:20)

---

9   In 1:13, the rhetorical questions expecting a negative answer focus these false divisions. "Was Paul crucified for you?" contrasts pointedly with "Christ crucified" (1:23).

In this sequence of rhetorical questions, the wisdom of unbelief that opposes the gospel is "the wisdom of the world," and the proponent of that unbelieving wisdom is "the debater of this age."

In 2:6–8, the wisdom of the gospel Paul communicates is "not the wisdom of this age or of the rulers of this age" (NIV). Furthermore, "None of the rulers of this age understood this [the "wisdom of God," 2:7]," otherwise, "they would not have crucified the Lord of glory" (2:8).

Then, toward the conclusion of this section, Paul writes (3:18–20):

> Let no one deceive himself. If anyone among you thinks that he is wise in this age, let him become a fool that he may become wise. For the wisdom of this world is folly with God. For it is written, "He catches the wise in their craftiness," and again, "The Lord knows the thoughts of the wise, that they are futile."

Here—in the counter-valuation of wisdom and foolishness between God and unbelief—the one who embraces "the wisdom of this world" is the one who is "wise in this age." "This age" and "this world" are functionally equivalent, virtual synonyms.

These parallel expressions show how, as in Ephesians 2:2 noted earlier, "world" (κόσμος) has come to function within the two-aeon construct, and thereby has been historicized and taken on a temporal association. In the passages just surveyed, "the world," where it is correlate with "this age," is implicitly "*this* world." A clear instance of this development is also found in 1 Corinthians 7:31: "For the form of this world is passing away" (NKJV, NASB 1995).[10]

Paul's polemic against the presumed wisdom and power of unbelief in 1 Corinthians 1–3 shows that the wisdom and power of God that believers have received—focused as it is in Christ crucified, "the power of God and the wisdom of God" (1:24)—is not merely opposed to the wisdom and power of unbelievers in a personal or individual sense. Rather, this opposition is ultimately nothing less than the opposition that exists between two opposed ages, two conflicting world orders.

10 Even though Paul (with the rest of the New Testament) does not speak of "that world [κόσμος]" or of "the world to come," in contrast with "this world," the former is implied, as the latter ("this world") clearly functions within the two-aeon construct.

To highlight this point, this passage teaches that the determination of the believer's knowledge and even beyond that, the believer's very existence (cf. Col. 3:3-4, discussed later)—what is decisive for our being and knowing as believers—has aeonic dimensions. We are pointed here to consider that in contrast to unbelievers, the knowledge of the believer is of a different age than the unbeliever. In light of the eschatological fulfillment inaugurated by Christ, believers and unbelievers are presently living in two different worlds. In the deepest sense of the word, belief and unbelief operate in different "universes of discourse," in terms of the two-aeon construction. The believer's knowledge, Paul tells us in our passage, is eschatological. It partakes of the wisdom of the age to come; it is, as we will see, new creation knowledge.

To be sure, these sweeping generalizations about the believer's knowledge cannot stand by themselves and are misleading without important qualifications. One is in the light of Paul's later declaration in 1 Corinthians: "For now we see in a mirror dimly" (13:12). Short of Christ's return, a provisional, preeschatological dimension cuts through all our present knowledge and limits it commensurately.

That fundamental limitation, however, is not a retraction by Paul or drawing back from what he has said earlier—even more fundamentally—in 1 Corinthians, specifically in 2:15-16, within the context beginning at 1:18 we have been considering: "the Spiritual person"—that is, the believer indwelt, motivated, and directed by the Holy Spirit (cf. 2:10, 12-14)—"judges [or "discerns"] all things, but is himself to be judged by no one" (2:15). That is so because the Spiritual person has "the mind of Christ" (2:16). This mind, presently possessed and shared in by believers in their union with Christ and (to be) the deepest dimension of their thinking, is the mind of the age to come.

The note on which Paul closes this section in 3:21-22 crowns as it reinforces the preceding observations:

For all things are yours, whether Paul or Apollos or Cephas or the world or life or death or the present or the future—all are yours, and you are Christ's, and Christ is God's.

First Corinthians 1:18-3:22 points to the radical epistemological difference Paul sees between believers and unbelievers, a difference that is on the order of a cleavage between two opposed ages, two opposing orders for creation.

In passing here but importantly, this passage offers strong exegetical support for a basic and repeated emphasis in the theological epistemology that underlies and has given rise to the presuppositional apologetics of Cornelius Van Til and others: there is no neutral epistemological point of contact between belief and unbelief; no common ground exists that believers and unbelievers share epistemologically, however one might want to factor that ground.

"Jews demand signs and Greeks seek wisdom" (1:22). Whether undertaken empirically or speculatively, whether by practical observation or by theoretical reflection, unbelief arrives at conclusions—measured by God's self-revelation in nature and Scripture as the ultimate source and standard for all valid truth claims—that are in conflict with "the mind of Christ," with the knowledge of God, and reject the wisdom of God.

Here, again, a qualification needs to be kept in view. To say—and this needs to be emphasized—that there is no common ground epistemologically between Christians and non-Christians is not to deny what both have in common and the genuine point of contact there is between them: Ontologically, both are image-bearing sinners living in God's creation. In and of themselves, both are sinners in need of the gospel and the saving and transforming work of the Spirit. Only by that work, experienced for the first time and maintained subsequently, are there those who are now made "Spiritual" and so share in "the mind of Christ," the source of all truly sound and ultimately coherent creaturely thinking.[11]

2 Corinthians 5:17

How does this verse advance understanding of Paul's use of the distinction between the two ages? The answer lies in determining and reflecting on the meaning of the first half of the verse, composed of a conjunction, a subordinate, conditional clause, and a main clause expressing the conclusion of the realized condition.

This main clause presents a couple of translation issues: (1) Should καινὴ

---

11 These comments on this passage have been developed at greater length in my "Epistemological Reflections on 1 Corinthians 2:6-16," in *Revelation and Reason: New Essays in Reformed Apologetics*, ed. K. Scott Oliphint and Lane G. Tipton (Phillipsburg, NJ: P&R, 2007), 13-40.

κτίσις be translated "new creation" or "new creature," and if the former, in what sense? (2) Since no verb is explicit in the Greek text, what verbal idea should be supplied, and how should the clause as a whole be translated?

The answer to the first of these questions is that κτίσις should almost certainly be translated "creation," not "creature." This Greek word as it is used here does not describe an individual person or, with "new," have in view the personal renewal experienced by the person who is in Christ, however undoubtedly true that renewal is on other grounds; this is not primarily but only by inference a proof text for individual regeneration. Rather, the reference is to the new creation, comprehensively considered, to which the one in Christ belongs, in which the one in Christ now exists.

Grounds favoring this understanding can be seen along several lines— lexical, syntactical, and contextual. Lexically, Paul uses κτίσις here, not κτίσμα, the word for a created person or thing (in Paul, cf. 1 Tim. 4:4). By itself, this observation is not conclusive because of the semantic overlap between the two words, and the fact that sometimes Paul does use κτίσις to refer to an individual created person or thing (Rom. 1:25; 8:39).

Still, the primary meaning of κτίσις—in Paul and, more broadly, in both biblical and extrabiblical Greek—is *creation* in a comprehensive sense, referring to the totality of created reality (e.g., Rom. 1:20; Col.1:15; Rev. 3:14). So, we may say, the lexical state of affairs tilts toward a comprehensive creation sense in 2 Corinthians 5:17.

The syntax of the first half of 5:17, masked in English translation, needs to be considered. Translated word for word, it reads, "Therefore if anyone in Christ, new creation." In the conditional ("if") clause, the verb "is" is plainly implied. The main clause, however, consists solely of "new creation," standing alone. So, the thought of the clause has to be determined from the context, by weighing contextual considerations.

A number of translations, opting either for *creation* in an individual sense or for *creature*, render with an implied "he is a": "he is a new creation" (e.g., ESV, NKJV, NET; "he is a new creature," NASB 1995). Others leave the sense of "creation" open or ambiguous and supply a generalizing "there is a" (e.g., NRSV, NASB 1995 mg.)

These various proposals are plausible as translations. But, as we have seen, vocabulary and syntax alone are not decisive, so that here, as is often the case, for determining meaning, "context is king." In fact, contextual factors, both immediate and broader, run counter to restricting the reference in 5:17a to the personal renovation or regeneration experienced by the individual believer, and for a more comprehensive reading.

First, 5:17b directly amplifies the meaning of 5:17a. "The old things" and "the new things" are both generalizing expressions.[12] As such, they are plausibly taken as having a broad, even environmental sense or scope and so giving that environmental meaning to the new creation itself.

Second, in the immediately following verses, the primary point is reconciliation and the ministry of reconciliation that has been entrusted to Paul (5:18-20). Pertinent to our interest is his emphasis on the *comprehensive* scope of the reconciliation that God has effected in Christ. Reconciliation concerns "all things" (τὰ πάντα; NKJV); coming at the beginning of 5:18, it links directly with and sheds light back on "the new things" of the new creation at the end of 5:17.[13] Furthermore, the object of the reconciliation is nothing less than "the world" (κόσμον, 5:19).

It might be argued that "not counting their trespasses against them," directly following in 5:19, limits "the world" to the world seen as made up of sinful human beings in need of reconciliation. Certainly, they are the primary objects of reconciliation, but that does not require restricting the scope of "the world" and of "all things" to them.

In fact, what Paul says elsewhere about reconciliation tells against that restriction and for a more comprehensive reference. In Colossians 1:20, the scope of reconciliation is clearly cosmic and universal: The object of reconciliation, effected "by the blood of his cross," is "all things," further delineated as nothing less than things "whether things on earth or things in heaven" (NIV). The reconciliation of sinners in Christ has a context, a cosmic environment that shares with them in their reconciliation.[14]

Third, 2 Corinthians 5:14-15 is one of those places in Paul where he provides a basic perspective on what has been effected in the death and resurrection of Christ. Here, his controlling point is that in and by his death, the "all" for whom Christ died have themselves died, a death such

---

12 In Greek, neuter plural adjectives used substantively and made definite: τὰ ἀρχαῖα, καινά (while the latter lacks the article, its implied definite sense is clear).

13 This direct link is clearer in the syntax of the Greek text than in English translations: ἰδοὺ γέγονεν καινά. τὰ δὲ πάντα ἐκ τοῦ θεοῦ τοῦ καταλλάξαντος ἡμᾶς ἑαυτῷ διὰ Χριστοῦ (5:17-18).

14 Cf. Rom. 8:19-23, where the creation as a whole will share in the future "redemption" and openly revealed "freedom" and "glory" of the church.

that "those who live might no longer live for themselves but for him who for their sake died and was raised."[15]

Second Corinthians 5:16–17 goes on, then, to shed light on this new life and matters related to no longer living for self but for Christ. "Therefore" at the beginning of 5:16 and then again at the beginning of 5:17 links these verses as consequences flowing from 5:14-15.[16]

In 5:16, "according to the flesh" is adverbial, not adjectival. It describes the manner of knowing or regarding anyone in general and Christ in particular, the kind of sinful knowledge that Paul "once" had but now repudiates and "no longer" has.[17] The statement, whether or not autobiographical, is intended to be representative of all believers and their present knowledge.

How is 5:16 pertinent for understanding "new creation" in 5:17? That can be seen by noting that in 1 Corinthians 1, Paul explicitly connects being "wise according to the flesh" (1:26 NASB, NKJV) with the wisdom of "the debater of this age" (1:20); "according to the flesh" is functionally equivalent and interchangeable with "of this age." Consequently ("therefore," 2 Cor. 5:17), in contrast to this fleshly wisdom, the wisdom and understanding of one who is in Christ, who now has "the mind of Christ" (1 Cor. 2:16), is of the age to come or, in other words, is the wisdom of those who belong to the new creation order that has dawned in the death and resurrection of Christ.

Fourth, in its context, along with the other considerations previously noted, Galatians 6:15—"For neither circumcision counts for anything, nor uncircumcision, but a new creation"—serves to put the comprehensive reference of the new creation in 2 Corinthians 5:17 on a firm basis, if not beyond question. Coming toward the close of Galatians and speaking autobiographically but in a way, again, that is surely to be true of all believers, in Galatians 6:14, Paul declares, "May I never boast" (NIV). There is, however, a singular exception to this sweeping renunciation of boasting: the cross of Christ; Paul's exclusive boast is Christ crucified (cf. 1 Cor. 2:2).

---

15 On the death and, by implication, life of the "all" in view in these verses, cf. elsewhere in Paul, esp. Rom. 6:1-14, to be discussed in some detail below.

16 Obscured in some English translations, "therefore" (ὥστε) is the first word in the Greek text of both verses, clearly signally a conclusion that is being drawn from what has proceeded.

17 "According to the flesh" does not modify the object of knowing, as if Paul is saying that his interest is no longer, as it once was, in the historical Jesus of the past but only in Christ as the heavenly being he now is—the way this verse has sometimes been misinterpreted.

What further qualifies this boast—the reason Paul gives here—is that by the cross of Christ "the world has been crucified to me, and I to the world" (Gal. 6:14). The death of Christ has effected a break, definitive and irreversible, for Paul and for all believers. It is a break that is surely and deeply personal but also more than individual. It is a break cosmic in its proportions, a break with "this world" (cf. 1 Cor. 3:19 and Eph. 2:2, already discussed earlier). Here, at the close of the letter, Paul echoes, in effect, its opening words, where we began this survey of his use of the two-aeon construction: by the death of Christ, believers have been delivered from "the present evil age" (1:4).

Galatians 6:15 amplifies 6:14 ("For" at the beginning of 6:15 establishes that connection). Syntactically, the similarities with 2 Corinthians 5:17 are evident, notably in the second half of the verse, which consists only of "but" followed by "new creation" and with no verb. The sense of the clause, then, as for the conclusion in 2 Corinthians 5:17a, has to be determined from the immediate context.

In that regard, the "new creation" in Galatians 6:15 corresponds to "the world" in 6:14 as its pointed antithesis. The new creation in view is not personal but cosmic and aeonic in its scope. It is, in other terms, the age to come, into which believers have been brought by the death and resurrection of Christ.

The first part of 6:15 reinforces this conclusion. The new creation, which is what now "counts," is juxtaposed in contrast to the old covenant order, in which the distinction between circumcision and uncircumcision did "count." But now, with the new covenant inaugurated by the arrival of the new creation, that distinction no longer counts.[18]

Fifth, returning now to 2 Corinthians 5:17, the contrast between old and new in the latter part of the verse is not only individual or experiential. The contrast as such is not limited to the change in the believer effected by personal regeneration and sanctification. Rather, as in Galatians 6:15, the scope of the contrast is broadly historical, in fact eschatological. It is a contrast between nothing less than two worlds—the old world order and the new world order.

---

18 The old covenant in view here was made with Abraham and confirmed with Israel under Moses. As such, it belongs to this age, the old aeon, as an administration of the covenant of redemptive grace introduced at the fall when this age, due to human sin and the guilt of sin, became subject to corruption and death. It has been *superseded* as it has been *fulfilled* by the inauguration of the new covenant (cf. 2 Cor. 3:6-18; Gal. 4:22-26).

The "old things" that have passed away are the things of the old fallen creation, the things of the unredeemed world in sin and misery—in other words, the things of this aeon, this present evil age. The "new things," in contrast, are the things of the new creation, of the final eschatological order that has been inaugurated by Christ—in other words, the things of the aeon to come.

To emphasize this point is not at the same time to polarize cosmic, sweeping redemptive-historical (*historia salutis*) and personal (*ordo salutis*) considerations in understanding 5:17. For in view is the situation and what is true for the individual, the person who is united to Christ. On balance, in 5:17, Paul is saying, as we might put it, to the one in Christ: the old things that have passed away have passed away for you, but it is more than just the things of your individual past that has passed away.

The point of 5:17a, then, is this: anyone in Christ is of the new creation, is already a participant, in a sense to be further clarified, in the final order for the creation, in the eschatological age to come.

I have approached the interpretation of 2 Corinthians 5:17 as a translation issue. How, then, should it be translated? Among existing translations I am aware of, the best are the NIV (2011): "Therefore, if anyone is in Christ, the new creation has come: The old has gone, the new is here!," and the REB (1989): "For anyone united to Christ, there is a new creation: the old order has gone; a new order has already begun."[19]

———

The passages considered so far show how the two-age distinction structures Paul's overall outlook on the comprehensive eschatological nature of the salvation accomplished in the death and resurrection of Christ, the consummate as well as cosmic magnitude of the redemptive-historical fulfillment revealed in his humiliation and exaltation.

This two aeon–shaped outlook is reflected in other passages, surveyed briefly here, that express in different ways the already realized eschatologi-

19 "This means that anyone who belongs to Christ has become a new person. The old life is gone; a new life has begun!" (NLT) is an example of a translation that misses the point of the verse by narrowing it anthropologically. My treatment of the verse here has built primarily on that of Vos, *The Pauline Eschatology*, 46-49, to which I especially refer readers, and Herman Ridderbos, *Paul: An Outline of His Theology*, trans. J. R. de Witt (Grand Rapids, MI: Eerdmans, 1975), 45-46, 55.

cal aspect basic to Paul's theology. I begin with the "bookends" of Romans, its opening and closing.

Romans 1:2

Here in the opening section of the letter, Paul, as its sender, having identified himself as an apostle "set apart for the gospel of God" (1:1) and before emphasizing that the content of this gospel is "concerning his Son" (1:3-4), adds that the gospel is what "he [God] promised beforehand through his prophets in the holy Scriptures" (1:2).

By this qualification, Paul does several things. For one, he affirms the essentially *prophetic nature* of the Old Testament as a revelation of the *gospel*. This serves as a reminder, important for interpreting the Old Testament, that its meaning is not self-contained or self-referential; it is open-ended for further revelation to follow and has to be understood in the light of that future revelation of the gospel in the New Testament.

Also, in light of 1:3-4 ("concerning his Son"), 1:2 indicates the *Christological character* of this revelation. As revelation of the gospel, the Old Testament is basically and pervasively a book about Christ.

Further, in 1:2, Paul qualifies his ministry of the gospel (and so any ministry that would build on it and be faithful to it). He positions it historically by indicating in effect its place in the history of revelation. The emphatic form of the verb translated "promised beforehand"—literally "pre-promised" (προεπηγγείλατο)—implies a comparison. In contrast to the promissory, prophetic, and provisional character of the Old Testament statement of the gospel—note yet again, the overall distinguishing concern of the Old Testament is the gospel—Paul's gospel ministry is in the context of fulfillment, of final revelation. In that sense, his is an eschatological ministry. He ministers an eschatological *content* in an eschatological *context*.

Romans 16:25-27[20]

Now to him who is able to strengthen you according to my gospel and the preaching of Jesus Christ, according to the revelation of the mystery that was kept secret for long ages but has now been disclosed and through

---

20 I assume here, without entering into the textual transmission debate, that these verses are the original ending of Romans.

the prophetic writings has been made known to all nations, according to the command of the eternal God, to bring about the obedience of faith—to the only wise God be glory forevermore through Jesus Christ! Amen.

The central element in this doxology with which Romans closes is "the revelation of the mystery." Given this closing context, this expression highlights a key element in the content of Paul's preaching.

In the syntax of 16:25, "my gospel," "the preaching of Jesus Christ," and "the revelation of the mystery" are not, as they may at first appear, parallel descriptions; the preposition "according to" (κατά) is repeated before the last of these three phrases, while the first two are coordinate in sharing that preposition without its repetition. Semantically, then, the last of these phrases, "the revelation of the mystery," is best seen as specifying the content of the first two: the revelation of the mystery is the subject matter of Paul's gospel preaching concerning Christ.

Three participial clauses (in Greek) modify "the mystery." It (1) "has been kept secret for long ages," (2) "has now been manifested," and (3) "has been made known through the prophetic Scriptures" (my translation). Note the difference there is between (2) and (3): the *manifestation* of the mystery is distinguished from its being *made known*.

Taken together, these three clauses clarify the meaning of "the revelation of the mystery." An important interpretive key is to recognize that it is *not* a noetic or cognitive category. That is, the revelation of the mystery does not refer to disclosure of teaching previously kept secret; it is not simply a body of newly revealed doctrine.

Rather, the revelation of the mystery is an event, in the sense that the mystery in view is not what was not known (unknown information) but what had not happened. This use of *mystery* has to do with the secret plan of God regarding salvation. It is a mystery insofar as it is fixed in God's eternal counsel but has not yet occurred in time. The revelation of the mystery is the actual realization in history of God's eternal plan of salvation.

To be more specific, the mystery, in a word, is *Christ*—not just information about Christ but Christ himself in his person and work, salvation as eternally purposed in him. And the revelation of the mystery is that purposed salvation, centered in his death and resurrection, as it has actually been accomplished and become a reality in history. The long ages' silence expressed in the first of the modifying participial clauses is the silence of non-eventuation,[21] of Christ having not (yet) appeared in history and his work not having occurred.

How little this mystery is purely noetic, a matter solely of not-yet disclosed verbal revelation,[22] is made clear by the third of the participial clauses. Distinct from its having been "manifested" (the second participial clause), the mystery has been "made known." Further, it is made known through "the prophetic writings," almost certainly a reference to the Old Testament (cf. Rom. 1:2). In other words, the mystery, though it was not yet "manifested" in the event sense just noted, had previously been "made known" in a noetic sense; verbal revelation concerning it was there all along in the Old Testament.[23]

In Romans 16:25-26, then, the "mystery" is Christ in his saving work as it was purposed from eternity, and its "revelation" is the realization in history of that eternal purpose. Note again how pronounced the element of fulfillment and finality is. The "now" (νῦν) of the revelation of the mystery stands in contrast to the "long ages" of silence. It has the sense of "now finally," "now at last"; it is, decidedly, an *eschatological* "now."

This understanding of the passage is reinforced in 1 Corinthians 2:1, if in the Greek text μυστήριον ("mystery" NRSV) is read instead of μαρτύριον ("testimony" ESV, NIV, NKJV, NASB).[24] In that case, "the mystery of God," which Paul proclaimed in Corinth, *is*, not just about, "Jesus Christ and him crucified" (2:2).

This sense of the mystery and its revelation is present in the similar pattern of expression found in 2 Timothy 1:9-10: salvation is a matter of "his [God's] own purpose and grace, which he gave us in Christ Jesus before the ages began, and which now has been manifested through the appearing of our Savior Christ Jesus" (cf. Titus 1:2-3). Outside of Paul, the event

---

21 The participle σεσιγημένου may also be translated, "kept silent."

22 To be clear, new verbal revelation is included in the revelation of the mystery inasmuch as characteristically in the history of special revelation redemptive deed (the mystery in this instance) is accompanied by explanatory revelatory word, such as Paul, by inspiration, provides here.

23 This is yet another New Testament indication that the Old Testament is about Christ and the gospel. Accordingly, Paul customarily preached Christ from the Old Testament (Acts 17:2-3: "as was his custom . . . from the Scriptures").

24 Both variants are fairly evenly attested, and each is defensible as original on contextual and transcriptional grounds.

of Christ's sacrificial death "was foreknown before the foundation of the world but was made manifest in the last times for the sake of you" (1 Pet. 1:19-20). In both of these instances, "manifested" is the same verb used in Romans 16:26, and in the latter, the event manifested is eschatological; Christ's death takes place "in the last times."

Relevant here, too, are other instances where Paul uses terms for verbal communication concerning Christ in a nonverbal historical event sense: his future return, the event, will be "the revelation of our Lord Jesus Christ" (1 Cor. 1:7 NASB); he himself, in his work, is "the wisdom of God" (1 Cor. 1:24; cf. 1:30); the event of his death is itself "the testimony given at the proper time" (1 Tim. 2:6).

Colossians 1:26-27

the mystery hidden for ages and generations but now revealed to his saints. To them God chose to make known how great among the Gentiles are the riches of the glory of this mystery, which is Christ in you, the hope of glory.

The similarity between these verses and Romans 16:25-26 is apparent, making it plausible that Paul echoes what he wrote earlier in Romans. But there are differences between the two passages, and these serve to clarify further how "the revelation of the mystery" (Rom. 1:25) is to be understood.

At the close of Colossians 1:25, Paul, in reflecting on his ministry (1:24), states that his God-given "stewardship" (or "commission") is "to make the word of God fully known." The clause that follows directly, then, states the content of that word.

Here, questions similar to those raised in interpreting Romans 16:25-26 present themselves: In what sense is the mystery as revealed the content of Paul's preaching? Does it consist solely in the disclosure of previously secret teaching, unknown information? Or, with the explanatory verbal revelation that accompanies it, is it a nonverbal event or reality?

Here, more pointedly than in the Romans passage, the answer is the latter. For Paul goes on to say that the mystery—long hidden, extending back into the depth of God's eternal purpose and now revealed[25]—is "Christ in

---

[25] Here, as in Rom. 16:26, "now" (νῦν) is contrastive and eschatological; it has the force of "now at last," "finally."

you, the hope of glory" (Col. 1:27). The revealed mystery is not previously unknown and now eventually disclosed information about Christ, but Christ himself. The ground and substance of the church's certain hope is Christ in his work, not heretofore arcane teaching about him.

This conclusion is reinforced as Paul continues his line of thought into the opening verses of chapter 2 and speaks of "the mystery of God, namely, Christ" (2:2 NIV). After weighing textual and syntactical considerations, "Christ" is best understood as being in apposition to "mystery"; Christ himself is the mystery. When Paul immediately adds that in Christ "are hidden all the treasures of wisdom and knowledge" (2:3), in context, this is best taken as meaning that Christ is the now revealed embodiment of the wisdom and knowledge resident in him as the mystery (cf. "Christ . . . the wisdom of God," 1 Cor. 1:24).[26]

This material in Colossians shows again how little the revelation of the mystery in view here and in Romans 16 is a purely noetic disclosure, wholly a matter of previously undisclosed verbal revelation. Rather, the mystery revealed is the event of salvation in Christ, as that salvation previously was not yet accomplished in history but now, finally, is. Moreover, the mystery as revealed is not just an aspect of that salvation. Rather, within the context of Colossians 1-2, the revealed mystery is Christ in all of his saving "riches" and "glory" (1:27), as in him the "fullness of God" has been manifested "bodily" (1:19; 2:9) in history to accomplish the salvation of the church. As the mystery revealed, Christ is specifically the exalted Christ, Christ crucified and now resurrected and indwelling the church (cf. 1:18).

In both of these passages, Christ as the revealed mystery is made known "to all the Gentiles" (Rom. 16:26 NRSV), "among the Gentiles" (Col. 1:27). In Ephesians 3, reference to the Gentiles is prominent in relation to the multiple occurrences there of "mystery" (3:3-6, 9; cf. 3:1).

Concerning this usage in Ephesians 3, the mystery "made known" to Paul "by revelation" and into which he has "insight" is "the mystery of Christ" (3:3-4). This is likely an instance where mystery is predominantly a category of verbal revelation, in this case new verbal revelation about Christ. If so,

---

26 Col. 4:3 speaks of "the mystery of Christ," on account of which Paul is imprisoned. Here the genitive "of Christ" is likely appositional; the mystery is Christ himself. Similarly, "the mystery of the gospel" (Eph. 6:19) is plausibly taken to mean that the content of the gospel is Christ, referred to indirectly as the mystery.

in the light of Romans 16:25–26 and Colossians 1:26–27, the content of that revelation is Christ himself as the revealed mystery (cf. Col. 2:2; 3:4).

This mystery has "now been revealed," more broadly, to "his [God's] holy apostles and prophets,"[27] in contrast to its not being "made known to the sons of men in other generations" (Eph. 3:5; cf. "the mystery hidden for ages in God," 3:9). This is essentially the same contrast concerning the mystery and its revelation in the Romans and Colossians passages.

The substance of the mystery in view here is the inclusion of Gentiles along with Jews as "fellow heirs, members of the same body, and partakers of the promise in Christ Jesus through the gospel" (3:6; cf. 2:11–22). Seen in relation to the revelation of the mystery in Romans 16 and Colossians 1, this event of Gentile inclusion is not the whole of the revealed mystery. It is, however, an integral aspect, an essential outcome of the salvation accomplished by Christ.

Verbal revelation about the mystery of this inclusion of the Gentiles is not foreign to or unknown in the Old Testament; in that sense, it is not, as it has been put, an "unforeseen mystery" there. Without taking the time here to show it, the Old Testament is replete with references to the future inclusion of Gentiles (e.g., Isa. 42:6; 49:6; cf. Luke 24:46–47: "Thus it is written, . . . repentance and the forgiveness of sins should be proclaimed in his name to all nations"; cf. Rom. 15:8-12 and the Old Testament passages cited there).

Conclusion. The way in which Paul associates his own ministry with the revelation of the mystery and qualifies it in a fundamental way with that descriptor makes clear, by this one expression, both the eschatological character of the content of his preaching as well as the eschatological context of his ministry. This point, in view at the beginning of Romans (1:2) as we noted, comes out again at its close.

Paul is clearly aware of what is nothing less than the eschatological character of his time and place in the history of redemption as an instrument of revelation. In view as well, by implication, without being able to dwell on it here—as important as it is—is the eschatological character of all new covenant ministry (cf. 2 Cor. 3:6). Again, the νῦν of the revelation of the mystery is the "now" of redemptive-historical fulfillment, in contrast to the

---

27 These prophets, contrasted here with past generations, are New Testament prophets; cf. 2:20.

preceding ages-long waiting for that fulfillment. The salvation manifested in Christ is what God has finally done after ages of expectation, after the accomplishment of that salvation had been "hidden for ages and generations" (Col. 1:26). The revelation of the mystery is yet another way of expressing the inaugurated arrival of the eschatological age to come.

Galatians 4:4; Ephesians 1:10; 1 Corinthians 10:11

This basic eschatological orientation comes out in still other distinctively Pauline expressions, like those in these verses:

> But when the fullness of time had come, God sent forth his Son, born of woman, born under the law. (Gal. 4:4)

> as a plan for the fullness of time, to unite all things in him, things in heaven and things on earth. (Eph 1:10)[28]

Note that in Ephesians 1:10, the fullness of time is associated with "making known . . . the mystery of his will, . . . which he [God] set forth in Christ (1:9), connecting with the use of "mystery" in Romans 16:25–26 and Colossians 1:26–27.

"The fulness of time" in these verses does not mean what it is often taken to mean. The point, undoubtedly true, is frequently made that developments in the first-century Mediterranean resulted in a confluence of significant geopolitical and cultural changes and trends, and that the way in which these factors came together provided a context that was optimal for the coming of Christ. "The fullness of time," then, is seen as capturing this point.

This point, as true as it is on other grounds, is not what the expression means or what the verses where it occurs have in view. By it, Paul is not referring to an especially opportune time midstream in the ongoing course of history. The fullness of time is not a matter of a certain historical "ripeness," an auspicious or strategic time reached during the course of history.

Rather, Paul means exactly what he says. He speaks here in an absolute sense of the fulfillment of "the time" and of "times." The fullness in view is

---

28 In the Greek text, these expressions vary in the time words used: τὸ πλήρωμα τοῦ χρόνου (Gal. 4:4), τοῦ πληρώματος τῶν καιρῶν (Eph. 1:10), but, within the two-aeon framework, they are fairly taken as having the same reference.

fulfillment understood in terms of finality, as the definite articles used serve to accent. With the coming of Christ and his work in history, the time of this world has been "filled up." History, comprehensively considered, has reached its consummation, its telos.

True, the fulfillment spoken of here is initial; it has a still-future aspect. We need to be sure that in our own work we do not lose sight of that future but give it due attention. But we must not tone down what Paul says here. The end of history has arrived. Its consummation has begun, really and truly. "The fullness of time" is yet another way of signaling the end of this age and the dawning of the age to come.

The eschatological force of the phrase is reinforced in Ephesians 1:10 by the immediately following correlative clause. The purpose associated with the filling up of time is "to unite all things in him [Christ]." As we might variously render this infinitive used here (ἀνακεφαλαιώσασθαι), what has been inaugurated is the "summing up" or "heading up" or "bringing together" of all things in Christ, bringing all things together under Christ as head (κεφαλή) (cf. 1:22: Christ as "head over all things to the church").

That is what has actually begun, nothing less than the consummate "getting it all together," if you will, in Christ. The note of universality or completeness is explicit and emphatic. "All things" are cosmic in scope; they are "things in heaven and things on earth."[29]

First Corinthians 10:11 is in the midst of a context where Paul is exhorting the church to resist temptation, particularly the temptation to idolatry ("flee from idolatry," 10:14). He does that by drawing an analogy between the New Testament church and Old Testament Israel in the Sinai desert. Much as the author of Hebrews does (Heb. 3–4), here Paul views the church as the new and final wilderness community, as the eschatological pilgrim congregation.

Having cited incidences of the wilderness generation's idolatry and rebellion (1 Cor. 10:6–10), he states (10:11), "These things happened to

---

29 Earlier versions of the NIV (e.g., 1984) have "when the times will have reached their fulfillment" in Eph. 1:10. That injects a note of futurity that is not present and misses the present emphasis that Paul is concerned to make. The latest (2011) version has "when the times reach their fulfillment." That rendering, though not explicitly future, is still too indefinite about the time of the fulfillment in view. The NLT ("At the right time he will bring everything together under the authority of Christ") similarly misses this point.

them as examples and were written down as warnings for us" (NIV; cf. "as examples for us," 10:6). This "us," he concludes, are those "on whom the end of the ages has come."

This is how the church is to understand itself in dealing with exposure to the continuing temptations of "the present evil age" (Gal. 1:4). It must not lose sight of the basic identity it has because it also already exists in the eschatological age to come that has arrived in Christ, his death and resurrection. With an eye to the immediately following verses (1 Cor. 10:16-22; cf. 11:23-26), participation in the Lord's Supper both confirms and serves as a continual reminder of this basic identity.

The redemptive-historical fulfillment that has taken place in Christ—at the center of Paul's theology and for which his use of the two-aeon distinction provides a clarifying framework, particularly the eschatological nature of that fulfillment—can be seen in two further instances.

2 Corinthians 6:2

For he says,

> "In a favorable time I listened to you,
> and in a day of salvation I have helped you."

Behold, now is the favorable time; behold, now is the day of salvation.

The immediate larger context unit here is 5:11-6:10.[30] In the opening verses of 2 Corinthians 6, Paul continues reflecting on his ministry as a ministry of reconciliation (cf. 5:18). In that ministry, he is "working together" with God (6:1), as he has been entrusted by God with "the message of reconciliation" (5:19). At the heart of that message are the appeals "be reconciled to God" (5:20) and "not to receive the grace of God in vain" (6:1).This latter appeal prompts our particular interest here: his citation and use in 6:2 of Isaiah 49:8.

Immediately noticeable in this interpretive handling is the emphatic two-fold occurrence of "now." This reminds of its usage in Romans 16:26 and Colossians 1:26 in connection with the revelation of the mystery. In fact, as

---

30 The placement of the chapter break at 6:1 obscures this.

we will see, here too this "now" is eschatological; it has broad redemptive-historical overtones and associations.

Reflecting the parallelism of Isaiah 49:8, "the favorable time" and "the day of salvation" predicated of the "now" are synonymous. How, then, should we understand their reference?

Answering that question is helped with a negative observation. Despite the many sermons preached on this text, in view is not a particular occasion or set of circumstances in the life of an individual sinner that must be taken advantage of before it passes away. The "time" and "day" do not refer to the chance or opportunity that the sinner has to repent and believe in Christ, which in God's eternal and inscrutable plan may be here today but gone tomorrow. That scenario is of course true on other biblical grounds, but that is not the point here. Analogous to what we have seen in 5:17 about the new creation, the favorable time/the day of salvation is not to be understood as referring to a merely individual state of affairs.

The meaning of these expressions comes from the context of the Old Testament citation that Paul uses here. Isaiah 49 is one of the so-called Servant Songs. As their exegesis is able to show, in them the servant speaking in the first-person singular provides a prophetic forecast of Christ and his work. In other words, the "you" singular (σου, σοι) in Isaiah 49:8 and 2 Corinthians 6:2, as Paul quotes from the Septuagint, refers to the servant; this "you" is Christ.

Isaiah 49:8 is intelligible only in light of the preceding context, especially the lament of the servant in the first half of 49:4 that he has toiled "in vain" and expanded his strength "for nothing," though this lament is not without the hope in the Lord expressed in the last half of the verse ("yet surely my right is with the LORD, / and my recompense with my God"). Isaiah 49:8, then, is part of the response of the Lord in the intervening verses, assuring the servant that his hope is well-founded and his labors are not in vain, because he, the Lord, has answered the servant and come to his aid. In view of the parallelism, we may gloss: the Lord has answered the servant by coming to his aid; the Lord's efficacious answer is the aid he gives.

The Pauline context is one of fulfillment of the Isaiah passage. "The favorable time" is the time marked by the death and resurrection of Christ (cf. 2 Cor. 5:15); it is the time when the Lord answered the servant eschatologically. Pointedly, the resurrection is the Lord's vindicatory answer to the servant.[31] Correlatively, "the day of salvation" is the day of reconciliation, for believers (5:18) and for the world (5:19).

Rather plainly, then, these expressions are to be taken in a broad redemptive-historical sense. The "time" and "day" is the end time of fulfillment that has come with Christ, the day of salvation appointed for the spread of the gospel to the nations; it is part of the Lord's helping response to the servant: "I will make you as a light for the nations, / that my salvation may reach to the end of the earth" (Isa. 49:6).

This conclusion prompts several additional observations. First is a hermeneutical reminder. The use of Isaiah 49:8 in 2 Corinthians 6:2 provides a good illustration of how in the New Testament use of the Old, the citation of a verse or passage is often (though not always) to its larger Old Testament context and its meaning.

Second, the church in the period between Christ's resurrection and return may be construed as part of the Lord's "answer" to Christ as the servant of the Lord. The church is "now" the "recompense" or "reward" promised to him (Isa. 49:4; 49:6: "I will make you as a light for the nations, / that my salvation may reach to the end of the earth"; cf. Luke 24:46–47). In this respect, it may be said, the church in the "now generation"!

Third, in contexts that are largely parallel and where Paul is exhorting the church concerning its life and the various relationships that Christians have (as husbands, wives, parents, children, masters, and slaves), Ephesians 5:16 and Colossians 4:5 speak of "making the best use of the time." In this phrase "the time" (with the definite article in Greek, τὸν καιρόν) most likely has the broad, redemptive-historical sense it has in 2 Corinthians 6:2; it refers to the whole of the time span between Christ's resurrection and return. In view, in other words, is not the relative amount of time granted to each individual believer, though this is how the phrase is often understood.[32]

---

31 This point is reinforced by noting that "the favorable time" is the same as "the year of the Lord's favor" (Isa. 61:2, in the context of another servant song), which in Luke 4:19 Jesus applies broadly to the time of his earthly ministry.

32 E.g., in many translations. Eph. 5:16: "making the most of your time" (NASB), "making the most of every opportunity" (NIV), "make the most of every opportunity" (NLT), "taking advantage of every opportunity" (NET); Col. 4:5: "making the most of the opportunity" (NASB), "make the most of every opportunity" (NIV, NLT), "making the most of the opportunities" (NET).

But what about "because the days are evil" in Ephesians 5:16? While it is the case that "the time" in this verse is, as we are proposing, a positive salvation-historical notion, there is an under- or dark side that needs to be recognized and taken into account. While the new creation has dawned, and while the age to come is present, the old aeon, "this present evil age" (Gal. 1:4) still continues.

Several other statements of Paul are plausibly, if not certainly, read in the same way as Ephesians 5:16 and Colossians 4:5. "Besides this you know the time, that the hour has come for you to wake from sleep. For salvation is nearer to us now than when we first believed" (Rom. 13:11). Here, too, "the time" (τὸν καιρόν), with "the hour" (ὥρα) for being alert, likely has in view the entire period until Christ's return, to which the approaching "salvation" in the latter part of the verse refers.

"The time has been shortened" (1 Cor. 7:29 NASB). Here "the time" (ὁ καιρὸς) is coterminous with "the form of this world" that is "passing away" (7:31 NASB 1995). It is the present period until Christ's return, in which "as if . . . not" is the principle that should mark the lives of believers in their basic relationships and activities (7:29b–31a).

Galatians 3:23, 25

Our interest in these verses is the references to faith and the arresting insight they provide into how controlling for Paul is his redemptive-historical outlook. In the broader context, 2:15–4:7, the main point is justification by faith and the related matter, it should not be missed, of the Galatians' reception of the Spirit (3:2, 5); the two, the forensic and the renovative aspects of salvation, are never separated for Paul.

The background here is the compromising and jeopardizing of the gospel among them by the insistence of some that circumcision is necessary for salvation. The main issue at stake in the passage, then, concerns the application of salvation, how salvation is received: is it "by works of the law, or by hearing with faith" (3:5)? In other words, this issue is an *ordo salutis* issue.

Almost as obvious as this primary concern, however, is the redemptive-historical framework Paul brings to bear in dealing with it. This becomes especially clear beginning at 3:15. All along, Paul has been developing and driving home one key point, the central thesis advanced at the beginning of the section: "a person is not justified by works of the law but through faith in Jesus Christ" (2:16).[33]

This emphasis gives rise—inevitably we may say—to the question of the law, its origin and function. In this regard, Paul maintains that despite the unrelieved antithesis between whether salvation (justification) is received by doing the works of the law or through faith in Christ—an antithesis at the *ordo salutis* level—God's giving of the law at Sinai is not contrary to his saving purpose. The law does not spring from some contrary motive; it is not a malevolent power. As Paul affirms elsewhere, "the law is holy, and the commandment is holy and righteous and good"; "the law is spiritual" (Rom. 7:12, 14; cf. 7:13).

The Mosaic law, coming as it does 430 years after the promises given to Abraham by the covenant God made with him, does not nullify but is for the sake of those promises (Gal. 3:17). The giving of the law is in the interests of bringing about their fulfillment and the realization of the inheritance promised to Abraham (3:18). In this respect, the law is a function of promise.

Specifically, the law "was added because of transgressions" (Gal. 3:19; cf. Rom. 5:20; 7:13), in order to bring about the salvation in Christ promised to Abraham and his offspring (Gal. 3:16, 29). To this promise, Abraham's faith, and faith like his, is the requisite response. This, briefly, is the gist of the historical perspective initiated in 3:6–9 and resumed at 3:16.

This sketch situates the references to faith in 3:23 and 25.

Now before faith came, we were held captive under the law, imprisoned until the coming faith would be revealed. So then, the law was our guardian until Christ came, in order that we might be justified by faith. But now that faith has come, we are no longer under a guardian.

Here, two related points are made about faith: (1) It is set over against the law in a broad historical sense. (2) It was not present until the time of Christ.

---

33 I leave to the side here the much debated question of whether in the prepositional phrase διὰ πίστεως Ἰησοῦ Χριστοῦ, the genitive Ἰησοῦ Χριστοῦ is objective ("faith in Jesus Christ") or subjective ("the faith [faithfulness] of Jesus Christ") and assume the objective understanding to be correct. The literature on this question is extensive. For a treatment establishing the objective view, see esp. Moisés Silva, "Faith Versus Works of the Law," in *Justification and Variegated Nomism*, vol. 2, ed. D. A. Carson, Peter T. O'Brien, Mark A. Seifrid (Grand Rapids, MI: Baker Academic, 2004): 215–48.

The contrast in these verses, then, is not between the law and faith in individual experience, in the application of salvation (*ordo salutis*). The "we" is rhetorical, for readers with Paul viewing the unfolding of covenant history. The role of the law as "guardian" (or "tutor," "guide," "custodian"— παιδαγωγός) is not personal but preparatory for the coming of Christ in the period prior to his coming.

Galatians 3:24 is often taken to describe the effect of the law in the life of the individual sinner as the law produces a conviction of sin and so drives the sinner to Christ out of a sense of need produced by that conviction. That scenario is certainly sound and biblical but is based on considerations other than are found here. The law has and is to have that effect in sinners, revealing their need of Christ and bringing them to faith in Christ, but that is not the point here. In the prepositional phrase εἰς Χριστόν (3:24), the force of the preposition is almost certainly not telic (indicating the goal or purpose: "to Christ," NASB, NKJV) but temporal; the sense of the phrase is "until Christ came" or "until Christ" (ESV, NIV).[34]

What, then, is the meaning of "before faith came" and "now that faith has come"? How is Paul using "faith" here? In Scripture, faith has two basic meanings. An established way of distinguishing the difference is the distinction between *fides quae creditur* ("the faith that is believed"; faith as a body of belief or doctrine) and *fides qua creditur* ("the faith by which it is believed"; faith as an act of believing). The classic biblical instance of the former sense is Jude 3 ("contend for the faith that was once for all delivered to the saints"). But that sense is hardly in view in these two occurrences. So in Galatians 3:23, 25, we are left with faith as the act of believing.

But how can Paul say this? He hardly means that no one believed or exercised faith before the time of Christ. For throughout this passage, beginning at 3:6, Abraham is the exemplary believer, the model of justification by faith.[35]

The answer lies in recognizing that in these two statements, "faith" is used in an abbreviating sense, as a metonym. The term for the exercise of faith refers here not to that exercise but to the object of faith exercised. The word

---

34 Translations that take the personal effect view of the law have to render with an interpretive gloss in italics: "*to lead us* to Christ" (NASB), "*to bring us* to/unto Christ" (NKJV/KJV).

35 Cf. Rom. 4, where David is also an example of justification by faith (4:6–8); note that the giving of the law at Sinai—before and after Sinai—makes no difference for being justified by faith.

for exercising faith is used to show that that exercise is inseparable from its object, that it is meaningless apart from that object, and depends on that object for its efficacy. Here "faith" stands for the salvation accomplished by Christ; "faith" is Christ as the object of faith.

So, "before faith came" and "now that faith has come" mean before Christ, as the object of faith, came and now that he has come. Their sense is equivalent to "until Christ came" (3:24), "until the Seed would come," (3:19 NASB; cf. 3:16, "'to your seed,' that is, Christ," NASB), or "when the fullness of time had come" in God's sending of his Son (4:4).

I have taken the time to consider this usage because it highlights in a striking way how pronounced and important is the historical qualification that Paul attaches to the exercise of saving faith. That point is perhaps obvious but can become obscured. Justification by faith is not a timeless arrangement or procedure of God. It is not experienced by the individual sinner directly on the basis of a pretemporal decree, as one might infer from a misreading of the "golden chain" sequence in Romans 8:30, although that predestinating decree is surely involved and determinative.

Nor is justification experienced as the realization of a suprahistorical or existential state of affairs. In view here is the understanding of Bultmann and others where faith is a constitutive act, where believing is, we may say, its own "justification."

Justification is not vaguely theological; in its specifically theological and fully Trinitarian and covenantal character, it is pointedly Christological. That is, justification is fully dependent upon and given its abiding validity by the coming of the Son in the fulness of time (Gal. 4:4). The God who justifies the sinner is the God who justifies in union with Christ (see Gal. 5:4) by what has been effected in his death and resurrection.

Justification by faith—including the justifying faith of Abraham, Paul's use of Abraham as the model for justification by faith—is valid and intelligible only in terms of the basic structure of the history of God's covenant with Abraham; that is, in terms of the distinction between the promise of that covenant and its fulfillment or, more pointedly, the fulfillment of the promise.

So thoroughly and exclusively is justifying faith dependent upon and inseparable from its object in a redemptive-historical sense that Paul can even speak of that faith as not being present until the object, the promised seed, Christ, is present and his saving work has been accomplished in history.[36] Here again is another indication of how for Paul the *ordo salutis* (the application of salvation) is controlled and given its meaning by the *historia salutis* (the accomplishment of salvation), how the history and experience of the individual sinner is related to and dependent on the work of Christ in history.

Summary and Conclusion

Living in the Fullness of Time

The objective in this section has been to survey a number of those passages in which Paul orients his message and ministry by using the two-aeon construct, and in other related ways, that reflect that construct, passages in which he indicates the basic nature of his ministry as an apostle, both as a writer of Scripture and as an apostle-missionary to the Gentiles.

What this survey demonstrates is the historical-eschatological perspective that permeates Paul's theology and informs it as a whole. The passages considered show the all-embracing redemptive-historical context in which he locates his ministry and which qualifies it in its entirety. Even more basically, these passages bring to light that it is within this redemptive-historical context that he locates himself and other Christians and qualifies their existence as believers in Jesus Christ.

Looking back over the passages surveyed: In all he is and does, Paul is among those "on whom the end of the ages has come" (1 Cor. 10:11). He is deeply conscious of living in "the fullness of time" (Gal. 4:4; Eph. 1:10), when, at last, God has sent his Son and when the new creation has already dawned (2 Cor. 5:17). His vantage point in history is characterized by the fact that he is privileged to be able now to look back on the climactic events of the history of redemption, the death and resurrection of Christ, as having occurred.

Using a sometimes-cited analogy from the Second World War, Paul knows himself to be among those for whom the great D-Day kingdom

---

36 So far as the actual exercise of faith is concerned, the faith of Old Testament (old covenant) believers and New Testament (new covenant) believers differs but has the same object. The essential difference is this: The faith of the former is in the promise *to be fulfilled*; the faith of the latter is the same promise *that has been fulfilled*. For both, the focus of their faith, from different vantage points in covenant history, is Christ as the fulfillment of the promise.

battle is over, for whom the era of conflict between the kingdom of God and the dominion of Satan is in the past and has been decisively resolved; the redemption of God's people is an accomplished and secure reality (Col. 1:13-14).

To use another analogy—this from the history of redemption itself—in a way that Moses and Israel at the Red Sea could only catch a shadowy glimpse, Paul is now able to "stand still, and see the salvation of the LORD" (Ex. 14:13 KJV). He is among those believers for whom the period of shadows is a thing of the past, for whom the provisional and anticipatory has given way to fulfillment, to the dawn of the final order of things in the creation.

Moreover, concerning this decisive, epochal transition, this aeon-ending turn of events, as it is the context of his ministry, it is, more importantly, its content. Apart from this content and context, the salvation experienced by the New Testament believer is largely unintelligible.

All this can be summarized otherwise by saying that Paul is a minister of "the mystery that has been hidden from ages and generations, but has now been manifested to the saints" (Col. 1:26, my translation; cf. Rom. 16:25-26).

The Age to Come

In summarizing the basics of Paul's message and ministry, it is essential to take note of an element that, on balance, has yet to receive the attention commensurate with the fundamental structural place it has. Assuming the results of the attention that we will subsequently give to this aspect, we may state the conclusion here: The presence of the age to come, the eschatological fulfillment already realized, does not eliminate an equal emphasis on the fulfillment that is still future, on what that future will bring. Using the Second World War analogy again, D-Day is not yet V-E Day.

From his vantage point in history, Paul looks not only to the past and the fulfillment that has already taken place in Christ but also to the future. There is one great event still outstanding in the unfolding of the history of salvation, a future event that, like the past fulfillment, also controls his outlook on the present life of the church. That event, with its concomitants, is, of course, the parousia, the return of Christ.

So, for instance, together with the Corinthians, Paul is "eagerly waiting for the revelation of our Lord Jesus Christ" (1 Cor. 1:7, my translation). He is among all those who are "waiting for our blessed hope, the appearing of the glory of our great God and Savior Jesus Christ" (Titus 2:13).

This still-future eschatological hope of the church is widely recognized. But it is often and typically embraced with little or no recognition of, much less appreciation for, the fully eschatological character of what has already taken place in Christ. For that reason, to this point in our work, I have put the emphasis on the latter, the realized eschatology. However, we should not become so preoccupied with this already realized aspect that we lose sight of the equally and, in its way, ultimately more consummate reality that is still future.

One Parousia, Two Phases

The preceding point brings into view the question of the relationship between present/past and future in Paul's eschatological outlook. Addressing that question briefly and in general terms here, Paul's dual eschatological focus on both the future and the past, on the already-realized as well as the still-future, does not betray some sort of uncertainty or confusion on his part, as some in the critical history of interpretation have argued in different ways.

In fact, it is the case—as we will see when we subsequently consider Paul's teaching on resurrection—that the future is given with the past. What has already happened in the past, just because of its nature as past, has in view not only the present but also the future and requires that future. The one cannot be conceived of apart from the other.

Putting this point with a grammatical analogy, in parsing the tenses of redemptive-historical consummation, the past tense—or, better, the Greek perfect tense—and the future tense belong together. They are inseparable as they are dependent on each other.[37]

In this regard, an observation made earlier in considering the kingdom proclamation of Jesus bears repeating here. As we consider the use of the Old Testament by Paul and the other New Testament writers, particularly their elaboration of the Old Testament expectation of the coming of the Messiah and the eschatological day of the Lord, that elaboration has given

---

37   The Greek perfect tense indicates the present state that results from a past action; e.g., of Scripture, "it is written" (γέγραπται, 1 Cor. 1:31); of Christ's resurrection, "he is raised" (ἐγήγερται, 1 Cor. 15:20, my translation).

rise to the customary distinction between the first and second comings of Christ. But given the way Paul and others in the New Testament in fact delineate that distinction, stressing as does Paul the eschatological nature of both comings, the first as well as the second, the two are more aptly seen not as two separate events but, no matter how much time has in fact elapsed between them, as two parts, the beginning and end, of the same event complex. There is one day of the Lord, one coming of the Messiah, one parousia of Christ, that occurs in two basic phases or stages.

The Imminence of Christ's Return

Some brief comment may be made here about the imminence statements concerning the return of Christ in the New Testament.

Paul and other New Testament writers speak about Christ's return as near or soon (in Paul, e.g., Rom. 13:11; 1 Thess. 5:1-2). The reason is not because they have some advance calendar information that they, for most part, have held back and left to us to figure out with our eschatological ingenuity.[38] Nor is it because they and Jesus were mistaken, a virtual presupposition of much historical-critical interpretation.[39]

To the contrary, their imminence pronouncements *about the future* are made based on what has occurred *in the past*. Because of what has already happened in Christ, his future return is so certain that it is spoken of as soon or near. These imminence statements have the nuance of "it's just a matter of time now," "it's inevitable now," no matter how many years, even centuries, have elapsed in the meantime. The imminence expressed, in other words, is a redemptive-historical category, an expression of redemptive-historical certainty.

The Conditioned Present

To reiterate a basic conclusion of our survey in this section, a key component and overall controlling qualification of Paul's teaching concerning

---

38 Church history is replete with exercises of this errant guesswork. Looking back over recent decades, Hal Lindsay, Harold Camping, and Tim LaHaye come to mind.

39 In this regard, it is important to keep in mind the distinction between what Paul and the other New Testament writers say and their understanding of what they say. What they say is, more ultimately and beyond their full comprehension, what God says. They may well have thought that Christ would return within the near future of their own lifetimes or, if not then, shortly thereafter. But that is not what they, by inspiration, say.

the present situation of believers is the conditioning of their present by the past and the future.

This conditioning and determination of their present by the past and the future does not have in view the personal past and personal future of each individual believer, but, as 2 Corinthians 5:17 especially shows, the redemptive-historical past and future. Concretely, a basic determinant of the present situation of the church is that it is bracketed by the resurrection and return of Christ. This bracketing is fundamental for understating the present existence of the believer and what that existence entails.

This eschatological bracketing is expressed perhaps most succinctly by Paul in what he writes to the Thessalonian Christians concerning reports that have come back to him about their reception of the gospel, specifically "how you turned to God from idols to serve the living and true God, and to wait for his Son from heaven, whom he raised from the dead, Jesus who delivers us from the wrath to come" (1 Thess. 1:9–10).

Here, the present life of the church is defined both by what it has been turned from and what it has been turned to. The church consists of those who in their personal lives have turned from idolatries of whatever sort to the service of the living and true God in all its aspects. This is a comprehensive description of what the church is all about: its worship and service of God (cf. Rom. 12:1–2).

But this service does not take place in a vacuum. It has a context, a determining historical context bracketed by the past and the future. The church's present service is "waiting service"—an active and engaged waiting for the future return of his Son. At the same time, that looking to the future entails looking to the past, to the death and resurrection of the Son, a backward look basic to and the source of its present worship and service, a looking back that also brings assurance of deliverance from condemnation in the future that Jesus will provide at his return. This bracketed service encapsulates the basic identity of the church in the interim between Christ's resurrection/ascension and return.

PAUL'S MODIFICATION OF THE TWO-AGE DISTINCTION: THE OVERLAP OF THE TWO AGES

In this chapter, our concern is with Paul's understanding of the eschatological fulfillment inaugurated by the salvation accomplished in the death and resurrection of Christ—or, more broadly, his humiliation and exalta-tion—and how that understanding is expressed by his use of the distinction between this world-age/aeon and the world-age/aeon to come.

At the outset, in considering the background to Paul's use of this construct, we noted that its origin is in Second Temple Judaism prior to the time of the New Testament and that from there it was taken over by Jesus, Paul, and the writer of Hebrews. However, we have also seen that in Paul's utilizing the two-aeon framework, an important and decisive difference is involved. That difference, formal and structural in nature, is not difficult to see. It concerns the coming or parousia of the Messiah as the division point between this age and the age to come. For Judaism then and orthodox Judaism still today, this event has not occurred; the Messiah has not yet come. For Paul, the Messiah has already come in the person of Christ. The end of this age has arrived; the age to come has been ushered in.

It is apparent, then, that Paul could not simply take over the two-aeon construct at hand in the Judaism in which he was raised.[40] For him to continue using it, now that Christ has come, basic structural modification was necessary. We have already gotten some indications of this modifica-tion in the passages we have so far examined. In the interim between the resurrection and return of Christ, the two ages are concurrent; the age to come has arrived, but the present evil age continues.

With a view to our subsequent work, it will be helpful at this point to reflect further on the modification required and formalize it. For that purpose, we may distinguish two basic modifications: one horizontal, the other vertical—keeping in mind that the two are inseparable and are really two aspects or dimensions of the modification involved.

The Horizontal Modification

In view of the fact that the Messiah has come, at a first glance, it might seem improper, even incongruous for Paul to continue thinking and writing in the present in terms of the contrast between this aeon and the coming aeon. After all, what from the traditional Jewish point of view was the aeon

---

40 See also Richard B. Gaffin Jr., "The Resurrection of Christ and the Age to Come," The Gospel Coalition, https://www.thegospelcoalition.org/.

to come has, in fact, ceased to be that, solely coming, only future; it has become a present reality.

Yet despite this initial impression of incongruity, Paul continues to think and write in terms of the two-aeon schema as relevant to the present. Without at all slighting the eschatological significance of Christ's work—the aeon-to-come inaugurating consequences of his cross and resurrection—Paul still continues to apply the antithesis between this aeon and the aeon to come to the historical situation postresurrection.

How is this antithesis still relevant now that the Messiah, Jesus the Christ, has come, now that the end of this age has occurred? The answer, the rationale for the continuing relevance of the antithesis, lies in the basic structural consideration we have already had occasion to note. For Paul, the arrival of the Messiah has a dual character: It takes place not as a one-time coming but in two successive stages or epochs. The coming of the eschatological day of the Lord, the end of the age, the parousia of the Messiah, occurs in two installments.

The first appearance of Christ is eschatological. It initiates the realization of Old Testament expectation, of the promises of the old covenant, of the hope of the faithful remnant in Israel. In other eschatological terms, it is the arrival of the *basileia*, of the hoped-for eschatological rule and realm of God; or, again, it is the dawning of the age to come. But still, making full allowance for the stupendous effect of Christ's coming, his coming does not mark the cessation of all historical expectation. Rather, what has taken place gives rise to a new complex of hope, a renewed focus on the future.[41]

The following observations apply to the interim phase of the parousia, to the interval between Christ's first and second comings.

First, this period is a combination of affinities between this aeon and the aeon to come. The present situation between Christ's resurrection and return is an admixture of characteristics of both the pre-eschatological order marked by sin and its results and the eschatological order of deliverance from sin and its consequences.

---

41 Vos seeks to clarify this development with a couple of analogies drawn from the area of biological reproduction: for one, cell separation; the coming aeon in its arrival involves yet another still to separate from it. Or at a higher level: the coming aeon in its arrival is a mother pregnant with a child yet to be born (Geerhardus Vos, *The Pauline Eschatology* [Grand Rapids, MI: Baker, 1979], 36).

Since this duplex situation will occupy us in some detail later, suffice it here to say that a large part of the program of New Testament interpretation or, putting it more personally, a large part of understanding your own existence as a believer, of what your life as a Christian is all about, lies in clarifying this distinctive admixture of the old and the new, of the pre-eschatological and the eschatological, of both having been definitively delivered from sin and yet continuing to sin.

Second, Paul continues to refer to this period—the interim between the first and second comings—as "this/the present age" (1 Tim. 6:17; 2 Tim. 4:10: Titus 2:12), using the language of the old or pre-eschatological aeon in the traditional construct to describe this period.

But with that noted—as the passages considered in the previous section are beyond clear in showing—Paul maintains that the eschatological age to come has already been inaugurated; the new age has already arrived. To borrow the language of the writer of Hebrews—almost certainly not Paul, but fairly expressing Paul's own view and what he could have stated—Christians presently experience "the powers of the age to come" (Heb. 6:5).

Paul calls the period between Christ's resurrection and return "the present age." But it is the present time in which the reality of the future aeon, the eschatological order, has arrived with its penetrating and transforming power.

Third, it is Oscar Cullmann who coined the term "taseology"[42]—from the Greek τάσις, one of whose meanings is "tension"—to characterize this present interim state of affairs. The notion of tension aptly captures the essence of this in-between situation of believers in the period between the resurrection and return of Christ (cf., e.g., 1 Thess. 1:9-10)—pulled as they are by the opposed forces of this aeon from which they have been delivered and the aeon to come into which they have been brought. Believers continue experiencing the tugs of conflicting attraction between the old, pre-eschatological order of sin and death and the new and final order of righteousness and life in Christ.

The Vertical Modification

What may be viewed as a second modification in Paul's use of the two-aeon schema brings us into contact with what is perhaps the most distinctive element in his eschatology.

---

42 Oscar Cullmann, *Salvation in History* (New York: Harper & Row, 1967), 172.

Historical Then Theological

The first modification, as significant as it is, maintains the linear or horizontal outlook essential to the original two-age doctrine. The overlap between the two ages beginning with Christ's death and resurrection occurs on the horizontal timeline moving forward toward the end of history at his return. In that sense, the two ages, while overlapping and concurrent, are still consecutive.

The second modification, or second aspect of modification, consists in the introduction of a vertical or perpendicular component into the overlap between the two aeons. This modification, as we will see, comes out more explicitly in Paul's later letters. Contrary to the way in which some historical-critical scholarship has argued, this second modification is not a matter of Paul eventually changing his mind during the course of his ministry, moving away from a horizontal to a vertical outlook. The second modification does not supplant the first and make it obsolete.

Rather, the two modifications have to be seen together; they supplement each other. Joined to the linear or horizontal orientation is a vertical or perpendicular outlook. The aeon to come is above as well as ahead. The eschatological kingdom in its coming is in heaven as it is also on earth (cf. Matt. 6:10).

Initially, these observations may seem paradoxical, perhaps even unintelligible. It may appear that injecting a vertical or perpendicular component amounts to a break with two-aeon scheme with its horizontal orientation that cannot be expressed meaningfully in terms of it or is even in conflict with it, as some historical-critical interpretation has argued.

Help in alleviating this impression comes from recalling that earlier in this chapter, in discussing the background to Paul's use of the two-aeon distinction as it emerged in Second Temple Judaism we noted the semantic development experienced by the Hebrew עוֹלָם and Aramaic אָעְלְמָ, and αἰών in Hellenistic Judaism, as they functioned in this construction and as αἰών was taken over and used in the New Testament. What in each instance was originally a time word took on as well a spatial meaning. A comprehensive word for time also comes to have an all-inclusive spatial sense; these words, as they are employed in the two-aeon scheme, can mean either "age" or "world."

Further, these two senses are interrelated. Αἰών has a dual force; it refers to a delimited spatiotemporal order, to a world-age.[43] In terms of its *world* sense, then, what we are considering as a second, vertical modification of the distinction between the two ages becomes not only possible but also conceptually intelligible.

This line of reflection, however, though relevant to the modification involved, is by itself misleading. At issue here is not simply a matter of theoretical possibility or conceptual potential, formally considered, at Paul's disposal, but a practical necessity of monumental proportions.

As with the first modification, so here too the factor that determines the direction of Paul's thinking is what has already taken place in the coming of Christ in the fullness of time. This is *the historical reality* that necessitates the modification in theory we are now considering. It is not as if the apostle is involved in some sort of abstract, merely theoretical speculation. Rather, it is the case here that "the historical was first, then the theological."[44]

Here again—a structural characteristic of the history of special revelation noted previously—revelatory word is focused interpretively on redemptive deed; the latter is the raison d'être that necessitates the former. First the historical event, then its theological explanation.

The Ascended Christ

In this instance, what may be viewed as the second modification in Paul's use of the two-aeon distinction was occasioned by Christ's resurrection and its consequences, by the activity of Christ as resurrected. The new state of affairs that doctrine had to keep pace with is, as it might be put, the abiding liveliness of Christ.

The empty tomb (1 Cor. 15:4) not only tells us where Jesus is not but also raises the question, Where then is he? In answering this question, the church has at times gone to extremes in reflecting on the implications of the resurrection and ascension. We run the risk of speculatively overstating and have to be on guard against falling into a kind of "theological astrophysics."

---

43 Throughout our discussion, we have been using "aeon" to signal this double meaning (*Doppelklang*).

44 Vos, *The Pauline Eschatology*, 41. This could well serve as an aphorism that, if heeded, would cut off a great deal of undue theological speculation.

However, in the concern to avoid undue speculation, we must not underplay or downplay what the New Testament does say. At least this much must be affirmed on the basis of its teaching: Christ is not here but *there*, with "there" being described characteristically as "the right hand of God" (in Paul, Rom. 8:34; Col. 3:1; cf. Acts 2:33; 7:55–56; 1 Pet. 3:22).

In other words, in his ascension, Christ has departed to a new sphere of existence. No matter how sublime, how difficult it may be for us to conceive, how "fourth-dimensional," Christ has departed to a new environment. I speak of an "environment" advisedly, because where he now is, is a place, a spatiotemporal order, appropriate to and in keeping with the continuing incarnate mode of his existence. In any event, the abiding liveliness of Christ resurrected and ascended is the liveliness of the *incarnate* Christ.[45]

The ascension of Christ means that the eschatological "center of gravity"[46] has shifted from the present world order to a new world order. As long as the present world continues its course, the eschatological world above will run concurrent to it. With the resurrection and ascension of Christ, the world to come has become a present reality, even though it is the case that only first in the future at his parousia will it come into its own in entirety, only then will the coming aeon be realized in all its fullness.

To make the basic point in view here, it could be said that the ascension of Christ results in a cosmic dualism or bifurcation. In speaking in that way, however, we need to keep clear to ourselves and as we communicate to others that this is dualism brought about in history, by the course of the history of redemption. It is effected in time and is of temporary duration. Accordingly, it is far removed from any sort of pagan Greek cosmology or timeless ontological dualism.

Paul, then, is the first and most explicit among the New Testament writers to add a new dimension to the eschatological outlook and interest of believers. Not only do believers continue to look to the future along the horizontal timeline of world history moving to its consummation, but in

45 It is worth noting that an inevitable indicator of false religion, a mark of certain cults, is a denial that the resurrected Christ is still incarnate. "The only redeemer of God's elect is the Lord Jesus Christ, who, being the eternal Son of God, became man, and so was, and continueth to be, God and man in two distinct natures, and one person, *forever*" (Westminster Shorter Catechism, 21; emphasis added).

46 Vos, *The Pauline Eschatology*, 37.

doing that, there is now also a vertical reference that enters in. Believers not only "wait for his Son from heaven" (1 Thess. 1:10; cf. Titus 2:13) but also "set [their] minds on things that are above" (Col. 3:2).

Note again, it bears repeating, this vertical interest, though more pronounced in his later letters, does not supplant but supplements the horizontal outlook. The introduction of the vertical is not, say, a desperate measure invented by Paul to counteract his disappointment over the delay of the parousia and his increasing fear that it would not occur.

Vital Union

More, however, is involved in this second modification than simply the believer's eschatological outlook and interest, as we just put it and as important as that is. Much more.

Nothing is more basic to Paul's teaching on salvation than the union that exists between Christ and believers, the reality of being "in Christ." Being united to Christ lies at the basis of all God's dealings with his people for their salvation from eternity to eternity—from their being chosen "in him" before the foundation of the world (Eph. 1:4-5), to their present life and freedom from condemnation for their sins "in Christ Jesus" (Rom. 8:1-2), to their future glorification "with him" in that union (Rom. 8:17).

Presupposing what more careful study than I can undertake here will show,[47] it needs to be recognized that the present union of the believer with Christ is not only representative or legal. It is that, but it is also *vital*. It is nothing less than a life-union, a union in life shared with Christ. In that sense, it is an aspect of what is characteristically called mystical union and is effected by the enlivening work of the Holy Spirit in the believer. In that sense, vital union, union in life with Christ, is also Spiritual.

As good an instance of this vital union as any in Paul is Galatians 2:20, often memorized and quoted, autobiographical yet also true of every believer: "I have been crucified with Christ and I no longer live, but Christ lives in me" (NIV). Here, it is apparent, the life in view is the life of Christ as crucified, resurrected, and ascended (cf. Eph. 2:5-6)—in other words,

---

47 For a brief overview of biblical teaching on union with Christ with some reference to other treatments in greater depth, see my chapter, "The Work of Christ Applied," in *Christian Dogmatics: Reformed Theology for the Church Catholic* ed., Michael. Allen and Scott R. Swain (Grand Rapids, MI: Baker Academic, 2016), 280-83.

the life specifically of Christ as he is now exalted, and the sharing of the believer in that exaltation life.

It is also apparent, then, that the ascension means more than only a shift in locality of "the center of gravity" of the eschatological outlook of believers. The ascension involves more than the movement of the object of their religious interest and devotion. For believers, the ascension has an import that is truly experiential or existential. The ascension means nothing less than the relocation of the actual life of the believer, in a sense to be clarified further.

Keeping this consideration in view—the vertical dimension not only of the eschatological outlook of believers but also of their existence in union with Christ—we can better understand and appreciate other statements of Paul about the Christian life, like Galatians 2:20, in something of their intended depth, as something more than loose rhetoric or unthinking doxology.

The import of vital or existential union with Christ for the vertical modification of the two-aeon construct is seen in the following passages.

EPHESIANS 1:3

> Blessed be the God and Father of our Lord Jesus Christ, who has blessed
> us in Christ with every spiritual blessing in the heavenly places.

Here at the beginning of the lengthy doxology that opens the letter (extending through 1:14), Paul speaks of the activity of God the Father in blessing the church. In view are blessings that are presently enjoyed.[48]

This blessing activity of the Father is qualified by three prepositional phrases: "in Christ," "with every spiritual blessing," and "in the heavenly places." In the syntax of the Greek text, these phrases are parallel, each beginning with the preposition ἐν. But semantically, their relationship is synthetic—that is, mutually explanatory, and gives rise to the following observations about the blessings presently enjoyed by believers.

First, these blessings are an existential reality. Believers are truly and actually there, in heaven. Second, this reality has a Christological basis. Believers are there, because and as Christ is there. The next occurrence of

---

48 These blessings, then, are not the future "inheritance, . . . kept in heaven for you, . . . ready to be revealed in the last time," in view in the doxology at the beginning of 1 Peter (1:4-5).

the phrase "in the heavenly places" (1:20) makes this explicit: Christ is now seated there by virtue of his resurrection. This Christological basis, in other words, is not timeless but redemptive-historical.

Third, the blessings in view have a Spiritual character; they are blessings brought about by the work of the Holy Spirit. "Spiritual" here does not limit the scope of the blessing but indicates its source. Implied is not a contrast with material blessings in distinction from those "spiritual" in the sense of "immaterial." Rather, if there is a contrast in view, it is with "fleshly un-blessing," with the misery and suffering associated with the sinfulness of "the flesh," in antithesis to the blessings produced by the Spirit.

EPHESIANS 2:6

> [God] raised us up with him [Christ] and seated us with him in the heav-enly places in Christ Jesus.

The first two points above—the existential reality for the believer and its Christological basis—are even more explicit here. This statement echoes Ephesians 1:3 and accents what is true by virtue of union with Christ in his death, resurrection, and ascension.

PHILIPPIANS 3:20

> For our citizenship is in heaven, from which also we eagerly wait for a Savior, the Lord Jesus Christ. (NASB 1995)

This statement not only confirms what we have seen in the Ephesians passages but, in doing that, also provides an important additional thought. In the Greek construction, the possessive "our" (ἡμῶν) is the first word, not where it would normally be in relation to "citizenship," which it modifies. This positioning catches the reader's eye and gives the word a certain accent: "*our* citizenship is in heaven." When it comes to evaluating the two worlds, the two realms, in which the believer exists, "heaven" has the priority; the believer more properly belongs and exists there. There, in heaven, is the ultimate citizenship and true homeland or residence of the believer.[49]

---

49 Akin to the meaning of βασιλεία, discussed earlier, πολίτευμα has the concrete sense, "com-monwealth" (NASB mg.) as well as the abstract "citizenship." The one sense implies the other.

The significance of the relative clause in the latter half of 3:20 should not be overlooked: it is from heaven, where their true citizenship is and where in their union with Christ they now exist, that believers are waiting for Christ to return (cf. 3:21). The horizontal and vertical modifications come together here in one sentence—clear evidence how little they are at odds or in tension with each other.

COLOSSIANS 3:3-4

Your life is hidden with Christ in God. When Christ who is your life appears, then you also will appear with him in glory.

The vertical dimension in its truly existential import for believers is plain and emphatic in these statements. Their life, ultimately considered, is "with Christ in God." In fact, in their union with Christ, their life is not only with him; without obliterating the personal distinction between Christ and the believer, he *is* their very life.[50]

For the present, their life is "hidden" with Christ. This hiddenness is the case because of where Christ is presently: in heaven "above, . . . seated at the right hand of God" (3:1). Again, as in the other passages looked at, it is Christ in his ascension, Christ as exalted, in whom believers exist and have their life, who is their life.

However, this present hiddenness of Christ's ascension life that believers share in is not permanent. Looking toward to the future, that life will become open when Christ, their life, returns and they will be (openly) glorified together with him (3:4; cf. Rom. 8:17-19; 2 Thess. 1:10). Note how here, as in Philippians 3:20, the two eschatological dimensions under consideration, the vertical and the horizontal, are both centered on the exalted Christ—Christ presently "in the heavenlies" and Christ coming "from heaven" in the future. With that common focus, they occur together and complement each other without any hint of incompatibility.

---

50 In the Greek syntax of 3:4, "your life" is in apposition to "Christ"—made clear by translating the beginning of 3:4, "When Christ, your life, appears . . ." Paul could not have expressed this identity in life more pointedly.

PAUL'S MODIFIED USE OF THE TWO-AGE DISTINCTION: SUMMARY AND CONCLUSION

In this chapter, our concern has been to set out the structure of Paul's eschatology. It will be helpful to summarize that survey here, along with a couple of added observations.

The Consummation of Redemption

The basic labels for Paul's eschatological outlook are "redemptive-historical" (or "salvation-historical") and "Christological" (the latter, without at all intending to eclipse, much less deny, its fully Trinitarian character). Eschatology for Paul is the climax or consummation of redemptive history, the consummation that has already dawned when "Christ Jesus came into the world to save sinners" (1 Tim. 1:15). To be more specific, that consummation has commenced in the exaltation of Christ—in his resurrection and ascension—after he had suffered and died for the sins of his people. Paul's eschatology has an indelible redemptive cast; for him, eschatology, as the consummation of history, is preeminently the consummation of redemption.

A Tridirectional Outlook

Any assessment of Paul's eschatology is bound to recognize and take into consideration three factors or strands. These are identifiable by noting that his eschatological outlook is tridirectional: backward, forward, and upward.

The first of these, the backward look, to which I have given the large part of our attention in this chapter, is where Paul emphasizes the eschatological fulfillment that has already taken place in the coming of Christ "in the fullness of time" (Gal. 4:4; Eph. 1:10). Coming into view here is all that pertains to the present eschatological reality inaugurated by the first coming of Christ, the initial stage of the parousia of the Messiah as the fulfillment of the eschatological hope of the Old Testament.

The forward look, to which I have not given nearly as much attention so far, is of equal, if not greater importance. In view, of course, is all that is still-future eschatologically, the fulfillment that will occur when Christ returns, with the second and final stage of the Messiah's parousia.

The third, upward look is the vertical perspective found particularly in those passages where in light of the ascension, Paul reflects on the present existence of Christ, and of believers in union with him, "in the heavenlies."[51]

The Relation of the Two Aeons

The presence of each of these three strands in Paul is indisputable. That raises the question of their mutual relationship: How in his view are they related to each other?

This question, it needs to be appreciated, is one posed by the Pauline materials themselves, and the most plausible answer lies in his use of the two-aeon distinction. This use provides him with the integrating framework for the three basic strands and how they relate to each other.

Paul's eschatology can no doubt be presented in different ways. However, doing that as we have—in terms of his use of the two-age construction—has the advantage of avoiding the risk of imposing an alien scheme that would be inappropriate to or otherwise distort his views. Paul's modified understanding and use of the two-aeon scheme is one of the deep structures of his theology that has its surface manifestation in various ways in his letters, fully occasional as they are.

The diagram[52] on the next page displays this modified use in its basic elements: the overlap of the two aeons, including the vertical, heavenly dimension, in the period between Christ's resurrection and return.

The Renovation of Creation

The diagram leaves open the relationship between heaven and earth following Christ's return and the absolute end of this aeon. That relationship is an aspect of the basic issue, long debated in the history of the church, whether the eternal state will mean the annihilation or the renovation of the present creation. Suffice it here to say that the latter, renovation, is plainly

---

51 In a largely overlooked paper, "Structural Strands in New Testament Eschatology" (given at the seventh annual meeting of the Evangelical Theological Society, December 29–30, 1954), John Murray labels these three strands, respectively, "anticipated," "prospective," and "projective." While other labels than these may be used, the value of the paper, building in large part on the work of his teacher, Geerhardus Vos, is in its identification and penetrating treatment of the three strands. The paper is available at http://www.kerux.com/doc/0603A2.asp.

52 Adapted from the diagram of Vos, *The Pauline Eschatology*, 38n41.

Paul's Tridirectional Eschatology

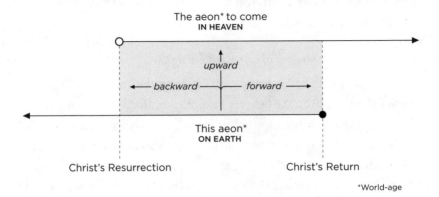

Paul's view, as Romans 8:19-22 especially shows. The present "longing" and "groaning" of "the whole creation" is not for its annihilation but rather to share with believers in their future hope of glory and, along with them, to be delivered from the "futility" and "bondage to corruption" that presently permeates creation.[53] The arrival of the age to come in its fulness at Christ's return will mean the disappearance not of the distinction but of the present disjunctive distance between heaven and earth.

Inaugurated Eschatology

If we look for an overall label for Paul's tridirectional eschatology, particularly with an eye to the situation in the period between Christ's resurrection and return—the overlap of the two aeons with its vertical component—Vos's proposal is "semi-eschatological."[54] This, however, has the disadvantage of leaving the impression that the fulfillment that has already taken place in Christ's first coming is less than truly eschatological. There is probably no one term that is fully satisfactory. Among various proposals that have been made, "inaugurated eschatology" is probably the best.

---

53 I have addressed this issue in the chapter, "What 'Symphony of Sighs'? Reflections on the Eschatological Future of the Creation," in *Redeeming the Life of the Mind. Essays in Honor of Vern Poythress*, ed. John M. Frame, Wayne Grudem, and John J. Hughes (Wheaton, IL: Crossway, 2017), 146-64.

54 Vos, *The Pauline Eschatology*, 38.

Final Observations

A couple of final observations will serve to round out our treatment of the structure of Paul's eschatology.

A Dualistic Understanding of Christian Living?

The vertical, "in the heavenlies" aspect can leave the impression that Paul teaches a basic split in the believer's experience, that with this aspect he inculcates a sharp dichotomy in the Christian life, a dualistic conception of Christian living. Is this impression accurate? This question may be considered from a couple of clarifying angles.

First, this teaching of Paul is in fact the basis for the otherworldliness or heavenly-mindedness that has always been a hallmark of genuine Christian piety. That mindset has often been abused and distorted in different ways. Various forms of asceticism and monasticism that have emerged over the history of the church come to mind. But leaving abuses to the side here, Paul's overall eschatological orientation does provide for what is fairly characterized as "otherworldliness" or "heavenly-mindedness" as a consequence of Christ's ascension.

Consider, for instance, Philippians 1:23. Faced with the uncertainty of the imprisonment situation in which Paul finds himself, unsure whether the outcome will be his imminent death and end of his ministry, his prevailing desire is "to depart and be with Christ." This is his preference, because being with Christ following his death, which will mean no longer "living in the body" (1:22 NIV), is, he says, "far better," "better by far" (NIV). He prefers personally to depart his present life on earth in order that he may be with Christ in heaven. This is certainly a kind of heavenly-mindedness.

Philippians 1:23 is autobiographic, made in the context of the particular life and ministerial situation in which Paul finds himself. It could be thought, then, that the preference he expresses is something of an exception and not necessarily applicable to other believers. However, that impression is countered by 2 Corinthians 5:8, where Paul expresses the same preference, but now, as it is clearly to be true of all believers, the preference is "to be away from the body and at home with the Lord" (NET, NIV; cf. 5:6).

What is particularly noteworthy, without going into the details of the passage (5:1–11), is that this is to be the believer's preference, even with the deep anomaly involved, as 5:3-4 put it graphically, of being "found naked" and "unclothed."

This—in passing here but important—is what disembodied existence means for divine image bearers, for whom the body is integral for that image in its wholeness. Such existence is attenuated. It is not to have left behind the body as the temporary and disposable prison house of the soul, but is an ultimate disintegrated nakedness. Paul's expressed preference for himself and other believers is to be spared this nakedness and rather for their present mortal bodies to be "clothed" (or "clothed over") with their resurrection bodies.

But however it turns out for believers (cf. 1 Cor. 15:51), Paul's preference for them—even with the profound abnormality of disembodied existence—is nonetheless the preference for absence from the body at death because of the "far better" presence with the Lord that will follow. We need to ask ourselves, then, to what extent his desire, this preference, is part of the makeup of our own outlook and piety.

On balance, for Paul, the *ultimate* eschatological hope of believers personally is the resurrection of the body at Christ's return. In the meantime, their *penultimate* hope is be with Christ "in the heavenlies" after bodily death.

Second, in light of the preceding observations, we may say, then, that a dualism, akin to what we noted earlier, is involved in the apostle's eschatological outlook. If we use "dualism" to help in making this point, then at the same time, we need to be clear that we are not in any sense talking about an ultimate or permanent dualism (metaphysical or cosmological) but a redemptive-historical dualism, a dualism resulting from the way redemptive history has unfolded. As such, it is a temporary dualism, occasioned by Christ's ascension and lasting until he returns.

Further and importantly, it does not entail any kind of dichotomizing or compartmentalizing of the present life of the believer. This can be seen in an instructive way in Colossians 3, a passage whose opening verses we have already considered and will come back to look at once again in some detail later in chapter 13.

In 3:1-2, Paul commands the church to "seek" and "set your minds on" "the things that are above."[55] This expression, in itself abstract and otherwise

---

55 τὰ ἄνω—the adverb "above" used substantively with the neuter plural article ("the things that are above") and indicating a general category.

undefined, is immediately qualified and made more concrete by the relative clause at the end of 3:1: "where Christ is, seated at the right hand of God." "The things that are above" are that because of Christ's ascension and his life as ascended, his ascension life in which, as we noted earlier, believers presently share in union with him (3:3-4).

In the latter part of 3:2 the pointed antithesis to the "things that are above" is the "things that are on earth."[56] These are the things believers are not to set their minds on. This antithesis in itself and without further qualification is flatly dualistic (above-below); it could leave the impression that Paul is here advocating a certain world-detachment, a renunciation and abandonment, as much as possible, of present life on earth, for which retreating into a monastery or some other form of ascetic existence would in fact be the ideal.

At a first glance, moreover, this impression may seem to be reinforced by the subsequent command in 3:5: "Put to death therefore your members that are on the earth" (ESV mg.). That impression, however, is dispelled by a correct understanding of the verse.

"Members" (plural, μέλη) describes the human body as a functioning entity; it brings into view bodily existence as it has the capacity to act and interact. As far as the syntax of 3:5 is concerned, although in the Greek text the sinful attitudes and action listed in the latter part of the verse ("sexual immorality . . . covetousness, which is idolatry") are in the same case (accusative) as "members," they are not adjectival. That is, they are not characteristics of bodily existence as such; the sins listed are not qualities innate to the body. The point of 3:5 is not the depreciation of the body, as if bodily existence, life "on earth," is inherently and inescapably sinful.

Note how the following translations, among others, easily lead, or at least dispose to, this misunderstanding: "Put to death therefore what is earthly in you" (ESV; RSV); "Therefore put to death your members which are on the earth" (NKJV); "Put to death, therefore, whatever belongs to your earthly nature" (NIV); "So put to death whatever in your nature belongs to the earth" (NET); "So put to death the sinful, earthly things lurking within you" (NLT); "Therefore, put to death what belongs to your worldly nature" (HCSB); "Put to death, then, the parts of you that are earthly" (NAB).

---

56 τὰ ἐπὶ τῆς γῆς, with the prepositional phrase "on earth" used substantively with the neuter plural article (the "things that are on earth") and again indicating a general category.

Rather, the sins listed function *adverbially*. They qualify the verb "put to death" by specifying sins that are the objects of that mortifying action, by indicating concretely what that mortification looks like. Believers are not to use their "members" for the sins enumerated; in their bodily existence and conduct, they are to avoid them.[57]

So, since seeking and minding the things above means negatively not using our "members" on earth for sinning, this seeking/minding consists positively in using our members for the opposite of sinning, for righteous living in our bodily existence.

This conclusion is reinforced by clearly parallel commands elsewhere in Paul as well as in the rest of Colossians 3:

> Do not present your members to sin as instruments for unrighteousness, but present yourselves to God as those who have been brought from death to life, and your members to God as instruments for righteousness. (Rom. 6:13; cf. 6:19)

> I appeal to you therefore, brothers, by the mercies of God, to present your bodies as a living sacrifice, holy and acceptable to God, which is your spiritual worship. (Rom. 12:1)

Seeking the things above, it turns out, is a thoroughly down-to-earth reality. The rest of Colossians 3 makes this abundantly clear by further detailing what Paul means by seeking the things above and mortifying our members on the earth. Giving no more than an overview of the passage here, that seeking takes place in the earthly life of believers in their relationships both within and outside the congregation (3:8–17), and in their day-by-day living in marriage, the home (parenting), and at work (3:18–4:1).

So, the vertical component in Paul's eschatology, far from dichotomizing the life of believers or depreciating their "members," facilitates worshiping and serving God in the full range of their bodily existence. As we will see later, what Paul teaches about the relationship between the exalted Christ and the Holy Spirit and the work of the Spirit in the church and within

---

57 The translation of 3:5 is admittedly difficult. I would suggest the following: "Therefore put to death using [*or* the use of] your members on the earth for sexual immorality, impurity, passion, evil desire, and covetousness, which is idolatry."

believers further clarifies how the heavenly and earthly aspects of their existence are integrated and held together.

Seeking the things above, as said, is very much a down-to-earth reality. For Paul, heavenly-minded believers are those who do the most earthly good.

The "Premillennial" Structure of Paul's Eschatology

The essential structure of Paul's eschatology, we may say, is "premillennial," using the word quite differently from its conventional sense. That is, it is premillennial in the sense of being pre, prior to, more basic than, and foundational to any further discussions of eschatology. The eschatological structure that we have considered in Paul is "pre" in the sense of being more fundamental than traditional evangelical debates about the millennium. It is a structure that introduces considerations that are more basic than those that have been predominant, at least characteristically, in those debates.

This is not to say that this structure gives ready answers to all of the questions that are traditionally discussed or renders them irrelevant. My point here is not simply to preempt that discussion, as if we should proceed by ignoring it in more or less sovereign indifference. The question still remains important: What, according to Paul and the rest of Scripture, are we to expect concomitant with the return of Christ, immediately before and after?

My concern, however, is to point out that taking into consideration the Pauline structure we have seen provides an important perspective for properly defining the right questions in debates about eschatology, and that such defining is always helpful for arriving at the right answers.

With an eye briefly to debates about the millennium, then, structurally, Paul's "premillennial" eschatology supports the amillennial view; it undercuts both the premillennial, whether dispensational or nondispensational, and classical postmillennial views.[58] On balance, I would be ready to defend the proposition that Paul is an "optimistic amil," always keeping in mind that this optimism has to be defined by what he teaches about the Christian life, some of which we will see as we move on to consider his teaching on the resurrection.

---

58   Some more recent postmillennial views agree with amillennialism to the extent that both recognize that the millennium is the entire period between Christ's first and second comings. For a further, more in-depth analysis and assessment of discussions about the millennium, see my chapter "Theonomy and Eschatology: Reflections on Postmillennialism," in *Theonomy: A Reformed Critique*, ed. William S. Barker and W. Robert Godfrey (Grand Rapids, MI: Zondervan Academic, 1990), 197-224.

The primary basis for the foregoing "millennial" conclusion is the inaugurated eschatology taught by Paul (consistent with the rest of the New Testament). If the coming and work of Christ "in the fullness of time" in fact brought to an end this age and the beginning of the eschatological age to come (i.e., the long-awaited coming of the promised kingdom of God, the dawning of the prophesied day of the Lord), then this initial and anticipatory but essentially eschatological era (i.e., the millennium) is no longer still future.

Given that the eschatological coming of Jesus as the promised Messiah is twofold—one initial, one final—structurally, there cannot be a twofold initial eschatological era. There can be only one such period, already present, followed by the eternal state, the age to come in its fullness, ushered in when he returns. The millennium is the entire interadvental period.

It strikes me as fair to observe that a large motive for the often-intense preoccupation with the millennium as still future and zeal for a particular view, whether premillennial or postmillennial, stems from the failure to appreciate the eschatology already inaugurated at Christ's first coming and its implications for the life of the church today. A pervasive characteristic of traditional discussions of eschatology, in other words, has been to "de-eschatologize" the present life of the church, to have an eye only for the eschatological "not yet" that misses the "already."

Labeling Paul's (amillennial) eschatology as "premillennial" in my redefined sense serves to underscore, once again, the importance of the point we have noted earlier: an eschatology that would be true to Paul and the rest of Scripture is elliptical; it has a dual focus and needs to be defined not only in terms of what is still future, not only by what will take place at Christ's return but also in terms of what has arrived and is now present with his first coming. To the extent that we do not recognize the truly eschatological finality of that coming, our understanding of both the salvation he accomplished, culminating in his death and resurrection (*historia salutis*), and the application of that salvation (*ordo salutis*) will be accordingly attenuated and impoverished.

We might say, then: "The question of eschatology is more than eschatological." That is, the question of eschatology considered biblically is always more than eschatological in the sense of traditional discussions about eschatology, including the millennium.

11

The Resurrection (Part 1)

Christ and Christians

INITIAL OBSERVATIONS

In chapter 9, we considered the question of the proper entrée into Paul's theology and whether it has a center. At the close of that chapter, we noted the statement of Herman Ridderbos, helpful for the perspective it provides on the unity in diversity of New Testament teaching: "Paul does nothing but explain the eschatological reality which in Christ's teaching is called the Kingdom."[1]

In chapter 9, we also saw that compared with the teaching of Jesus, kingdom language, while occurring in the same present-future pattern we find in Jesus, recedes in Paul. Instead, Paul explains the kingdom proclamation of Jesus by focusing on those impending events that Jesus himself sees to be decisive for the coming of the kingdom—namely, his own death and resurrection (Matt. 16:21, 28; Mark 8:31; 9:1; cf. the reference to his transfiguration as a preview of his resurrection glory in Matt. 17:9). With this death-and-resurrection focus, Paul's eschatology is, as Ridderbos puts it succinctly, "Christ-eschatology."[2]

In chapter 10, we saw how Paul expounds this eschatology in various ways within the framework of the distinction between the two ages/aeons and their overlap that structures his thinking as a whole. Clearly, then,

---

1 Herman Ridderbos, "Redemptive-Historical Character of Paul's Preaching," in *When the Time Had Fully Come: Studies in New Testament Theology* (Grand Rapids, MI: Eerdmans, 1957), 48–49.
2 Herman Ridderbos, *Paul: An Outline of His Theology*, trans. J. R. de Witt (Grand Rapids, MI: Eerdmans, 1975), 49 ("Christus-eschatologie," in the original Dutch).

further consideration of Paul's theology proceeds appropriately by exploring the significance of the death and resurrection of Christ—those events "of first importance" for the gospel that is at the center of his theology (1 Cor. 15:3-4).

Christ's death and resurrection are, of course, inseparable. Particularly applicable to Paul is the observation made at least as early as Calvin that in Scripture, references to the death alone or to the resurrection alone are synecdochic.[3] To speak of the one in its significance always has in view the other in its significance. They are unintelligible apart from each other; each conditions the meaning of the other.[4]

I call attention to this inseparability toward the beginning of this chapter, because in it and the following chapters, our study of Paul's theology will focus primarily on his teaching about the resurrection, with little attention to the death of Christ. This narrowing of our focus is not because Paul considers Christ's resurrection more important than his death or his death less important than his resurrection. Rather, our focus on the resurrection is for reasons of a broad church-historical sort.

As we look at the history of doctrine, a fair generalization is that in the area of soteriology, the theological tradition of the Western church—Roman Catholic as well as Protestant—has tended to concentrate heavy and at times almost exclusive attention on the death of Christ. Particularly since the time of Anselm (1033/34-1109), the atonement and the accomplishment of salvation, the work of Christ and atonement, have been virtually synonymous. Debate over the salvation accomplished in Christ has concentrated on his death and its significance.

In the modern period, especially in the face of challenges emerging since the Enlightenment with its rationalistic and moralistic emphases, the church—where it has remained true to Paul and the rest of Scripture—has been intent on making emphatically clear that the death of Christ is a

---

3 John Calvin, *Institutes of the Christian Religion*, ed. John T. McNeill, trans. Ford Lewis Battles (Philadelphia, PA: Westminster, 1959), 2.16.13 (1:521): "So then, let us remember that whenever mention is made of his death alone, we are to understand at the same time what belongs to his resurrection. Also, the same synecdoche applies to the word 'resurrection': whenever it is mentioned separately from death, we are to understand it as including what has to do especially with his death."

4 See also Richard B. Gaffin Jr., *By Faith, Not by Sight: Paul and the Order of Salvation*, 2nd ed. (Phillipsburg, NJ: P&R, 2013), 25–26.

genuine atonement for sin; that, more than an ennobling and challenging example, which it also is, his death atones as a substitutionary sacrifice for the sins of others, a penal substitution that removes the guilt of sin; that his death is a sacrifice for sin in order to satisfy divine justice, a provision of God's love in order to propitiate his just wrath. In the theology of the Western church, the dominating, at times exclusive, focus in soteriology has been on the death of Christ and its atoning significance.

In drawing attention to this development here, it should be clear, my interest is not at all to challenge its validity or even its necessity. Nor am I calling into question the conclusions reached about the atoning character of Christ's death. However, it does need to be recognized that in this predominant preoccupation with the death of Christ, the resurrection has been eclipsed in significant ways. In particular, the doctrinal or theological significance of the resurrection has tended to be overlooked.

Certainly, the importance of the resurrection has been and is widely recognized. But characteristically, that importance is seen primarily and almost exclusively in terms of its evidential and apologetic value: The resurrection, seen as the greatest evidence for the truth of Christianity, is valued as a stimulus to faith in Christ and support for Christian faith.

Unquestionably, the resurrection does have important apologetic and evidential significance. But in the case of Paul, failure to appreciate and emphasize the theological meaning of the resurrection is particularly impoverishing, because his writings contain substantial material that brings to light the doctrinal significance of the resurrection. To be more specific, this material shows the decisive soteriological importance of the resurrection.

In this and the following chapters, then, our attention will be given to what may aptly be called Paul's resurrection theology. The question that will occupy us, posed in various ways, is this: What, according to Paul, is the redemptive efficacy of Christ's resurrection? How is Christ's resurrection integral to our salvation? What specifically is the significance of Christ's resurrection both for the once-for-all accomplishment of redemption (*historia salutis*) and its ongoing application (*ordo salutis*)?[5]

---

5 Much of the substance of the content that follows is also found in my *Resurrection and Redemption: A Study in Paul's Soteriology*, 2nd ed. (Phillipsburg, NJ: P&R, 1987), though presented and developed here along somewhat different lines.

THE UNITY BETWEEN THE RESURRECTION OF CHRIST AND THE RESURRECTION OF CHRISTIANS

Our focus is the resurrection of Christ. It might seem surprising and even questionable, then, to begin, before anything else, by bringing into view the resurrection of the believer as well. Does not doing that blur our focus on Christ's resurrection?

While this initial impression may be understandable, proceeding as we will quickly shows that in fact nothing is more fundamental to Paul's understanding of the resurrection of Jesus than this: When we are concerned with his resurrection in all of its uniqueness—in its historical particularity as the event that took place three days after his death on the cross—precisely then Paul would have us recognize the close connection there is between Christ's resurrection and the resurrection of believers, in fact the unbreakable bond that exists between Christ and believers in resurrection. This fundamental unity will become clear as we consider the following passages.[6]

1 Corinthians 15:20

But in fact Christ has been raised from the dead, the firstfruits of those who have fallen asleep.

I begin with this affirmation because nowhere else is the unity that it is important for us to grasp made clearer than here: in his resurrection and as resurrected, Christ is "the firstfruits of those who have fallen asleep" (cf. "Christ the firstfruits," 15:23). Nowhere is the solidarity between Christ and believers in resurrection presented so pointedly and as graphically as here.[7]

Concerning this use of firstfruits (ἀπαρχή), one commentator states, "This little word contains a thesis."[8] By itself, of course, a word does not contain a proposition or thesis; a word has its meaning only in the syntactical unit of which it is a part and as it functions within its immediate

---

6 Some of the content in discussing these passages and elsewhere throughout this chapter is also found in my essay, "The Resurrection of Christ and the Age to Come," The Gospel Coalition, https://www.thegospelcoalition.org/essay/the-resurrection-of-christ-and-the-age-to-come/.

7 Throughout 1 Cor. 15, the resurrection of believers in view is their future bodily resurrection.

8 Johannes Weiss, *Die erste Korintherbrief*, 10th ed. (Göttingen: Vandenhoeck & Ruprecht, 1925), 356.

context. Still, the statement just quoted, however questionable linguistically, is not far off the mark.

Implicit in the use of "firstfruits" in context here is the controlling thought that underlies the entire argument, or at least much of the argument, in this epochal chapter on the resurrection. In fact, this thought not only controls the development of much of the teaching in this chapter but also, as we will see, underlies much of Paul's teaching on the resurrection as a whole.

Firstfruits is (by vintage!) an agricultural term. In using it here, Paul likely has in view its Old Testament background, where the term primarily has cultic significance, describing the firstfruits sacrifices that are brought each year at the beginning of the spring grain harvest in Israel (e.g., Ex. 23:16, 19; Lev. 23:10, 17, 20; Prov. 3:9). In this usage, importantly, the word is more than just an indication of temporal priority. The notion of organic connection is also apparent and essential. The firstfruits as the initial portion of the harvest is in view as it is inseparable from the whole harvest and represents the whole. Offering up the first part of the harvest to God was an act of thanksgiving, acknowledging the entire harvest as his gift to Israel.

With this Old Testament background likely in Paul's mind (it is difficult to see that it would not have been), 1 Corinthians 15:20 shows that the resurrection of Christ and the resurrection of believers cannot be separated. Why? Because Christ's resurrection is the "firstfruits" of the resurrection "harvest," as Paul surely intends the metaphor to be extended; to talk about a firstfruits without a harvest at least implicitly in view is pointless.

An important parenthetical observation is necessary at this point for keeping clear the focus of this passage, as well as the rest of the chapter. In 1 Corinthians 15, all told, the resurrection of unbelievers is not in view. When Paul says that Christ is the firstfruits of the resurrection harvest, he is not including unbelievers in that harvest. They are outside the purview of this passage.[9]

In fact, the resurrection or revivification of unbelievers for final judgment is barely touched on in Paul's teaching. He does affirm it in appearing before Felix (Acts 24:15), but does not reflect on it elsewhere. The focus

---

9 That is also the case in 1 Thess. 4:13–18. There is nothing in this passage either, one way or another, about a future resurrection of unbelievers presumably distinct and separated in time from the resurrection of believers.

throughout 1 Corinthians 15 is exclusively soteriological; it concerns the resurrection of believers.

With this qualification noted, we must be sure not to miss the full impact of 15:20. On the basis of this passage and others, it is often said—in Easter sermons and elsewhere—that Christ's resurrection is the guarantee of our resurrection in the sense that God has decreed and promised our resurrection, that because he raised Jesus, he promises that he will raise believers.

That is true and not to be discounted. But it does not go far enough in getting at what the apostle is saying in 15:20. Rather, Christ's resurrection is the guarantee of our resurrection in the sense that his resurrection is nothing less than "the actual beginning" of the "general epochal event."[10] The general event of resurrection that will include believers, 15:20 teaches, begins with the resurrection of Christ. In Christ's resurrection, God has begun fulfilling the promise that includes our resurrection.

As we might put it to make this point, if we were to have Paul at a prophecy conference or some other venue and were to ask him, "When, Paul, will the resurrection event take place in which believers share?" The first thing he would likely say is, "It has already begun." In Christ's resurrection, the final harvest of bodily resurrection has become visible. He will argue that in some detail later in the chapter, particularly in 15:42-49.

To sum up, two related considerations, fundamental for Paul's resurrection theology, come to light in 1 Corinthians 15:20. The first is the eschatological significance of Christ's resurrection. His resurrection, as it occurred three days after his death on the cross, is certainly a stupendous event in the past. However, it is not, as it might be viewed, a more or less isolated miracle there in the distant past. Rather, we may say on the basis of this passage, as an event that has taken place in the past, the resurrection of Christ in fact belongs to the future. It is the initial part of the eschatological harvest of resurrection at the end of history and from there has entered into history.

In the wider context of Paul's teaching, 1 Corinthians 15:20 confirms that with Christ's resurrection, the age to come begins, the new creation dawns, the eschatological fulfillment is inaugurated.

Second, clear here as well is the unity or solidarity that exists between Christ in his resurrection and believers in their resurrection. Even though

10 Geerhardus Vos, *The Pauline Eschatology* (Grand Rapids, MI: Baker, 1979), 45.

presently separated by more than two thousand years, they are not so much two events as two episodes of the same event. In terms of the firstfruits metaphor, they are the beginning and the end of the one-and-the-same harvest of resurrection.[11]

1 Corinthians 15:12–19

In this paragraph leading up to 15:20 the same notion of unity is present and controls the argument. Here, Paul has not yet come to the ringing declaration of 15:20. Instead, he argues hypothetically, employing an argument that has its validity and force as it anticipates and presupposes the truth affirmed in 15:20.

1 Corinthians 15:12 asks rhetorically, "Now if Christ is proclaimed as raised from the dead, how can some of you say that there is no resurrection of the dead?" Coming into view here is the opposition that Paul is having to deal with throughout this chapter, opposition that will concern us in detail subsequently. For now, his point by the question he poses is clear: If the proclamation concerning Christ's resurrection is true, then the resurrection of believers from the dead cannot be called into question. To affirm the resurrection of Christ implies the resurrection of believers.

Not to be missed is the fact that Paul also expresses himself conversely: "But if there is no resurrection of the dead, then not even Christ has been raised" (15:13). "We are even found to be misrepresenting God, because we testified about God that he raised Christ, whom he did not raise if it is true that the dead are not raised" (15:15). "For if the dead are not raised, not even Christ has been raised" (15:16). To deny the future resurrection of believers carries with it a denial of the resurrection of Christ.

The clear assumption here, the reason Paul can argue as he does, is that the two resurrections are integrally and inseparably related. The one is given with the other, so that he can argue both ways: if Christ's resurrection, then the believer's resurrection; if the future resurrection of believers, then Christ's past resurrection.

---

11 How are we to view those resurrections that antedate the resurrection of Christ, like that of Lazarus, of those mentioned in Matt. 27:52–53, and of those in the OT? Suffice it here to say that these are impermanent revivications; in each instance, those brought back to life eventually died again and were buried. They were not raised with the eschatological resurrection body that Christ has.

Noteworthy also is the primary emphasis of the argument in this section: from the resurrection of believers in the future to the resurrection of Christ in the past. Not the reverse, from the past resurrection of Christ to the Christian's future resurrection—as we might expect and do find Paul arguing elsewhere. This emphasis is another indication of just how firm and close is the bond between the two resurrections in Paul's thinking. It confirms, as we have already put it in looking at 15:20, that the two resurrections are not so much separate occurrences as two episodes of the same resurrection-harvest event.

Colossians 1:18

He is the beginning, the firstborn from the dead.

On stylistic grounds, the immediate context unit, 1:15–20, is widely held to be a hymn that Paul either fashioned himself or had at his disposal. With 1:15–17 paralleling 1:18–20, our interest is in the second strophe, where in the flow of ascriptions to Christ in 1:18, he is identified as "the firstborn from the dead."

This description expresses virtually the same thought as "the firstfruits of those who have fallen asleep" in 1 Corinthians 15:20. There is, however, this difference: "Firstborn" does not bring out the element of organic connection in the way that "firstfruits" does. Still, in combination with the prepositional phrase, "from the dead" (ἐκ τῶν νεκρῶν), the thought is plainly the solidarity of Christ with the dead.

As in 1 Corinthians 15, here too the "dead" in view are dead believers. So the prepositional phrase brings out the unity of Christ with dead believers. Within this group, as he is "from" it ("from among the dead" NIV), he is "firstborn," the first to be raised (cf. Christ as "the firstborn from the dead," Rev. 1:5 NIV). The other descriptions in the immediate context show that he is in view as alive and reigning.

"Firstborn" (πρωτότοκος) is almost certainly not to be understood in the sense that the resurrection of Christ is being likened to the process of birth. Although the statement is sometimes read that way, it gets us on a wrong track.

Rather, as it is used here, the term has the metaphorical sense it already has in the Old Testament, documented by its usage in the Septuagint. There it indicates special dignity, exalted status, supremacy, and special relationship. So, for instance, as chosen and set apart by God, Israel as a nation is his "firstborn son" (Ex. 4:22). David (foreshadowing Christ), as the Lord's "chosen one" and "anointed" by him (Ps. 89:3, 20), is "the firstborn" and, as such, "the highest of the kings of the earth" (89:27; 88:28 LXX).

In the flow of Colossians 1:18, "firstborn" has its sense together with the designation, immediately preceding, of Christ as "the beginning" (ἀρχή). This term, too, has its Old Testament background where it not only is an indication of temporal priority but also can denote special standing and headship or origin/source (see Gen. 49:3; Deut. 21:15, 17, where in the LXX πρωτότοκος and ἀρχή occur together as parallel descriptions).

Taken together, "the beginning" and "the firstborn" accent the unique headship and supremacy of Christ as resurrected. This is confirmed by other expressions in the immediate context, particularly in the rest of 1:18 that he is "the head" of the church and "preeminent" in everything. Together they also give rise to the thought that the general resurrection for believers begins with the resurrection of Christ.

On balance, then, "firstborn" accents the uniqueness of Christ, while "from the dead" brings out the aspect of solidarity. Again, as in 1 Corinthians 15:20, present are both the eschatological significance of Christ's resurrection and the unity with believers involved.

There are two other references in Paul to Christ as "firstborn." Within this Christ hymn, parallel with its use in 1:18, he is "the firstborn of all creation" (1:15). This also is clearly an indication of exalted status or supremacy—here, however, without any notion of solidarity. The sense of "of all creation" (the genitive case in the Greek text is relational, not an indication of source or origin) is not to identify Christ with the creation, as though he were a created being, as Arians, ancient as well as modern like Jehovah's Witnesses, maintain. Rather, in relation to the creation, he is its creator.

Colossians 1:16–17 immediately go on to make that emphatically clear. As "the firstborn," he is the creator of everything, and as its creator, providentially sovereign over everything in the creation. This parallel description intersects with his headship and exalted status in redemption as resurrected "firstborn" in 1:18, coupled there with the notion of solidarity brought out, as we have seen, by "from the dead" (cf. Eph. 1:22).

In Romans 8:29, the ultimate goal of God's predestinating purpose, its omega-point for believers, is "to be conformed to the image of his Son." This image-conformity, in turn, is to the further, even more ultimate end that he, the Son, might be "the firstborn among many brothers." The tie to Colossians 1:18 is not difficult to see: as "firstborn from the dead," Christ is "firstborn among many brothers"

The predestined conformity to the image of the Son is specifically to the image of the resurrected Son. Elsewhere, Paul makes clear both that believers are already being transformed into the image of Christ ("being transformed into the same image [of the Lord] from glory to glory," 2 Cor. 3:18 ESV mg.) and that in their bodily resurrection they will be perfectly conformed to that image ("as we have borne the image of the earthly one [Adam], we will also bear the image of the heavenly one [Christ]," 1 Cor. 15:49, my translation).[12]

2 Corinthians 4:14; 1 Thessalonians 4:14

In the light of the three passages we have considered in detail, one needs to do little more than read these two verses to recognize that reflected in them is the same organic unity between Christ and believers in their bodily resurrection:

> knowing that he who raised the Lord Jesus will raise us also with Jesus and bring us with you into his presence. (2 Cor. 4:14)

> For if we believe that Jesus died and rose again, even so God will bring with Him those who have fallen asleep in Jesus. (1 Thess. 4:14 NASB 1995)

In the latter verse, the prepositional phrases are best taken as distributed so that "in Jesus" (or "through Jesus" [διὰ τοῦ Ἰησοῦ]) modifies "have fallen asleep," while "with him" modifies "will bring," rather than both viewed as modifying "will bring." Death for believers does not sever their union with Christ (as *resurrected*).[13]

---

12 Both of these passages will occupy us in detail below.

13 The Westminster Catechisms, Larger (answer 86) and Shorter (answer 37), both appeal to this verse to support the statement that the bodies of dead believers, awaiting resurrection, are "still united to Christ."

Ephesians 2:5–6; Colossians 2:12–13; Romans 6:4–13

The passages so far examined are clear about the organic unity existing between Christ's past resurrection and the resurrection of believers as *future and bodily*. However, in order to get the full picture concerning this bond in resurrection, another strand of passages needs to be considered. These are places where Paul speaks of the resurrection of the believer, not as future, but as in the past (using the aorist tense in Greek), passages that state, more particularly, that believers have already been raised with Christ. A key text in this regard is Ephesians 2:5–6. That passage will be our primary focus, with supporting references to the other passages listed above.

> even when we were dead in our trespasses, made us alive together with Christ—by grace you have been saved—and raised us up with him and seated us with him in the heavenly places in Christ Jesus.

What does Paul mean that believers (the "we" in view) have already been raised with Christ? That question has been given different answers. Frequently, it is thought that Paul has in view the involvement of believers with Christ at the timepoint of his resurrection, in the sense of their being contemplated in Christ when he was raised. On this understanding, believers are said to have been raised with Christ because he was raised for them; their resurrection is in view in his, as he is their representative.[14] There is certainly an element of truth in this view, and it would be wrong to eliminate it from these passages.

Less plausible is the view of some of older commentators—some Puritan commentators, for instance—who contrast the verbs of resurrection and ascension with Christ (2:6) with "made . . . alive . . . with Christ" (2:5), referring the latter to the enlivening that has already taken place for believers in their regeneration, the former to their future bodily resurrection and glorification. On this view, since Christ in his resurrection and glorification is their representative and surety, aorist tenses are used in 2:6 to emphasize the good-as-realized certainty of that future resurrection.

---

14   This apparently is the view of Herman Ridderbos in *Paul: An Outline of His Theology*, trans. J. R. de Witt (Grand Rapids, MI: Eerdmans, 1975).

What, then, is the past resurrection with Christ in view in these passages? Is it only a representative union with Christ in his resurrection? In fact, a careful reading of these passages in their contexts discloses another aspect, an aspect that is crucial not to suppress or ignore.

When Paul says to the church that we have been raised with Christ, he is referring not only to our resurrection being contemplated in Christ's, as he is our representative/surety. That aspect is there. But also—and I would say primarily—these passages bring into view an involvement that is existential, in the sense of what has taken place in the actual existence or life history of the individual believer, when a sinner is first united to Christ by faith.

Experiential might also be used to describe this resurrection event and its resultant state. However, it carries the liability of suggesting that having already been raised results in an experience in the sense of a specific and identifiable psychological state. Certainly, this experience has undeniable and important psychological implications for the believer, as we will see; it is radically transformative personally. But it is not an experience to be defined in terms of a particular psychological condition.

What are the grounds for this "existential" view? In Ephesians 2:5-6 and Colossians 2:12-13, the enlivening by union with Christ in his resurrection is what God, "rich in mercy" because of his "great love" (Eph. 2:4), has done "when we were dead in our trespasses" (2:5; cf. "dead in trespasses and sins," 2:1; Col. 2:13). How this deadness in trespasses and sins and the transition to resurrection life in Christ are to be understood and "when" that transition occurred are particularly clear in Ephesians 2.

Ephesians 2:5-6 may be seen as the pivot or turning point within the immediate context (2:1-10), where a key notion is walking—used as a metaphor for a way of life, a lifestyle, actual conduct. The passage opens with the past, pre-Christian "walk" of believers (2:1-3). In view is their former depraved deadness manifested in sinful conduct, in conformity to this aeon ("the age of this world," my translation). At its other end, however, the passage closes on this note: "For we are his workmanship, created in Christ Jesus for good works, which God prepared beforehand, that we should walk in them" (2:10). Now the present "walk" of believers is in view. The idea of "walking" brackets the passage, and its central theme is the contrast, in fact the antithesis, between their past and present walks, between their former pre-Christian, this-age way of life in the deadness of their sinning and their present new creation (i.e., age to come) life in Christ manifested in their good works.

What effects this transition, this radical reversal in walk, this 180-degree reversal in conduct? The answer is there in about the middle of the passage, the pivot point of its flow (2:5–6). What brings about this death-to-life turnaround in walk is being made alive with Christ by union with him in his resurrection and ascension, by being united to him as he now is as resurrected and ascended.

This existential understanding of past resurrection with Christ is reinforced in the other related passages listed above. In Colossians 2:12, having been raised with Christ occurs "through faith" (cf. Eph. 2:8). In Colossians 3 and Romans 6 (both passages to be looked at in some detail later), in context, the past resurrection of the believer (Col. 3:1; Rom. 6:4–5) is the effective basis of personal obedience, the dynamic that produces holy living. The resurrection in view describes the reality of personal transformation, the radical change that has taken place in the life of the believer.

Also, in Colossians 2 and Romans 6, baptism is in view. Being raised with Christ is among the benefits that are signified and sealed by baptism— in other words, among those benefits of the actual appropriation of salvation.

For these considerations, then, we are brought to the conclusion that while the representative aspect is surely involved, the resurrection in view in these passages is real, an actual experience of resurrection in the life of the believer. It is not merely true, as it is sometimes put, "in principle"—if by that is meant that it is not really or not yet true, less than a real resurrection.

To put this conclusion another way, the resurrection in view refers primarily to the application of salvation, not its once-for-all accomplishment. While the language, referring to Christ's resurrection, belongs to the latter (the *historia salutis*), the reality described primarily concerns the former (the *ordo salutis*), the application of salvation to the individual believer. Union with Christ by faith links the two.

Summary and Further Observations

Three Elements of One Resurrection Harvest

In Paul's teaching on the unity between Christ and believers in resurrection, there are three components: the resurrection of Christ three days after his crucifixion, the past resurrection of the believer in being united to Christ by faith, and the future bodily resurrection of the believer.

The organic connection between these three elements needs to be kept in view. In terms of the firstfruits metaphor (1 Cor. 15:20), controlling much of Paul's teaching on the resurrection, all three are part of one harvest. The unity that exists between the resurrection of Christ and the resurrection of believers is such that the latter, the resurrection of believers, consists of two episodes in the existence of the individual believer: one that is past—the believer has already been raised with Christ—and one that is still future—the believer is yet to be raised with Christ.

Both of these aspects of the believer's experience of resurrection are integrally related to each other, and together they are integrally related to the resurrection of Christ in the sense that they constitute a whole, a unity. So, it could be said that this unity is such that Jesus's resurrection is refracted into the experience of the individual believer in this twofold fashion, already and not yet, past and future.

Note too—and this should not be missed—how the formal structure of Paul's eschatology discussed in the previous chapter—his use of the distinction between the two ages—qualifies and is reflected in his teaching on the resurrection: The two ages overlap in the time between the resurrection and return of Christ, so that the eschatological age to come, the new and final order for the creation, has both already begun and is still future. So too, commensurately, in this period, the resurrection of the believer—the fundamental eschatological event for the person of the believer—has both already occurred and is still future.

The Question of Terminology

What labels are available for distinguishing these two aspects of the believer's resurrection—the realized and the future? Various possibilities are more or less useful.

The future resurrection is "bodily," suggesting "nonbodily" for the realized resurrection. "Nonbodily," however, is not a positive designation. Other distinctions provide a positive designation: internal-external, invisible-visible, secret-open. These are useful, as long as it is also made clear that the realized resurrection, labeled "invisible" or "secret," is to have, as we will see, very visible and open manifestations in the life of the already raised believer.

The distinction spiritual-physical as an alternative for the other distinctions just noted is not useful. In fact, it is misleading if we use *spiritual*, as we should, in its pervasive Pauline sense, to refer to the activity of the Holy Spirit. There is no question that the past resurrection of the believer is "Spiritual" (the adjective capitalized to keep the reference to the Spirit clear); it is the enlivening work of the Spirit.

However, the physical, bodily resurrection of the future will be even more "Spiritual." As 1 Corinthians 15:42-44 makes clear, the resurrection of the body is the consummate completion of the Spirit's work in renovating the believer, so that the one-word label that Paul uses there for the resurrection body is "Spiritual" (15:44). So, "Spiritual" does not serve to differentiate between the two resurrections (past and future) of the believer; the one is as Spiritual as the other.

To answer our question, Paul would likely direct us to 2 Corinthians 4:16: "Therefore we do not despair; even if our outer self[15] is perishing, our inner self is being renewed day by day" (my translation). Here Paul, looking at the person of the believer, makes a categorical distinction between the inner and outer self. This is a fundamental anthropological distinction also implicit in references to the "inner" self elsewhere in Paul (Rom. 7:22; Eph. 3:16).

Several comments about this distinction are in order. Negatively, it is not a distinction between two entities. The distinction is not partitive, as if the Christian is a dual personality, a sort of hybrid consisting of two persons ("selves"). While there are surely partitive implications, the outer-inner distinction intersects with, but is not equivalent to, the distinction between body and soul.

Rather, the distinction is best taken as *aspectival*—that is, as two ways of viewing the person of the Christian as a whole. It is the one "I"[16] existing as both inner self and outer self that is the single subject of the main verb "do not despair." That subject is not the inner in distinction from the outer self.[17]

What Paul means by the outer self ("body" or "members") is more than narrowly physical. It is the psychophysical totality I am. It is who I am in

---

15 "Man" (ἄνθρωπος), used generically.
16 While Paul uses the plural, 2 Cor. 4:16 describes what is true of every Christian as an individual.
17 The outer self is interchangeable elsewhere in Paul with the "body" or "members," while the inner self is usually in view in his frequent references to the "heart." For a helpful survey of the anthropological terms Paul uses, see Ridderbos, *Paul*, 114-21.

my functioning, as a functioning person, as I am able to think, will, speak, act, enter into relationships, etc. The outer self is the functioning I.

In distinction (not separation!), the inner self ("heart") is the core of the being of the I, the deepest recesses of the I. The inner self is who I am in my prefunctional disposition, the disposition, more basic than my functioning, that gives rise to that functioning and decisively controls and finds expression through that functioning.

Here, Paul does express a certain definite, even fundamental "split" in the person of the Christian. But he is not bifurcating the Christian or dichotomizing the personal makeup of the Christian in terms of an inner core that really counts and an outer shell or covering, more or less disposable.

On balance, what is now true of the Christian as inner self is not yet true for the outer self. For the present—that is, until Jesus comes—what is true of the inner self of the believer is true only within the outer self, within the outer for which the inner is inner. While the daily renewal that Paul affirms here is not yet true *for* the body, until death, it is true only *in* the body, to trade on the prepositions italicized. Paul holds these two distinct aspects together: only in the body, but not yet true for the body.

To clarify further and clear away a misunderstanding that sometimes clouds this passage, the distinction between the inner self and the outer self is not the same as the distinction Paul makes elsewhere between "the old self" and "the new self." Anticipating what we will see in detail subsequently, Paul is clear: for Christians, the "old self was crucified with him [Christ]," so that they are "no longer . . . enslaved to sin" (Rom. 6:6). The believer has "put off the old self with its [sinful] practices" and "put on the new self" (Col. 3:9-10). The "[corrupt] old self" belongs to the believer's "*former* manner of life" that has been "put off" (Eph. 4:22). Galatians 3:26-27 shows that to put on the new self is by faith to have "put on Christ." Putting off the old self and putting on the new self is realized by being united with Christ by faith.

So, in 2 Corinthians 4:16, as we have noted, it is the single subject, the whole person, who is not despairing. That single subject, the whole person, is the new self in Christ. At the same time, Paul says here, that new self exists in the modes of the inner self and the outer self.

Finally, as this passage makes clear, "outer" and "inner" refer to opposite, in fact, antithetical realities operative in the Christian, realities that are as antithetical in their outcome as death and life. The outer self is the person of the believer undergoing decay and perishing, eventually resulting in bodily death. The inner self is that person marked by resurrection life and ongoing, day-by-day renewal.

So, to the question about labels for distinguishing the past from the future resurrection of the believer, this is Paul's answer: inner self–outer self. The inner self has already been raised; the outer self has yet to be raised.

Our consideration of Paul's teaching on the unity in resurrection between Christ and the Christian carries this basic conclusion: If you are a believer in Christ, united to him by faith, then at the core of your being (the heart), in the deepest recesses of who you are, you will never be more resurrected than you already are. This has obvious and profoundly important implications for Paul's understanding of the Christian life, some of which we will see.

Further Confirmation of Resurrection Unity

The unity or solidarity between Christ and believers in resurrection seen in the passages we have so far considered is confirmed throughout Paul in an indirect yet pervasive way, a way that itself also proves to be instructive. This occurs in those statements where he refers to the resurrection of Jesus without any particular amplification, where in one way or the other he simply affirms the fact of Christ's resurrection. These statements are of two kinds. In both, the main verb, almost exclusively, is ἐγείρω ("raise," "raise up"). A survey of these statements reveals a consistent and unmistakable pattern.

In the one group, the verb is in the *active* voice, God is *the subject*, and Christ or Jesus is the *direct object* (e.g., "if you . . . believe in your heart that God raised him from the dead," Rom. 10:9; cf. 1 Cor. 15:15; Acts 13:30, 37). Similarly, Jesus or Christ is the direct object of the subject, "the one who raised" (Rom. 4:24 NET; cf. Col. 2:12). Concerning this subject, Paul is specific: it is God the Father (Gal. 1:1; cf. Eph. 1:17 with 1:20; 1 Thess. 1:9-10: ". . . his Son, . . . whom he raised from the dead").

In the other group of statements, the verb is in the *passive* voice (in either the aorist or perfect tense), and Christ, variously designated, is the *subject*. Approximately half of the references to the resurrection in Paul are in this category (e.g., aorist tense: "Jesus our Lord, who . . . was . . . raised for our justification," Rom. 4:24-25; "who for their sake died and was raised" 2 Cor. 5:15; perfect tense: the firstfruits theme verse, 1 Cor.

15:20, cf. 15:12, 13, 14, 16, 17; 2 Tim. 2:8: "Remember Jesus Christ, raised from the dead" NIV).

It is true that in some instances, these passive tense forms have an intransitive-active sense ("rose"). In Paul's use, however, in light of the first group, they are true passives ("was raised").[18]

Two points stand out in these references to the resurrection. First, it is God in his identity as Father who raises Jesus. Second and correlative with the first, Jesus is passive in his resurrection. This viewpoint, as far as I can see, is held consistently, without exception by Paul. Nowhere does he say that Christ was active in his own resurrection or that he contributed to his resurrection. Much less does he teach that Jesus raised himself. To put it pointedly, Paul never says that Jesus "rose" from the dead, always that he "was raised."[19] The stress everywhere is on the creative power and enlivening action of the Father of which Christ is the recipient and beneficiary.[20]

This pattern of expression—the enlivening action of the Father and Jesus as passive in his resurrection—is theologically significant. It reflects as it reinforces Paul's central conception of the unity that exists between the resurrection of Christ and the resurrection of believers. Christ's passivity in his resurrection shows his identification with them that slept as "firstfruits" (1 Cor. 15:20), his solidarity with the dead as "firstborn" (Col. 1:18).

This question is bound to surface: How is this uniform emphasis of Paul to be understood in the light of statements of Jesus himself in the Gospels that he will be active in his resurrection? For instance, "Destroy this temple, and in three days I will raise it up" (John 2:19), where the context makes clear he was speaking of his resurrection (2:21-22). Or, speaking of his impending death and resurrection, "I lay down my life that I may take it up again. . . . I have authority to lay it down, and I have authority to take it up again" (John 10:17-18). Other statements in the Gospels express this

---

18 For a full discussion of this survey of Paul and the rest of the New Testament, see John Murray, "Who Raised Up Jesus," *Collected Writings* (Edinburg: Banner of Truth, 1982), 4:82–91.

19 A question could be raised about 1 Thess. 4:14: "Jesus died and rose (ἀνέστη)." This no more affirms that Jesus was active in his resurrection than the related statement also with the intransitive use of the same verb in 4:16, "the dead in Christ will rise (ἀναστήσονται)," means that believers will be active in their resurrection. In both instances, the active agent of resurrection, the one who raises, is not indicated.

20 See also Richard B. Gaffin Jr., "Redemption and Resurrection: An Exercise in Biblical-Systematic Theology," in *A Confessing Theology for Postmodern Times*, ed. Michael S. Horton (Wheaton, IL: Crossway, 2000), 233.

activity, that in the active sense, Jesus "rose" from the dead. How does Paul's emphasis relate to these statements? Is there a contradiction between Paul, on the one hand, and Jesus and the Gospel writers, on the other?

Without addressing this issue here in any detail or depth, we should recognize that facing us here is the ultimate and sublime mystery of the two-natured person of Jesus—his true deity and his genuine humanity. In this regard, the Chalcedon formulation (AD 451), true to Scripture, is not only helpful but also essential for sound exegesis of New Testament teaching about the person of Christ and what we can know about how the two natures relate to each other. Chalcedon is not to be seen, as some hold, as an imposition of alien Hellenistic philosophical categories on the New Testament.

Chalcedon affirms that in the person of Christ, the two natures are united "without confusion, without change, without division, without separation." An important corollary, then, is that what is true of either nature is true of the whole person. Accordingly, what Jesus says in John's Gospel is true in terms of his deity, whereas Paul has in view what is true in terms of his humanity. There is no conflict between Paul and Jesus in John's Gospel, as some would want to argue. Elsewhere, Paul is quite clear in affirming the deity of Christ (e.g., Rom. 9:5; Col. 1:15-17, 19; Titus 2:13)

CONCLUSION

To conclude our examining Paul on the unity in resurrection between Christ and Christians, and as a transition to our further consideration of his resurrection theology, it should be clear by now, and important to recognize, that for him the significance of Christ's resurrection does not lie where the difference between Christ and his people is most profound, in his deity in contrast to our humanity. Rather, the primary significance of Christ's resurrection is found in what he and his people have in common, in their shared humanity (except that Christ is without sin, Rom. 8:3).

For Paul, Christ's resurrection is in view not as an evident display of his divinity, as a powerful proof of his deity, in distinction from his humanity. Rather, the significance of the resurrection lies in the vindication of the incarnate Christ in his suffering and obedience unto death. The resurrection, as Paul sees it, is as well the powerful transformation of Christ in his humanity. His resurrection, as we have already noted in discussing

Colossians 1:18, constitutes him "the firstborn among many brothers," as the "image" to which believers are being and will be "conformed" (Rom. 8:29).

On balance, for Paul, the resurrection of Christ is thoroughly messianic, just as much as are his sufferings and death, just as necessarily representative and vicarious as is his death. That comes out perhaps most explicitly in 2 Corinthians 5:15, linking his death and resurrection: believers should "no longer live for themselves but for him who for their sake died and was raised."[21]

---

21 "For their sake" (ὑπὲρ αὐτῶν) modifies "was raised" as well as "died."

12

The Resurrection (Part 2)

Christ and the Holy Spirit

OUR FURTHER EXPLORATION of Paul's resurrection theology will probe in greater detail the significance of the resurrection, first for Christ (the history of salvation, *historia salutis*) and then for the Christian in union with Christ (the order of salvation, *ordo salutis*).[1] This chapter will deal with the former, the next chapter with the latter.

In considering the redemptive-historical significance of the resurrection, in particular what his resurrection meant and entails for Christ *personally*, nothing is more significant than the relationship between Christ and the Holy Spirit dating from his resurrection. Examining several passages will make that clear.

1 CORINTHIANS 15:45

The last Adam became the life-giving Spirit. (my translation)

I begin with this statement because, embedded in its immediate context, it expresses a fundamental reality for both Paul's Christology and Pneumatology. Addressing two questions serves to clarify the meaning of this statement: (1) What is the reference of the noun πνεῦμα? (2) Since the

---

1 Some content in this chapter, based on my class lectures, is also found elsewhere in my writings over the years; see, e.g., Richard B. Gaffin Jr., "'Life-Giving Spirit': Probing the Center of Paul's Pneumatology," *Journal of the Evangelical Theological Society* 41, no. 4 (December 1998): 573–89; Gaffin, "The Resurrection of Christ and the Age to Come," The Gospel Coalition https://www .thegospelcoalition.org/essay/the-resurrection-of-christ-and-the-age-to-come/."

life-giving πνεῦμα is what Christ "became" (ἐγένετο), what is the time of this becoming?

As we will see, the answer to the first question is the person of the Holy Spirit, to the second, the resurrection. While establishing these answers is my primary interest in this section, I will broaden my treatment with some observations pertinent to understanding 15:45 within its immediate and larger context in 1 Corinthians 15 and for the theology of Paul as a whole.

The Immediate Context

The immediate context of 15:45 is 15:42–49. Concerning 15:45–49 (along with 15:22), John Murray has written that they provide "one of the most striking and significant rubrics in all of Scripture."[2] This is not an overstatement. For instance, from a doctrinal, systematic-theological perspective, present here are considerations fundamental for virtually every locus—the doctrines of creation, including the creation of man (male and female) as God's image, of the fall and sin, Christology, soteriology, and eschatology. Something of how that is the case will emerge with our focus on Christ and the Spirit.

Within 1 Corinthians 15 as a whole and especially the turn the discourse takes beginning with 15:35, Paul is concerned with the resurrection of believers as future and bodily. First Corinthians 15:35 raises two questions, a "how" question and a "what" question—questions, in other words, about the mode of the resurrection and the nature of the resurrection body: How are the dead raised? With what kind of body do they come?

These questions were apparently posed by opponents confronting Paul and likely in a derisive fashion. This ridicule would explain the sharpness with which he begins his response (15:36)—a single word in the Greek text, abrupt and emphatic: "Fool!" (ἄφρων).[3]

This interchange brings into view the opposition that Paul is having to deal with in 1 Corinthians 15 and, as we will see, elsewhere in the letter. What was the nature of that opposition? Evidently, it centered in a denial of the resurrection as both future and bodily. Beyond that, the exact nature and the grounds for this denial are more difficult to determine, at least

---

2 John Murray, *The Imputation of Adam's Sin* (Grand Rapids, MI: Eerdmans, 1959), 39.
3 NET, NRSV. Other translations needlessly blunt or tone down this sharpness: e.g., "You foolish person!" (ESV), "Foolish one" (NKJV), "How foolish!" (NIV), "What a foolish question!" (NLT).

conclusively, and interpreters are divided in their further understanding of the opposition.

At 15:12, Paul begins a section (15:12-19) dealing with this opposition with a rhetorical question: "Now if Christ is proclaimed as raised from the dead, how can some of you say that there is no resurrection of the dead?" From this question, it appears that the opponents were confessing Christians, making some sort of Christian confession, and were within the congregation; they were "some of you." Further, from 15:12, it appears that there was agreement, at least formally in some sense, that Christ has been raised.

What was this sense? With whatever differences there are among interpreters, a fairly wide consensus exists that Paul is having to confront some form of belief influenced by pagan Hellenistic anthropology, a dualism that involved depreciation of the human body and, more generally, of the material world. Most satisfactory, it seems, is the view that Paul is having to deal with a protognostic error, an incipient gnostic heresy.

The thinking that marked this heresy likely made a sharp distinction, even opposition, between the Christ of the present and the Jesus of the past. On the one hand, it regarded Christ as a heavenly and pneumatic being—"pneumatic" or "spiritual" in the sense of immaterial, nonbodily— a being with which the believer is identified in substance. In distinction, it depreciated the earthly historical Jesus of the past. This flesh-and-blood being living on earth previously has no significance for Christian faith.

Accordingly, we can posit that this view of Christ, with the kind of disjunction just noted, involved a spiritualization in the sense of an immaterialization of the resurrection of believers, a denial of a truly physical bodily resurrection. Regarding the time element, it appears that this spiritualized resurrection of the believer was understood solely in terms of what has already happened to the believer: an experience of regeneration understood as a change in substance—a conception that involved a thorough distortion of Paul's teaching on the enlivening work of the Holy Spirit. Resurrection, construed in terms of this sort of substantial change, judges the true self, the spiritual, immaterial essence of who I am, as already brought to perfection, because absorbed into and now part of the pneumatic, heavenly Christ.

One virtually inevitable and quite practical consequence of this view is that the body has no positive significance. The body is a thing of indifference, so that its impulses may be either suppressed or indulged. The body can be misused either, at one extreme, through different forms of asceticism or, at the other extreme, in various sorts of licentiousness, particularly sexual license. The latter perhaps had become more of an issue in the church in Corinth. A plausible connection can be drawn between the error of those he is correcting here in 1 Corinthians 15 and the kinds of sexual immorality he confronts earlier in 1 Corinthians 5-7.

Worth considering, also, is the view that Paul may be dealing with a distortion of his own teaching in passages like Ephesians 2 and Romans 6: a distorted and one-sided misappropriation of his teaching that the believer has already been raised with Christ. Along this line, there is perhaps as well a connection between the error in Corinth and the position of the two individuals mentioned in 2 Timothy 2:17-18, Hymenaeus and Philetus, who by "saying that the resurrection has already happened" were "upsetting the faith of some." For them too, apparently, the resurrection of the body was not a future hope.

The Nature of the Resurrection Body

Whatever may be said further about his opposition, Paul picks up on the two questions in 15:35 and treats them, in effect, as a single compound question; the two questions—the how and the what of the resurrection body—are obviously related. Dealing with these questions structures his discussion beginning in 15:36 to the end of the chapter.

For our purposes, skipping over the intervening verses to 15:42, beginning there through 15:49, we see that Paul reasons antithetically by developing a contrasting parallelism between the resurrection and preresurrection body of the believer, between the eschatological body that believers will have and their present pre-eschatological bodies—the latter, more specifically, the body under the curse on sin, the body "sown"/buried in death (cf. 15:36-37). In light of the formal structure of Paul's eschatology, discussed in chapter 10, the shaping control of the two-aeon construct, even though the terminology is not explicit, is unmistakable.[4]

---

4   For the following observations on 15:42-49, I am especially indebted to the penetrating insights of Geerhardus Vos, *The Pauline Eschatology* (Grand Rapids, MI: Baker, 1979), 166-71. These pages, including n19, 169-70, repay careful reading and reflection; cf. Geerhardus Vos, "The Eschatological Aspect of the Pauline Conception of the Spirit," reprinted in Richard B. Gaffin Jr., ed., *Redemptive History and Biblical Interpretation: The Shorter Writings of Geerhardus Vos* (Phillipsburg, NJ: P&R, 1980), 105-7.

On the one side of this parallel contrast, the resurrection body is marked, in turn, by "incorruption" (NKJV, KJV) or being "imperishable" (ESV, NIV, NASB), "glory," and "power." In contrast, each of these three predicates corresponds antithetically, in turn, to each of the three predicates of the preresurrection, sin-cursed body: "corruption" (NKJV, KJV) or being "perishable," "dishonor," and "weakness" (15:42–43).

The first half of 1 Corinthians 15:44, then, provides an all-embracing summary description of the two bodies being contrasted. In a word, the future resurrection body is "Spiritual"[5] (πνευματικόν); the present preresurrection body is "natural" (ψυχικόν[6]). These one-word labels, all told, best describe these two bodies, respectively.

Applied to the resurrection body, the adjective πνευματικόν, as we will see, refers to the Holy Spirit and his work. It is important to be clear about this reference in light of certain persisting misconceptions. For one, the adjective is not anthropological—that is, "spiritual" in the sense of referring to the human spirit. This is the view, for instance, of Charles Hodge in his commentary on this passage: the spiritual body is "a body adapted to the πνεῦμα," understood as "the rational, immortal principle of our nature."[7] Hodge is not someone easily or often disagreed with, but this view is not sustainable.

Much more widespread is the misunderstanding that the adjective has a compositional force—that is, "spiritual" describes what the resurrection body is made of, the material out of which it is composed. On this view, the resurrection body is "spiritual" because it is made of an immaterial spiritual substance. This view clearly involves a denial of the genuinely physical character of the resurrection body. As Vos observes,

This adjective Pneumatikon [Spiritual] expresses the quality of the body in the eschatological state. Every thought of immaterialness, or etherealness or absence of physical density ought to be kept carefully removed from the term. Whatever in regard to such qualifications may or may not be

---

5   This adjective is capitalized here, contrary to standard current English usage, to make clear that it does not mean "spiritual" in the sense of "nonphysical," "immaterial." That sense as a description of the resurrection body would be a serious error.

6   The difficulties that beset the English translation of this adjective (rendered "natural" by most English translations) will be addressed below.

7   Charles Hodge, *An Exposition of the First Epistle to the Corinthians* (New York: Robert Carter & Brothers, 1857), 347.

involved; it is certain that such traits, if existing, are not described here by the adjective in question. In order to keep far such misunderstandings the capitalizing of the word ought to be carefully guarded both in translation and otherwise: πνευματικόν almost certainly leads on the wrong track, whereas Πνευματικόν, not only sounds a note of warning, but in addition points in the right direction positively. Paul means to characterize the resurrection-state as the state in which the Pneuma [Spirit] rules.[8]

The Role of the Spirit

To this point, I have done little more than assert rather than argue that in 15:44, πνευματικόν as a description of the resurrection body refers to the work of the Holy Spirit. Several mutually reinforcing grounds support that view, as well as, in turn, that the noun πνεῦμα in 15:45 refers to the person of the Holy Spirit.

The Ψυχικόν-Πνευματικόν Distinction

Within the New Testament—and for that matter, in early Christian literature beyond the New Testament—this contrast is found only in Paul and in only one other place, earlier in 1 Corinthians in 2:14-15. In other words, within the New Testament and occurring within the same document, this contrast is distinctively Pauline.

Without documenting or going into the details here, this distinction does have an extrabiblical background in the terminology found in some gnostic materials, of which Paul would likely have been aware. In that case, his use of the distinction lays hold of gnostic categories in order to make a decidedly and emphatically antignostic point.

In 2:14-15, the contrast is between "the natural person" (ψυχικὸς ἄνθρωπος) and "the Spiritual person" (ὁ πνευματικὸς). "Natural" here has a decidedly negative sense. The person it describes is not only unwilling but even unable to accept "the things of the Spirit of God." In view with this use of the adjective is who and what has now become "natural" as determined and defined by the fall. Here, "natural" refers to all that results from the fall and pertains to unrelieved human sinfulness resulting from the fall. The contrast between the two persons, then, is a contrast between the unbeliever and the believer.

---

8   Vos, *The Pauline Eschatology*, 166-67.

In the immediate context, beginning at 2:10, a major emphasis is on the necessity of the Spirit's activity in revelation. That stress, coupled with the explicit reference to the Spirit in 2:14 ("the things of the Spirit of God"), shows clearly that the adjective "Spiritual" in 2:15 refers to what is associated with the working of the Holy Spirit. The believer is a "Spiritual person" in the sense of being renewed, indwelt, and controlled by the Holy Spirit.[9]

This conclusion is supported by the near, if not exact, parallel to the natural-Spiritual contrast in Jude 19, where unbelievers are described as "natural, not having the Spirit" (ψυχικοί, πνεῦμα μὴ ἔχοντες; my translation). Unbelievers, in their "natural" (i.e., sinful) conduct, are without the presence and work of the Holy Spirit in their lives ("They follow their natural instincts because they do not have God's Spirit in them," NLT). In other words, they are "un-Spiritual."

Paul's Other Uses of Πνευματικός

There are multiple occurrences of the adjective used alone. With one exception noted presently, they always refer to the activity of the Holy Spirit. Occasionally, Paul does use the noun πνεῦμα anthropologically (e.g., Rom. 1:9; 1 Cor. 2:11; Gal. 6:18), but never the adjective.

The following are some instances of his use of the adjective clearly referring to the work of the Spirit: "the law is Spiritual" (Rom. 7:14); "you who are Spiritual" (Gal. 6:1); "every Spiritual blessing" (Eph. 1:3); "all Spiritual wisdom and understanding" (Col. 1:9). The sole exception is its antithetical meaning in Ephesians 6:12: "the spiritual forces of evil in the heavenly places."

At this point, then, we have sufficient grounds for concluding that the adjective πνευματικός in 1 Corinthians 15:44, as well as its use in 15:46 as we will see, refers to the activity of the Holy Spirit.

A Spiritual Body

While my primary interest in this section is in the meaning of "the last Adam became a life-giving πνεῦμα" in 15:45, it will be worth commenting

---

9 A trichotomist anthropology erroneously maintains that the adjective in 2:15 is anthropological (as well as the cognate adverb "spiritually" in 2:14); the human spirit, in distinction from the soul, is seen as the center or organ of God-consciousness and worship, awakened and become ascendant in the believer. A trichotomist anthropology is not sustainable biblically. For a refutation of trichotomy, see, e.g., John Murray, "Trichotomy," in Collected Writings of John Murray, vol. 2 (Edinburgh: Banner of Truth, 1977): 23–33; on 1 Cor. 2:13–15, see p. 28.

further at this point on Paul's description of the believer's resurrection body as "Spiritual" in 15:44.

As we have already seen from the contrasting parallels in 15:42-44, "Spiritual" is the one-word label that Paul sees as best describing the resurrection body, all told. His comprehensive descriptor for this body—in view of its attendant qualities of imperishability, glory, and power—is "Spiritual." In contrast, the preresurrection body of the believer—the body that because of the curse on sin is marked by perishability, dishonor, weakness—is inevitably going to be "sown," as Paul puts it graphically, buried because mortal. The resurrection body, then, is not another body, but this "sown" body so thoroughly transformed by the Holy Spirit, so thoroughly indwelt and renovated by the Holy Spirit, that no single term better describes it than "Spiritual."[10]

To counter a widespread misunderstanding, the adjective, as we noted earlier, does not describe the composition of the resurrection body, as if in view is a body made up of some spiritual substance, usually with the emphasis that the resurrection body is nonphysical. To the contrary, what the apostle has in view, all told, is the present body of the believer with its physicality so thoroughly transformed by the Spirit that it will be suited to a new and consummate order of physical existence—in that sense, an eschatological order suitable for Spirit-transformed bodily existence.[11]

In discussing this and related passages, N. T. Wright has coined the term "transphysical" for the resurrection body.[12] This proposal, as he intends it, is helpful in capturing the sense that the resurrection body, far from being nonphysical, will be transformed in its physicality, and in that sense is a transphysical body.

The Relationship between 15:44b and 15:45

The balanced antithetical parallelism begun in 15:42 and continuing through 15:44a is replaced in 15:44b by an *if-then* conditional construction; the existence of the resurrection body is inferred from the existence

---

10 Cf. "who will *transform our lowly body* to be like his glorious body" (Phil. 3:20).

11 It should be kept in mind that the body here is not narrowly corporeal but refers to the human person as a functioning psychophysical entity, what Paul elsewhere calls the "outer self" (2 Cor. 4:16; cf. 1 Cor. 15:51: "We shall not all sleep, but we shall all be changed").

12 N. T. Wright, *The Resurrection of the Son of God* (Minneapolis, MN: Fortress, 2003), 477, cf. 612, 661, 678-79.

of the preresurrection body: "If there is a natural body, there is also a Spiritual body." 1 Corinthians 15:45, among other considerations, functions to support this argument with an appeal to Scripture ("So also it is written," NASB).

A link in vocabulary between 15:44 and 15:45 is significant for our inquiry. On the one side of the contrast between Adam and Christ, the noun πνεῦμα (15:45) corresponds to the adjective πνευματικόν (15:44b). This correspondence carries with it the conclusion that as the adjective, for sufficient grounds we have already seen, refers to the activity of the Holy Spirit, so its cognate noun refers to the person of the Holy Spirit.

This conclusion drawn from the correlation between adjective and noun is reinforced by another element in 15:45. Paul does not simply say that as the last Adam Christ became the Spirit but qualifies with the participial expression "life-giving" (πνεῦμα ζῳοποιοῦν); he became "the life-giving Spirit."

This qualification—describing the activity of giving or producing eschatological life—Paul elsewhere associates specifically and broadly with the Spirit. This association is most explicit in 2 Corinthians 3:6: the new covenant, all told, is marked by the fact, using the same verb, that "the Spirit gives life" (τὸ δὲ πνεῦμα ζῳοποιεῖ).

There is no question that the reference here is to the Holy Spirit. As Paul is a minister of the new covenant (3:6), the Corinthian church is "a letter from Christ delivered by us, written not with ink but with the Spirit of the living God" (3:3); the new covenant is "the ministry of the Spirit" (3:8). Note as well the close connection between the Spirit and life elsewhere in Paul: "the Spirit of life" (Rom. 8:2); "the Spirit is life" (8:10; cf. 8:6; Gal. 6:8).

In view of (1) the link between the adjective πνευματικόν meaning "Spiritual" (1 Cor. 15:44) and the noun πνεῦμα (15:45) and (2) the qualification of πνεῦμα as "life-giving," the answer to the first of the two key questions we raised at the outset of this chapter is that πνεῦμα is a reference to the person of the Spirit. First Corinthians 15:45 states that "the last Adam became the life-giving Spirit" in the sense of the Holy Spirit.

This is a remarkable statement. Particularly for readers who have not previously considered 15:45 carefully, questions no doubt come to mind. How is this statement to be related to Scripture's clear and pervasive

teaching concerning the tripersonal nature of God? How is such a statement compatible with orthodox Trinitarian doctrine? These questions are
understandable and certainly need to be addressed head-on.

1 Corinthians 15:45–49

Before doing that, however, it will be useful for further understanding 15:45
and the implications of the relationship between the resurrected Christ
and the Holy Spirit expressed there to trace the course of the rest of Paul's
argument in this section through 15:49.

1 CORINTHIANS 15:45

Here, Paul now begins to broaden the contrast begun at 15:42. The contrast between bodies—between the buried ("sown") and resurrected body
of the believer—is now expanded to include whole persons, whole living
persons. On the one side, Adam is brought into view as a "living being"
(ψυχὴν ζῶσαν); on the other side, Christ, the last Adam, is in view, as we
have discussed, as the "life-giving Spirit" (πνεῦμα ζῳοποιοῦν).

Paul introduces Adam into the contrast by quoting Genesis 2:7—in other
words, Adam not as fallen (the Adam of Genesis 3) but as he was before
the fall, by virtue of creation. The contrast in 1 Corinthians 15:45, then, is
between pre-fall Adam and Christ, the resurrected last Adam.

This broadening of the contrast points to a significant aspect of Paul's
argumentation that is typically passed over or simply missed in the exegesis
of this passage. His interpretive citing of Genesis 2:7 shows that a consummation was in view for the creation from its beginning. An eschatology
that was forfeited by Adam in his disobedience and fall (Gen. 3) has been
achieved by Christ, the last Adam, in his obedience unto death (Phil. 2:8)
and resurrection (cf. Rom. 5:12-19; 8:19-22).

Paul sees Genesis 2:7, with its description of the creation of Adam
in the image of God ("the man became a living being"; cf. Gen. 1:27),
as having in view an eschatological fulfillment. That may be seen from
(1) the glossing of "man" in the quotation with "first" and "Adam," and
(2) "became" from the quotation as the verb implicit in the latter part of
the Greek text of 1 Corinthians 15:45. This way of including 15:45 ("the
last Adam became life-giving Spirit") in quoting Genesis 2:7 shows that,
for Paul, Christ as the life-giving Spirit fulfills the meaning of Genesis

2:7. Given the fall, the forfeiting first Adam anticipates the fulfilling last Adam; fallen Adam becomes "the type of the one to come" (Rom. 5:14, my translation).

As whole persons, Adam and Christ are introduced in 1 Corinthians 15:45 not simply as individuals, as random or isolated persons. Each is plainly a representative or head, a key figure. Adam, created in the image of God (Gen. 1:27), is the primary exemplification of that bodily existence that Paul dubs "natural" (ψυχικόν); Christ as resurrected, is the primary exemplification of the bodily existence Paul calls "Spiritual" (πνευματικόν). Adam is the natural one par excellence. Similarly, Christ is *the* Spiritual one.

Clarifying a detail of the passage, important for its understanding, is necessary at this point. The two occurrences of "natural" (ψυχικόν) in 1 Corinthians 15:44 do not have the same reference. In 15:44a, as we have seen, "natural" is a summary label for the preresurrection ("sown") body marked by the effects of the fall and the curse on sin (corruption, dishonor, and weakness, 15:42–43). In 15:44b "natural" describes the body of Adam before the fall.[13]

This difference reflects the significant difference in syntax between 15:44a and 15:44b. In the antithetical parallelism of 15:44a, "natural" on the one side describes the sin-cursed preresurrection body. In the positive argument (if-then) of 15:44b, "natural" designates the original, unfallen pre-eschatological body, from which Paul infers the eventual existence of the eschatological body. Concerning this difference, Vos makes the important observation: "From the abnormal body of sin no inference could be drawn as to that effect. The abnormal and the eschatological are not so logically correlated that the one can be postulated from the other."[14]

This prompts the further observation that from the "natural" (ψυχικόν) vantage point of the original, pre-fall creation (15:44b), the "natural" (ψυχικόν) of 15:44a (and 1 Cor. 2:14), marred by sin, is in fact decidedly "unnatural." The marks of the fallen, sin-cursed "natural" body—corruption,

13 The noun ψυχὴν in 1 Cor. 15:45 (from Gen. 2:7) grounds the use of its cognate adjective ψυχικόν in the *argument* of 1 Cor. 15:44b (just as we have already seen above, πνεῦμα grounds πνευματικόν). This cognate link (ψυχὴν-ψυχικόν), clear in Greek, is apparently impossible to capture in English translations, at least in current English usage (some older commentators expressed this link with "soul"-"soulish").

14 Vos, *The Pauline Eschatology*, 169n19.

dishonor, and weakness—are not predicable of the pre-fall "very good" (Gen. 1:31) "natural" body.

Bringing Adam and Christ into view as whole, living persons in 1 Corinthians 15:45 at the same time entails even more. Bodily existence is not an abstraction; it does not take place in a vacuum, at least if it is a living, functioning body. Rather, bodily existence implies a context, an environment, an overall ecology, if you will. A body is an index, a pointer to an environment; it is exponential of the context in which it exists.

1 CORINTHIANS 15:46

It is not the Spiritual that is first but the natural, then the Spiritual. (my translation)

This verse makes clear the broadening scope of Paul's reasoning. The neuter singulars τὸ ψυχικόν ("the natural") and τὸ πνευματικόν ("the Spiritual") are best taken substantively. They are generalizing expressions referring to contrasting orders of existence. That broadening becomes explicit in 15:47–49.

It is a mistake, then, missing this broadening, to read an elided "body" (σῶμα) after the neuter singular expressions in 15:46, as do some commentators and even some translations (e.g., CEB, NLT), as if only the bodies of 15:44 are again being contrasted (these bodies are of course included in the generalizing expressions).

The question may be asked why Paul expresses himself exactly as he does in 15:46. The balanced two-member contrasting parallelism in 15:42–45 and resumed in 15:47–49 is broken up with a *not this . . . but this . . . and then this* construction. The likely answer lies in recognizing that Paul expresses himself as he does to correct the Hellenistic thought pattern of his opponents. According to that pagan way of thinking, "the spiritual" in the sense of the ideal is first in the sense of being the protological or archetypal realm that lies in back of the material world, the world as we experience it. The spiritual is understood as the ideal in the sense of having atemporal priority and superiority to the phenomenal material world.

At any rate, whatever the accuracy of this suggestion, we should not miss that here, once again, Paul clearly reveals the historical-eschatological direction of his thinking. Perfection, the consummate ideal, is not to be sought either at the *beginning* of history or *above* history but at the *end* of history. Perfection is realized by the unfolding of history to its consummation.

1 CORINTHIANS 15:47–49

These verses confirm and at the same time elaborate the comprehensive scope expressed in 15:46. Here, Paul resumes his balanced two-term contrast, his two-member contrasting parallelism, but with a shift in terms—with "earth" (γῆ), on the one side, "heaven" (οὐρανός), on the other, with their respective correlate adjectives (χοϊκός, ἐπουράνιος) replacing the contrast between "natural" (ψυχικόν) and "Spiritual" (πνευματικόν) and their respective cognate nouns (ψυχή, πνεῦμα). Several things are noteworthy about this contrast.

First, it is certainly not synonymous with the contrast in 15:42–46; there is an important semantic significance to the shift in terms. The basic frame of reference, however, is the same. The cosmological and spatial terms introduced make explicit the comprehensive environmental context already anticipated with the contrast between bodies begun at 15:42.

Second, the contrast between earth and heaven with its explicitly cosmological terms is, at the same time, *historical.* Heaven, on the one side of the contrast, is heaven become what it now is because of Christ's ascension, because it is where the *incarnate* Christ was not previously but now is, the place of his heavenly session; in being there, he is now "from heaven" (15:47). Christ, as the life-giving Spirit, is the resurrected and ascended Christ, Christ glorified, no longer in his earthly state of humiliation but in his heavenly state of exaltation. Heaven has now become, until his return, the locus of eschatological redemption.

Third, the comprehensive scope of the contrast comes out further in the way in which Paul compares Adam and Christ in these verses. Clearly, as in 15:45, they are not in view simply as lone individuals but as representatives. This is clear from the linking of singular and the plural expressions on both sides of the contrast.

Adam, as "the first man" (15:47), is preeminently and archetypally "the earthly one" (ὁ χοϊκός; my translation); so he has associated with him "those who are earthly" (οἱ χοϊκοί; my translation)—that is, all human beings as they descend from Adam (15:48). In contrast, Christ, as "the second man" (15:47) is preeminently and archetypally "the heavenly one" (ὁ ἐπουράνιος; my translation); so he has associated with him "those who are heavenly" (οἱ ἐπουράνιοι; my translation), believers in view of their union with Christ as ascended.

Note that in 15:47, the prepositional phrases "from the earth" (ἐκ γῆς) and "from heaven" (ἐξ οὐρανοῦ) should be taken adjectivally, synonymous with being "earthly," on the one side, "heavenly," on the other. In the Greek text, these phrases are not genitives of source or origin but indicate place or location.

In the case of Christ, "from heaven" is an exaltation predicate, referring to his present place of residence (cf. Phil. 3:20: it is "from heaven"—Christ's place of exaltation, where, in union with him, their "citizenship," their true homeland, is—that believers await Christ's return). To take "from heaven" as a reference to Christ's origin out of his state of preexistence in his incarnation significantly misses a key point of the passage.

1 CORINTHIANS 15:49

> As we have borne the image of the earthly one [the man of dust], we shall also bear the image of the heavenly one. (my translation)

This capstone declaration brings the argument in the section to its climax and, at the same time, back to the point of departure in 15:42. At their future resurrection, believers will bear bodily the image of the heavenly one. By virtue of their solidarity with Christ, believers will experience the complete Spiritual transformation, the transphysical renovation, of their bodily existence. "The image of the heavenly one" (cf. Rom. 8:29) is another way of describing the "Spiritual body" (1 Cor. 15:44).

The Time of Christ's Becoming the Life-Giving Spirit

With these observations on the flow of 15:42–49, I turn to the second question raised at the beginning of our now somewhat-lengthy consideration of this passage. The first question ordering our discussion concerns the meaning of πνεῦμα in 15:45, and we have seen that it refers to the person of the Holy Spirit. Since the life-giving Spirit is not what Christ, as the last Adam, is eternally or timelessly but what he "became," our second question concerns the timepoint of this becoming.

From our analysis of the passage so far, there should be little difficulty in recognizing that the answer is Christ's resurrection or, more broadly including the ascension, his glorification. A couple of considerations make this answer clear.

First, in the immediate context (15:42–45), included in Christ becoming the life-giving Spirit—whatever else that involves in its fullness as we have been considering it—is the fact that he is the first instance of the Spiritual body that believers will receive in their future resurrection (15:44–45); he is the primary exemplification and manifestation of that resurrection body. Also, as the life-giving Spirit, Christ is "the heavenly one," whose image believers, as "the heavenly ones," will bear bodily at their resurrection (15:48–49). So, by analogy, it follows that as believers will be glorified in their resurrection, so Christ has been glorified, including becoming the life-giving Spirit, in his resurrection.

Second, looking at the passage in its broader context, the entire discourse in chapter 1 Corinthians 15 beginning at 15:12, as we have already seen, concerns the resurrection of Christ and the unity that exists between Christ and believers in resurrection. The controlling consideration, as much as any, is Christ as "the firstfruits" in the resurrection harvest that includes believers (15:20, 23; cf. 15:12–19).

With that being the case, it would make little sense for Paul to construct his argument as he does if Christ were already life-giving prior to or apart from his resurrection. It would not be convincing to stake everything on the unbreakable bond between Christ and believers in resurrection if he were qualified to be the giver of resurrection life by virtue of anything other than his own resurrection.[15]

In other words, Christ is not constituted as life-giving by virtue of his preexistence, although his preexistent deity is surely in the background as an absolutely essential precondition and is not in any way diminished by what Paul says. Nor is it his incarnation that makes Christ life-giving.[16]

As "the firstfruits" (15:20), Christ is "the life-giving Spirit" (15:45); as "the life-giving Spirit" he is "the firstfruits." His resurrection is clearly the timepoint when Christ became the life-giving Spirit.

---

15 Jesus's declaration "I am the resurrection and the life" (John 11:25) is made and has its validity in view of his still future glorification, consisting in his being "lifted up" in his death and resurrection (John 3:14; 8:28; 12:32, 34; cf. 7:39).

16 See the comment above about "from heaven" (15:47) as an exaltation predicate, not an indication of origin out of preexistence.

The Relation between Christ and the Spirit

That in 1 Corinthians 15:45 the life-giving Spirit Christ became in his resurrection is the Holy Spirit rests on firm exegetical grounds. But that leaves a key question still to be addressed for necessary clarification and to avoid possible serious misunderstanding: What is the sense of this becoming experienced by Christ? In other terms, what is the nature of the unity or equation or identity between Christ and the Spirit that Paul expresses here?

In answering this question—this is the crucial, all-important consideration—what must be recognized and constantly kept in view is the historical scope of the apostle's statement in 15:45 and the immediate context (15:42–49). He is not addressing essential, eternal inner-Trinitarian relationships. Those relationships are outside his purview here. Keeping this historical focus in view, then, the affirmation in 15:45 is obviously not to be taken in an ontological sense, as if Paul is denying or obliterating the personal distinction between the second and third persons of the Trinity.

Rather, in view is what happened to Christ, what he experienced, in history, what he "became" in the unfolding of redemptive-history to its resurrection-consummation. Furthermore, in view is what he experienced in his specific identity as "the last Adam" and "the second man" (15:45, 47)—in other words, as incarnate, in his assumed humanity, not in his deity as the immutable eternal Son.

The point of 15:45 in its immediate context is this: His resurrection-glorification brought about a conjunction or oneness between the incarnate Christ and the Holy Spirit that did not exist previously. For Christ, the resurrection resulted in (1) an unprecedented possession *of* the Spirit and (2) an unprecedented transformation *by* the Spirit. This possession and transformation was so climactic, so complete and permanent, that Christ and the Spirit are now one. Paul deems that oneness expressed adequately and appropriately by saying that Christ, as the last Adam, became the life-giving Spirit.

This oneness, however, exists in a specific respect; it consists in the activity of giving life. If we look for labels for this oneness or equation, in terms of the classical theological distinction between the *ontological* and *economic* Trinity, this equation reflects the latter (economic), always keeping in mind that it concerns the transformation experienced by Christ in his humanity. Other possible designations are *functional*, understood in terms of the consequent activity involved, or, given the quality of the resurrection life in view, *eschatological*.

At any rate, in view is their conjoint, unified saving activity, an activity that does not obliterate or compromise the personal Trinitarian distinction between Christ and the Spirit. Dating from his resurrection and in his exaltation, it is now the case not simply that the Spirit makes alive but that Christ, the last Adam, as the Spirit makes alive.[17]

That 15:45 refers to the Holy Spirit is recognized across a broad front in monographs and commentaries, including among Reformed interpreters—for instance, Herman Bavinck, Geerhardus Vos, John Murray, and Herman Ridderbos. Hence, it remains a source of disappointment that those English translations produced and most used by evangelicals continue to resist capitalizing and render with lowercase "spirit" and without the definite article in 15:45.[18]

This disappointment is all the more puzzling since it has to be asked: Within the outlook of Scripture in general, and of Paul in particular, what meaning could "a life-giving spirit" possibly have as a description of Christ after his resurrection? The response of Christ to the fearful apostles after his resurrection would appear to counter any such notion: "For a spirit (πνεῦμα) does not have flesh and bones as you see that I have" (Luke 24:39; cf. 24:37).

Presumably one reason for evangelical resistance to capitalizing stems from the concern that to do so appears to lend credence to the

---

17 Questions could be raised about the activity of the Spirit in the creation as a whole, both in its origin and subsequent preservation, in the creation of Adam, and with Adam and Eve prior to the fall. Such questions are also outside of Paul's purview in this passage. The life-giving in view is specifically *soteriological* and *eschatological*.

18 E.g., the ESV, NASB, NIV, NET, and NKJV/KJV. Commendable exceptions are the HCSB, GNT, and NLT, which have "Spirit," although GNT and NLT translate the verb with "is" instead of "became," which misses or perhaps even distorts the timed and dynamic/transformative force here of "became." Of the translations I have seen, only the GNT has the definite article before "life-giving Spirit" (or "spirit").

It should be noted that references in Paul to the (Holy) Spirit are always definite, whether or not the definite article occurs; the presence or absence of the definite article in the Greek text is not determinative for whether the reference is to the third person of the Trinity. See the substantiating conclusion in this regard reached, after a careful survey of Paul's usage, by Gordon Fee, *God's Empowering Presence: The Holy Spirit in the Letters of Paul* (Peabody, MA: Hendrickson, 1994), 24.

anti-Trinitarian and purely functional Spirit-Christology argued by some interpreters of Paul. But that hesitation, however understandable, is unnecessary. When the scope, the salvation-historical focus, of the passage is kept in view, it is not only unnecessary but also completely unwarranted to find here a denial of or any incompatibility with the personal distinction between Christ and the Spirit that would be irreconcilable with clear biblical teaching about the Trinity and later church formulation of Trinitarian doctrine.

Paul's Trinitarian conception of God underlying this passage and essential to his theology as a whole is clear enough elsewhere. It is explicit, for instance, in the personal and parallel distinction between God (the Father), Christ as Lord, and the (Holy) Spirit in 1 Corinthians 12:4-6, 2 Corinthians 13:14, and Ephesians 4:4-6.[19]

My hope, then, is that from now on, when readers see "a life-giving spirit" in one or another translation they may have in hand, they will think "Spirit" and recognize the eschatological oneness in their activity between the incarnate Christ and the Holy Spirit that Paul affirms here.

Clarifying Observations

Our primary interest in 1 Corinthians 15:45 has been in the relationship Paul affirms there between the Holy Spirit and Christ dating from his resurrection. In considering the meaning of that affirmation, we have already noted how deeply embedded it is in its immediate context (15:42-49). Three additional clarifying observations conclude our examination of this passage.

First, in the light of teaching elsewhere in the New Testament concerning the relationship between Christ and the Spirit—teaching, for instance, in Luke-Acts that we considered in part 1—the relationship in view in 1 Corinthians 15:45 is best understood in terms of the staging or phasing principle involved, as Christ in his earthly ministry passes from his state of humiliation, culminating in his death, into his state of exaltation, beginning with his resurrection. First Corinthians 15:45 hardly means that Christ's relationship with the Holy Spirit begins with his resurrection. Rather, that

---

19 For a thorough demonstration of Paul's Trinitarian view of God, see Fee, *God's Empowering Presence*, 825-45, esp. 839-42.

relationship originates with his birth—in fact, at his conception by the Spirit (Luke 1:35)—heightens with his endowment with the Spirit at the onset of his public ministry in his baptism at the Jordan (Luke 3:22), and reaches its climactic and consummate realization in his resurrection.

Second, and related to the preceding observation, the last clause of 1 Corinthians 15:45 is helpfully viewed as Paul's one-sentence commentary, in effect, on the significance of Pentecost. The multiple elements that Peter delineates as a single complex of events in his Pentecost sermon—resurrection, ascension, reception of the Spirit in the ascension, and outpouring of the Spirit on Pentecost (Acts 2:32–33)—Paul telescopes and encapsulates by saying that in his resurrection, the last Adam has become the life-giving Spirit.[20]

It needs always to be kept in mind that this is a redemptive-historical affirmation. Paul is not denying, for instance, the Spirit's life-giving activity among God's people prior to the resurrection. Here, if nothing else, we can take note of what Paul says about the Old Testament wilderness generation in 1 Corinthians 10:3–4. With all of the thorny hermeneutical questions this passage poses, those who "were baptized into Moses" (10:2), "all ate the same spiritual food, and all drank the same spiritual drink," and in doing that, "they drank from the spiritual Rock that followed them, and the Rock was Christ."

Taking this threefold use of the adjective πνευματικός here as a likely reference to the Holy Spirit ("Spiritual"), the situation under the old covenant is marked by the presence and activity of the Spirit in ministering the active presence of the preincarnate Christ. But this conjoint presence, as efficacious as it undoubtedly was (*ordo salutis*), was no more than anticipatory (as an event in the *historia salutis*). It anticipates the fulfillment on which it depends, the fulfillment that inaugurates with the incarnation of Christ "in the fullness of time" (Gal. 4:4).

First Corinthians 15:45 affirms what is true as the culmination of that fulfillment: Now, at last and finally, the Spirit is present and at work among God's people (1) on the stable basis of the finished, once-for-all work of Christ in his earthly ministry and (2) as the Spirit is the transformer of

20 See also Richard B. Gaffin Jr., "Redemption and Resurrection: An Exercise in Biblical-Systematic Theology," in *A Confessing Theology for Postmodern Times*, ed. Michael S. Horton (Wheaton, IL: Crossway, 2000), 237.

Christ in his humanity. This is the fulfillment in view in saying that Christ, as the last Adam, has become the life-giving Spirit.

Third, a striking feature of 15:42–49 is the comprehensive scope it opens up. These verses are part of Paul's answer to the question posed to him about the mode of the resurrection and nature of the resurrection body (15:35). This is surely an important question but, considered in its own terms, rather specific in its focus. So the turn his answer takes, as he develops the antithetical parallelism begun in 15:42, may be surprising and come across initially as an exercise in "theological overkill."

Asked a specific and practical question about the resurrection body, he proceeds to develop an outlook that is nothing less than cosmic in its scope. In response to a question about the nature of the resurrection body, he generates an answer that opens up a viewpoint encompassing nothing less than the whole of history, from its beginning to and including its consummation. That does not overstate what takes place in these verses.

This cosmic, history-encompassing perspective appears from the way in which Adam and Christ are introduced and function in Paul's argumentation. Their respective roles are aptly highlighted by the numerical adjectives used to identify each. In the order and scope of Paul's thinking here, Adam is "the first" (ὁ πρῶτος, 15:45, 47); no one before Adam "counts," or matters. In contrast, Christ, in his adamic identity, is "the second" (ὁ δεύτερος, 15:47); no one between Adam and Christ counts. At the level of Paul's overarching outlook here, not Noah, not Abraham, not Moses, not David, not Israel as a nation, not anyone between Adam and Christ comes into consideration. But as "the second," Christ is also "the last" (ὁ ἔσχατος, 15:45); no one after him counts; Christ is literally the eschatological man.

As we have already had occasion to note, in this passage, Adam and Christ are key figures; they are plainly representatives and heads. As such, they bring into view two orders of life, two environments of existence. On the one hand, the order of Adam is first by virtue of creation and has become subject to corruption through sin. In contrast, the order of Christ, the new Adam, is second and last, and is incorruptible.

So, triggered by the question about the resurrection body, Paul's answer brings into view two orders of life, beginning at creation and reaching to and including the consummation, orders of life, one preeschatological, the other eschatological, that are consecutive, comprehensive, and antithetical.

In other words, recalling our earlier discussion about the formal structure of Paul's eschatological outlook, it is not difficult to recognize that the two-aeon distinction shapes as it underlies the argumentation in 15:42–49.

This is the virtual sense of 15:46 and the two generalizing expressions there: "the natural" (become unnatural because of the fall) and "the Spiritual" designate successive and contrasting aeons, this age and the age to come, two world orders, creation and its consummation, creation and the new creation, each beginning with an Adam of its own.

What should not be missed, particularly prominent in this passage, is the large megapoint that keeps coming out as we consider Paul's theology: the way in which his eschatology both shapes and is shaped by his Christology, and with that, his soteriology. Unmistakable in this passage is the nothing-less-than-eschatological character of Christ's saving work. The eschatological age to come, the new and final creation, begins with the resurrection of Christ, when, having been "delivered up for our trespasses and raised for our justification" (Rom. 4:25), he was constituted the life-giving Spirit.[21]

2 CORINTHIANS 3:17–18

Now the Lord is the Spirit . . . the Lord who is the Spirit.

These expressions are closely related as they presuppose what Paul has previously written to the Corinthian church in 1 Corinthians 15:45 concerning the relationship between Christ and the Spirit. So, with that background in view, this passage may be treated much more briefly here.

In 2 Corinthians 3:6, Paul identifies himself as a minister of the "new covenant" and contrasts it, as the following verses make clear, with the old covenant (cf. 3:14). This contrast structures the discourse to the end of the chapter.

In 3:7–11, so far as distinguishing persons are concerned, Moses (3:7) stands for the old covenant, the Spirit (3:8) for the new. On the new covenant side, as virtually all translations and most, if not all, commentaries and monographs recognize, the reference is to the Holy Spirit. That is clear, if nothing else, from "gives life," the verb of which the Spirit is the subject

---

21 For a more extensive treatment of 1 Cor. 15:45 and related passages, see my "The Last Adam, the Life-Giving Spirit," in *The Forgotten Christ: Exploring the Majesty and Mystery of God Incarnate*, ed. Stephen Clark (Nottingham: Apollos, 2007), 191–231, and the literature cited there.

(3:6; cf. "the Spirit of the living God," 3:3), the same verb (ζῳοποιέω) that Paul uses for "the life-giving Spirit" in 1 Corinthians 15:45.

In the section that begins in 3:12, a shift in the contrast occurs on the new covenant side. While Moses continues on the old covenant side (3:13-15), Christ (3:14) enters the picture and replaces the Spirit. This raises the question, in effect: What explains this change, this interchangeability between the Spirit and Christ on the new covenant side of the contrast? 2 Corinthians 3:17 provides the answer: because "the Lord is the Spirit."

That here "the Lord" is Christ—not, as some argue, a reference to the Spirit—seems clear for the following reasons:

First, the removal of the veil of unbelief occurs "when one turns to the Lord" (3:16, alluding to Exod. 34:34). That is so, in context, "because only in Christ is it taken away" (3:14 NIV). The veil is removed when, in faith, one turns to Christ as Lord. Additionally, turning to the Lord in faith understood as turning to the Holy Spirit, instead of to Christ, is an odd notion biblically, certainly without precedent elsewhere in Paul.

Second, in 3:18 "the glory of the Lord," into whose image believers are being transformed as they behold (or reflect) that glory, can hardly be any other than the glory of Christ. Romans 8:29 and 1 Corinthians 15:49 (cf. Phil. 3:21) should put that beyond question, along with "the glory of Christ, who is the image of God" just a few verses later (2 Cor. 4:4).

Third, "The Spirit of the Lord," immediately following in 3:17, distinguishes the Spirit from "the Lord" (cf. "the Spirit of Christ," Rom. 8:9).

For these three reasons, in 2 Corinthians 3:17-18, "the Lord" is Christ and "the Spirit" is the Holy Spirit. This is the sense of "the Lord (Christ) is the Spirit" at the beginning of 3:17 as well as "the Lord who is the Spirit" at the end of 3:18.[22]

The clarifying comments made concerning 1 Corinthians 15:45 apply here as well. Here, as there, Paul's focus is historical, on what has transpired in the history of redemption with the incarnate Christ, in terms of his humanity. Here again, eternal and essential inner-Trinitarian relationships are outside Paul's purview. Here, as there, it is not only unnecessary but also unwarranted to see a denial of the distinction between the second

---

22 In the expression ἀπὸ κυρίου πνεύματος (3:18), πνεύματος is best taken in apposition to κυρίου, referring to Christ: "the Lord, the Spirit" (NASB) or "the Lord who is the Spirit."

and third persons of the Trinity in conflict with teaching elsewhere in Paul and the rest of the New Testament, and later church doctrinal formulation based on that teaching.

"The Lord" in 2 Corinthians 3:17-18 is specifically Christ as exalted, and the identity affirmed between Christ and the Spirit is based on the consummate and unprecedented transformation by and possession of the Spirit experienced by Christ in his resurrection. The identity in saying that "the Lord is the Spirit" is a oneness or unity in their activity, an identity that does not deny but keeps intact and unchanged the personal distinction in deity between them.

In 1 Corinthians 15:45, that conjoint activity consists in giving resurrection life. In 2 Corinthians 3:17, in view is the eschatological "freedom" inherent in that life. The regimen or order ("law") put into effect by the new covenant is such that "the Spirit of life in Christ Jesus has set you free" (Rom. 8:2; "the life-giving Spirit in Christ Jesus has set you free" NET).

The apostle would expect his original readers in Corinth, and all subsequent readers, to understand that the "is" (ἐστιν) in 2 Corinthians 3:17 is based on the "became" (ἐγένετο) in 1 Corinthians 15:45. In his resurrection, Christ, the last Adam, became the life-giving Spirit. Consequently, he, the exalted Lord, is the Spirit. He is now and forever who and what he became once for all.

ROMANS 1:3-4

This passage merits our careful attention for the way in which it advances our understanding of the significance of the resurrection for Christ personally, particularly its importance for his relationship to the Holy Spirit and their resulting conjoint activity.

The Immediate Context

The immediate context, 1:1-7, follows the standard format for beginning letters in the Hellenistic period with its three basic elements: first identifying the sender(s), then the recipient(s), followed by a greeting.

In following this form, Paul does not do that in a merely formal or minimalist fashion. Instead he expands on it, sometimes extensively, in distinctively personal and gospel-centered ways, sometimes to highlight matters of substance that are then dealt with more fully in the main body of the letter. We have already seen an instance of such expansion in considering Galatians 1:4 in chapter 10.

Here, where a simple "Paul" (Παῦλος, in the nominative case in Greek) would have satisfied the form for identifying the sender, an extended expansion occurs continuing all the way through 1:6. The recipients, the "saints" in Rome (in the dative case), are then indicated in 1:7a, followed by the greeting, Christianized, in 1:7b.[23]

In 1:1, Paul first identifies himself with three additional descriptions. Syntactically parallel to each other, they are in apposition to "Paul." But semantically, a progression from each one to the next seems apparent: as "a servant of Christ Jesus" he has been "called to be an apostle," and as a servant-apostle he has been "set apart for the gospel of God."

This mention of the gospel at the end of 1:1 leads Paul to qualify it, first with a relative clause in 1:2 and then with a prepositional phrase at the beginning of 1:3. Looking at this sequence in reverse, the gospel "concerning his Son" is what God "promised beforehand . . . in the holy Scriptures." God's Son—"his own Son," whom he "did not spare" but sent in "the fullness of time" (Rom. 8:3, 32; Gal. 4:4; Eph. 1:10)—is the content of "the gospel of God" as it was promised by him in the Old Testament.[24]

This reference to the Son, in turn, prompts the rest of 1:3–4, which in English translation consists of two relative clauses (attributive participial clauses in Greek, both modifying υἱοῦ) that further describe the Son, note, as the content of the gospel:

> who was born of the seed of David according to the flesh, who was declared to be [or appointed] the Son of God in power according to the Spirit of holiness by the resurrection from the dead. (my translation)

It is not difficult to see that these two clauses present a contrasting parallelism, with each clause introduced by a controlling participle (in Greek): "born" or "became" (τοῦ γενομένου), contrasted with "declared" (τοῦ

---

23 By way of contrast, compare this lengthy elaboration, with another letter opening, following the standard form in its bare essentials: "Claudius Lysias, to his Excellency the governor Felix, greetings" (Acts 23:26).

24 For the discussion to follow, note that in light of Rom. 8:3, 32, cited parenthetically in this sentence, "his Son" at the beginning of 8:3 already indicates and thus affirms his deity.

ὁρισθέντος). This parallelism is further displayed in the chiastic (a-b-b-a) contrast between elements internal to the two clauses: "of the seed of David" contrasts with "by the resurrection from the dead,"[25] and "according to the flesh" with "according to the Spirit of holiness."

This literary structure has prompted a number of commentators and others to posit that the two clauses have a pre-Pauline origin as a confessional or hymn fragment. That could well be. One argument in favor of this view is that if these clauses are elided, there is still a smooth, uninterrupted flow between the beginning of 1:3 to the end of 1:4: "concerning his Son, . . . Jesus Christ our Lord."

My own view is that we can neither exclude nor be insistent on a pre-Pauline origin. The important consideration for interpretation is that whether or not these clauses originated with Paul, he includes them because he wishes to highlight what he deems essential about the Son as the content of the gospel.

Understanding the Contrast

How, then, should these clauses in their details and the overall contrast between them be understood? For our purposes here, as a fair generalization looking at the history of interpretation, there are two basic views. One we may dub *ontological*. According to this view, the contrast is between the two coexisting sides or components in the makeup of the person of the Son, between contrasting parts in the constitution of his person. Specifically, "flesh" (1:3) is his human nature, "Spirit of holiness" (1:4), his divine nature. Accordingly, on this view, these clauses teach explicitly, perhaps more explicitly than anywhere else in Scripture, the hypostatic (personal) union of Christ's two natures, the doctrine of the two-natured person of Christ.

This is the view, for instance—limiting ourselves to Reformed interpreters, but they are representative of interpreters, past and present, from other traditions—of Calvin[26] and Charles Hodge[27] in their commentaries on Romans, and of Warfield.[28]

---

25 This pairing is clearer in Greek: both phrases begin with the same preposition (ἐκ, ἐξ).

26 John Calvin, *Commentaries on the Epistle of Paul the Apostle to the Romans*; trans. and ed. John Owen (Grand Rapids, MI: Eerdmans, 1948), 43–47.

27 Charles Hodge, *A Commentary on the Epistle to the Romans*, new ed. (Grand Rapids, MI: Louis Kregel Publisher-Bookseller, 1882), 24–30.

28 This view of the passage is defended at length by B. B. Warfield, "The Christ That Paul Preached," in *Biblical Doctrines* (New York: Oxford University Press, 1929), 235–52.

The other view can be labelled *redemptive-historical*. On this view, the contrast is between two successive stages in the experience or history of Christ, between two consecutive modes of his existence. The contrast, then, is not between the two natures of Christ, human and divine, but between his two states, his state of humiliation (1:3) followed by his state of exaltation (1:4).

This is now the prevailing view across a broad front of interpreters, adopted among Reformed interpreters by Vos[29] and also by Murray and Ridderbos in commentaries on Romans appearing independently of each other in 1959.[30]

When it comes to a decision between these two views, Calvin, Hodge, and Warfield are certainly a formidable combination. Furthermore, the two-natures view has a certain *prima facie* plausibility. It is probably the view most average readers come away with, given the importance of the doctrine of Christ's two natures and its influence in the doctrine and life of the church down through its history. Upon more careful examination, however, this view is beset with difficulties. Three may be noted here.

First, if the evident parallelism between the two clauses is maintained and "flesh" (1:3) is taken to refer to Christ's human nature, then this view requires taking "the Spirit of holiness" as a reference to Christ's deity, to his divine nature. But that means giving "Spirit," as well as the contrast between "Spirit" and "flesh," a sense they do not have elsewhere in Scripture and is foreign to Paul.

Hodge in his Romans commentary seeks to respond to this objection.[31] He counters it by pointing to the uniqueness of "Spirit of holiness" (πνεῦμα ἁγιωσύνης), that this expression occurs only here in the New Testament. This uniqueness—he reasons contrary to what some in his time were apparently arguing—is an indication that its reference is other than the many references to the Holy Spirit in Paul and the rest of the New Testament, which always have the modifying adjective "holy" (ἅγιον), but not, as here, the qualifying noun, "holiness" (ἁγιωσύνης). Accordingly, on his under-

---

29 Vos, *The Pauline Eschatology*, 155-156n10.

30 John Murray, *The Epistle to the Romans. The English Text with Introduction, Exposition and Notes* (Grand Rapids, MI: Eerdmans, 1959), 5-12; Herman Ridderbos, *Aan de Romeinen* (Kampen: N.V. Uitgeversmaatschappij J. H. Kok, 1959), 24-26.

31 Hodge, *Romans*, 28.

standing of the antithetical parallelism between the clauses, specifically that "flesh" (1:3) is an unambiguous reference to the Son's human nature, Hodge concludes that "Spirit of holiness," distinctive as it is, clearly refers to his divine nature.

Upon more careful reflection, however, this response does not hold up. "Spirit of holiness" is clearly a Semitism—that is, it has its provenance and gained its currency in Hebrew and Aramaic during the Second Temple period. In other words, πνεῦμα ἁγιωσύνης is translation Greek.[32]

Important for determining its meaning here are its equivalent Hebrew occurrences in the Old Testament: רוּחַ קָדְשְׁךָ (Ps. 51:13; 51:11 English translations), רוּחַ קָדְשׁוֹ (Isa. 63:10-11). Most English translations correctly render them with "Holy Spirit." Significantly, this translation is reinforced in the Septuagint: for all three occurrences (Ps. 50:13 LXX), it has τὸ πνεῦμα τὸ ἅγιόν, "the Holy Spirit."

Additionally, in the pseudepigraphic *Testament of Levi* (18:11), πνεῦμα ἁγιωσύνης refers to the divine Spirit given to the Messiah and his people. In light of this background, then, there is a fair presumption, to say the least, that in Romans 1:4, "the Spirit of holiness" refers to the Holy Spirit, not the Son's deity.

A second difficulty facing the ontological or two natures view is that it takes 1:4 to mean that the resurrection was declarative in the sense of making evident the deity of the Son *in distinction from and in contrast to his humanity*. But, as we have seen, such a reading runs counter to Paul's sustained emphasis on the unity between Christ and Christians in resurrection (Christ as "the firstfruits" of the resurrection harvest) and the *adamic* significance of the resurrection for him (as "the last Adam" and "the second man").

A further, third difficulty for the ontological view is that, as noted, these clauses are embedded in Paul's elaboration as the sender of Romans, specifically as he is "set apart for the gospel of God . . . concerning his Son." In other words, these clauses are best taken as a summary of the gospel, as expressing the gospel in a nutshell. This prompts what I leave here as a rhetorical question, to which I will return below. The doctrine of the two

---

32 This, by the way, may be an indication of the pre-Pauline origin of the clauses, addressed briefly above.

natures, of the two-natured person of Christ, is surely integrally important for the gospel, but is it a *summary* of the *gospel*?

Upon reflection, then, along these three lines of difficulty, especially when they are seen together, the ontological or two natures view of the contrast, despite its apparent plausibility and cogency, fails to find a place within Paul's theology; it does not fit plausibly within the framework of his thinking.

This, however, is not the case for the redemptive-historical or two-states view.

An important key for understanding Romans 1:3-4, serving to support the redemptive-historical view, lies in seeing that the contrast between "flesh" (1:3) and "Spirit" (1:4) has the customary and distinctive sense that it has throughout Paul. In fact, this contrast, at times antithesis, is among the most basic and prominent elements in his teaching. With that being the case and since we have not given it due attention so far in considering his theology (other than at several points in the history of interpretation), I introduce a survey of the contrast at this point, as a kind of excursus, that goes somewhat beyond the immediate demands of exegeting Romans 1:3-4. When that survey is done, I will return with its results to complete the treatment of this passage.

The Flesh-Spirit Contrast in Paul: A Brief Survey

The major passages where this contrast occurs are found in Romans 8:1-17 and Galatians 5:16-25 (cf. 6:8). In considering these and other related passages here, my primary, overriding interest is to show how this antithesis ties into Paul's eschatology, to point out its historical nature, that a historical factor controls Paul's use of the contrast.

Recognizing and appreciating this historical qualification is all the more important because of the unmistakable tendency throughout church history not to associate the two in Paul—the flesh-Spirit contrast and his eschatology—in any clear or definite way. Indeed, the tendency has been to set them in opposition, as has happened at times particularly within the historical-critical tradition where flesh and S/spirit have been construed in terms of pagan Hellenistic influence on Paul, on the one hand, and his eschatology seen as the Jewish/Old Testament side of his thinking, on the other. A perception of tension, even conflict, between the two has been the inevitable result.

The tendency, in general, has been to "philosophize" on the contrast in Paul and to view it as either a metaphysical or an anthropological contrast. That is often the case even when it is correctly seen that on the one side the Holy Spirit is in view. The work of the Spirit is typically viewed in an essentially timeless—that is, historically unconditioned—way. Hence my interest here in pointing out how the contrast, particularly Paul's conception of the work of the Spirit dovetails with his eschatology.[33]

I proceed here by first considering the flesh side of the contrast, then the Spirit side, before drawing some overall conclusions.

Flesh (σάρξ)

Paul's use of "flesh" may be surveyed by noting at least three different, quite distinct senses it has. One use, closest to our English word *flesh*, refers to corporeal existence, particularly of human beings. This usage is more or less equivalent with "body" (σῶμα). For instance, in the parallelism in 2 Corinthians 4:10-11, "in our mortal flesh" occurs interchangeably with "in our bodies"; "in my flesh" (Gal. 4:14 NKJV) refers to Paul's bodily or physical condition (in the light of 4:13; cf. Col. 1:24). More broadly, "flesh" can refer to the corporeality of various animate beings, not just human beings, like land animals, birds, and fish (1 Cor. 15:39; cf. 15:38-41).

It should be noted that this usage, closest to our widespread English usage, is the least frequent for Paul. This leads to the not inconsiderable problem that in English this corporeal sense may easily be read into Paul's other much more frequent and distinctive uses, which we have yet to consider, resulting in significant misunderstandings.

A second sense in Paul are instances where "flesh" refers not to a part, the corporeal aspect, of the makeup of human beings but, in light of the meaning of בָּשָׂר in the Old Testament (e.g., Gen. 6:12-13; Isa. 40:6), to the whole person: for example, "by the deeds of the law no flesh will be justified in His sight" (Rom. 3:20 NKJV, citing Ps. 142:2 LXX; cf. also Gal. 2:16). "No flesh"—that is, "no one" (NIV), "no human being" (ESV)—will be justified by the works of the law (cf., similarly, "no flesh should glory in His presence," 1 Cor. 1:29 NKJV).

---

33 In this regard, I cannot commend too highly for careful reading and reflection Vos, "The Eschatological Aspect of the Pauline Conception of the Spirit."

In this sense, "flesh," referring to the whole person, is a one-word index for what is specifically human.[34]

Romans 11:14 is an instance of an even broader use. One motive Paul has as "an apostle to the Gentiles" (11:13) is that in carrying out that ministry he might "somehow provoke my flesh to jealousy and save some of them" (my translation). Here "my flesh" singular (μου τὴν σάρκα) has a clearly plural, suprapersonal sense: "my fellow Jews" (ESV), "my own people" (NIV), "my fellow countrymen" (NASB 1995). This use of "flesh" has a collective force; it expresses a genetic connection, racial solidarity.

This suprapersonal instance, thirdly, may serve as a transition to considering Paul's most distinctive and theologically most pregnant usage. Here, "flesh" refers to a historically or temporally qualified sphere of existence. "Flesh" takes on an atmospheric quality, as it refers to the present order of the creation, with all that is characteristic of human life and necessary for its maintenance. In this sense, it is fair to say, "flesh" is the environment in which human beings live. This usage finds its expression primarily in the distinctively Pauline phrases, "in the flesh" (ἐν σαρκί) and "according to the flesh" (κατὰ σάρκα).

Here are some examples. Ephesians 5:15–6:9, a passage that deals with what it means in various basic relationships of life for Christians to be filled with the Spirit (5:18), includes in 6:5 the exhortation to bondservants (or slaves) to obey "your masters according to the flesh" (NASB, NKJV; τοῖς κατὰ σάρκα κυρίοις). Here, "flesh" hardly has the sense it has in Romans 11:14; Paul is not telling slaves they need be concerned to obey only masters with whom they have a genetic connection. Rather, they are to obey those who are their masters in terms of the present sociocultural order of things. Their "earthly masters" (ESV, NIV) gets at the sense helpfully, though with an important qualification I will make clear below.

In Philemon 15, Paul says concerning the runaway slave, Onesimus, who Paul is sending back to his master, Philemon, "he was parted from you for a while, that you might have him back forever." Here a distinction is made in the master-slave relationship between the temporary and the eternal. In Philemon 16, this relationship is further in view, with the

---

34 This second sense of σάρξ parallels the use of ψυχή ("soul") in 1 Cor. 15:45 (quoting Gen. 2:7) and elsewhere (Acts 2:41, 43; Rev. 18:13) to refer to the whole person, not just a part.

hoped-for potential for Onesimus to be more than a slave, to become "a beloved brother"—for Philemon as well as Paul—"both in the flesh and in the Lord."

Here, in the parallel between Philemon 15 and 16, "in the flesh" correlates with "for a while," with what is temporary; "in the Lord" correlates with "forever," with what is eternal. Juxtaposed are a relationship characteristic of the present earthly order ("flesh") and the permanent transformation of that relationship brought about by the gospel.

In passing but importantly, it should not be missed how this approach of Paul to the social structure involving slavery is ultimately subversive of it.

The pattern of usage in 1 Corinthians 1:18–3:23 is particularly instructive. Those who reject the gospel as foolishness are the wise, powerful, and well-born "according to the flesh" (1:26 ESV mg.). In this rejection, they exemplify "the debater of this age" (1:20), who is associated with "the wisdom of the world" (1:20), the "wisdom of this age" (2:6). They embrace "the wisdom of this world" (3:19) as they are "wise in this age" (3:18).

According to this pattern of expression, the person who is wise according to the flesh is the person who is wise in this present aeon, this present world-age. Here "according to the flesh" is virtually synonymous with "of this world" or "in this age."

With this temporalized or historicized use of "flesh," then, we once again find ourselves squarely within Paul's basic eschatological structure. "Flesh" refers to a comprehensive state of affairs, a world order; "flesh" is functionally equivalent with "this age," the old aeon. "Flesh" brings into view man (generically considered) in this world, human existence and human nature "in this age."

Flesh and Sin

In this aeonic usage, "flesh" characteristically, though not always, has a depreciatory, ethically negative sense. This sense can be seen clearly, for instance, in the key passages where flesh is contrasted with the Holy Spirit.

Romans 8:4 states a key purpose of the death of God's Son as an atonement for sin (8:3): "in order that the righteous requirement of the law might be fulfilled in us, who walk not according to the flesh but according to the Spirit." The immediately following verses (8:5–8) show what gives rise to these two contrasting "walks" or ways of life and conduct.

On the one side, walking according to the flesh stems from the thinking or disposition[35] of those, unbelievers, whose controlling focus is "the things of the flesh" (8:5). That disposition, further, is manifested by a deeply rooted "hostility toward God" (my translation) that not only does not but cannot submit to his law (8:7); it renders those controlled by it incapable of pleasing him (8:8).Those who are determined by and manifest this disposition of hostility toward God are those who are "according to the flesh" (8:5) and "in the flesh" (8:8).[36]

This mindset of unbelief is antithetical to the mindset of those who are believers, who exist and live "according to the Spirit" and "mind the things of the Spirit" (8:5, my translation). These two dispositions are as antithetical in their ultimate outcome as are "death," on the one hand, "life and peace," on the other (8:6).

The ethically negative, sin-qualified sense in which Paul uses "flesh" is evident in Galatians 5, where "the works of the flesh"—sinful attitudes and conduct such as sexual immorality, idolatry, enmity, jealousy, etc. (5:19-21)—are set in unrelieved antithesis to "the fruit of the Spirit" (5:22-23).

This use of "flesh," interchangeable with "this age" and associated with sin, needs to be qualified in an important respect. There is nothing originally inherent in the constitution of the flesh that explains why Paul depreciates it and sees it as a source of sin. Here again, keeping in view the apostle's historical perspective is essential. The flesh is the source of sin not per se, particularly in its corporeal or physical aspect, but because of what has unfolded in history. By and because of the disobedience of Adam, the flesh has become weak; the original creation order has become subject to corruption; the order of fallen Adam and his posterity has become the order of sin and death.

Spirit

With this comprehensive aeonic as well as ethically negative use of "flesh" noted, we turn to consider further the Spirit side of the antithesis. The ethi-

---

35 In these verses, φρονέω and φρόνημα have in view a basic attitude, mindset.

36 The translation decision (e.g., the NLT) to render σάρξ with "sinful nature" in this and other passages expresses an important truth. However, it masks the likewise important truth that while sin is personal and individual, sinners (having a sinful nature) do not sin in isolation or a vacuum. Their sinning has aeonic dimensions. In the case of unbelievers, their unrelieved being in the flesh and walking according to the flesh is because they have not been "deliver[ed] . . . from the present evil age" (Gal. 1:4).

cal aspect hardly needs demonstration. The Spirit is inherently "the Spirit of holiness" (Rom. 1:4), separated from sin and the polar opposite of all that pertains to sin and sinning. The preeminent adjective for the Spirit, used often, is "holy" (e.g., Rom. 5:5; 2 Cor. 13:14; Eph. 1:13). This attribute, implicit in the antithesis in disposition and conduct in view in Romans 8:4-6, comes out explicitly in Galatians 5:19-23 in the listing of the fruit of the Spirit (love, joy, peace, etc.), set in opposition to the works of the flesh.

Requiring more attention is Paul's inherently aeonic, more specifically comprehensively eschatological conception of the Spirit and his work. The Spirit in his redemptive working is the Spirit of the age to come; the age to come is the age of the Spirit's redemptive working.

This comprehensive eschatological conception of Spirit finds its focused and sweeping expression, as a virtual aphorism, in 1 Corinthians 15:46, considered earlier: "But the Spiritual is not first but the natural, and then the Spiritual" (my translation) Here, "the Spiritual" (τὸ πνευματικόν—the adjective, neuter singular, used as a substantive) is a generalizing expression. It refers to the order as a whole that has begun with the resurrection of Christ (cf. 15:44-45), the order of the resurrection life of the age to come. The eschatological order for the (re)new(ed) creation is, in a word, the Spiritual order, the order of the Spirit.

In addition to this more abstract summary statement, Paul uses a couple of well-chosen concrete metaphors that effectively communicate his eschatological conception of the Spirit and his working. One is from commercial life, the other has an agricultural background.

The Spirit as "Deposit" or "Down Payment" (ἀρραβών):
2 Corinthians 1:22; 5:5; Ephesians 1:14

This word may also be translated as "first installment," "pledge," or "guarantee." A Semitic loan word (cf. its use in Gen. 38:17-20), it had a wide currency in commercial transactions throughout the Mediterranean world at the time Paul was writing, documented in extant nonliterary extrabiblical papyri from that period, where it is used for an initial payment made as a good faith commitment toward payment in full (cf. "the earnest" KJV).

An aspect of this extrabiblical usage is important for understanding Paul's use. The "deposit" was ordinarily not a down payment in another species, but payment in kind. It was not a quantity of grain, say, followed subsequently by a consignment of oil to complete the deal. Rather, it was a few cattle in anticipation of the rest of the herd to come, or a sum of money toward the balance in cash.

Accordingly, in "the deposit of the Spirit" (2 Cor. 1:22; 5:5, my translation), "the Spirit" is in apposition to "deposit" (in the Greek text, τοῦ πνεύματος in the genitive case is appositional); its sense is "the deposit which is the Spirit," "the deposit that consists of the Spirit." The basic thought in these two passages is that the present possession of the Spirit in his working anticipates and looks forward to a full possession of the Spirit and his work.

The specifically eschatological character of the possession of the Spirit communicated by this metaphor also needs to be made clear. Paul's use is intended to communicate that the Spirit is an eschatological gift both present and future. The present possession of the Spirit is an eschatological gift in anticipation of its full possession in the future.

That is made particularly clear by Paul's other usage in Ephesians 1:14, coming as the climax of the long doxology that begins back in 1:3. "The promised Holy Spirit," with which believers have been "sealed" (1:13) is "the down payment of our inheritance" (ESV mg.). As such, it is the Spirit "by whom you were sealed for the day of redemption" (Eph. 4:30), where the "redemption" in view is future and interchangeable with "inheritance" in 1:14.

Here as elsewhere in Paul (Eph. 5:5; Col. 3:24), the inheritance in view is unambiguously eschatological. The thought is that the Spirit is the deposit, the actual "goods" if you will, not just on any inheritance but on an inheritance that is specifically eschatological. In God's way of working, an eschatological installment plan is underway. The Spirit presently within the church and indwelling believers is the initial installment in that eschatological arrangement.

This eschatological dimension is also plain in 2 Corinthians 5:5, where the down payment of the Spirit is the guarantee specifically for the resurrection body (cf. 2 Cor 5:1-4)—that is, the eschatological body that, recall, with the one-word label Paul gives it elsewhere (1 Cor. 15:44), is "Spiritual," enlivened and transformed by the work of the Spirit.

Further, it needs to be kept in mind, without arguing it here, that this metaphor does not describe the Spirit as received only by some believers in distinction from others, as if some believers have this eschatological down payment but others do not. Rather, involved is a categorical affirmation concerning the Spirit presently indwelling all believers and in the full range and diversity of his working in the church.

The Spirit is the down payment on the eschaton, which is itself an anticipatory realization of the eschaton. The Spirit in his working is the first installment of eschatological existence, the down payment on new creation existence. The presence of the Spirit is the guarantee that what is already received initially will be received in its fullness at the parousia.

So, how this metaphor works for Paul is apparent. Its use is calculated to bring out pointedly the presently realized and still-future structure of his eschatology, brought to bear on the Spirit. To say the Spirit is "deposit" says it all eschatologically in a single word: already in part, not yet completely.

The Spirit as "Firstfruits" (ἀπαρχή): Romans 8:23

This is the other metaphor, from agricultural life, that Paul uses to express his eschatological conception of the Spirit. We have already considered its application in 1 Corinthians 15:20 to describe Christ as resurrected. Because Christ became the life-giving Spirit in his resurrection (15:45), these two uses of this metaphor—for the resurrected Christ and for the Spirit—are surely related. In receiving and being united to Christ, the resurrected firstfruits become the life-giving Spirit, believers have received the Spirit as firstfruits.

As in 1 Corinthians 15:20, this use of this metaphor likewise has its Old Testament background in the firstfruits sacrifices brought at the beginning of harvest time. Here, however, in contrast to that background, Paul's use of the metaphor involves a reversal. The firstfruits is not an offering presented to God but a gift given by God: "we ourselves, who have the firstfruits of the Spirit" (Rom. 8:23).

Also and importantly, here too, as in 1 Corinthians 15:20, the firstfruits is not simply an indication of temporal priority. The notion of organic connection is also essential. As the first part of the harvest, the firstfruits is inseparable from the rest of the harvest. As the initial portion, it signals the full harvest to come.

Paul associates the Spirit as firstfruits specifically with "the redemption of our bodies" (Rom. 8:23). The Spirit presently given to believers is the firstfruits of the full eschatological harvest of bodily resurrection (redemption) in the future, note again, consisting of those bodies that are consummately, in one word, "Spiritual" (1 Cor. 15:44).

Here, too, the metaphor captures both the Spirit as presently active and yet looking toward his fuller working in the future. To have the Spirit as "firstfruits," as well as "down payment," is to have an initial and provisional experience, in itself eschatological, of the eschatological redemption and transformation that will be realized in its fullness by the Spirit at Christ's return.

In Romans 8:23, the resurrection of the body is called "the adoption." This is striking inasmuch as a few verses earlier Paul has just written that believers have already received "the Spirit of adoption" and are presently God's adopted sons and children (8:14-16). For Paul, the adoption of the believer is both present and future. The distinction is that the adoption of believers, their present status as God's adopted sons and Christ's brothers (8:29), will be openly revealed (8:19, 21) in the transformation that will take place in the resurrection of their bodies. In this respect, the Spirit as firstfruits is the Spirit of adoption.

Flesh and Spirit

With this survey of Paul's use of "flesh" and then of his references to the Spirit, some further comments about the antithesis between them can serve to round out this excursus before we return to the interpretation of Romans 1:3-4.

Paul's use of "flesh" certainly has anthropological and personal implications that include the sinful nature of human beings. That implication is clear and prominent in its multiple uses in Romans 8:4-8, Galatians 5:16-17, 19, and elsewhere. However, to render "flesh" in these instances with "sinful nature" and like expressions, as some translations do, runs the risk of obscuring the more than personal aspect integral to this personal usage.

The antithesis between flesh and Spirit is fundamentally a comprehensive historical contrast, a contrast between two ages, two world orders—one that is present and one that is coming, one that is old, the other that is new. The order of the flesh is transient and passing away; the order of the Spirit is permanent and abiding (cf. 1 Cor. 7:31; 2 Cor. 4:18).

Once again, we see that the antithesis has its place within the framework of Paul's eschatology. "Flesh" is the power of the present evil age. Or said better, in the light of the way Paul countervalues power and weakness in 1 Corinthians 1:24–27, "flesh" brings the present age into view in its weakness, because ultimately the power of this age amounts to no more than weakness.

Considered from the vantage point of the gospel and what has been accomplished in Christ, as the flesh is the order of weakness, so, in antithesis, the Spirit is the power of the age to come, the power of the eschatological aeon. When, concerning the present activity of the Spirit in the church, the writer of Hebrews speaks of "the powers of the age to come" (Heb. 6:5), that expression precisely captures the essence of Paul's eschatological conception of the work of the Spirit.

It should not be missed that the fundamental aeonic dimensions of the flesh-Spirit contrast also come out indirectly yet quite unmistakably in various ways. A number of passages are best understood against that two-age background. This shows the value of analyzing Paul, in light of the occasional nature of his letters, in terms of the underlying structure that finds its surface expression in the text at hand.

A couple of examples will suffice here. At the beginning of Romans 12 and the major transition in the overall flow of the letter there, Paul's appeal to the church includes the comprehensive, first order exhortation: "Do not be conformed to this age, but be transformed by the renewal of your mind" (12:2 ESV mg.). Here the antithesis to conformity to this age is the transformation that consists in the renewal of the mind.

Within the larger context of Paul's teaching, this mind-transforming renewal is plainly the work of the Spirit (cf. "the renewing of the Holy Spirit," Titus 3:5 NET). So here, implicitly, the Spirit in his working is the power of the eschatological aeon. Romans 12:2 says, in effect, "Don't be conformed to this age but be transformed according to the age to come." The renewing of the believer's mind by the Spirit, antithetical to being conformed to this aeon, is brought into view as a fundamental eschatological reality.

The eschatological, age-to-come dimension of the Spirit's work comes through similarly in 1 Corinthians 2. The "wisdom . . . taught by the Spirit" (2:13) is not antithetical, as elsewhere, to "fleshly wisdom" (2 Cor. 1:12 KJV, NKJV) but, equivalently, to the "wisdom of this age or of the rulers of this age" (1 Cor. 2:6)

Finally, in bringing to a close our survey of the Spirit-flesh contrast in Paul, every association of an individual with "flesh" does not entail attributing evil or sinful qualities to that person. Particularly instructive in this regard is the overall picture brought into view in 2 Corinthians 10:3. The church is to follow Paul's example in "bringing every thought captive in obedience to Christ" (10:5, my translation), because "though we walk in the flesh, we do not wage war according to the flesh" (10:3, my translation) Or transforming slightly without changing the general sense: "For though we live in the flesh, we do not live according to the flesh." Here "in the flesh" is ethically neutral, "according to the flesh," ethically negative.

Note, against the background of Paul's eschatology, how this statement captures the present situation of the believers: in the flesh, but not according to the flesh. Presently, short of the return of Christ, Christians continue to exist "in the flesh," within this age. But they do not conduct themselves "according to the flesh" (cf. "the weapons of our warfare are not fleshly," 10:4, my translation), according to the sinful standards of the present evil age. The ongoing challenge to the church is to recognize and not lose sight of both of these dimensions and so to avoid falling into the extreme of some form of triumphalist thinking, on the one hand, or of no longer being able to distinguish itself from the present evil age, on the other.

Then, finally, there are also the occurrences of "flesh" in Romans 1:3 and 9:5 applied to Christ, obviously without associating sin with him personally. The former occurrence brings us back full circle, in light of this survey of the Spirit-flesh contrast in Paul, to our interpretation of Romans 1:3–4.

Contrast between Humiliation and Exaltation

As we noted above, an important key for interpreting Romans 1:3–4 is to take the contrast between flesh and Spirit there in the sense that contrast has elsewhere in Paul. With that in mind, the meaning of the verses may be spelled out as follows:

First, note again that the subject of the two parallel clauses is made explicit at the beginning of 1:3: "his [God's] Son"—the Son in his identity as God's own Son, whom God sent and did not spare (Rom. 8:3, 32). In other words, the deity of the Son is brought into view before anything said about him subsequently in the clauses; the Son as the divine person he is, is the subject of the clauses.

Second, the contrasting parallelism between the clauses is also *progressive*. According to the clause in 1:3: by birth, the eternal Son of God became incarnate ("born of the seed of David," NKJV) and thereby entered into the order of flesh (cf. "in the days of his flesh," Heb. 5:7)—that is, sin excepted, he otherwise became fully participant in this present evil age

According to the clause in 1:4, by resurrection, the incarnate Son of God was in his human nature transformed by the Holy Spirit and entered the eschatological order of the Spirit's working—that is, he became fully and finally participant in the age to come.

Third, with 1:4, then, we find ourselves squarely within the same orbit of thought concerning the relationship between Christ as resurrected and the Spirit as 1 Corinthians 15:45 and 2 Corinthians 3:17.

Fourth, the basic direction of thought in Romans 1:3-4 concerning the Son is from preexistence to humiliation to exaltation.[37] The contrast between the two clauses is between his states of humiliation and exaltation, not his two natures. Elsewhere, in 1 Timothy 3:16, the same contrasting parallelism is expressed more succinctly: "manifested in the flesh, / justified in the Spirit" (NKJV).[38]

The Validity of the Two-States Interpretation

Toward the beginning of our consideration of the contrast in Romans 1:3-4, we noted certain difficulties along three lines with the ontological or two natures view, despite its initial plausibility. Now we can note how the redemptive-historical or two-states interpretation is not beset with but passes the test at those points of difficulty.

First, we are able to take "the Spirit of holiness" as a reference to the Holy Spirit, not the deity of the Son. We are able to explain the Spirit-flesh contrast here consistent with Paul's usage elsewhere rather than having to find an exception, while at the same time doing justice to the parallelism of the clauses.

Second, the resurrection is seen to be significant for the Son in terms of his humanity, not his deity, consistent with the emphasis, as we have seen, on the adamic character of the resurrection throughout Paul.

---

37 The same pattern is especially notable in Philippians 2:6-11: preexistent deity (2:6)—humiliation (2:7-8)—exaltation (2:9-11).

38 Outside of Paul, on the most likely reading: "put to death in the flesh, but made alive in the Spirit" (1 Pet. 3:18 NASB).

Third, recall, as I pointed out above, that Paul is intent in the opening verses of Romans on giving an encapsulated summary of the gospel ("the gospel of God . . . concerning his Son"). The redemptive-historical exegesis of 1:3-4 meets that requirement. These verses express the heart of the gospel in a nutshell by expressing the *history* of Christ in a nutshell.

The gospel is *not* the person of Christ, but the person *and* work of Christ. The gospel is not Christ, the God-Man, but Christ, God who became man, and who, as such, entered the sin-cursed present evil age with all of the humiliation, weakness, suffering, and ultimately death for sin associated with that existence in the flesh ("in the likeness of sinful flesh and for sin, he condemned sin in the flesh," Rom. 8:3), and who by the Holy Spirit was resurrected from the dead and constituted the possessor and source of the eschatological life and power of the age to come.

This is the gospel with its basic implications that the apostle goes on to give such unsurpassed development to in the remainder of Romans, especially in 1:16–11:36.

The Son of God in Power

The controlling participle of the clause in 1:4 is "declared" or "appointed" (ὁρισθέντος). This is not the most natural or expected contrast with "born" or "became" (γενομένου) in 1:3. We might rather anticipate something like "resurrected" or "made alive." This choice of verb functions to bring out an aspect of the resurrection of the Son that is not immediately apparent and might be missed: his resurrection has declarative significance; as an event, it "speaks." Specifically, by his resurrection, he is effectively "declared to be the Son of God in power."[39]

This wording (ὁρισθέντος υἱοῦ θεοῦ ἐν δυνάμει) gives the content of the resurrection as a declaration. Commentators debate whether here "in power" (ἐν δυνάμει) is adverbial or adjectival. In other words, does this prepositional phrase modify "declared" or "Son of God"? Does the phrase have in view the power manifested in the act of raising the Son or the power that marks the state of the Son resulting from his resurrection? Should the translation be "powerfully declared to be the Son of God" or "declared to be the powerful Son of God" ("the Son-of-God-in-power," NET)?

---

39 The alternative translation of the verb, "appointed" (NIV, NET) amounts to an effective declaration.

On the redemptive-historical two states understanding of the contrast in 1:3-4, the answer is almost certainly the latter. By his resurrection, the incarnate Son became and now is and continues to be what he was not before: "the Son of God in power." Christ's resurrection, seen as a declarative event, has adoptive significance. Taking the participle with its other possible meaning ("appointed"), his resurrection is his de facto, effective appointment that inaugurates his consummate status and state as the incarnate Son. As the resurrection of believers will be their open manifestation of their adoption (Rom. 8:23), so Christ's resurrection as "the firstfruits" manifests his adoption, in the sense that it ushers him into the climactic stage of his messianic Sonship.

"For he was crucified in weakness, but lives by the power of God" (2 Cor. 13:4). This statement—plainly a contrast between Christ's pre- and the postresurrection states—sheds light on the contrast in Romans 1:3-4: "crucified in weakness" corresponds to the clause in 1:3, "lives by the power of God" to the clause in 1:4. His preresurrection ministry, even including the displays of power manifested in his miracles, was, all told, a matter of weakness, relatively speaking, compared with the power that is now his and exercised as resurrected, as by his resurrection he has become, what he was not before, the Son of God in power.[40]

CONCLUSION

Twin lines explored in this chapter concerning the relationship between Christ and the Spirit in the light of the resurrection are worth highlighting. This will include some repetition and further elaboration.

1. The Holy Spirit and the Last Things (Pneumatology and Eschatology)

Unmistakable, especially in 1 Corinthians 15:45 and Romans 1:4, read in the overall context of Paul's theology, is his eschatological conception of the work of the Spirit. This bears emphasizing in view of a persisting tendency, noted above, in historic Christianity to isolate the present activity of the Spirit and eschatology from each other. This tendency, it's fair to say, has

---

40 On Rom. 1:3-4, see as well my *Resurrection and Redemption: A Study in Paul's Soteriology* (Phillipsburg, NJ: P&R, 1987), 98-113.

entered the life of the church because of the broader underlying tendency to divorce the present existence of the church and circumstances of Christian living from its eschatological future. This has resulted well-nigh exclusively in a concern with what God by his Spirit is doing in my life right now, to be occupied with the present work of the Holy Spirit in the inner life of the believer and in interpersonal relationships, both within the church and of believers with unbelievers.

The problem here is not with this quite proper and necessary concern but with focusing on the present work of the Holy Spirit and the dynamics of spirituality without any particular reference or connection to God's eschatological program. Over against such a tendency, what needs to be underlined in light of what we have seen of Paul's teaching is that while the work of the Spirit is surely intimate and personal, affecting me in the deepest depths of who I am as an individual and in all my relationships (again, that is not at issue here), that work is not a merely private matter. The Spirit's work concerns individuals, but it is not to be understood individualistically or as narrowly personal.

Rather, as Paul sees it—and this would be true of the other writers of the New Testament as well—the present work of the Holy Spirit in the church and within the believer is, as it might be put, of one piece with the great work that God is doing at the end of history in renovating the entire creation. What is happening to me as an individual believer under the impact of the Holy Spirit, of the Spirit's work in my life, has to be seen as part of that large consummating work of God in renovating the entire creation, looking toward the end of history. According to Romans 8:19-22, "the whole creation" (8:22) and those who have "the firstfruits of the Spirit" (8:23) are presently conjoined in "groaning" (8:22) for that consummation.

The present work of the Spirit in the life of the believer is one with the work that God has begun in sending his Son in the fullness of time and will complete at his return. The metaphors that Paul uses to categorize the Spirit given to believers show that link. The Spirit's working in them is the "down payment" toward the fullness of their eschatological inheritance, the "firstfruits" with a view to their place in the great eschatological harvest. Along the lines of the use of these impersonal metaphors and borrowing from a (now bygone!) insurance commercial, in their present possession of the Spirit, believers are privileged to "get a piece of the [eschatological] rock" now.

The line of Paul's thinking on the Spirit is from the future back to the present, rather than the reverse. It may also be looked at the other way around, the future as an extension or outworking of what is given in the present. However seen in terms of the firstfruits-harvest model, Paul's thought moves from the full-harvest future back to its present firstfruits-beginning. The future is not so much an extension of the present as the present is an anticipation of the future.

The writer of Hebrews describes the present working of the Spirit in the midst of the people of God as "the powers of the age to come" (Heb. 6:5). This, as already noted, captures Paul's inherently eschatological conception as well. Paul's Pneumatology is inseparable from his eschatology.

2. The Holy Spirit, Christ, and the Christian (Pneumatology, Christology, and Soteriology)

This point, related to the first, will also serve as a useful segue into considering the Christian life in the next two chapters. The way Paul expresses himself in Romans 8:9–10 is particularly instructive here:

> You, however, are not in the flesh but in the Spirit, if in fact the Spirit of God dwells in you. Anyone who does not have the Spirit of Christ does not belong to him. But if Christ is in you, although the body is dead because of sin, the Spirit is life because of righteousness.

As we saw earlier, beginning in the latter part of 8:4, Paul addresses, in a pointedly antithetical fashion, the difference between belief and unbelief, between those who "walk . . . according to the flesh" and those who "walk . . . according to the Spirit," culminating in the stark assessment on the one side that "[t]hose who are in the flesh cannot please God" (8:8).

In contrast, in 8:9 and the beginning of 8:10, those who are not "in the flesh," believers, are variously characterized in relation to the Spirit and to Christ: (1) they are in the Spirit; (2) the Spirit is in them; (3) by positive inference from the negative form of expression, having the Spirit of Christ, they belong to him; that is, they are in Christ; (4) Christ is in them. This pattern of expression includes all four combinations for believers in relation to the Spirit and Christ: you . . . in the Spirit; the Spirit . . . in you; you . . . in Christ; Christ . . . in you.

By this pattern, Paul is obviously not looking at the situation of believers in a pie-chart-like fashion and factoring it into different sectors, as if in their lives the Spirit in you, you in the Spirit, Christ in you, and you in Christ is each a part separate from the other three. Rather, he is describing their situation in its fullness in terms of the different angles from which it is to be viewed. So, from one angle, for instance, those in Christ are—at the same time and as that is the case—those in the Spirit, those in whom the Spirit dwells, and those in whom Christ dwells. These various expressions are functionally equivalent.

In the life of the church and the experience of the individual believer, Christ and the Spirit are interchangeable. Negatively, as Paul puts it here (8:9c), there is no union with Christ that is not at the same time a relationship with the Holy Spirit; there is no relationship with Christ that is not also fellowship with the Spirit (cf. Phil. 2:1).[41] To have Christ is to have the Spirit; to have the Spirit is to have Christ. That is so because in the life of the church, there is an unbreakable unity, an inseparable bond between Christ and the Spirit.

Another instance of this inseparability is seen in Paul's eloquent prayer to the Father for the church in the latter part of Ephesians 3. It includes the petition that believers "be strengthened with power through his Spirit in your inner self, so that Christ may dwell in your hearts through faith" (3:16–17, my translation). Here "his Spirit in your inner self" and "Christ . . . in your hearts" are parallel and mutually interpreting.[42] For the Spirit to be at work in the inner self is for Christ to dwell in the heart; Christ indwelling the heart means the Spirit is powerfully present in the inner self.

This bond is undeniable from the way Paul expresses himself in these passages. But what explains it? Its basis or origin is not, as it might be thought, that God has determined, more or less arbitrarily, that there be this unity in the experience of the believer. As we look into Paul more broadly, especially the passages considered in this chapter and most specifically 1 Corinthians 15:45 and Romans 1:4, it is apparent that this inseparable conjunction between Christ and the Spirit exists not because God has determined that it first begin with the experience of the believer or is ultimately based or constituted by what occurs in that experience.

41 See also Gaffin, "Redemption and Resurrection," 238–39.
42 In Paul's usage, the inner self (man, person, being) and the heart are interchangeable, in effect synonymous.

Rather, the ultimate basis of this unity between Christ and the Spirit in the experience of believers lies in back of their experience in the experience of Christ, in what transpired in the course of his definitive once-for-all accomplishment of their salvation. The inseverable bond between Christ and the Holy Spirit in the experience of believers (in the *ordo salutis*), expressed in Romans 8:9-10, exists because, prior to their experience (in the *historia salutis*), Christ has become "the life-giving Spirit" (1 Cor. 15:45), and the Spirit is "the Spirit of Christ" (Rom. 8:9; cf. Gal. 4:6; Phil. 1:19).[43]

---

43 It perhaps bears repeating here that this inseparability in no way compromises or eclipses the personal distinction between Christ and the Spirit.

6

13

The Resurrection and the Christian Life (Part 1)

Indicative and Imperative

OUR POINT OF DEPARTURE for considering Paul's theology of the Christian life should be apparent from what we have seen in previous chapters.[1] For him, no vantage point on the Christian life is more basic than the resurrection. The Christian life in its entirety is to be subsumed under the category of resurrection. Pointedly, the Christian life is resurrection life. It is part of the resurrection-harvest (cf. 1 Cor. 15:20) that began with Christ's resurrection. United to the resurrected Christ, the believer's place in that harvest is not only in the future but also now—not yet but also already. For Paul, there is no deeper perspective on the Christian life than that it is a display and outworking of the life of Christ, resurrected and ascended.

When, for instance, Paul writes autobiographically, but also representatively for all Christians, "I have been crucified with Christ and I no longer live, but Christ lives in me" (Gal. 2:20 NIV), that is not an enthusiastic exaggeration but, however surely doxological, a measured assessment. It is not an expression of overstated rhetoric but of literal reality. At the core of their being, in the deepest recesses of who they are, in the "inner self" (2 Cor. 4:16), Christians will never be more resurrected, literally, than they already are. God has already done a work of resurrection in the believer, a resurrecting work that will never be undone.

---

[1] Some of the content of the chapter, likewise based on my lecture notes, also appears in Richard B. Gaffin, *By Faith, Not by Sight: Paul and the Order of Salvation*, 2nd ed. (Phillipsburg, NJ: P&R, 2013), 77–89.

Elsewhere, when Paul expresses confidence that "he [God] who began a good work in you will bring it to completion at the day of Jesus Christ" (Phil. 1:6), this good work begun is rooted in nothing less than a work of resurrection in the believer united with the resurrected Christ.

The resurrection life of the believer is "eternal life" (e.g., Rom. 5:21; 6:23; 1 Tim. 6:12). It bears emphasizing, to avoid misconceptions, that for Paul this eternal life is *eschatological* life. As eternal, it is not above or beyond history; it is not in that sense timeless or ahistorical, detached from history. Believers have eternal life because they share in the resurrection life that will be revealed in its fullness at the end of history and has come to them out of that future. For them, the life that belongs to the consummation of history, the life of the age to come, is present as they live in this age.

That the Christian life, all told, is resurrection life obviously has wide-ranging implications. These can be further explored profitably in a number of different ways. In this chapter, my aim is to probe an essential aspect of Paul's understanding of sanctification—namely the role of the hortatory or parenetic element, his commands addressed to the church, as that understanding comes to light in the relationship between these imperatives and the indicatives of salvation.

In doing that, as it could also be put, we will be considering the intersection of eschatology and ethics in Paul, his resurrection ethics.

In considering the indicative-imperative theme, I begin by examining a key passage, take note of several related passages, and draw some conclusions along the way.

COLOSSIANS 3:1-4

If then you have been raised with Christ, seek the things that are above, where Christ is, seated at the right hand of God. Set your minds on things that are above, not on things that are on earth. For you have died, and your life is hidden with Christ in God. When Christ who is your life appears, then you also will appear with him in glory.

We looked at this opening paragraph of Colossians 3 earlier in chapter 10. I return to it here because it proves particularly instructive for the focus and direction it gives to our present interest.

A Present Possession and a Goal

The first thing to be noted is the twofold way the resurrection life of the believer comes into view in these verses. On the one hand, the believer's resurrection is an already accomplished fact, expressed grammatically in the past tense (in the Greek text, the aorist passive indicative second plural, συνηγέρθητε): "You have been raised with Christ" (3:1)

"With Christ" points to union with the exalted Christ, union that entails sharing in his resurrection life. As Paul has made explicit earlier in Colossians 2:12, it is effected through faith ("you were also raised with him through faith"). The union with Christ in view is existential, by-faith union.

The resurrection life presently enjoyed by believers in union with Christ also comes out in the past tenses of the verbs in 3:3: "you have died" (ἀπεθάνετε, aorist indicative), and "your life is hidden with Christ in God" (κέκρυπται, perfect indicative; cf. "Christ who is your life," 3:4). Again, it bears emphasizing, this is not figurative language. It is not just loosely metaphorical for some otherwise undefined dynamic reality, but is to be taken literally for what is true for believers in the inner self (2 Cor. 4:16).

On the other hand, interwoven with these past (Greek aorist and perfect) tense expressions affirming the present reality of the believer's resurrection life, are two commands, two present tense imperatives with their objects: "seek the things that are above" (ζητεῖτε, 3:1) and "set your mind on things that are above" (φρονεῖτε, 3:2).[2] These commands are virtually synonymous or at least largely overlapping in their meaning: to seek the things above is to have one's mind set or intent on the things above.

The direct object of both imperatives is "the things . . . above"—in the Greek the adverb used substantively with the neuter plural article (τὰ ἄνω). "Above" by itself is abstract and indefinite. But the relative clause that immediately qualifies its first occurrence makes it concrete and specific: "above" is "where Christ is, seated at the right hand of God" (3:1).

This qualifying clause is important. The "above" in view is not a Platonic above, the above of a timeless metaphysical dualism. It is, rather, as it may be dubbed, a redemptive-historical above: It is the above become what it

---

2 In context, both verbs likely have a progressive or iterative force: "keep seeking" (NASB, NET); "keep thinking about" (NET).

now is because it is where the resurrected Christ has gone in his ascension and is now located. It is the above that is presently marked and conditioned by the session of Christ there at the right hand of God (cf. "in the heavenly places" as the location of the ascended Christ, Eph. 1:3, 20; 2:6; cf. 1 Cor. 15:47–49). "The things above," then, can have reference only to the things of resurrection or ascension life, what pertains to that life.

With these two imperatives, the resurrection life now becomes a matter of aspiration, something to be attained as well as something possessed. In some sense, still to be clarified, resurrection life is to be sought. So we may fairly transpose the commands: "seek resurrection life"; "direct your thinking and willing toward resurrection life."

In this passage, then, resurrection life is in view as both a present possession and a goal to be sought, as both a gift already received and a task to be undertaken.[3] This concurrence can be captured with the command: "Seek after, set your mind on what you already have"; put less paradoxically: "Seek in one sense what in another sense you already have."

The Indicative-Imperative Pattern

This teaching is no doubt capable of being expressed in different ways. But of interest—and numerous commentators have noted this—is how it is reflected by and shapes the grammar Paul uses. This is seen, for instance, in the syntax of Colossians 3:1.

In its basic structure, this verse is composed of a subordinate clause and a main clause. In categories used for constructions in Greek, the opening clause is a first-class conditional or simple past particular supposition. In that conditional subordinate clause (the protasis), the verb is in the indicative mood: "If then you have been raised with Christ." The main clause (the apodosis), the remainder of the verse, is the consequent that follows from this conditional; in it the verb is in the imperative mood: "seek the things that are above."

So, expressed in grammatical categories, the structure of the verse is this: if the indicative, then the imperative. Or, transposing in terms of the content: if you have resurrection life, then seek resurrection life. Assuming, as the context makes clear, the realized character of the condition, that the

---

3   Expressed in German, resurrection life is both "Gabe und Aufgabe."

hypothetical expresses an actuality, the conjunction may be rendered by "since" rather than "if" (as does the NIV: "Since, then, you have been raised with Christ"; cf. NLT). So Paul is saying: Because you have resurrection life, seek resurrection life.

The indicative-imperative pattern of teaching in this verse and elsewhere in Paul has been the object of much discussion, particularly in the modern period—since the middle of the nineteenth century when a focus began on Pauline theology as a distinct entity within the New Testament. It has become something of a convention, particularly for those taking the historical-critical approach, to refer to "The Problem of Indicative and Imperative in Paul."

Certainly, there is a challenge here—an enriching challenge at that, particularly in considering the relationship between the indicative and the imperative. But rather than seeing that as a problem, it is preferable to speak, instead, of "The Pattern of Indicative and Imperative in Paul."

Other Passages

Before giving some attention to that relationship, it will be useful to bring together here other occurrences of the pattern in addition to Colossians 3:1–2—a survey that shows just how pervasive and characteristic it is in Paul.

Galatians 5:25: "If we live in the Spirit, let us also walk in the Spirit" (NKJV). The grammar here is almost identical to Colossians 3:1. If we transpose the sense of "walk" as a metaphor for a way of life (ESV and NIV have "keep in step"), then we have in effect: "If we live in the Spirit, let us also live in the Spirit." Or, given that the conditional is realized: "Since we live in the Spirit, let us also live in the Spirit." The common denominator of life in the Spirit is both an indicative and an imperative.

Galatians 5:1: "For freedom Christ has set us free; stand firm therefore, and do not submit again to a yoke of slavery." It is not difficult to see the elemental thrust, fairly transposed: "You are free, therefore be free"; you are free (indicative); be free (imperative).

Ephesians 5:8: "Now you are light in the Lord. Walk as children of light." This reduces fairly to: "You are light; walk as light."

First Corinthians 5:7: "Cleanse out the old leaven that you may be a new lump, as you really are unleavened." This is addressed corporately to the congregation as a whole in view of a discipline situation Paul is having to confront. But it is also applicable to each member individually (cf. 3:17: the church as a whole is God's temple; 6:19: each believer is a temple of the Holy Spirit).

Here the pattern is the reverse of the preceding examples: the imperative comes first, then the indicative. The first clause ("Cleanse out . . . new lump") says, in effect: "Become unleavened," giving the basic meaning: "Become unleavened, because you are unleavened."

Romans 6:2: "[You have] died to sin"—the indicative. Romans 6:12: "Let not sin therefore reign in your mortal body"—the imperative.

The pattern also emerges from correlating statements from different contexts.

Galatians 3:27: "You . . . have put on Christ"—the indicative. Romans 13:14: "Put on the Lord Jesus Christ"—the imperative. While the latter verse reportedly led to Augustine's conversion, it is not addressed primarily to unbelievers. Both verses are directed equally to Christians.

Colossians 3:9-10: "seeing that you have put off the old self with its practices and have put on the new self"—the indicative. Ephesians 4:22-24: "to put off your old self . . . and to put on the new self"—the imperative. This instance is less certain since in the Ephesians 4 passage, the verbs (infinitives in Greek) may have an indicative rather than imperative force.

The indicative of "the fruit of the Spirit" (Gal. 5:22), fruit produced by the work of the Spirit, is also "your fruit" (Rom. 6:22 NKJV, KJV), the result of obeying imperatives attendant on being "slaves of God." Similarly, love, first among the fruit of the Spirit, is also the first and greatest of the commandments (Rom. 13:8-10).

These instances, to which others could be added, suffice to illustrate the presence of the indicative-imperative pattern or phenomenon throughout the Pauline corpus. Taken together, they have prompted the observation that Paul's exhortations to the church—his resurrection ethics in their entirety, his teaching on sanctification and the Christian life—may be summed up by the epigram: "Become what you are"; become (imperative) what you are (indicative).

This epigram is helpful as a summary but also carries a liability. To avoid any suggestion of self-sufficiency or autonomous self-assertion—like its equivalent, for instance, present in the ethics of Stoic philosophy contemporary with Paul—it needs always to be rephrased, or at least read implicitly, with an all-encompassing Christological gloss: "Become in Christ what you are in Christ."

THE RELATIONSHIP BETWEEN INDICATIVE AND IMPERATIVE

Union with Christ and Covenant

A great deal is at stake in this relationship. Positively, it takes us to the heart of Paul's understanding of the Christian life. Negatively, misconstruing it strikes at the core of that teaching and with that, of the gospel.

Without being able to develop the point here, this relationship, properly understood, shows how thoroughly Paul is a committed covenantal theologian. The covenant bond established by God with his people at the beginning of redemptive history has been given its final, eschatological form in Spirit-worked union between the exalted Christ and believers. Union with Christ is the climactic realization of the covenant relationship structured by the promise, "I will be their God, / and they shall be my people" (2 Cor. 6:16; cf. 6:18; Lev. 26:12; Jer. 32:38; Ezek. 37:27).

This relationship, seen in terms of God's activity on the one hand, is unilateral and sovereignly monergistic from beginning to end—in its origin, its maintenance, and its consummation. At the same time, as it engages his people, it is fully bilateral in its realization and outcome.

Antinomy or Contradiction?

In the modern period, much exegesis—for the most part taking the historical-critical approach—has concluded that the coexistence of indicative and imperative as we find it in Paul amounts to an antinomy or even a contradiction. This perception has been negotiated in different ways. I limit myself here to providing a sketch that indicates those ways without documenting or going into detail.

For some, the contradiction is not real but apparent, and the sense of contradiction between the indicative and the imperative is softened by, in effect, eliminating the one as a way of emphasizing or at least expressing the other—viewing the indicative as a disguised imperative or, alternatively, seeing in the imperative a hidden indicative.

For others, the contradiction is outright. The explanations go in one of two basic directions. Some argue that the imperative is the inconsistency. It amounts to a relapse on Paul's part back into Jewish legalism, either as a necessary adjustment because of the failure of an imminent parousia to materialize as expected, or as a temporary measure he adopts until greater spiritual maturity is observable among Christians.

Still others argue that the indicative is the inconsistency, an indication that Paul has been carried away by a certain idealism, an ideal that cannot be maintained in the light of reality. In passing without pursuing it here, I suspect that this is the practical outlook, if not in theory, of many Christians (How can Paul say that I have "died to sin," Rom. 6:2?).

On this view, Paul is caught in a kind of theory-praxis polarity. The theory, expressed in the indicative, sounds good, but the imperative is the necessary qualification of quite impracticable theory. The imperative amounts to Paul the idealistic visionary having to become Paul the practical pastor.

I leave this sketch with the observation that these various approaches are hardly satisfying or persuasive in light of what we have already seen in our own survey of Paul. It is not as if, in a disjointed fashion, here he writes in the indicative, over there in the imperative. Rather, in a number of places he connects them deliberately and explicitly in the very same sentence, as we see, for instance, in 1 Corinthians 5:7, Galatians 5:25, and Colossians 3:1.

In considering their relationship here, then, I proceed on the assumption that in Paul indicative and imperative belong together without contradiction and coexist in a *positive, nonpolar, nondialectical* relationship.

The Content of the Indicative and Imperative

Indicative and *imperative* are by themselves abstract terms. So it is important, especially in using them repeatedly, to be clear about their concrete reference and keep that reference in mind.

The indicative is the salvation accomplished once for all by Christ and received by being united to him by faith produced by the Spirit. The heart of the indicative is justification, adoption, and the definitive aspect of sanctification.

The imperative is the law of God, specifically its moral core. This conclusion, disputed by some, can be established along the following lines.

Paul writes to the church in Corinth, "For neither circumcision counts for anything nor uncircumcision, but keeping the commandments of God" (1 Cor. 7:19). Two other statements elsewhere in Paul also open with the assertion (protasis) that the circumcision-uncircumcision distinction no longer avails:

> For in Christ Jesus neither circumcision nor uncircumcision counts for anything, but only faith working through love. (Gal. 5:6)

> For neither circumcision counts for anything, nor uncircumcision, but a new creation. (Gal. 6:15)

All three of these syntactically parallel statements contrast the situation of the new covenant (cf. 2 Cor. 3:6), inaugurated by the cross and resurrection of Christ, with the old covenant order, where the distinction between circumcision and uncircumcision did matter, decidedly and fundamentally. Correlating the consequent (apodosis) in each of the three statements, what now matters ("counts") for the church is (1) the arrival of the "new creation" in Christ, (2) as that arrival entails "faith working through love," and (3) is manifested in "keeping the commandments of God." For Paul, commandment-keeping has an integral place in the life of the church as the new covenant people of God.

What Paul means by "the commandments of God" continues to be disputed. Some hold that in view is the ethical teaching of Jesus during his earthly ministry and elsewhere in Paul, with no direct reference to the Ten Commandments.

Romans 13:8–10, however, point to a different and sounder conclusion. There, echoing the teaching of Jesus (Matt. 22:36–40; Mark 12:28–31) and citing several of the commandments, Paul sees the Decalogue, summarized and fulfilled in the love command, as incumbent in the life of the church (cf. also the use of the fifth commandment in Eph. 6:2).

This conclusion regarding the continuing positive function and applicability of the moral law as expressed in the Ten Commandments, with some modifications made (notably the change of the weekly Sabbath from the seventh to the first day, in view of the resurrection of Christ), is reinforced by the course of Paul's argumentation in Romans 8:1–8.

Those united to Christ ("in Christ Jesus") are "therefore" no longer under condemnation (8:1)—that is, they are now justified (cf., Rom. 8:33-34). As such, they have been set free from "the law [regimen] of sin and death," because ("for") they are now under the regimen ("law") of "the Spirit of life . . . in Christ Jesus" (8:2).

Consequently, the end in view purposed for them by the sin-condemning atoning work of Christ (8:3) is that "the righteous requirement of the law might be fulfilled in us" [note: "in," "within," not "for," "on behalf of"], as they "walk not according to the flesh but according to the Spirit" (8:4).

The verses that immediately follow expand on this Spirit-flesh antithesis in "walk"—in outlook, life, and conduct. On the negative side (8:7), the "mindset" (CSB; τὸ φρόνημα), or basic disposition, of the flesh (cf. 8:6) is marked by enmity (KJV, NKJV) toward God. Singled out as the distinguishing manifestation of this hostility or enmity is that it does not, in fact cannot, "submit to God's law." As a result of this inherent law-submitting inability, "Those who are in the flesh cannot please God" (8:8).

From this we should surely conclude, on the other side of the antithesis, that those who possess and are animated by the mindset of the Spirit (8:6) are those who do submit to God's law, and that, in doing so, however imperfectly, they are pleasing to God, as their "delight is in the law of the LORD" (Ps. 1:2). Paul is clearly a proponent of what subsequently has been dubbed "the third use of the law"—the law as a positive guide for living in covenant with God—which after all, as Calvin for one has rightly said, is its "principal use."[4]

The Relationship of the Indicative and Imperative

With this clarification in hand regarding the concrete content of the indicative and the imperative, their relationship in Paul can be further addressed by first highlighting two considerations: the relationship is both irreversible and inseparable.

From what we have already seen, it should be clear that the relationship is *irreversible*. This is so in the sense that the indicative has the priority. The indicative is foundational; it grounds the imperative. The imperative is the consequent fruit of the indicative, and not the reverse. Paul's gospel

---

4 John Calvin *Institutes of the Christian Religion*, ed. John T. McNeill, trans. Ford Lewis Battles (Philadelphia, PA: Westminster, 1960), 2.7.12 (1:360).

as the good news of freedom from the guilt and power of sin stands or falls with this irreversible priority.

To put it negatively, it is not as if the indicative is constituted by (responding to) the imperative or expresses only a possibility that is first actualized by the imperative (the view, for instance, influenced by existentialist philosophy still influential in various forms); the imperative is not the actualization of the indicative, constantly in need of being reactualized.

Rather, the indicative provides the impulse or dynamic for the imperative, the incentive for fulfilling the imperative. Paul never writes to the church in the imperative without first writing in the indicative or the indicative at least being implicit. As a good pastor, he knows all too well, as many subsequent preachers regrettably do not, that "it does no good to beat a dead horse." Christians can never be exhorted effectively apart from being reminded who Christ is and who they are and what they have been given in him. Where that gospel reminder is lacking, the imperative inevitably becomes an oppressive burden on the congregation.

At the same time, this irreversible relationship is also an *inseparable* relationship. Paul, we may also generalize, never writes in the indicative without having the imperative in view, at least implicitly. On balance, the imperative without the indicative leads inevitably into some form of soteriological *legalism*; it leaves us with Paul the *moralist*. On the other hand, the indicative without the imperative tends to *antinomianism*; it leaves us with Paul the *mystic* or *quietist*. Moralism and its twin, morally indifferent mysticism, are the outcomes when indicative and imperative become disjoined and their inseparability lost sight of.

It needs to be kept clear that the indicative does not describe a reality that is true for the believer without the imperative. The indicative does not have in view a situation where (a heart for) the imperative, where being disposed to obey and respond positively to the imperative, is not yet present but follows as a subsequent and presumably detachable and not truly integral addition. The indicative does not exist apart from a disposition to a positive response, however imperfect, to the imperative, apart from a heartfelt desire for doing the will of God and obeying his law.

To be true to Paul, we must appreciate that indicative and imperative are given together, and obedience in response to the imperative is the consequence and attestation apart from which the indicative is nonexistent.

Such obedience is indispensable as "the fruits and evidences of a true and lively faith."[5] There is no resting in the indicative that is not also restless—at least incipiently, in its basic disposition—for the imperative. The indicative of sharing in salvation in Christ and the consequent imperative to do his will and to please him are inseparable. The one does not exist without the other in their irreversible relationship.

We may certainly and properly speak of "The Moral Effects of a Free Justification."[6] But in doing so, we must guard against seeing that as an automatism, as if those moral effects follow automatically in the life of those justified. The hortatory element, the need for the church to be exhorted, that permeates Paul's writings is a clear indication that the life of new obedience does not result automatically in those united to Christ and justified in him. Such obedience happens surely, necessarily, but not apart from their active and willing engagement.

The imperative, then, has a critical or discriminating function. Where, by faith, the indicative of salvation in Christ is in fact present, where resting in Christ and his work is a reality, there a concern for the imperative must and will also be a reality that finds expression—however minimally, however imperfect that obedience may be.

In discussing this coalescence of indicative and imperative in Paul, Herman Ridderbos is helpful in striking the requisite balance: The imperative, no less than the indicative, is the concern of faith. It is not as if faith is concerned only with the indicative and then involvement with the imperative somehow goes beyond faith.

The imperative, no less than the indicative, is the concern of faith. Both indicative and the imperative are the object of faith, as faith in Christ, and they are that together and inseparably. Faith in its receptivity answers to the indicative; faith in its activity corresponds to the imperative.[7]

---

5 The language of the Westminster Confession of Faith, 16.2, in describing the good works of believers.

6 The title of an essay by R. L. Dabney in Robert L. Dabney, *Discussions*, ed. C. R. Vaughan (Richmond, NJ: Presbyterian Committee of Publication, 1890), 1:73–106.

7 Herman Ridderbos, *Paul: An Outline of His Theology*, trans. J. R. de Witt (Grand Rapids, MI: Eerdmans, 1975), 256. His discussion as a whole of the indicative-imperative relationship (253–58) has substantially influenced my comments here.

Section 2, chapter 14 ("Of Saving Faith") in the Westminster Confession of Faith helpfully reflects the distinction that Ridderbos makes as a matter of Pauline theology. That section ends by accenting "the principle of acts of saving faith"; namely, "accepting, receiving, and resting

PHILIPPIANS 2:12–13

> Therefore, my beloved, as you have always obeyed, so now, not only as in my presence but much more in my absence, work out your own salvation with fear and trembling, for it is God who works in you, both to will and to work for his good pleasure.

The penetrating and comprehensive perspective these verses provide serves to round out our consideration of indicative and imperative and their relationship in Paul.

Here the imperative comes first (at the end of 2:12): "work out your own salvation." This command, general in its terms and quite sweeping in its scope, does not have in view a one-time occurrence but calls for action that is to be ongoing, as the Greek verb tense (present/progressive) indicates. For believers, working out their salvation is to be a constant, continuing concern. It is also to be done "with fear and trembling"—an indication not of anxious or terrified uncertainty but of reverent and fully engaged involvement.

The indicative that follows (in 2:13) is equally sweeping—in fact, more than equal in its all-encompassing sweep: "It is God who works in you, both to will and to work for his good pleasure."

The way in which indicative and imperative are joined here needs especially to be appreciated. Notice what Paul does *not* say. He does not say that believers are to work while God works alongside them; his working is not parallel with theirs. Nor does he say that believers are to work up to a certain point and then God will take it from there and complete what is lacking in their working; God's working does not supplement theirs. And he certainly does not say that believers are to be at work, and in spite of that, in spite of their efforts marred by their sin, God is at work in some remedial and compensatory fashion. While that is true on other grounds, it is not the point here.

To the contrary, believers work, "for" (γάρ)—giving the all-important reason—God works in them. Why are they to work? Because of and based upon God's work. The imperative of their working is grounded in the irreversible priority of the indicative of God's working in them. His working is sovereignly determinative, decisive, and all-controlling for theirs.

---

upon Christ alone for justification, sanctification, and eternal life." This is the receptivity of faith. The section begins and builds up to that culminating statement by describing the activity of faith, what faith does in responding to the commands of God's word.

In view of this coalescence in working, one could speak of the "synergy" involved. Using that term may be inadvisable since it is subject to considerable misuse and misunderstanding. Still, it should be recognized how that language is fairly defended here (cf. "working together [Συνεργοῦντες] with him [God]," 2 Cor. 6:1).

Whether or not we speak of synergy here, it is important to be clear— to reiterate—that in view is not a divine-human partnership in the sense of a cooperative enterprise with each side making a contribution of its own. It is not as if Paul here contemplates a fifty-fifty undertaking—50 percent God and 50 percent ourselves. It is not even in that regard, 99.44 percent God and the minuscule rest us (to borrow on the math of a soap commercial of the distant past).

Rather, involved here, as it has been put, is the mysterious math of God's covenant with his people, where 100 percent plus 100 percent equals 100 percent. Sanctification as a process is 100 percent the work of God and just for that reason, γάρ, it engages the full 100 percent activity of the believer.

Coming into view here is the mystery of the work of the Holy Spirit in sanctification, the mystery of the life of faith—that mystery that we must not compromise or violate in our theologizing: the mystery of the sovereign working of God that comprehends the fully involved activity, the total engagement, of the believer.

To be clear, this is not just another instance of the general truth that divine sovereignty and human responsibility cohere and both must be affirmed. That truth is, of course, in the background. But here, Paul is not making a general anthropological statement but expressing a specifically soteriological truth: the saving truth revealed and maintained in union with Christ and through the Spirit.

That truth, bringing both its elements together, can be stated in different ways. Here we may express it as the mystery whereby the God of the covenant in grace promises, "I will be their God, and they shall be my people" (Jer. 31:33), the grand indicative echoed explicitly or in substance in Paul and elsewhere in Scripture, and at the same time, no less in grace, commands, "Be holy, for I am holy" (Lev. 11:44–45), the sweeping imperative that, while applied explicitly to the church outside of Paul (1 Pet. 1:16), is surely his concern here.

With a view toward the truth expressed in Philippians 2:12–13 and elsewhere in Paul (and Scripture as a whole), there is probably no theological technique, no golden doctrinal formulation, that will invariably succeed in keeping the imperative from becoming an occasion for moralism or the indicative from being heard as an invitation to antinomianism or quietism.

But recall how Ridderbos puts it: the imperative no less than the indicative is the concern of faith. With that in mind, those who until Jesus comes again "walk by faith, not by sight" (2 Cor. 5:7) will be able to negotiate the narrow ledge underfoot here, the proverbial razor's edge between the truth and error. Faith will always understand—faith as Paul understands it and would have the church understand it—that the signpost on the path of sanctification reads, differently, to be sure, but no less than for justification: In Christ alone, by grace alone.

ROMANS 6:1-7:6: SOME OBSERVATIONS

The intersection or interpenetration of eschatology and ethics, to put it formally, seen in the indicative-imperative pattern in Colossians 3 and elsewhere in Paul is quite prominent in this passage, particularly in the way Paul relates the death and resurrection of Christ to the Christian life. At the risk of overstatement, no other single passage in Paul—or, for that matter, in the entire New Testament—provides a more basic perspective on sanctification and the Christian life.

To the extent that we are able to look into this passage here, our consideration divides into several subsections.

Romans 6:1-2

The background to this passage, which also motivates it in large part, is what Paul has had to say previously in the letter, particularly beginning at 3:21 about the totally free and gracious character of justification. Justification, signalized by key expressions, is not "by works," "by works of the law," "through the law"; rather it is "by faith, in order that it might be according to grace" (4:16, my translation).

This teaching, according to some interpreters, is summarized in the immediately preceding section, 5:12-21. Others hold, in view of the comprehensive sweep of the Adam-Christ contrast in this section, that it is transitional, both looking back on his preceding reflections on justification as well as forward to where he is headed beginning in Romans 6. I am inclined to take this latter, transitional view.

In 6:1, then, Paul takes up an objection to his teaching on justification. He poses this objection in the form of a rhetorical question that echoes his own language a couple of verses earlier ("where sin increased, grace abounded all the more," 5:20): "Shall we continue in sin that grace may abound?" (NKJV).

This question raises a question of its own. Is Paul confronting a real objection he has already encountered? That may be the case in light of the substantially identical question in 3:8 ("And why not do evil that good may come?—as some people slanderously charge us with saying"). Or is it rather that Paul, anticipating a possible objection, proceeds to head it off by rebutting it?

This question—I incline toward the former view of an objection already encountered—does not need to be settled here. Whether actual or antici- pated, at issue is surely a live danger that Paul considers important, even necessary, to address.

The question at the end of verse one is immediately negated, and sharply: "By no means!" (6:2),[8] and then countered by another question: "How shall we who died to sin still live in it?" For exegesis, it is important to recognize that this rhetorical question specifies the central thesis on its negative side that governs the entire argument from this point through 7:6.

That thesis, glossed to include its positive side, is this: Believers have died to sin and have been made alive to God and to righteousness (cf. 6:11). The death and life in view are in the past tense—believers have died and been made alive; consequently now, presently, they are dead to sin and alive to God.

This thesis raises a key question, posed here in light of past and pres- ent interpretation of the passage: In what sense have believers died to sin? How are they now dead to sin? The answer will emerge in the course of our further exposition.

Romans 6:3–5

Pertinent to that answer is the way in which Paul goes on immediately to ground and develop the central thesis expressed in the question of 6:2.

---

8 μὴ γένοιτο: "May it never be!" (NASB 1995), "Certainly not!" (NKJV), or, in the forceful dy- namic equivalence (!) of the KJV, "God forbid."

He does that by appealing to the significance of baptism and in doing so provides one of the key statements in Scripture in that regard.

Baptism signifies and seals union with Christ, incorporation into Christ, pointedly union with Christ in his death and resurrection. When we think about baptism, to be true to Paul, we must not lose sight of this redemptive-historical factor. That consideration is decisive here. In view is union with Christ as he now is by virtue of his death and resurrection. Baptism signifies and seals union specifically with the exalted Christ, with Christ crucified, resurrected, and ascended, with all the saving benefits of that union.

Baptism takes on this soteriological efficacy by faith, as Paul will make clear elsewhere (Col. 2:12). So—to keep the focus on the controlling structure of Paul's argument here—for those united by faith with the exalted Christ, his death is their death; his resurrection is their resurrection.[9]

With the question posed above in mind—how, in what sense is the believer dead to sin—recall what we saw earlier in Ephesians 2:1–10 in discussing the teaching of that passage about the past resurrection of believers, that they have already been raised with Christ. As in Ephesians 2 (as well as in related passages; cf. Col. 2:12–13; 3:1), so here too in Romans 6, the union in view is not simply representative or vicarious. In view here is not only past historical union with Christ, the union of Christ with his people contemplated as one with him at the actual time of the cross and resurrection after three days. Rather, the union in view is vital, a union in life. In that sense, it is experiential or, in older Puritan idiom, experimental.

Why can we say that? Why do we need to be insistent that the union, signalized by baptism, grounds a reality that is clearly experiential or existential? The answer is in the exegetical consideration, already noted, that the union in view grounds the undeniably experiential reality expressed in the thesis of 6:2: believers have died to sin so that they no longer live in it.

This is the same thought as that present in Ephesians 2:1–2 ("you were dead in the trespasses and sins in which you once walked"). The deadness in sin from which believers have been delivered is that they no longer "walk" in it; unrelieved sinning is not their way of living, the pattern for their conduct.

---

9   Union with Christ in his death and union with Christ in his resurrection are not two separate or even distinct experiences, as if the one experience follows the other. As indicated above, in view is a single union with Christ as crucified and resurrected.

The positive side of the union in view, signified by baptism, comes out in Romans 6:4: "in order that, just as Christ was raised from the dead by the glory of the Father, we too might walk in newness of life." The positive implication of the thesis enunciated on its negative side in 6:2—that believers have died to sin and no longer live in it—is an opposed "walk," an opposite way of life, a lifestyle characterized as "newness of life." Romans 6:4 makes explicit the resurrection-dimension of the union and the new life it brings. The newness of the new life is the newness of resurrected living.

The opening verses of Romans 6 teach that by virtue of their union with Christ believers have experienced a decisive break with sin. A key point is that in being united to Christ, a definitive, once-for-all cleavage has occurred between believers and sinning as a "walk" or way of life. As the terms of the passage make clear, this once-for-all break is with sin as the controlling power in their lives.

Paul is not here denying the reality of indwelling sin in the believer (cf. Rom. 7:20), but he is affirming that while sin is indwelling, it is not dominating. Sin, sinful conduct, is not what ultimately rules in the life of the believer. As a consequence of their "old self" having been crucified with Christ in union with him, believers are no longer "enslaved to sin" (6:6); they have been "set free from sin" (6:7, the verb for justification elsewhere used here in this distinctive sense). This freedom from sin is from sin and sinning as lord or overmastering, enslaving power.

The preceding observations show that in the controlling thesis implicit in the rhetorical question in Romans 6:2, the death to sin in view is not, as some have argued and still argue, death to/freedom from the guilt and legal liability of sin. In other words, the reference is not to justification. In view, rather, is deliverance from the enslaving and corrupting power of sin—the definitive break with the deadness of sin in that sense—and the correlative enlivening in union with Christ, with a view to walking in the newness of his shared resurrection life. In other words, the question of Romans 6:2 is about sanctification ("definitive sanctification"[10]). The reference is to the gospel indicative of deliverance from the enslaving power of sin,

---

10 John Murray, "Definitive Sanctification" and "The Agency in Definitive Sanctification," *Collected Writings of John Murray*, vol. 2 (Edinburgh: The Banner of Truth Trust, 1977), 277–93.

the indicative that is the basis and provides the dynamic for the ongoing sanctification of the believer.

Romans 6:11

So you also must consider yourselves dead to sin and alive to God in Christ Jesus.

This verse sums up and draws together the key threads from what Paul has been saying in the chapter to this point.

First, the considering (or reckoning) called for here is with reference to being both "dead to sin" and "alive to God."[11] What this reference entails specifically has to be determined from the context. In light of Paul's argumentation leading up to 6:11, some of which we have noted, that reference concerns the power that controls the believer. Negatively, believers are dead to sin as their master; they are no longer sin's slave (cf. 6:6; 6:14, "For sin will have no dominion over you"). The basic issue in Romans 6, as much as any, is the issue of lordship: Who is your Lord? Who has the dominion in your life? Whom are you serving? Is it God or sin?

Romans 6:11 makes explicit an inference made above. The thesis implicit in the question of 6:2 is in the past tense: believers *have* died and been made alive. The thesis of 6:11 is in the present tense: believers *are* dead to sin and alive to God. The connection is unmistakable. Because of the definitive, once-for-all break with sin, the death-to-life transition, that has occurred for those who by faith have been united to Christ as crucified and resurrected, their present and permanent condition is that they are dead to sin and alive to God.

Second, the main or controlling verb in 6:11 is an imperative. Believers are commanded how they are to consider themselves, how they are to continue evaluating who they are in relation to sin and God.

To be clear about this command, in light of actual and potential misconceptions, in view is not the positing of an ideal that does not really correspond to the reality of the believer's situation—whether that positing be conceived of as occurring in a bold and assertive manner or as a wistful sort of longing. In other words, the command does not express a limiting

---

11 In the Greek text, both expressions are datives of reference or respect.

concept that believers are to hold before themselves but does not really measure up to the reality of their situation.

Neither, related to that idealist misconception, does Paul, in quasi-Kantian fashion, have in view an act of postulation where what is reckoned is realized or actualized by the act of reckoning. To put it in plainer terms, Paul is not saying: "Make it so by saying it is so." Despite the way the passage has sometimes been read, Paul is not sponsoring some form of power of positive thinking or message of self-esteem.

Rather, the reckoning that Paul calls for here is the reckoning of *faith*. It is a matter of what *believers* are to take into account, how they are, in fact, to understand themselves, what they must presuppose about themselves, about who they really are. With that said, however, "in Christ Jesus" at the end of 6:11 is (as always!) decisive. The reckoning of faith is a reckoning not of who believers are in and of themselves but who they are by virtue of their union with Christ and all they have in him.

Third, the command of 6:11 is linked directly with 6:10. Romans 6:11 draws a parallel with 6:10, indicated by the comparison-closing conjunction "so also" (οὕτως καὶ) at the beginning of the verse. Note that the direction of the parallel drawn is from Christ to the believer, not from the believer to Christ. What is first of all true for Christ, what is true in his experience, is consequently true for believers and their experience.

The line of Paul's reasoning is this: Because the death that Christ died was death to sin and because the life that Christ now lives he lives to God, therefore it is the case that believers, united with him by faith, are dead to sin and alive to God, and so are to reckon themselves as such. Moreover, in view of the parallel, the "once for all" (ἐφάπαξ, 6:10) stated explicitly for Christ applies to believers as well. As for him, so for them the death to sin in view is definitive and permanent.[12]

The culmination of the argument to this point in Romans 6 is that believers are rid of sin as the dominating, controlling power in their lives. They have been delivered from sin as lord over their lives, and that has happened

---

12 Romans 6:10 states that in his death, Christ "died to sin." In view of the sustained emphasis in 6:2-11 and the parallel between 6:10 and 6:11, the reference here is not to his having borne the guilt of sin, but rather, while being personally sinless, to his continuing under and being subject to the power of death as the consequence of sin, as an aspect of his state of humiliation throughout the course his earthly ministry. For a full discussion of 6:10, see John Murray, *The Epistle to the Romans* (Grand Rapids, MI: Eerdmans, 1959), 1:224-25.

once for all. For believers, the resultant state of being dead to sin and alive to God is permanent and secure, as permanent and secure as it is for Christ, with whom they are united.

Romans 6:12–13

Therefore do not let sin reign in your mortal body, so that you obey its lusts. And do not present your members as instruments of unrighteousness to sin, but present yourselves to God as alive from the dead, and your members as instruments of righteousness to God. (my translation)

The exhortation in these verses is general (akin in that respect to the exhortation in 12:1–2). It flows ("therefore") from the indicative of being dead to sin and alive to God affirmed in 6:11. As such, it indicates the direction of what follows in the rest of Romans 6. Making a permissible transformation of the surface construction serves to bring out the controlling place of the motif of resurrection, as well as the correspondence with Colossians 3:1–4 and related passages we have looked at: since you are alive from the dead, do not present your members as instruments of unrighteousness to serve sin, but as instruments of righteousness to serve God.

Correlating two phrases in these verses serves to bring out a fundamental perspective on the Christian life as a whole: "in your mortal body" and "alive from the dead."

Alive from the dead, in the mortal body. Nothing better brings to a focus the structure—the tension or dialectic in a positive, nonpolar sense—that marks the present existence of the believer. Nowhere do we find a more basic perspective on the existence of those who, on the one hand, have already been raised from the dead and yet, on the other, still need to be raised.

Looking back at passages we have already considered, this "dialectic" can be expressed in various other ways:

Believers are those who are alive with the life of the age to come as they continue to live in "the present evil age" (Gal. 1:4).

They are those already participant in the "new creation" (2 Cor. 5:17), but within "the present form of this world [that] is passing away" (1 Cor. 7:31).

They are those "who walk not according to the flesh but according to the Spirit" "in the flesh" (bringing together Rom. 8:4 and 2 Cor. 10:3).

They are those who "walk by faith, not by sight" (2 Cor. 5:7), where, in context, sight comes with future bodily resurrection.

In sum, overlaying the indicative-imperative distinction on the two phrases in Romans 6:12–13 (or vice versa) provides this basic perspective on the present existence of the believer:

- "Alive from the dead" pinpoints the *present* indicative of the eschatological, age-to-come salvation *already* experienced in union with Christ, the life-giving Spirit, and so also specifies the *source* and *dynamic* for fulfilling the imperative. This is what the congregation needs, by faith, to hear and know about itself before anything else.
- "In the mortal body" points to the *future* indicative of the eschatological, age-to-come salvation *not yet* revealed in Christ, and so also indicates the *need* for the imperative and its *scope*. This is why the congregation needs to be exhorted.

The Body and Sin

The possessive pronoun "its" translates αὐτοῦ in the Greek text (almost certainly the correct reading) and so refers back to "body" (σώματι), not to "sin" (ἁμαρτία), as English translations may seem to indicate. In the syntax of 6:12, then, "its lusts" are those of the body, not sin. The sinful desires believers are to resist belong to the body.

In a similar vein, elsewhere in Romans, Paul speaks of "the body of sin" (6:6) and also of "this body of death" as the source of sin (7:24). Further, "the deeds of the body" are those that mark living "according to the flesh" with its sinful disposition to sinning and with death as the ultimate outcome (8:12–13; cf. 8:6).

This association of sinful desires and sinning with the body demands reflection. What explains it?

The answer is not a lapse by the apostle into pagan Hellenistic dualism with its depreciation of the physical or material aspect of the world in general and the human body in particular as the source of evil. Rather, this association of sin with the body is intelligible only in terms of his basic historical-eschatological outlook.

Here again, the decisive consideration is akin to what we saw earlier in considering Paul's use of "flesh" (σάρξ). The bond that exists between the body and sin is not ultimately physical or metaphysical and substantial, but *historical and ethical*. It is not the result of creation, of a defect in its original constitution or in the corporeality of our being, in our makeup as persons created in God's image, as that image includes the body. Rather, this bond between sin and the body is the result of the fall and God's curse on human sin, as the Adam side of the contrast in Romans 5:12-19, for one, shows, and because in the case of believers, they too continue to exist, unresurrected bodily, in the present evil age.

What the believer is in Christ and by faith is true—and is only true— *in* the body, but it is not (yet) true *for* the body. In terms of the anthropological distinction basic for Paul, the renewal true of the "inner self" is true only *in* the "outer self," but that renewal is not (yet) true *for* the "outer self" (2 Cor. 4:16). The trade-off in the preceding sentences between the prepositions "in" and "for" is pivotal.

Consequently, inasmuch as it is in yet unresurrected bodies that believers function in their concrete, historical existence, the body—proximately but not ultimately—is a continuing source of sin in that the body is the *access way* or *entrée* for sin. The body is the locus of exposure to sin. Though for the believer, sin's dominating power—if not its inevitability (sin though no longer overpowering remains indwelling)—is broken through and terminated.

In making these observations, it is important to maintain a balance that takes us to the heart of Paul's soteriological anthropology. On the one hand, in terms of the already-not-yet dialectic of the believer's existence determined by the overlap of the two ages, Paul distinguishes the "I" (the "inner self") from the body ("members," "outer self"), from psychophysical existence, and sets them over against each other—as the "I" is both subjected to the body and yet reacts against the body (notably, in Rom. 7:17-23, esp. 7:22–23).[13]

---

13 On the much-mooted interpretation of Rom. 7:14-25, my view is that the subject of the conflict with sin is the Christian, as documented by Paul's own representative experience as a Christian. I make no effort to argue that view here—except to observe that despite arguments to the contrary, it is entirely compatible with the realized–still future eschatological structure of Paul's soteriology: in terms of the overlap of the two ages, Rom. 6:1–7:6 (and then Rom. 8) look at the present situation of believers from "above," from the perspective of the age to come as already present; Rom. 7 considers that situation from "below," from the perspective of the age to come as still future and their continuing to be in this (present evil) age.

On the other hand, Paul never uses this distinction between the "I" and the body, between the inner self and the outer self, to excuse sin in the believer or to distance believers from their sinning. His expressed anthropological duality is not the dualism of an essential inner core (the soul) and the body as the outer shell—disposable because it is not integral to who I am, so that its functions are a matter of indifference, with no ultimate significance.

Rather, "the deeds of the body" (Rom. 8:13) are an expression and assertion of the whole person. The whole person functions in the body and only in the body. Man (male and female) in the body is not only a corporeal but also a spiritual being. Embodied human existence has an inward side. The sinful deeds of the body are not only "the sins of the flesh"—the promiscuous and deviant sexuality and the wanton and unwarranted violence that Hollywood and other entertainment media love to dwell on. These sinful deeds are also spiritual in nature as the partial listing of "the works of the flesh" shows (Gal. 5:19-21): idolatry, enmity, jealousy, anger, dissensions, envy.

Conversely, sexual promiscuity has a spiritual or inward side, as 1 Corinthians 6:13-20 especially shows clearly. In the case of Christians, sexual sin is sin against one's own body as a temple of the Holy Spirit (1 Cor. 6:18-19; cf. 1 Thess. 4:7-8).

In passing but importantly, in his unsparing indictment of human sinfulness in Romans 1, Paul introduces homosexuality as he does (1:25-27) not primarily because it is undeniably unnatural (1:26-27) but ultimately because of the deeply rooted idolatry it manifests, because of the radical self-worship of the creature rather than the Creator that it is.

SYSTEMATIC-THEOLOGICAL AND CHURCH-HISTORICAL REFLECTIONS

What we have seen in Romans 6 and related passages lends itself to some broader reflections of a systematic-theological and church-historical sort concerning sanctification.

The Necessity of Sanctification

Romans 6 especially shows how integral sanctification is to the salvation revealed and applied in Christ, how necessary and essential an aspect of that salvation sanctification is. This point needs to be stressed in view of a tendency prevalent to some extent within the churches of the Reformation and contemporary evangelical Christianity: the tendency to view salvation and the message of the gospel exclusively in terms of justification as the free forgiveness of sins. Often this tendency is more or less unreflecting, but sometimes it is also made explicit.

Where this tendency or outlook takes hold, sanctification tends to be seen as the believer's response for salvation defined in terms of justification. The animating attitude is something like this: If Jesus did that for you, shouldn't you at least try to do this for him? Since he died for you so that your sins might be forgiven, shouldn't you try your best to please him?

Sanctification, then, becomes the response, particularly an expression of gratitude, on the part of believers for justification, for the free remission of sin, usually with an accent on the imperfection and the inadequacy of the gratitude expressed.

Sometimes the impression is even left that while sanctification, a concern for holy living, is highly desirable and its lack certainly shows an unbecoming lack of gratitude, it is not really essential for the believer. An emphasis on gratitude for justification is in fact made in a way that sanctification is not truly integral to salvation. By integral to salvation, I mean an essential part of what it means to be saved from sin and apart from which there is no salvation. Salvation is indeed from the guilt of sin, but it is also from the corruption and enslavement of sin, however imperfect and incomplete in this life.

Where this outlook takes hold—and, again, it may often be more unreflecting than a matter of explicit teaching—justification and sanctification are effectively separated and disjoined. Justification, on the one hand, is what God does, sanctification, on the other, what we do, typically with an accent on how inadequately we do it.

At its worst, this understanding—justification is what God does, sanctification what I do—can lead to a deadening moralism. That happens by the (no doubt, often unintended) reintroduction of what amounts to a works principle divorced from the faith that justifies and in tension with justifying faith. Works—self-affirming, self-securing, self-assuring efforts—so resolutely resisted at the front door of justification are smuggled in through the back door of sanctification.

Let me be clear at this point. Surely, gratitude for justification is important, supremely important. Nothing I am saying in my reflections here is intended or should be allowed in any way to eclipse not only the appropriateness but also the importance of expressing that gratitude. Along with the apostle, how could we be anything but profoundly grateful for the free forgiveness of our sin and the imputed righteousness of Christ? That note of gratitude is as unmistakable as it is pervasive in Paul. Gratitude as our response for justification is not the issue here.

Also, there is no question that as sanctification involves our doing, all these efforts are, at best, imperfect and flawed by our continuing to sin. With the Heidelberg Catechism, we must confess and without hesitation that "in this life even the holiest have only a small beginning of this obedience."[14]

Sanctification Is What God Does

But now, focusing again on what we have seen in Paul, we must not depreciate this "small beginning," for it is a nothing less than an *eschatological* beginning. If I have not mischaracterized the tendency and its existence I am concerned with here, Paul sounds a different and much more radical note about sanctification and the good works of Christians. For Paul, the key and controlling consideration is that first and foremost, sanctification is not a matter of what we do but of what God does.

This is expressed most emphatically in Philippians 2:12-13. Why is it that we are to be intent on "working out" our salvation, and as that is to engage us fully, "with fear and trembling"? It is "because" (γάρ), because God is at work in us. This "because" is decisive and all-determining. Sanctification is ultimately God's gracious doing, no less than justification.[15]

Furthermore—this comes out clearly in Romans 6—the most basic and essential consideration about sanctification is that it is not only a process involving us in our activity. First of all and antecedent to any activity of ours, sanctification is rooted in a decisive act of God, a definitive, once-for-all act of God that underlies our ongoing activity.[16]

---

14 Heidelberg Catechism, answer 114, Christian Reformed Church (website), https://www.crcna .org/.

15 Cf. this truth as expressed in the Westminster standards: Sanctification is a "work of God's free grace," as justification is "an act of God's free grace" (Shorter Catechism, 33, 35; cf. Larger Catechism, 70, 75).

16 On this definitive aspect, see esp. Murray, "Definitive Sanctification" and "The Agency in Definitive Sanctification," in *Collected Writings of John Murray*, 277-93. Much of his treatment, which has decisively influenced my own thinking, is based on Romans 6.

A central point of Romans 6–7 considered together is that sin is an undeniable and grievous reality in the life of the believer and in no way to be minimized or excused. But for believers in their continuing depravity and ongoing struggle with sinning, there is this consideration deeper than their depravity: sin is not their lord, their master. The believer—united to the crucified, resurrected, and ascended Christ—is not any longer sin's slave; sin no longer owns the believer as it does the unbeliever.

On balance, for the believer, sin is *indwelling* (Rom. 7:17, where the expression "indwelling sin" comes from), but it is not *overpowering*; indwelling sin in the believer is not enslaving sin. All manner of pressing pastoral and personal issues come into view here. Believers, as they are burdened by their continuing to sin, may even perceive that sinning as enslaving. Nonetheless, with the apostle, they must understand about themselves—with the liberating experience from specific sins that self-understanding ought to and does foster—that they are not "bound" (I use the word advisedly here) to sin; they are no longer sin's slaves.

In this regard, the motif of resurrection as a motive for holy living bears reemphasizing. Sanctification is an outcome of the resurrection already experienced by the believer. It does not overstate to say that, in both its definitive and ongoing aspects, sanctification has no deeper perspective from which it can be viewed than in terms drawn from Romans 6:11–13: Sanctification is a continual being "alive to God" by those who are "alive from the dead . . . in the mortal body."

Good Works and God's Work

A comment on the good works of the believer is in order at this point. As the capstone assertion of the section Ephesians 2:1–10, which we looked at earlier, 2:10 is perhaps the most decisive biblical pronouncement on good works. Noteworthy is the way this verse follows from 2:8–9. Just those who are saved "by grace . . . through faith" and "not a result of works" are those who have been "created in Christ Jesus for good works, which God prepared beforehand, that we should walk in them."

Here "works" are counterposed in two antithetical senses. On the one hand (2:8–9), works are *decisively negated* where they are in opposition to salvation by grace, where they serve the futility of boasting in self-saving, self-justifying efforts (cf. Rom. 4:2). On the other (2:10), works are *emphatically affirmed* where they are the manifestation of saving grace. The good works of sanctification belong to the new creation that has arrived in Christ

G. C. Berkouwer has made the particularly helpful observation—primarily in light of Ephesians 2:10—that "the path of good works runs not from man to God, says Paul, but from God to man."[17] Good works, biblically considered, are not the way of the sinner to gain God's saving grace, but the way of God's saving grace with and in the sinner.

What constantly needs to be kept in view, especially as we speak, as we often and appropriately do, about "our good works" is this: For the apostle, good works, ultimately considered, are not ours but God's, his work begun and continuing in us, his being at work in us "both to will and to work for his good pleasure" (Phil. 2:13 once again; cf. "he who began a good work in you," 1:6). This is why, without any necessary tension, the faith that rests in God the Savior is a faith that is restless and active to do his will.

The wisdom of this world (cf. 1 Cor. 1:18–3:23), with its various efforts at establishing and maintaining what it deems good works in an autonomous and self-sufficient manner, will obviously never be able to understand Ephesians 2:10. But then, I am inclined to say, neither will faith where it has become so narrowed in its vision that it is able to see the good works of the believer only as "my" works, with all their flaws and imperfections.

Faith, the apostle prompts us to say, is (to be) the faith of those who "with unveiled face, beholding as in a mirror the glory of the Lord, are being transformed into the same image from glory to glory, just as from the Lord, the Spirit" (2 Cor. 3:18 NASB 1995). Where faith has this transforming vision, reflecting the transforming glory of the resurrected Christ, and holds fast to this Christ, then faith will have no uncertainty about the answer to those perennial and searching questions that Paul puts to the church: "What makes you different from anyone else? What do you have that you did not receive? And if you did receive it, why do you boast as if you did not?" (1 Cor. 4:7, my translation).

Faith understands that the answer to these questions, clearly rhetorical, is the same for sanctification no less than for justification. The deepest motive for sanctification, for holy living and good works, is not our psy-

---

17 G. C. Berkouwer, *Faith and Sanctification*, trans. John Vriend (Grand Rapids, MI: Eerdmans, 1952), 191.

chology—how I feel about Jesus, how warmly disposed I am toward God, or my sense of gratitude.

That gratitude is not to be diminished; it surely has its place. But that is not the deepest motive. The deepest motive for sanctification is not anything in us, even our faith. Rather, that deepest of motives is its source—found not in ourselves but in Christ and his resurrection power, in the new creation we have already been made participants by and in Christ, and as he indwells us as the life-giving Spirit.

The Relationship between Justification and Sanctification

It is clear by now that my reflections are involving us in a perennial issue for the doctrine and life of the church and also for Paul's theology. That issue is the relationship between justification and sanctification, to which I limit myself here to the following observations.

For Paul, justification and sanctification are inseparable. They are not to be confused, but they are inseparable. They are not to be confused, particularly when sanctification is in view as an ongoing process over time in the life of the Christian. In that case, justification is the absolutely necessary and settled precondition for sanctification (though not its source or cause, as some argue).

But why are they inseparable? The answer is not because God has determined that to be the case in a more or less arbitrary, nominalist fashion: no sanctification without justification, no justification without sanctification. Their relationship is not a matter of a conjunction between otherwise separable entities or benefits quite capable of existing independently from each other, as if one could exist without the other. It is not as if God forgives sinners and then additionally, in an unrelated way, wants forgiven sinners to serve him.

Such reasoning is flawed because it loses sight of what is more central here; better, not what but who is central. The reason that justification and sanctification are inseparable is because of Christ, because of who he is as our righteousness (1 Cor. 1:30). His is the righteousness that is the final, eschatological answer to any and every charge against God's elect, the justifying and intercessory righteousness of God reckoned as ours (cf. Rom. 8:33–34).

But Christ, the living exhibition of the imputed righteousness that avails for us at God's right hand, is the lifegiving Spirit. As we consider the relationship between justification and sanctification, specifically the necessary inseparability of sanctification, the Christ of our concern is Christ who is what he now is in the fullness of his exaltation glory and redemptive triumph and because we have been united with this Christ.

Justification and sanctification are inseparable because, as Calvin, for one, stresses repeatedly both in the *Institutes* and throughout his commentaries, our union is not with a partial Christ or a half Christ.[18] Calvin's point: union with Christ is not just for some of his benefits, but that union is with the whole Christ and all of his benefits. Because of who Christ is and who we are in union with him, this union involves an all-or-nothing proposition: we either have the whole Christ or we have no Christ.[19]

In fact, at stake here are the "alones" for which the Reformation contended so resolutely. Each *sola* is exclusive only as it is inclusive, as it involves a *tota*—an "all." The Reformation *solas*, we may fairly say, are graciously totalitarian. Faith has everything or it has nothing. Specifically, by faith we receive the whole Christ or we have no Christ.

Faith is "the alone instrument of justification: yet is it not alone in the person justified, but . . . is no dead faith, but worketh by love."[20] As the alone instrument of justification, faith is never alone but in those justified is also always sanctifying. To miss this balance, for no matter what apparently impeccable Protestant or evangelical motivations, runs the risk of lapsing into moralism, which can prove eventually to be a halfway house on a pilgrimage back to Rome.

The Righteousness of God

Finally, an observation based on the structure of Romans. The main body of the letter is 1:16–15:13, for which in its entirety, not just through 4:25

---

18 To cite just one instance but the one that is most directly pertinent, the opening words in his Romans commentary on chapter 6: "Throughout this chapter the Apostle proves, that they who imagine that gratuitous righteousness is given us by him, apart from newness of life, shamefully *rend Christ asunder*" (John Calvin, *Commentaries on the Epistle of Paul the Apostle to the Romans*; trans. and ed. John Owen [Grand Rapids, MI: Eerdmans, 1948], 217; emphasis added).

19 This is a key and controlling point in Calvin's, in many respects, peerless development in book 3 of the *Institutes*, of the doctrines of justification and sanctification ("regeneration") in their relationship to each other. Together and inseparably, they form the "double grace" that flows from union with Christ ("partaking of him"). See Calvin, *Institutes*, 3.11.1.

20 Westminster Confession of Faith, 11.2.

(or 5:21), the controlling theme is the gospel as "the power of God for salvation," and in which "the righteousness of God is revealed from faith to faith" (1:16-17 NASB).

The meaning of "the righteousness of God" (1:17) continues to be much debated. Concerning that debate, it is surely God's acquitting and justifying gift. This is the truth that the Reformation recaptured and its heirs have seen so clearly. But, it may be plausibly argued, as the discourse in Romans unfolds, that the righteousness of God is not only that justifying gift. It is also and inseparably a subduing and enslaving power. The gospel-righteousness of God revealed in Christ includes enslavement—the enslavement, it is important to note, that brings to human beings the only true and genuine freedom they can know. The righteousness of God revealed in the gospel, as the power of God for salvation, is not only forensic but also renovative. It both justifies sinners and also transforms them.

This dimension—the righteousness of God as transforming power—comes out with particular pointedness in the latter part of Romans 6. Christians have been delivered from the "dominion" of sin (6:14), in the sense that they are "no longer . . . enslaved to sin" (6:6). As that is the case, "having been set free from sin, [they] have become slaves of righteousness" (6:18). Equivalently, "But now . . . you have been set free from sin and have become slaves of God" (6:22). To be "slaves of righteousness" is to be "slaves of God."

To be a slave of righteousness, in other words, is to be enslaved to "the righteousness of God," to be a slave of the righteousness that comes from God, with "sanctification" as its "fruit" (6:22; cf. "as slaves to righteousness leading to sanctification," 6:19). In contrast, the antithesis to this righteousness-enslaved, sanctifying state of Christians is their pre-Christian past: they were "slaves of sin" specifically as they were "free in regard to [this gospel-enslaving] righteousness" (6:20).

The gospel, of which Paul is not ashamed and which has as its center the revelation of the righteousness of God (1:16-17), is, we need to appreciate, not just in some peripheral way but at its core, the gospel of liberating captivity to God.

That is good news for sinners. The gospel is the good news of free remission of the guilt of sin and of freely imputed righteousness. That, of course, is at its heart and must never be lost sight of or obscured. But the gospel is as well and equally the good news of liberating enslavement to righteousness. Noteworthy is the way, as reported by Luke, that Barnabas and Paul proclaim the gospel in the response to the idolatrous crowd in Lystra: "we bring you good news, that you should turn from these vain things to a living God" (Acts 14:15; cf. 1 Thess. 1:9).

There are, of course, many ways to evangelize, and we need always to remember that we cannot and need not say everything at once. Certainly, with the emphasis I am making, I do not want in any way to be heard as saying anything other than that it remains true in our own day that the first word sinners need to hear is the word that concerns the reconciling righteousness of God in Christ and the free forgiveness of sins, the gratuitous justification of the ungodly solely by faith.

But in light of Paul's argumentation in Romans, any presentation of the gospel that is not at least oriented to the truth of Romans 6, that maintains or leaves the impression that liberating enslavement to the righteousness of God is not a part of the gospel but a less or nonessential addendum to the gospel, is lacking as a presentation of the gospel as the revelation of the righteousness of God. It veils that revelation in its fullness, and so to that extent is not "the power of God for salvation for everyone who believes" (1:16).

14

The Resurrection and the
Christian Life (Part 2)

Christian Suffering

PAUL'S THEOLOGY of the Christian life is rooted in the resurrection life of Christ and in sharing in that life. To be united with Christ in his resurrection—in terms of the firstfruits metaphor of 1 Corinthians 15:20, to have a place in the end-time resurrection harvest inaugurated by his resurrection—is not only a future hope at his return but also a present reality.

This reality, as fundamental as it is comprehensive, is obviously open to being probed beyond what we have seen so far. How further, then, is the resurrection life of the believer to be understood? As we could put the question, For believers raised with Christ in the period between his resurrection and return, what is their quality of life, its complexion? In terms of categories drawn from Romans 6:12-13, what does ongoing, day-to-day living look like for those who are "alive from the dead" . . . "in [the] mortal body"? What further qualifies that way of life? What aspects are constitutive of their resurrection experience?

Among a number of different directions that could be followed in answering such a large and wide-ranging question, the answer I have chosen to explore in this final chapter is, in a word, suffering. My thesis, as paradoxical as it might at first sound, is that for Paul, suffering is an essential mark of the believer's present experience of resurrection. Suffering specifies as fundamental a dimension as any of the Christian life, precisely as that life is sharing in the life of the resurrected Christ.

The decision to take our discussion in this direction is prompted, in part, by the need to head off a certain misunderstanding. The truth of the Christian life as resurrection life is an exhilarating and elevating truth. As a result, it is subject to being distorted and used to minister a false presumption, an easy resurrection triumphalism, leading to one or another sort of prosperity Christianity that always seems to be out there.

My concern here, negatively, is that the undeniable triumph of the believer in Christ, the triumph of already being united to him in his resurrection, not be misconstrued and misappropriated into a deceptive triumphalism. Positively, at issue here is an aspect of the present resurrection life of the believer, as essential as any for Paul, that may not be missed or minimized.

Our procedure will be to look at several key passages and take note of basic conclusions about the Christian life that follow from them.

2 CORINTHIANS 4:7-12

> But we have this treasure in jars of clay, to show that the surpassing power belongs to God and not to us. (4:7)

Focusing on two key expressions in this statement, "this treasure," for one, has its sense from the immediately preceding section, 3:17–4:6 (the chapter break is not in the best place). The treasure in view is, in general, the gospel. Materially, it is salvation—just expressed in 4:6, utilizing Genesis 1:3, as the saving "light" of the new creation "in our hearts," the light that consists in "the knowledge of the glory of God in the face of Jesus Christ."

In a word, then, "this treasure" is Christ. The treasure is the exalted Lord who is the Spirit (3:17; cf. "the life-giving Spirit," 1 Cor. 15:45), who indwells believers (cf. Rom. 8:9-11; Eph. 3:16-17). The confident "we have" accents that the treasure is the actual possession of believers. From the context, then, "this treasure," all told, is the eschatological, new creation glory of God in Christ possessed by Christians in union with him.

Secondly, this treasure possessed is in "jars of clay." In view with this image is not some ceramic masterpiece, but, in terms of the culture of that time, something both cheap and fragile, an item picked up at little cost and disposable (if it gets broken, just throw out the shards and get another).[1]

---

1   "Perishable containers," as an earlier version of NLT (1996) has it.

The clay jars are believers considered in themselves. As "this treasure" is Christ, the "clay jars" are Christians.

How the basic profile we noted in Romans 6:12–13 comes out here should not be missed: "this treasure" corresponds to "alive from the dead," "jars of clay" to "in [the] mortal body."

Second Corinthians 4:7–12 is autobiographical. Paul is speaking of himself and his own experience; in 4:12, he explicitly distinguishes himself ("in us") from those he is addressing ("in you"). But while there is this autobiographical aspect and it is no doubt prominent, the autobiography involved also has representative significance. Despite the argument of some that the passage is uniquely apostolic or only about Paul as an apostle, Paul expresses himself here in a way that has implications for all believers. The "we" as the subject of the main verb in 4:7 is not stylistic but is fairly seen as having a numerically plural reference that includes all believers. Note here, if nothing else, "jars" (plural), not "jar" (singular).

Second Corinthians 4:8–9 amplifies the thought of 4:7. Grammatically, in the Greek text, these verses are composed of four parallel sets of contrasting participial clauses that are subordinate to as they modify adverbially "we have" in 4:7. Semantically, they spell out something of the circumstances or condition of those who have this treasure in clay jars (NASB 1995):

afflicted in every way, but not crushed
perplexed, but not despairing[2]
persecuted, but not forsaken
struck down, but not destroyed[3]

The apostle has obviously given some attention to fashioning this parallel pattern of contrasts as he has, with their left-right cadence. The one, left-hand side in each of the four contrasts ("afflicted" . . . "perplexed" . . . "persecuted" . . . "struck down") describes the experience of the clay jars. In each instance, the other, right-hand side expresses what is also true of

---

2 For this contrast, Philip Hughes, *Paul's Second Epistle to the Corinthians* (Grand Rapids, MI: Eerdmans, 1962), 138n7, suggests the alliterative pair: "confused, but not confounded"—an apt description of believers!

3 Insofar as Paul's own experience is reflected in these contrasts, cf. esp. the specific persecutions and hardships enumerated in 2 Cor. 11:23–28; also 6:4–10.

their experience but also alleviates it. The fragile jars that believers are, are not empty; they contain the treasure of the sustaining power of the resurrected Christ indwelling them. The rhythmic fourfold repetition of "but not" (ἀλλ᾽ οὐκ) adds a rhetorically effective accent.

Here, we may say, rhetoric is shaped by reality. This "but not" theology captures an essential aspect for believers of the situation of overlap of the two aeons in the period between the resurrection and return of Christ.

Second Corinthians 4:10—"always carrying about in the body the dying of Jesus, so that the life of Jesus also may be manifested in our body" (NASB 1995)—both summarizes and further amplifies 4:7-9. It also gives a unifying focus to the contrasts in 4:8-9. Syntactically, this subordinate participial clause ("always carrying about"), like those in 4:8-9, also modifies "we have" back in 4:7. Second Corinthians 4:7-10 is one long sentence in the Greek text. It is written to present a single total picture.

The composition of 4:10 differs from 4:8-9, in that the right-hand side of the contrast is—significantly, as we will see—a purpose clause ("so that"). The contrast now, within the bodily, clay jar existence of the believer, is between "the dying of Jesus" and "the life of Jesus."

"The life of Jesus" corresponds to "this treasure" in 4:7; the life of Jesus in the believer's body is the treasure in the clay jars. "The dying of Jesus," in contrast, encapsulates all of the suffering and adversity in view in 4:8-9. The noun that Paul uses here (νέκρωσις, *nekrōsis*) is a verbal noun (cf. its only other New Testament use, in parallel with its cognate verb νεκρόω in Rom. 4:19). That verbal force should be maintained here and translated "dying" (NASB, NKJV), rather than "death" (ESV, NIV).

In other words, this noun does not have in view death as a terminal state but exposure to death, not the fact of having died but the deadly and imperiling conditions that lead to death and can result in death. Its sense is that of the parallel description in 2 Corinthians 4:11: "being given over to death (εἰς θάνατον)." As Paul contemplates believers in their bodily existence, he accents, as we might put it, their "necrotic" (not "neurotic"!) condition. This necrosis consisting of suffering and adversity, he says, is not an end in itself but serves a purpose—namely, "so that the life of Jesus may also be manifested in our bodies."

Second Corinthians 4:11—"For we who live are always being given over to death for Jesus' sake, so that the life of Jesus also may be manifested in

our mortal flesh"—is a new sentence in the Greek text. With slight variations, however, it is virtually identical to 4:10.[4] For our purposes, we may
fairly view 4:11 as repeating for emphasis the summarizing focus of 4:10
on the situation of the treasure in clay jars.

This parallel between 4:10 and 4:11 prompts the following observations:

First, as already noted, "the dying of Jesus" is to be understood as "being
given over to death for Jesus's sake." The dying of Jesus hardly refers to
a continuing vestige of mortality and suffering experienced by him personally within or along with his life as resurrected and ascended, as if his
state of humiliation has not been entirely left behind in his state of exaltation. Rather, his dying is realized as and in the sufferings of believers for
him ("for Jesus's sake"), in some instances, no doubt, ending in physical
death. It is his dying because he is united with them, without that union
obliterating the personal distinction and present bodily distance between
him and them.[5]

Second, in each verse, an adverb meaning "always" (πάντοτε, 4:10; ἀεί,
4:11) is in a position of emphasis at the beginning of the construction in
the Greek text. This accentuates that the state of affairs in view for believers is ongoing and enduring, in fact permanent for as long as their mortal
bodily existence continues.

Third, with the virtually identical purpose clause with which each verse
ends, we arrive at the culminating point of the entire passage. "The life
of Jesus" in each clause is his resurrection life, his life as resurrected and
ascended. These purpose clauses show how the manifesting of this exalted
life in the mortal bodily existence of believers is related to the dying of Jesus,
understood as their suffering for his sake. The point is hardly to separate
or compartmentalize the two, the dying and the life, as if the one has to do
with the believer's bad, down days, the other with good, up times.

---

4 2 Cor. 4:10 has "in our bodies," while 4:11, "in our mortal flesh." This is an instance in Paul's
varied use of "flesh" (σάρξ), where it is synonymous or interchangeable with "body" (σῶμα)
and without the sinful, ethically negative sense it has elsewhere in antithesis to the Holy Spirit.
Paul sees bodily resurrection as the resurrection of the flesh (cf. 1 Cor. 15:50 with 15:54). So,
properly understood, there is no objection to that language.

5 This is the sense of the words of Jesus to Paul underway to Damascus (Acts 9:4–5; cf. 22:7–8;
26:14–15): "Saul, Saul, why are you persecuting me?" . . . "I am Jesus, whom you are persecuting."
In persecuting the church, Paul was persecuting the ascended Jesus with whom the church is
united as one.

Rather—and this is the primary takeaway from this passage for our discussion of it—clearly it is in the suffering of believers in the mortal body that the resurrection life of Jesus is manifested (not alongside of, in addition to, or in spite of, but in those sufferings). Second Corinthians 4:10-11 show that the locus or manifestation mode of the resurrection life of Christ is the suffering of Christians for him. This life of Jesus comes to expression in the mortal bodily existence of the believer as the dying of Jesus. In this way, back to 4:7, the treasure in the clay jars is to the end of showing that just in their suffering, "the surpassing power belongs to God and not to us."

Second Corinthians 4:12—"So death is at work in us, but life in you"—concludes the passage with an important consequence. Here Paul distinguishes himself from his readers: the Corinthians' reception of the gospel is an instance of the life of Jesus manifested as the dying of Jesus realized in his ministry to and among them (cf. 2 Cor. 3:2-3).

But this extension of the gospel is exemplary and can surely be replicated in and by others. Second Corinthians 4:12, along with several other passages we have yet to address in light of this passage, provide an important missiological principle, an evangelizing consideration of fundamental significance for the mission of the church. The gospel at work in the church with its life-in-death implications of suffering and the sacrificial giving of self—sacrificial suffering in the giving of self—is a decidedly effective means of bringing others into the church and under the saving and life-giving dominion of "the Lord who is the Spirit" (3:18).

PHILIPPIANS 3:10-11

That I may know Him and the power of His resurrection and the fellowship of His sufferings, being conformed to His death; if somehow I may attain to the resurrection from the dead. (NASB)

Embedded as these verses are in their immediate and broader context (3:2-11), some contextual observations are in order.

Philippians 3:2-6

The sharply worded threefold warning ("Look out," 3:2) is voiced about those who insist that Gentile believers must be circumcised. In pushing this false, gospel-undercutting view of circumcision, they are "those who mutilate the flesh" (cf. Gal. 5:11-12; 6:12-13 for Paul's similarly forceful and unsparing tone in dealing with false teaching related to circumcision).

In contrast to these false teachers, Christians are the true circumcision, as evidenced by their worship and service (Phil. 3:3). They worship "in the Spirit of God" (NASB), as their lives are marked by a fundamental contrast: they "glory in Christ Jesus and put no confidence in the flesh."

This contrast focuses a basic difference between believers and unbelievers, akin to what we see, for instance, in the latter part of Romans 6: Inevitably, human beings are boasters. They either boast with confidence in themselves in one way or the other, which always leads to some form of idolatry, or their boast and confidence is in Christ and all he is to them.

The autobiographical verses that follow (3:4-11) expand on this foundational contrast. In them, Paul juxtaposes the antithesis in boasting/confidence between his pre-Christian past and presently as a Christian. The former, his "confidence in the flesh," was his Jewish pedigree and performance as a Pharisee (3:4-6).

Philippians 3:7-11

These verses describe basic dimensions of the radical and sweeping change in Paul's life brought about by his newfound boast and confidence in Christ rather than himself. Here, even more clearly than in 2 Corinthians 4:7-11, the autobiography is representative and exemplary for all Christians.

What he had previously prized so highly about himself, everything that he had considered "gain," he now estimates, all told, as "loss because of Christ" (διὰ τὸν Χριστὸν, 3:7 NASB), "because of the surpassing worth of knowing Christ" (3:8). In this gain-loss calculus, he now in fact reckons his Pharisaic past in its totality as "dung" (σκύβαλα[6]), and he does that "in order that I might gain Christ and be found in him" (3:8-9)—in other words, that he might be united to Christ.

Paul's gain, the gain of believers, has its focus in union with Christ and the benefits of that union. "The surpassing worth of knowing Christ" (3:8) is more than merely notional, theoretical. It is union-knowledge, the full

---

6 A word for excrement of various kinds, including fecal matter, used here for its intended shock effect; "dung" (KJV, NET) better captures this effect than the milder "garbage" (NIV, NLT) or "rubbish" (ESV, NKJV).

knowledge of personal relationship, an experiential knowing, existential knowledge, as 3:10 will show.

In 3:7, Paul's reckoning of gain is in the past tense (the perfect tense in Greek); it is a settled gain. In 3:8, that reckoning is in the present tense, and union with Christ is expressed in a purpose clause (3:8–9)—that is, as a present aspiration.

This hardly means that union with Christ is somehow transitory or impermanent and has constantly to be regained. But it does show that, for Paul, being united to Christ at the inception of the Christian life, once and done as it surely is, is not just an event in the past. Union with Christ, while definitive, is an ongoing reality. Nothing is more important for Paul than the maintenance of that union, than continuing to be found in Christ.

The rest of 3:9 into 3:10-11 spells out basic benefits of being united to Christ, matters about that union Paul wishes to highlight. For one, union with Christ means "not having a righteousness of my own" (3:9), the law-produced and law-enhanced righteousness of his Pharisaic past (cf. 3:6). Rather, that union brings with it "the righteousness from God," righteousness that is received by faith in Christ and in that sense is dependent on faith (cf. "the righteousness of faith," Rom. 4:13).

Philippians 3:9, then, is best understood as referring to justification. Paul's desire is to be found in Christ that he might have the righteousness of God revealed in Christ as his. Elsewhere, Paul shows that believers have this justifying righteousness by imputation—that is, by being counted or reckoned righteous by faith (e.g., Rom. 4:1-12; 5:18-19[7]). Here, Paul makes clear that the imputation involved in justification is not an isolated act, an isolated imputative occurrence, but is anchored in being united to Christ. For Paul, justification flows from union; it does not occur prior to or apart from union.[8]

---

7   In 5:19, "made righteous" or "constituted righteous" (my translation) is best taken as referring to a forensically constitutive declaration—that is, imputation.

8   "Therefore, that joining together of Head and members, that indwelling of Christ in our hearts—in short, that *mystical union*—are accorded by us the highest degree of importance, so that Christ, having been made ours, makes us sharers with him in the gifts with which he has been endowed. We *do not, therefore, contemplate him outside ourselves from afar in order that his righteousness may be imputed to us but because we put on Christ and are engrafted into his body—in short, because he deigns to make us one with him*. For this reason, we glory that we *have fellowship of righteousness* with him." John Calvin, *Institutes of the Christian Religion*, ed. John T. McNeill, trans. Ford Lewis Battles (Philadelphia, PA: Westminster, 1960), 2.16.13

Philippians 3:10-11

These verses are our primary interest in this passage for the depth of insight they provide concerning suffering as an essential aspect of the Christian life, specifically as sharing in the resurrection life of Christ.

Philippians 3:8-11 is one sentence in the Greek text, in which 3:10 expresses a further purpose stemming from the overall purpose of being found in Christ (3:9).[9] Paul desires and aspires to be united with Christ, not only for justification but now also for sanctification, for the particular facet of sanctification that he is concerned to bring out here. Union with Christ brings both justification and sanctification.

To utilize these standard systematic-theological categories here (union, justification, sanctification) is not to impose a structure alien to Paul. To the contrary, these categories, properly understood, have their validity as they derive, in part, from this and other Pauline passages.

Philippians 3:10 begins, "in order that I may know him [Christ]." Here—and this is an all-important key to understanding 3:10 as a whole and the purpose it expresses—this knowing is not bare cognition, not merely notional, not just information about Christ, although sound doctrinal understanding is involved. Rather, the knowledge in view is the personal, relational knowledge that comes from being united with Christ. It is the same knowledge in view in 3:8, of "surpassing worth" in its *fullness*. It is not a first step, in need of being supplemented or added to by the subsequent items in 3:10. Instead, the sequence in the rest of 3:10 spells out what this full and experiential union-knowledge includes.

The sequence is not, as might be expected suffering-death-resurrection, but resurrection-suffering-death. In it, the two occurrences of "and" should not be taken as coordinating or additive but as explanatory or epexegetical. As we might picture this sequence, it is not like cars in a train lined up one after the other, each with its separate load, but like nested Chinese boxes or Russian dolls, where in opening one, inside is another, and inside that yet another, and so on.

To know "the power of his resurrection," then, is not in addition to knowing Christ but a constituent aspect of that union-knowledge. To

---

(1:521); emphasis added. Calvin may not have thought in terms of a distinct theology of Paul, but he has well understood the mind—and heart—of the apostle.

9   Those wanting to test their Greek skills can take on the challenge of diagramming the syntactical relationships in 3:8-11!

know Christ is to share in the power of his resurrection life. But to know this resurrection power is, in turn, to know the "fellowship of his sufferings" (KJV, NASB). Experiencing the fellowship of Christ's sufferings is not in addition to experiencing his resurrection power. Rather, the former is a function of the latter; resurrection power is displayed in the fellowship of suffering. Paul is saying, Do you want to know what it means to know Christ? It means experiencing the power of his resurrection *as* the fellowship of his suffering.[10]

The fellowship of suffering is not present in the life of the believer in distinction from the power of resurrection. It is not as if I am to look into my life and ask in factoring fashion, Where is the resurrection part, and where is the suffering part? That misunderstands the apostle's "ands" entirely. He tells us here that sharing in Christ's suffering in knowing him is not an experience in addition to or distinct from experiencing the power of his resurrection. Rather, here as in 2 Corinthians 4, the resurrection life of Jesus, Christ's resurrection power, is realized in the suffering of believers. Their sharing in suffering for him is the manifestation mode of his resurrection power. Christian suffering is the locus of Christ's resurrection power.

The participial clause at the end of Philippians 3:10 reinforces this, by bringing everything to a focus. "Being conformed to his death" (NASB, NKJV; cf. "the dying of Jesus," 2 Cor. 4:10) does not introduce a distinctly new notion. It does not so much add a thought as summarize what it means to know Christ and the power of his resurrection in the mode of suffering. That, all told, is being conformed to his death.

For Paul, Christ's resurrection power is to have a cruciform effect. The impact of Christ's resurrection life in the church, the impression or imprint that the resurrection ought to leave in the life of the believer, is, as much as anything, the cross.

The ultimate goal of predestination for believers is "to be conformed to the image of his [God's] Son" (Rom. 8:29). Until Jesus comes again, this as much as anything is what it means to be conformed to that image, to have "Christ . . . formed in you" (Gal. 4:19): to be conformed to his death as the manifestation of his resurrection life.

10 This linking together of resurrection and suffering is reinforced in the likely most reliable Greek text, where the definite article is not repeated but the two share a single definite article ("the power of his resurrection and fellowship of his suffering").

Philippians 3:11 adds a still further purpose to the purpose of knowing Christ in his surpassing fullness: "if somehow I may attain to the resurrection from the dead" (my translation). "Somehow" (πως) here is not an expression of doubt or a mood of uncertainty but brings out Paul's fully involved and resolute engagement ("that by any means possible," ESV), looking from the present to the future.

Taking 3:10-11 together, the full sequence is resurrection-suffering-death-resurrection. Resurrection is the reality that both brackets and forms the existential union-knowledge of Christ: resurrection now—as suffering now, as death now—and as resurrection beyond suffering and death in the future. Here, the Christian life is patterned by the already and not-yet of resurrection. As the resurrection is the basis of the Christian life, its grand and comprehensive indicative, it also sets its great imperative and final goal.

The conclusions about resurrection and suffering reached in our discussion of the 2 Corinthians 4 and Philippians 3 passages are reinforced and can be expanded on in the light of other passages in Paul. The subpoints that follow distinguish between the death and resurrection of Christ. This distinguishing is not meant, contrary to what we have just seen, to compartmentalize and lose sight of their interrelationship in the life of the Christian but to underline and be more precise about the different angles from which Paul views Christian suffering.

CHRISTIAN SUFFERING AND THE DEATH OF CHRIST

As we have seen, the sufferings of believers are categorized as "the dying of Jesus" (2 Cor. 4:10), and their sharing in Christ's suffering as "being conformed to His death" (Phil. 3:10 NASB).[11]

Elsewhere, Christians, on the one hand, in fact "share abundantly in Christ's sufferings" (2 Cor. 1:5), while, on the other, they are to suffer with Christ: "provided we suffer with him in order that we may also be glorified with him" (Rom. 8:17). Suffering with Christ permeates the whole of the Christian life, from beginning to end, so that it is both a given and a calling, an indicative and an imperative.

---

11 I should perhaps have noted earlier—what should be obvious—that not all suffering by Christians is Christian suffering. Paul would certainly agree with the distinction Peter makes in addressing Christians between their God-glorifying suffering "as a Christian" and their suffering as the consequences of their sinful conduct (1 Pet. 4:15-16).

Such statements, it bears reemphasizing, have their meaning and validity given to them by the union that exists between Christ and the Christian. The "with Christ" of Christian suffering is integral to their suffering and may never be eclipsed. This prompts the observation that, for Paul, the suffering of Christ culminating on the cross, on the one hand, and the suffering of believers, on the other, are bracketed together. In a manner that is important to qualify against serious misunderstanding, Christ's own suffering plus Christian suffering form a unit; their shared suffering is seen as a single entity.

Colossians 1:24 includes the most striking assertion of this bond between Christ's sufferings and those of believers: "Now I rejoice in my sufferings for your sake, and in my flesh I am filling up what is lacking in Christ's afflictions for the sake of his body, that is, the church." How are we to understand this statement of the apostle? What can he mean that in the afflictions Christ endured, there is a "lack"?[12]

In answering this question, it is imperative to be clear about what Paul does *not* mean. He is not contradicting what he plainly teaches elsewhere. He is not denying the crucially important respect in which Christ's sufferings culminating in his death are unique, *sui generis*, in a class of their own, and, as such, are in no way lacking.

Christ's afflictions are those of God's "own Son," his one and only Son, whom he "did not spare . . . but gave him up for us all" (Rom. 8:32; cf. 8:3). This points to the atonement as the unique and inimitable accomplishment of Christ. Paul, then, is not saying that Christ's death is insufficient as an atonement for sin. He does not mean that Christ's death as an atoning sacrifice—a sacrifice that removes sin's guilt (Rom. 8:1, 33–34), propitiates God's just wrath on sinners (Rom. 3:25), reconciles him to them and them to him (Rom. 5:10–11), and delivers them from sin's enslaving power (Rom. 6:6)—has somehow to be supplemented by the sufferings of believers.

If, for instance, it should come to mind that Colossians 1:24 means that the sufferings of Christians serve to reconcile them to God, then to dispel that notion, all one needs do is back up a few verses in the immediate context, where Paul affirms that reconciliation, comprehensively considered, has been fully and finally accomplished by Christ's death:

---

12 Literally, "the things lacking" (τὰ ὑστερήματα), pointing to a plurality of the lack.

For in him all the fullness of God was pleased to dwell, and through him to reconcile to himself all things, whether on earth or in heaven, making peace by the blood of his cross. And you, who once were alienated and hostile in mind, doing evil deeds, he has now reconciled in his body of flesh by his death, in order to present you holy and blameless and above reproach before him. (1:19–22)

In 1:24, Paul has hardly forgotten this emphatic affirmation of the finished, definitive character of the reconciling of God in the cross of Christ. Clearly, he is not saying that in their atoning efficacy, there is some deficiency or lack to be made up in Christ's afflictions.

Furthermore, these observations about the atonement carry with them that Paul does not mean that Christ's obedience unto death (Phil. 2:8; Rom. 5:18–19) is not the sufficient and exclusive basis for the believer's justification.

Being clear about what Paul does not mean in Colossians 1:24, however, still leaves the question: What, then, does he mean? The answer lies along the following lines.

Having accented the reconciliation accomplished by the cross of Christ (1:19–23), Paul in 1:24 shows that there are aspects—other than reconciling, atoning aspects—in terms of which the sufferings of believers and the sufferings of Christ himself are to be seen together, so that their sufferings are identified as his.

Colossians 1:24 is autobiographical, but like the other passages we have looked at in this section, the autobiography is representative. In view is not what is uniquely apostolic or limited to his ministry, as if in his suffering, Paul is identified with Christ in a way that is no longer applicable to others. He would have the church understand that all Christians experience suffering, as he has, as Christ endured suffering.

This shared suffering is best labeled *missiological*. In no sense is it *soteriological*. In view is not some insufficiency in the accomplishment of salvation that has to be supplemented, some lack in that accomplishment in need of being filled up or completed. In view, rather, is the evangelizing truth of 2 Corinthians 4:12, noted above: "So death is at work in us, but life in you." That principle, also autobiographical but replicable in other Christians, is important for the advance of the gospel and how it spreads.

Statements of Jesus in John 17:18 and 20:21 help in interpreting Colossians 1:24: "As you sent me into the world, so I have sent them into the world." "As the Father has sent me, even so I am sending you." This linking in sending—of the Father sending Jesus and of him, in turn, sending his disciples/the church into the world—prompts the choice of *missiological* to categorize the joint afflictions in view and at the same time to avoid, in distinction, any sort of soteriological confusion or muddiness.[13]

As we consider the solidarity between Christ and Christians in suffering, the truth Colossians 1:24 expresses is this, in the strikingly incisive words of John Murray: "Their [God's children's] sufferings are regarded as filling up the total quota of suffering requisite to the consummation of redemption and the glorification of the whole body of Christ (cf. Col. 1:24)."[14]

In the necessity of this totality of suffering, in the realization of this sum total—what Murray refers to as the "total quota" made up of Christ's own sufferings plus the sufferings of the church—is found a facet in the reason for the delay of the parousia. One reason for the now-prolonged period between the first and second comings of Christ, an aspect providing us with a rationale for the extent of that period, is that in this period, until Jesus returns, the church in its mission in and to the world is engaged in "filling up what is lacking in Christ's afflictions."[15]

Some hold that by its evangelizing efforts, the church can determine and accelerate the time of Christ's return, can "hasten the day," as it's put. The idea is that the more aggressive and successful the church is in spreading the gospel, as that effort includes the suffering involved, the sooner Christ will return. If an appeal is made to Colossians 1:24 in support of this notion, that clearly over-exegetes the "filling up" Paul has in mind.

---

13 That confusion is seen particularly in some Roman Catholic exegetes who have had something of a field day ("not without malicious joy," Ernst Käsemann, *Commentary on Romans* [Grand Rapids: Eerdmans, 1980], 57) using passages like Col. 1:24 in seeking to undercut the fundamental emphases of the Reformation, and in support of the soteriological nature and necessity of Rome's sacramental system. My comments here, though not in any full way, provide the basic lines of a response, so far as this verse is concerned.

14 In his commentary on Rom. 8:17, a passage that we will be looking at presently: "If so be that we suffer with him that we might be glorified with him." John Murray, *The Epistle to the Romans* (Grand Rapids, MI: Eerdmans, 1959), 1:299.

15 Cf. "until the number of their fellow servants and their brothers should be complete" (Rev. 6:11). My thanks to Dennis Johnson for drawing my attention to Rev. 6:9-11 and its relevance.

CHRISTIAN SUFFERING AND THE
RESURRECTION OF CHRIST

Second Corinthians 4:10–11 and Philippians 3:10, examined above, clearly show the close connection between Christian suffering and Christ's resurrection, the intimate bond between the two because believers are united with Christ as resurrected. As we have also seen, fundamental to Paul's understanding of salvation and the Christian life is that by virtue of this union, believers have already been raised with Christ, have ascended with him, and are seated with him "in the heavenly places" (Eph. 2:5–6 esp. makes this explicit; cf. Col. 3:3: "your life is hidden with [the ascended] Christ in God").

So, we may say, for Paul, believers suffer not in spite of the fact that they are raised up with Christ, not even alongside of that fact or in addition to it. Rather, they suffer because, united to Christ, they are raised up and seated with him in the heavenlies.

It is certainly true that Christians also suffer because they are not yet in heaven, not yet "away from the body" at death (2 Cor. 5:8), and because they are not yet raised bodily, in the "outer self" (4:16). But it is no less true that Christians suffer on earth—in the mortal flesh (4:11), in the clay jars they are (4:7)—just because, united with Christ, they are in heaven.

Christians suffer because they are in heaven. They, we can even say according to Paul, are raised up and ascended with Christ for a purpose: in order that they may suffer on earth, may "fill up what is lacking in the afflictions of Christ" (Col. 1:24). From this vantage point, then, we can appreciate further how their suffering is an expression of his resurrection glory and power, particularly as that manifestation is realized through the presence and power of his Spirit.

CHRISTIAN SUFFERING, CHRIST'S RESURRECTION,
AND THE SPIRIT

The passages so far considered concerning the resurrection and Christian suffering make no mention of the Holy Spirit. This silence can be puzzling. It may mislead to thinking that the Spirit is not involved with Christians in their suffering with Christ.

This silence will remain puzzling as long as what is fundamental both to Paul's Christology and his Pneumatology, as we spent considerable space in establishing in chapter 12, is not kept firmly in mind: In his resurrection, Christ "became the life-giving Spirit" (1 Cor. 15:45; cf. "the Lord is the Spirit," 2 Cor. 3:17-18). Christ—specifically as he is incarnate, crucified, resurrected, and ascended—and the Holy Spirit, while the two continue to be the distinct persons they are eternally, are one in their working, identified with each other in their in-tandem presence and activity in the church and within believers.

Life in the Spirit is the resurrection life of Christ (cf. esp. Rom. 8:9-11; Eph. 3:16-17). Through their joint and unified activity, then, the present locus of Christ's resurrection power, where his resurrection power is presently operative through the Spirit, is in the suffering of the church.[16]

Second Corinthians 12:9-10, another autobiographic but also paradigmatic instance not yet considered, should be read in this light. Second Corinthians 12:9a—"My grace is sufficient for you, for my power is made perfect in weakness"—is the response of the Lord to Paul's plea, beset by "a thorn . . . in the flesh," that he remove it (12:7-8).[17]

The power of the exalted Christ, as the Lord, "who is the Spirit" (3:17-18), is perfected in Paul's weakness—not apart from, in addition to, or to diminish or eliminate that weakness. For that reason, Paul, in turn, responds, "I will boast all the more gladly of my weaknesses." Why? "[S]o that the power of Christ may rest upon me" (12:9b).

Further, for Christ's sake, in this boasting, Paul is "content" in the full range of his weakness-sufferings—further detailed as "insults, hardships, persecutions, and calamities." Why this settled contentment? "For when I am weak, then I am strong"—through the indwelling Spirit of the resurrected Christ, we may surely gloss.

This, if you will, is the "perfectionism" taught by Paul and the rest of the New Testament: the power of the resurrected Christ—the life-giving Spirit, the Lord who is the Spirit—perfected in the weaknesses of believers.

---

16   Cf. Peter, writing to the church in much the same vein as Paul: "insofar as you share Christ's sufferings, . . . the Spirit of glory and of God rests upon you" (1 Pet. 4:13-14).

17   The nature of this "thorn," whether or not it was a physical malady, remains uncertain. "Three times" should not be read as meaning *only* three times and then he gave up, but, to the contrary, is best seen as an idiom for the fullness of Paul's pleading.

RESURRECTION, SUFFERING, AND THE CHURCH TODAY

Our reflections to this point on the resurrection and Christian suffering raise an inevitable question: Assuming that this teaching of Paul is valid and applicable for the entire interadvental period until Christ's return, as it in fact is, and that I have represented it with some accuracy, how then does it apply to the church today?

This question can and should be perplexing, even discomfiting to Christians in the West enjoying the religious freedom and relative lack of suffering for Christ they do (despite hardly negligible and rapidly accelerating secular animosity). A gaping disparity is obvious; inescapably evident is the blatant oppression and overt persecution of the suffering being experienced increasingly by Christians in most Islamic majority countries, mainland China, and elsewhere.

Why God permits the burden of suffering of the church to be distributed as he does in such an unequal fashion around the world at any one time in history, including ours, has no easy and final answers. Ultimately, we are faced with a mystery known only to God in his sovereign and wise purposes. But those purposes we know, as the apostle assures us (Rom. 8:28), even when we cannot fully comprehend them, are always for the good of the church.

Still, some help is provided in answering our question regarding how Paul's teaching continues to be applicable today to all Christians, by recognizing the broad understanding he has of Christian suffering and its implications—broader than is often recognized. That breadth can be seen by revisiting Romans 8, particularly 8:18-23.

As we noted earlier, 8:17 conditions future glory for believers, as heirs of God and co-heirs with Christ, on suffering with Christ: "provided [εἴπερ] we suffer with him in order that we may also be glorified with him." This conditional clause, in turn, triggers the verses that immediately follow. In them the main theme is suffering in the hope of glory, the incomparable contrast between present suffering and future glory (cf. 2 Cor. 4:17: the "eternal weight of glory" is "beyond all comparison" with the present suffering of the church).

Romans 8:18 speaks of "the sufferings of this present time." An important key for interpreting this passage as a whole is that "this [or 'the'] present time" (τοῦ νῦν καιροῦ) is not simply limited to the generation of Paul and his original readers in the church in Rome. Rather, it has a much more sweeping, comprehensive reference. It is equivalent—in terms of the two-aeon distinction—to this aeon, this "present evil age" (Gal. 1:4), in distinction from and in contrast to the eschatological age to come.[18] This present time is any and all times until the resurrection-redemption of the body (Rom. 8:23) at Christ's return. This time, this present time, Paul says, is marked fundamentally by suffering; it is categorically and comprehensively a time of suffering.

How broadly Paul conceives of this pervasive suffering, his wide-angle vision on suffering, appears in the way he sees "the whole creation" (8:22), along with believers, implicated in suffering (cf. the multiple references to the creation in 8:19–21). In what amounts to a brief commentary on the events of the fall in Genesis 3 and the result of God's curse on the creation because of human sin (8:20–22), the entire creation, including Christians, is, in a fundamental way, "subjected to futility" (8:20) and in "bondage to corruption" (8:21).

In this passage, Paul reminds the church that we live in a creation, with all that remains good about it, that is nonethelesssignificantly disordered and that the creation as a whole will remain in this disordered state until Jesus returns. Because of the curse on human sin, a massive futility factor pervades the entire creation. An inescapable decay/corruption constant cuts through everything in it, including ourselves and everything we do, frustrating even our best aspirations and accomplishments. We live in a creation where for now, this present time, put bluntly, too often "things just don't work right," including ourselves.

Paul graphically captures this situation with the image of the groans associated with the pains of childbirth, an image applied to believers together with the creation (8:22–23). This omnipresent groaning, like that of childbirth, is in fact bittersweet; there are two sides to it. Negatively, it is groaning from being under the duress of the ever-present futility and corruption already noted. But, positively, at the same time, it is groaning in eager anticipation (8:19); it is a groaning "in hope" (8:20), a sure hoping of the creation and believers together of eventual relief and of deliverance into "the freedom of the glory of the children of God" (8:21).[19]

---

18 Cf. "in this time" (ἐν τῷ καιρῷ τούτῳ), contrasted explicitly with "the age to come" in Mark 10:30.

19 The repeated references in this passage to the creation, in distinction from Christians, are to the impersonal creation personified, to the creation as the environment in which the church exists. Satan and those in submission to him, whether fallen angels or human beings who

Coming to light in this passage, then, is a much more broadened conception of suffering, including Christian suffering, than is usually entertained. Christian suffering is not only the monumental martyrdom or physical persecution. It is that, to be sure. In making the emphasis I am here, in no way do I mean to diminish such evident oppression or in any way slight the open and vicious opposition that some Christians, in distinction from others, are called to bear in "this present time."

Paul, however, points us to consider that Christian suffering is not only those sufferings that are glaring and monumental. It also involves the mundane and unspectacular. The sufferings of the present time are not only those that are occasional or exceptional, however unforgettable some of them may be. These present-time sufferings also inevitably mark our daily existence. Here Paul sheds light on the call of Jesus to discipleship that *anyone* desiring to follow him must "take up his [own] cross *daily*" (Luke 9:23; cf. 14:27). Christian suffering, all told, is (to be) an everyday matter for all.

The scope of Christian suffering is all-encompassing. It comprehends all that believers experience daily and in a myriad of ways—small as well as great, menial as well as monumental. Christians suffer as they continue to be subjected to the enervating futility and corrupting bondage that presently permeates the creation and impinges on their lives inescapably and at every point.

Suffering with Christ, then, is everything about this present-time existence with its inevitable stresses and difficulties, small as well as great, experienced in the various basic relationships of life—in marriage and the home, on the job, and elsewhere—endured for Christ's sake and in following him. Christians suffer with Christ as the burdens and frustrations undergone daily are borne in living out the demands that follow from the gospel in serving God and others. For Paul, to be a Christian is inevitably to suffer as a Christian.

Philippians 1:29, a perennially timely word to the church, makes this clear: "For it has been granted to you on behalf of Christ not only to believe in him, but also to suffer for him" (NIV). Here the apostle speaks of the "givenness" of Christian suffering. The main verb used (ἐχαρίσθη) may be fairly paraphrased "graciously given" or "given as a gift." Paul's point is not

---

remain unrepentant, do not share in the conjoint groaning and eager longing of the creation and believers in view.

that suffering is good for its own sake, as an end in itself. But as a matter of God's grace, suffering is constitutive for the church as church in living for its Lord. Faith in Christ and suffering for him are inseparable correlates. It is not the case that all Christians believe but only some suffer. The Christian life is a *not only–but also* proposition: not only believing but also suffering.[20]

CONCLUSION

The center of Paul's theology is God's work of redemption in sending his Son in "the fullness of time" (Gal. 4:4-5), the eschatology that has been inaugurated in Christ's death and resurrection (1 Cor. 15:3-4). This eschatological salvation from sin and its consequences, its guilt and corruption, Christ has accomplished by his obedience, by obediently enduring a lifetime of suffering and humiliation that culminated in his death on the cross. Because of that obedience, God has "highly exalted" him (Phil. 2:8-9). His state of humiliation is now behind him definitively; in his resurrection and ascension, he has entered his permanent state of exaltation as Lord (2:11).

In Romans 8, and indicated as well in other passages we have considered, a central concern of Paul is to make clear that in the matter of humiliation and exaltation—suffering now, glory to come—the church is one step behind its Lord. For "this present time"—the time until his return, coincident with and not ending at some point prior to the consummation-renovation of the creation as a whole, as 8:19-23 make clear—the church is and will remain in what is fundamentally a state of humiliation, filling up the afflictions of Christ, until at his return it enters its state of exaltation.

But while in this way the church is one large step behind its Lord, he has not left it behind. The church is not on its own or abandoned. For in its state of humiliation its exalted Lord is present in the power of his Spirit. Already, not just in the future, he, become the life-giving Spirit, is active as "head over everything for the church" (Eph. 1:22 NIV). And in its suffering, his resurrection life and power are being perfected. This is why, we may say, Christ's present eschatological victory is for the church an eschatology of suffering.

Toward the close of Romans 8, after detailing aspects of the suffering Christians do and potentially experience—"tribulation, or distress, or

---

20 See my "The Usefulness of the Cross," *Westminster Theological Journal* 41 (1978-79): 232-42, for a fuller discussion of the passages on suffering treated so far in this section.

persecution, or famine, or nakedness, or danger, or sword," and constant exposure to death (8:35-36)—Paul adds, "In all these things we are more than conquerors through him who loved us" (8:37).

Notice what Paul says and does not say here. He does not say, "*after* all these things"—afterward, for instance, in some presumably still-future, peaceful conflict-free or conflict-minimal provisional era (millennium), then the church will be victorious. No, "*in* all these things"—in "the sufferings of this present time" (8:18) in their all-pervading fullness—just there is the locus, the place presently, until Christ returns to usher in the age to come in its full finality, of the church's surpassing conquest, its eschatological victory.

For Paul, the sufferings of the church and the success of the gospel are directly, not inversely, proportional. The success that the church is bound to have in discipling the nations (Matt. 28:18-20) will not eliminate those sufferings. Rather, that success will be realized only through those present-time sufferings. Recall again the evangelizing principle of 2 Corinthians 4:12: "So death is at work in us, but life in you."

According to Jesus, his disciples will not have drunk the last drop from the shared cup of his suffering until he returns in his consummation-glory (Matt. 20:21-23; Mark 10:37-39). With this point, Paul the apostle—in his person, in his ministry, and in his theology—fully agrees. Until Jesus comes again, this point the church evades at the risk of losing its identity, this point the church avoids at the cost of failing to be faithful to its Lord in its mission in and to the world.

As I noted at the outset, there is not only one right way of approaching Paul's theology. So, too, there is not only one right way of concluding a study of his theology. I dare say, however, none is more appropriate and necessary than the note on which this study ends.

General Index

Scripture Index